GEORGE DIXON

SPORT, CULTURE & SOCIETY

DAVID K. WIGGINS, SERIES EDITOR

GEORGE DIXON

The Short Life of Boxing's First
Black World Champion, 1870–1908

JASON WINDERS

The University of Arkansas Press
Fayetteville
2021

978-1-68226-178-1 (cloth)
978-1-68226-177-4 (paperback)
978-1-61075-752-2 (e-book)

25 24 23 22 21   5 4 3 2 1

Manufactured in the United States of America

Designed by Liz Lester

♾ The paper used in this publication meets the minimum requirements of the American National Standard for Permanence of Paper for Printed Library Materials Z39.48-1984.

Library of Congress Cataloging-in-Publication Data

Names: Winders, Jason, author.
Title: George Dixon: the short life of boxing's first Black world
    champion, 1870–1908 / Jason Winders.
Description: Fayetteville: The University of Arkansas Press, [2021] |
    Series: Sport, culture, and society | Includes bibliographical
    references and index. | Summary: "Biography of Canadian-born,
    Boston-raised boxer George Dixon (1870–1908), the first Black world
    champion of any sport and the first Black world boxing champion in any
    division"—Provided by publisher.
Identifiers: LCCN 2021005735 (print) | LCCN 2021005736 (ebook) | ISBN
    9781682261774 (Paperback: acid-free paper) | ISBN 9781682261781 (Cloth:
    acid-free paper) | ISBN 9781610757522 (eBook)
Subjects: LCSH: Dixon, George, 1870–1908. | Boxers (Sports)—Canada—
    Biography. | Athletes, Black—Biography. | Boxing—Records—19th century. |
    International Boxing Hall of Fame. | Boxing—History.
Classification: LCC GV1132.D538 W56 2021 (print) | LCC GV1132.D538
    (ebook) | DDC 796.83092 [B]—dc23
LC record available at https://lccn.loc.gov/2021005735
LC ebook record available at https://lccn.loc.gov/2021005736

CONTENTS

SERIES EDITOR'S PREFACE

Sport is an extraordinarily important phenomenon that pervades the lives of many people and has enormous impact on society in an assortment of ways. At its most fundamental level, sport has the power to bring people great joy and to satisfy their competitive urges while allowing them to form bonds and a sense of community with others from various walks of life and diverse backgrounds and interests. Sport also makes clear, especially at the highest levels of competition, both the lengths that people will go to achieve victory and its close connections to business, education, politics, economics, religion, law, family, and other societal institutions. Moreover, sport is about identity development—how individuals and groups, irrespective of race, gender, ethnicity, or socioeconomic class, have sought to elevate their status and realize material success and social mobility.

Sport, Culture, and Society seeks to promote a greater understanding of the aforementioned issues and many others. Recognizing sport's powerful influence and ability to change people's lives in significant ways, the series focuses on topics ranging from urbanization and community development to biographies and intercollegiate athletics. It includes monographs and anthologies that are characterized by excellent scholarship, accessible to a wide audience, and interesting and thoughtful in design and interpretations. Singular features of the series are authors and editors who represent a variety of disciplinary areas and adopt different methodological approaches. The series also includes works by individuals at various stages of their careers, both sport studies scholars of outstanding talent just beginning to make their mark on the field and more experienced scholars of sport with established reputations.

This newest volume in the series is a biography of the great Black Canadian boxer George Dixon. Using a wide range of primary and secondary materials, Jason Winders furnishes a fascinating account of the life and boxing career of Dixon, the diminutive Black fighter who fought literally hundreds of bouts during some twenty years in the ring. Recounted here are Dixon's most famous matches, including his featherweight championship fight in 1892 against Jack Skelly at the Olympic Club in New Orleans. Part of a three-day pugilistic festival that also included a lightweight championship fight between Billy Myer and Jack McAuliffe, and a heavyweight championship fight pitting the "Boston Strong Boy" John L. Sullivan against James J. Corbett, Dixon's pummeling of Skelly to capture the featherweight championship enraged the white citizens of New Orleans to such an extent that no interracial fights were permitted in the Crescent City until the next century. Importantly, Winders provides important information about Dixon's life outside the ring, despite the fact the talented Black fighter left behind "no journals, no letters, no grand autobiographies." Stitching together newspaper accounts and other seldom-used sources, Winders delineates Dixon's complex personality and difficulties in navigating the world amid the hardening racial lines of late-nineteenth-century America. Unfortunately, like so many other boxers through the years, Dixon's personal life did not always mirror the many successes he experienced in the squared circle.

David K. Wiggins
Series Editor

ACKNOWLEDGMENTS

Of all the words contained on these pages, these are the ones I fear writing the most. As I have lived with Dixon for nearly a decade, a cast of hundreds has helped me, focused me, cheered me on to the finish. They got me moving when stuck, made me laugh when I didn't much feel like it, even taught me how to properly use a French press. Any attempt to list them all would be folly and fraught with unintentional omissions. Even unnamed, I hope they understand what their efforts have meant to me. I will one day repay their kindness.

There are some specific contributions to the text I would like to note.

Thank you to the family of boxing researchers, including my fellow members of the International Boxing Research Organization, who showed incredible support during my research process while answering what may have seemed like some oddball questions from the guy in Canada. Among those members, special thanks go to Colleen Aycock, Bob Caico, Lauren Chouinard, Patrick Connor, Dan Cuoco, Mike DeLisa, Lou Eisen, Tony Gee, Darryl Glenn, Stephen Gordon, Todd Greanier, Henry Hascup, Christopher LaForce, William Mays, Don Majeski, Daniel Oakes, and Bob Yalen. I remain in awe of their generosity—and jealous of their vast holdings.

These pages boast some amazing, rarely seen images, provided via the patient and kind hands of Joanne Bloom, Photographic Resources Librarian, Fine Arts Library of the Harvard Library.

This work has roots in my doctoral dissertation. Thanks go to those who helped shape this work in its earliest days, including Don Abelson, Nancy Bouchier, Michael Heine, Don Morrow, Darwin Semotiuk, Kevin Wamsley, and Jim Weese. Special thanks to my supervisor and friend Robert K. Barney, who has been there every step of the way.

My sincere thanks also go to the University of Arkansas Press team, which has treated this work as if it were their own. It has been an amazing experience and the culmination of a lifelong dream.

To all, I say thank you.

GEORGE DIXON

George Dixon. Albumen silver print on card. Photo by Elmer Chickering. *Courtesy of Special Collections, Fine Arts Library, Harvard University.*

Chelsea, Massachusetts, October 19, 1926

GEORGE DIXON HAD been forgotten for a generation by the time Lt. Edward Riley dragged the champion's memory into the darkened streets of Chelsea, Massachusetts, on an October night in 1926. Sparked by a defective switch in the basement of A. K. Mann's hardware store, a fire worked its way through the Mann Building, and then spread next door into a dry goods store owned by Louis Klickstein. Given the hour, both buildings were unoccupied, so firemen worked from the safety of the 300 block of Broadway, which had been closed to streetcar and automobile traffic. Louis Golden walked the short distance from his home to join the crowd gathered to watch the commotion. He saw Riley, an Engine No. 2 fireman, enter the store and pull from it a single item—a $2,500 jewel-studded championship belt. (He perhaps watched too intently, as the next day, Golden filed a police report claiming his pockets were picked of $2 as he stood staring.)

All gathered saw that the belt, even slightly singed, was a work of art by any standard. *National Police Gazette* editor and proprietor Richard Fox had presented Dixon with the belt in the boxer's heyday as feather-weight champion of the world. Emblazoned with the name *Police Gazette* across the top, the belt featured a pair of silver chains linking three silver shields, each semi-surrounded by rubies, diamonds, emeralds, and sapphires, and flanked on either side by flags representing the boxing powers of the United States, England, and Ireland. The center shield bore the likeness of Dixon inset in porcelain. During Dixon's reigns as champion, the belt would arrive a few days ahead of him in the city where the next match was to be held. It would hang in the windows of taverns, stores, and anywhere with high enough visibility to generate interest in the upcoming bout. Prior to the fire, the now-retired belt had been on display in

Mann's hardware store, on loan from its current owner, Red Chapman, a highly ranked contender for the featherweight world championship in the mid-1920s. In its October 20, 1926, edition, the *Boston Daily Globe* reported on the excitement of the previous evening. Under the headline, "George Dixon's Belt Rescued during Fire," it read, "Memories of George Dixon, great little boxer of a generation ago, and his reign over the Featherweights of the World, were awakened in Chelsea last night."[1]

It was the first time the paper had written about the city's adopted hero since his death nearly two decades earlier. Perhaps that silence foreshadowed the coming century, which would rarely pause for Dixon's name despite the unconventional path the diminutive champion paved for all who followed him.

———

He was a showman, a barnstormer, a man crowned world champion on three continents. He was an innovator, a scientific curiosity, a physical specimen deemed worthy of study and emulation. He was a Canadian celebrated for his unyielding defense of American virtue, a Black man elevated to unprecedented heights by white society. For a decade leading into the twentieth century, few Black men were as wealthy and none were more famous. Above all, George Dixon was a flawless fighter, a self-taught genius whose peerless exploits in the ring inspired a previously unseen pride among Black America that often spilled into city streets across the country. He fought constantly as a professional—maybe against a thousand opponents in his lifetime. While most were exhibitions against rather faceless foes, a hundred or so of those bouts were chronicled by both Black and white presses. A half dozen came to define an era. His championship reign ushered in an embrace of Black athletes at the highest echelons of sport. To a Black culture cementing its first national heroes, George Dixon was the single-most significant athlete of nineteenth-century America.

In June 1892, Dixon's defeat of British featherweight champion Fred Johnson was seen as a stirring victory for the United States—a moment of national revelry led by a young Black man. None other than John L. Sullivan, heavyweight champion of the world and a boastful racist, leapt to his feet at fight's end to shout, "Good for Boston—and the United States!" This was an America only a generation removed from Black slaves being bought, sold, and consumed for the gain of white men. Now, a Black man was asserting his manhood by way of sport, beating white men with his near-bare hands, rising to heights higher than any man his size no matter what color. It was a delicious irony not lost on Black America. Among the coast-to-coast accolades, the *New Orleans Crusader* wrote perhaps the most powerful words about a Black athlete's standing in Jim Crow America: "If he handled a Winchester as well as he does his fists, regulators would be scarce and lynchings rare occurences [*sic*]."[2] Hard to imagine the weight of that burden laid upon young shoulders.

But George Dixon was a complicated man with a complicated legacy. Beyond the cheering crowds, he was a drunk, a gambler, an incompetent spendthrift businessman who lost fortunes with spectacular ease. He was a puppet, a sucker, a willing captive of numerous unscrupulous white men. In public, he was prone to violent outbursts and fits of rage. In private, he was beholden to his own dark vices. For a decade after his entry into the twentieth century, few Black men were as pitied, and none named more frequently from public square and pulpit as a cautionary tale of modern excesses. He tried to live the part of a "sporting man" while knowing his place as a Black man in a white world, all with little guidance and opportunists at every turn.

Dixon was also a man who could be indifferent to his race. Never the activist, he neither drew race lines of his own nor punished clubs that encouraged them; he fought anyone, anywhere, for a paycheck. There were sympathies for fellow Blacks, certainly. You see them in the small stories of his interactions with individuals. But his hand was equally open to whites. He was a generous soul. Yet those stories do not overtake the overwhelming indifference Dixon had to race when it came to his life's work. In the ring, he was a hero to the Black man. But it is difficult to portray him among revolutionary race leaders of his time. He lived in a white world rather contentedly—with white managers and associates, as so many Black boxers had, and also a white wife, the sister of his most powerful and influential manager. He was comfortable in his confinement. Yes, he challenged Jim Crow when his drunken temper took over. But Dixon often combated the racism directed at him by becoming what was expected of him—a Black champion who accepted a place dictated by white men. Night after night, Dixon replayed the experiences of a Black body in captivity by enduring continual display—and battering—for the amusement and financial gain of others.

Unlike later fighters, however, he never became fully self-aware of this relationship and, thus, never seized the opportunity to control his own exhibition and ultimately keep the majority share of the profits he generated. A decade after Dixon's death, heavyweight Jack Johnson was, if not the first, then arguably the most successful such Black boxer at doing just that, paving the way for the greats of the mid-century era who found vast financial and cultural opportunities. Books like *Papa Jack* by Randy Roberts, *Unforgivable Blackness* by Geoffrey Ward, *Jack Johnson, Rebel Sojourner* by Theresa Runstedtler, among dozens of other academic works and hundreds of popular depictions, have rightfully positioned Johnson as iconic figure. But they all skip over Dixon's prelude. That is an unfortunate oversight. Despite his flaws, Dixon must be central to the discussion of the Black athlete, as he was a necessary transition toward independence.

Maybe Dixon was not the hero Black America needed. He never sought a balance between his worlds. He shed one aspect of himself to don another when others deemed it appropriate for his success. It was a trade-off he was more than willing to make. Lots of talented individuals from that era remain unknown to this day because they were unable to navigate these conditions.

These decisions came at a price, however, as they hastened Dixon's fade from memory. During the 1960s, US civil rights leaders recruited popular figures in the public eye to help with their campaign, including singers, actors, and athletes. The movement embraced current athletes to lend credence to the cause, including Jackie Robinson and Curt Flood, Althea Gibson and Arthur Ashe, Bill Russell and Jim Brown, Tommie Smith and John Carlos, and, of course, Joe Louis and Muhammad Ali. The contributions of these individuals to civil rights extended well beyond their performance venues—fields, courts, tracks, and rings. They continue to be of deep cultural significance, too, and have been well documented in biographies and films. While rooted in the present, civil rights leaders and scholars were also reclaiming the past by reviving the racial legacies of the likes of Paul Robeson, Jesse Owens, and Jack Johnson. Although their accomplishments were of another era, these men and women—and others like them—were worthy of distinction for their steadfastness in the face of oppression. Thanks to this exposure to new audiences, these figures' legacies experienced a popular rebirth. But not George Dixon's. Although the most famous Black man in America for a time, and certainly the most successful Black athlete of his age, Dixon was ignored by the modern civil rights movement. He therefore missed his biggest opportunity to be revived in the popular consciousness. Dixon sat somewhere in the past, somewhat lost, almost forgotten, a trivia answer.

But he should be viewed as far more. Until Dixon, every Black athlete in America had a similar story. After him, however, they began to face individual decisions about their lives and careers, weighing the risks and rewards. Would they lash out against the racial injustices they faced? Would they earn opportunity through reticence and conformity? Would they seek a middle ground between the two? This was a long journey that continues even today, but Dixon was the start of that journey.

It is not an easy story to tell. The main sources for most of Dixon's life suffer from what Robert Rinehart's describes as "historical nostalgia," an intentional embellishment of the past due to a perception that the subject matter—sport—is relatively frivolous and, therefore, there is less at stake in fond recollection.[3] Such was the case for much of boxing history during Dixon's era. At best, boxing provided a pastime and environment in which men wagered and drank, but rarely was it considered important enough to chronicle in great detail beyond the parlay. Therefore, historians working to define Dixon or his contemporaries are forced to confront head-on Rinehart's notion that "history is not made up of singular 'moments,' well represented and finalized for posterity by the sport historian, but, rather, that sport history is contextual, colored by individual standpoints and agendas, contested and malleable. The writer of traditional history may object to this stance, but for non-traditionalists, the very argumentativeness of 'history' is what makes it exciting and alive. *The* history becomes *A* history, part of a larger series of contested and possibly hanging histories."[4]

Such is especially the case for Dixon, who sits tantalizingly, even frustratingly, close to us—just over a century ago. Surely his life should be too recent to be lost to time already. In other disciplines, we view the late-Victorian and early Edwardian eras with a confident familiarity. Yet when it comes to the sporting landscape, and boxing in particular, the eras can be distant. Dixon's prime fell within one of boxing's many "Dark Ages," as legendary *New Yorker* writer A. J. Liebling once described the time between great heavyweight champions.[5] Dixon's prime fell between the end of John L. Sullivan's decade-long reign as heavyweight champion in 1892 and the rise of Jack Johnson in 1908. Aside from Dixon, the era was one of champions with little staying power and challengers of little distinction in all weight classes. Combine those circumstances with the sport's questionable legal and moral standing around the globe, as well as white-dominated media who painted Black boxers in a biased light, and one sees how the memories of many from that time have faded. Hence, for us today, George Dixon remains a curious historical paradox—familiar yet foreign.

His paper trail is long, and well-worn in places by would-be popular chroniclers. Yet it remains remarkably limited. During his lifetime, Dixon's story "inside the ring" was richly told, as his major post-1890 bouts were covered in great detail. However, little exists outside the ring, and all but nothing in Dixon's own voice—no journals, no letters, no grand autobiographies. Only *A Lesson in Boxing* (1893), an instructional pamphlet he wrote—a popular pursuit for fighters of his era—offers anything by Dixon's hand. It presents little by way of biographical or personal information. Besides this, there are only breadcrumbs: newspapers covered his final days in the signature, overtly flowery prose of that era's reporting; his former manager praised him in magazine articles after his death; years later, opponents' books describe their fights against Dixon. But all feed the image of "Dixon: The Boxer," never "Dixon: The Man."

In trying to explain Dixon, too many would-be chroniclers have depended on too few sources and were unwilling to admit there are many parts of this man's life that we will never know. Fighters of these years have confusing and contradictory histories. Scattershot coverage, outright false reporting tinged by bias against race or nationality, and far too few first-hand accounts led historians to cling to a handful of sources seen as definitive. But despite being far from complete, these sources echo through the ages.

This dearth of detail has resulted in only two full-length posthumous popular-history biographies on this important figure—the first written by *The Ring* magazine founder and longtime editor Nat Fleischer in 1938, as part of his *Black Dynamite* series,[6] the second by Steven Laffoley in 2012.[7] Beyond that, little scholarship on Dixon exists beyond the anecdotal— passing mentions, short chapters, but no in-depth study. Historians have placed Dixon at the forefront of boxing pioneers, but they often don't seem to know why, beyond a few lines related to his ring résumé.

Much of Dixon's story has been left in the hands of Fleischer. Although he is an icon to many, not all are enamored by Fleischer's ability to recount the past. Historian Kevin R. Smith characterized the famed author's five-volume *Black Dynamite* series, which chronicles Black fighters, as "both heavily flawed and repetitious," and parts of Fleischer's also imprecise *Lives and Battles of Famous Black Pugilists* as outright theft from the *National Police Gazette*. Published by Richard K. Fox, *The Lives and Battles* was not an original work of history, but rather a cobbled-together series of biographies assembled from Pierce Egan's *Boxiana*, Henry Miles's *Pugilista*, and the *Police Gazette* itself. So, if *Lives and Battles* is nothing more than a "rehash of old hat, hastily put together by an over-ambitious editor," then Smith argues that Fleischer's work can be at least partly viewed as little more than the continuation of unfounded mythmaking —no matter how many historians continue to reference the series.[8] Smith argues that Fleischer was "unabashed in his use of poetic license, making up sources and fictionalizing events when unable to unearth the true facts. Some of his conclusions are downright ludicrous and have done more to further mystify and confuse the history of several of these fighting men than to clarify their lives, careers and impact."[9] When we talk about the story of George Dixon, we are talking about a story largely repeated from the third volume of this *Black Dynamite* series, a story that has been echoed over and over again. Some of those words will be used here, but so will words from a range of sources, and where they conflict, contradictions are presented and context offered.

I pause here to mention the matter of my observation point— attempting to view Dixon's world as a white historian already a decade older than Dixon when he died. My experiences are in no way those of Dixon. More to the point, I am especially aware of the possibility of falling woefully short as a qualified commentator on the Black experience when discussing Dixon's trials and tribulations. I approach this project with eyes open to these limitations, and when confronted by them, I either look to fortify my opinions with further research or openly admit my assumptions. As such, this is a story of Dixon—but not the only story. I hope this book inspires others to take up Dixon and view his life through new perspectives. He is worthy of far more scholarship than he has received. On a related note, some of the language of race I quote in this work is troubling. The words are not presented here to titillate or incite, but rather to reveal the world Dixon confronted daily. I do not treat them lightly. In fact, I shudder at writing many of them. Admittedly, some of the racist terms need further explanation as they have, fortunately, fallen out of favor and instead sound completely foreign to our modern ears.

On these pages, I set out to revive the memory of Dixon, expand his story beyond the myth it has found itself wrapped in and repeated, and reposition him as central to the history of Black boxers in America. Yet historians want to start with Jack Johnson. But why not Dixon? By ignoring him, we have lost the point where the story of the modern Black athlete in America begins. We miss the origin of issues that remain unresolved or ignored in professional sports still today. While the dollar figures are wildly different, the dynamics of exploitation remain: rich young men putting their bodies and lives on the line for a few years of elite standing, to make richer men money for a lifetime.

Dixon was the moment where it all began.

CHELSEA, MASSACHUSETTS, OCTOBER 19, 1926　　9

George Dixon, approximately 1881. Photo by Asa Bushby and George Macurdy, Bushby and Macurdy Studio, Boston, Massachusetts. *Courtesy of Nova Scotia Archives.*

CHAPTER 1

Origins

THAT NIGHT WAS CHAOS inside and outside the ring. Johnny Murphy, the Rhode Island/New England featherweight champion, was a brawler of some note in that moment. Murphy is better known as a Harvard boxing instructor rather than for his six-year-long professional career, which featured a handful of bouts and little success.[1] However, he was at his height of fighting fame when he stepped into the ring with George Dixon on October 23, 1890.

Newspaper accounts spoke of Dixon dominating the bout, bloodying his white opponent for forty rounds until Murphy's corner threw in the sponge despite protests from their fighter and a crowd heavily invested in a Murphy victory. The bout stands among Dixon's most technically perfect—barely scratched by his opponent while delivering a brutal punishment.[2]

The performance becomes all the more impressive when considering the conditions of that execution. Dixon nearly missed the fight entirely, arriving late when a huge, all-white mob prevented his team from entering the Providence, Rhode Island, club. Police cleared a path; the fight started an hour late. Throughout the bout, the crowd showered Dixon with racist taunts to distract or anger him. Others attempted to start fights with Dixon's corner men, including his white manager, Tom O'Rourke. A crowd of men pressing closer and closer to ringside reached out and beat Dixon constantly with canes. The raps on his skin forced the fighter to the center of the ring throughout the bout; a blow to his head during a clinch almost sparked a riot. The pressure from the crowd never abated even as the betting swung heavily in Dixon's favor. As Murphy's fate grow more certain as the bout wore on—his ear was near ripped from his head in the closing rounds—one of his followers tried to cut the ropes and spill a mob into the ring. When they were prevented from entering, another free-for-all started when the hoodlum attempted to knife the man who stopped him.

Dixon never got over this bout. A week later, he was still bragging about the beating he delivered: "Murphy is in bed yet—with a silver tube in his left ear. I made him black and blue from head to foot."[3] That turned to anger, acceptance, and a tinge of sadness over the years, including in an April 1891 article published under his signature (seemingly augmented with a bit of O'Rourke boastfulness):

> Some of the worst thugs in the country were engaged to go to that affair for the express purpose of preventing me from winning. I knew of the job and what each man was called upon to do, according to the plans made. I did not worry the least bit, for I knew that the majority of the spectators and the referee would not stand any such nonsense.
>
> As soon as I began winning the thugs commenced to do their work, and they found such a strong opposition against them that they quickly stopped their dirty tactics. If that battle was fought three years ago, I am satisfied that I would not have won, and not only that, but I would have received a good beating from the hoodlums.
>
> I have done many favors for some of those that were in the plot, but they forgot all about my kindness when they saw me fighting one of their own color.[4]

Even in and around his Boston home, Dixon rarely squared off against just one man—he was also taking on the mindset of a nation. He wrote, "Whenever I sparred a white lad, I had to put my opponent out in quick time in order to get a decision. Finding they could not stop me from winning, they took other means of getting back at me."[5]

Far from an outlier, nights like this were the norm for the young Black man in the ring. This was the world of George Dixon.

———

George Dixon was born near Halifax, Nova Scotia, Canada, to Charles E. and Maria "Mary" (Dulliver) Dixon on July 29, 1870. In the race-obsessed parlance of the day, Dixon was occasionally referred to as a "quadroon," meaning he was one-quarter white, as his grandfather was reportedly white.[6] Newspapers published during his career fed this claim, and boxing historians and journalists continue to report it today, although nothing in the known family history supports the contention. One rather odd mention of his ancestry came in 1897 when John McCormick's *The Square*

Circle: Stories of the Prize Ring claimed that "Dixon is a chocolate-colored man, whose mother was a negress, but whose father is reputed to have been a white British soldier."[7] There is zero evidence of this claim beyond those pages. Nevertheless, the quadroon label stuck his entire career, even though the term was usually reserved for predominantly white individuals with a recent Black ancestor. Whites were given a far broader spectrum to definite their race. Predominantly Black individuals—like Dixon—with a recent white ancestor were still, in the eyes of the public, considered Black. Witness the emergence of "one-drop" laws at the time— stating that a mere single drop of Black blood in your ancestry defined you as Black. When it came to race, nuance was not considered.

Like many of the details surrounding his earliest years, Dixon's day-to-day life, and even the duration of his time in Nova Scotia, remain hazy. According to the Census of Canada 1881, the Dixon household was composed of eight members: Charles, fifty-two; Maria, forty-four; and their children William, twenty-four; Charles Jr., twenty-two; John, nineteen; Henry, thirteen; George, ten; and Teresa, four.[8] George Dixon was actually eleven at the time, as Census takers incorrectly listed his birth year as 1871. The entire family's ethnic origin was listed as "African"; their religion was listed as "Baptist."

Dixon's childhood in Nova Scotia came during a transitional moment for Canada's Maritime provinces. For three decades prior to Dixon's birth in 1870, and for another half a century afterward, Nova Scotia, New Brunswick, and Prince Edward Island endured a period of industrialization and transformation characterized by dramatic economic peaks and valleys. In the mid-nineteenth century, British financiers—based in both Great Britain and in the colonies that would become Canada in 1867—invested heavily in these eastern provinces. This injection led to an evolution in the region's traditional industries of shipping, agriculture, forestry, and fishing. Each ached with the growing pains necessary to keep up with rapid shifts in technology and tastes, both domestically and abroad. Take fishing, for example. At the beginning of the 1870s, large companies that had held century-long quasi-monopolies over the fishing industry went bankrupt. Fishermen previously employed by these companies now found themselves without access to boats and, therefore, without prospects of work. In addition to this corporate restructuring, catches diversified as well. Bottom fish like cod historically had constituted the largest part of the catch, but as tastes changed, specialty seafood and particularly lobster took on greater importance. Along with the diversification of catches came an emerging canning industry, which facilitated an exploding export business.[9] All this change was contained within a generation or two. Coal, the lifeblood of industrialization, was the only industry to remain stable during the decade, aided by John A. Macdonald, Canada's first prime minister.

Elected in 1878, Macdonald and his Federal Government stabilized the region with his National Policy, which enacted a series of specific measures, including customs tariffs of 30 percent on foreign textiles, iron, steel, coal, and oil. The Federal Government also financed the building of railways that spirited manufactured goods from the Maritimes to major markets in Quebec and Ontario, and subsidized manufacturing industries like Nova Scotia's steel industry. The result was dazzling, unprecedented economic and industrial growth. With only 20 percent of the total population of the Dominion of Canada, the Maritimes of the 1890s boasted eight of Canada's twenty-three cotton-spinning factories, two of its seven rope and cordage factories, three of its five sugar refineries, and the only two steel plants in the country. The region urbanized as the population migrated into industrial centers like St. John, Moncton, Sydney, and Halifax.[10]

Personal reflections on Dixon's time in Halifax are limited to a handful of mentions by the pugilist himself, as well as an impressive amount of conjecture by fight journalists and historians. When Dixon was born, his family was settled in Ward No. 5, District No. 9, Sub-district F, and Division 1, Halifax City. He was raised there, even attended school in the area for two years.[11] He rarely spoke publicly of his immediate or extended family, but many were quite accomplished in the arts and athletics, both in the United States and Canada. Later in life, if Dixon's fame were to be challenged among the immediate family, it might have been by his brother John Dixon, a beloved musician in Boston, a member of the Boston Brass Band and Victorian Orchestra. Upon John's death in 1930, the *Chicago Defender* wrote of him: "He was well-known to both races and had the reputation of having more friends of the white race than any of the 'old Bostonians.'"[12] George Dixon also had extended family making names for themselves on the ice. Perhaps the best known of his cousins, James E. Dixon, played in goal for the 1898 Halifax Eurekas championship team of the Colored Hockey League. The next year, he joined the Africville Seasides as player and secretary. He played professionally until 1922. Joining James on the newly formed Eurekas was his brother and George Dixon's cousin Wallace Dixon, who played forward and cover point until 1904. Wallace later served in the No. 2 Construction Battalion during the First World War. During the 1920s, the brothers owned J. W. Dixon Groceries in Halifax. Another cousin, Allen Dixon, played forward/point/rover for the Africville Seasides from 1899–1904, as well as one game with the Eurekas. Allen's father was the Rev. Edward Dixon, East Preston Baptist United Church.[13]

George Dixon's Canadian experience remains a mystery today. What we do know is that he was certainly not unique. Eastern Canada was a major pipeline for pugilistic talent at the turn of the century. Limited opportunity, and the legal uncertainty of the sport in Canada, drove many fighters to seek opportunity south of the border. The history of the Maritimes, and their deep roots set into the United States, especially among Black populations, has been documented on numerous occasions. These connections are often ignored when explaining the Canadian roots of fighters from Dixon's era and how those Maritime connections led to different experiences for these men versus those of fighters from Toronto, Ontario, Montreal, Quebec, or even from the United Kingdom. In the press of the day, and in writings since, all Canadian fighters are simply credited as being "of Canada," as if all experiences are equal. However, while Dixon's specific day-to-day Maritimes life may be murky, his Canadian experience can be understood through his life among the Black families of the Maritimes. Here we see that Dixon was never a Canadian—only an American waiting to return home.

Persons of African descent landed in what would become Canada when the first slave was sold in New France around 1628. By the early 1700s, with the region's economy focused on the fur trade, the need for slave labor was already eroding (unlike in the American colonies, where slavery was just gaining momentum). By the mid-1700s, there were only about eleven hundred persons of African descent—mostly slaves—living in Montreal.[14] Ironically, between 1787 and 1800, fugitive slaves from Canada fled south into New England and the Northwest Territory, reversing the more widely known direction of flow.[15] In the Maritimes, two major conflicts between the upstart nation to the south and its British masters, the American Revolution and the War of 1812, wrote the story of Black residents by infusing into these communities thousands of former slaves and British Loyalists. During the American Revolution, 1776–83, more than three thousand Black Loyalists fled the United States for Nova Scotia. More followed in 1812, when further conflict provided Blacks in the United States with the opportunity to escape slavery. When the

British blockaded the US East Coast in 1813, approximately 3,500 slaves successfully escaped their plantations, primarily in Georgia, Maryland, and Virginia, and sought refuge aboard British ships. In April 1814, Vice Admiral Sir Alexander Cochrane issued an official proclamation offering freedom to anyone who joined the British side, promising resettlement in the British colonies in North America and the West Indies. Nearly two thousand "Black Refugees," as they came to be known, were transported to Nova Scotia.[16] The new homes for these refugees, however, did not allow for a completely fresh start, free from the oppression they left behind.

To be part of the nineteenth-century British Empire, including Canada, was to be white. The nation discounted the presence of Blacks. This produced a "painful sense of invisibility" for Black Canadians, who were not only few but also continually reminded of their outsider status.[17] In the Maritimes, the white population resented the Black Refugees and refused to accept them as equal members of society. Provincial authorities protested that the refugees were "unfitted by nature to this climate, or to an association with the rest of His Majesty's Colonists." The poverty many Black Refugees found themselves mired in was considered proof to some in power that the Black population was more suited to slavery than freedom. Lieutenant Governor Lord Dalhousie recommended they be returned to the United States—or sent to Sierra Leone. Layered onto that social pressure, the new residents, many of whom arrived as farmers, also battled nature. Entire fields were destroyed by hordes of mice that swept across Nova Scotia's countryside in 1815. The following year became known as the "Year without a Summer," as the ground remained frozen until June; ten inches of snow fell that same month. Even when the Black Refugees achieved some success in producing crops, the long, cold winters depleted their resources. Many were forced to rely on government assistance and private charity despite their best efforts to become independent.[18]

The Dixons were one of eight families who made the second of the voyages between September 1813 and August 1816 on both naval and chartered transports. Allen Dixon, a refugee Black who migrated to Nova Scotia around 1813–16, initially settled in the Preston area, northeast of Halifax. However, by 1849, he had moved to Africville, a small community on the southern shore of Bedford Basin, just north of Halifax, where he was listed as an officer of the Community Church. Allen was the forefather of one of the larger Africville families, patriarch to a line that would one day produce George Dixon.[19] In fact, many of the original Black Halifax families—Arnold, Bailey, Brown, Carvery, Dixon, Fletcher, Grant, and Hill—settled in the Nova Scotian enclaves of Preston and Hammonds Plains. Once landed, most of these families faced the harsh reality of unemployment and racial prejudice in the region and sought jobs as laborers or artisans on the docks of Halifax, the region's largest economic draw by the 1830s.

In 1834, slavery in Canada was officially abolished. Soon afterward, Black men gained the rights to vote, serve on juries, join the military, and own property. This served as a beacon to Blacks south of the border. By the 1850s, Nova Scotia's population of people of African descent rivaled those in Massachusetts and Connecticut. Approximately two thousand Blacks lived in Boston. In Halifax, that number was seventeen hundred.[20] As Blacks moved across the border, however, they did not shed national identity. Among the most famous of the lot, Henry Bibb, was born into slavery in Kentucky, escaped at age twenty-two, and became a well-known anti-slavery author and lecturer. Following the 1850 passage of the Fugitive Slave Act in the United States, Bibb moved to Canada, fearing recapture by his former owner. That act, among other things, required all escaped slaves, upon capture, to be returned to their masters—even if that capture took place in a free state. Part of the larger Compromise of 1850, a pact designed to ease tensions between the free North and slave-holding South, the Fugitive Slave Act was nicknamed the "Bloodhound Law" among Abolitionists. In 1851, Bibb started Canada's first Black newspaper, *Voice of the Fugitive*. During his life, he rarely referred to himself as a Canadian or even as a British subject. He forever saw himself as a fugitive from the United States, not a permanent resident of a new homeland.[21] His perception of his identity was not unique. In fact, part of this reluctance of Black Americans to embrace a Canadian identity can be traced to their frequent encounters with Canadian racial animosities.

For the most part, Nova Scotia's Black community segregated themselves into Africville. Originally named for the road it grew around, Campbell Road, the earliest documented use of the name Africville is found in a petition from William Brown Sr. dated March 21, 1860, stating, "That your Petitioner is the owner of a lot of land situate at Africville in the City of Halifax." The first land deed to use the name was issued in 1866. The Halifax property that eventually became Africville comprised three five-acre lots in Division "Letter K" of the city's final land grant survey. Much of this land that became Africville—a community with no direct Africa connection, oddly enough—was purchased from whites, many of whom were former slave owners and traders.[22]

The origins of the community are, admittedly, nebulous, but between 1835 and 1840, its early residents started to coalesce in the area from the surrounding communities of Preston and Hammonds Plains. Shunned by their white neighbors, they took comfort in their religious institutions. Under the leadership of the Rev. Richard Preston, the African Baptist Church was founded in Halifax in 1832, leading the way for the creation of other Black churches in adjacent areas. These churches became the focal point of community life and provided the Black population with a sense of security and strength in hardship. Gradually, other social and religious organizations were founded, including the African Friendly Society, African Abolition Society, and, in 1854, African United Baptist Association, which became a lynchpin for social justice.

Africville was rural in character and remained so into the twentieth century. People kept chickens, pigs, goats, and horses, supplementing their tables by fishing in the Bedford Basin. The community rose to self-sufficiency—schools, churches, a post office, small stores—yet most employment was in nearby Halifax. But by the latter half of the nineteenth century, Halifax's industrial expansion started to consume Africville. Tracks laid by the Nova Scotia Railway Company in the 1850s resulted in the demolition of several homes in the community. After building a prison overlooking Africville, the City of Halifax placed a "night soil" facility—a pond holding human excrement collected throughout the night from buckets, cesspools, and outhouses in the prison—on the eastern edge of the community. Over the next few decades, several large-scale industries started to crowd in further—an oil storage facility, a bone mill, a cotton factory, two slaughterhouses, a coal-handling facility, a foundry. In the 1870s, just after George Dixon's birth, the city built an infectious-disease hospital, and soon afterward a trachoma hospital, overlooking the community. The contaminated waste from those facilities was poured onto the Africville soil.[23]

Such developments continued into the twentieth century, with a stone-crushing plant and an abattoir built on the edges of the settlement. Finally, Halifax moved the large, open city dump, labelled a health menace by the city council and resisted by residents in other areas, to a site less than 350 feet from the westernmost group of Africville homes. Halifax City Council minutes clearly indicate that, in addition to using the area for facilities not tolerated in other (white) neighborhoods, the eventual industrial use of Africville lands was planned. As Halifax experienced industrial expansion, the city council adopted several resolutions to expropriate Africville's territory. While for one reason or another these resolutions were not acted upon, the city's policy was spelled out in the following response to an interested business in 1915: "The Africville portion of Campbell Road will always be an industrial district and it is desirable that industrial operations should be assisted in any way that is not prejudiced to the interest of the public; in fact, we may be obliged in the future to consider the interests of industry first." During the late 1960s, the community and its dwellings were ordered destroyed and residents evicted ahead of the opening of the nearby A. Murray MacKay Bridge, related highway construction, and the Port of Halifax development at Fairview Cove to the west.[24]

From the beginning, a weight hung upon those with Africville roots. Those who stayed behind faced the constant pressure of government-sanctioned racist attitudes and policies that sometimes seemed the products of inconceivably sadistic minds. But those who left carried pieces of this community with them as well. This was not a legacy soon forgotten. We do not know what Dixon saw on the streets as a young boy, the stories his father told him of working with men in the community, the experiences his older siblings faced in schools. We do not know how Dixon's days in Africville shaped his attitudes on race. What we do know, however, is the family soon sought—and found—opportunity elsewhere.

———————

If the American Revolution and the War of 1812 marked the influx of Blacks into the Maritimes, then the American Civil War signaled the beginning of their departure. That conflict, which continues to define the United States to this day, also demonstrated the extent to which Black immigrants in Canada continued to see themselves as Americans in exile. During the decades before the Civil War, the Canadian press often chastised the United States. The *Toronto Globe*, fountainhead of abolitionism in Canada, repeatedly pointed out how Americans spoke of their liberty and yet imprisoned those who helped slaves escape. The ills of Canada, the *Globe* opined, were light in comparison. In 1812, pro-slavery US senators spoke of adding Canada to the Union as free territory in exchange for northern support in acquiring Cuba and portions of Mexico, then ripe for slavery expansion. In 1852, Canadians again were warned that the United States wished to add Canada to its thirty-two states. The fact of slavery—the "dread ulcer, eating and destroying the otherwise healthy frame"—made this idea quite unattractive.[25]

The war rekindled allegiances for many Black expatriates because of the events of Emancipation and the early years of Reconstruction. Redress and reform were intoxicating ideas from afar. By the time the Civil War ended in April 1865, Black migration back to the United States, specifically into New England, was a defining characteristic of the Maritimes. As the original refugees had children and grandchildren, some of the younger generations started to "engage in a redefinition" of the border.[26] First-generation refugees defined the border in sharp terms—slaveholding United States to the south, free British North America to the north. Yet many of their children and grandchildren never experienced slavery first-hand, and, therefore began to migrate toward opportunity instead of being ruled by history. As opportunity dwindled in the Maritimes, more people looked south. This migration did not go unnoticed, or uncommented upon, in Nova Scotia:

> The United States, with her faults, which are many, has done much for the elevation of the colored race. She has given to the race professors in colleges, senators, engineers, doctors, lawyers, and mechanics of every description. Sad and sorry are we to say that is more than we can boast of here in Nova Scotia. Our young men, as soon as they receive a common school education, must flee away to the United States to seek employment.... Very few ever receive a trade from the large employers, even in the factories, on account of race prejudices, which is a terrible barrier, and a direct insult to Almighty God.... When young mechanics have arrived in our city (Halifax) from the West Indies, they could not obtain a situation, simply on account of color. They had to accept something very menial, and, subsequently, they had to leave our city to go to the United States to prosecute their mechanical skill.[27]

As the Dixons were starting their family in the Maritimes, the American Civil War dominated dinner table discussions more than Canadian Confederation. Close and longstanding economic, social, and family ties between the region and the northeastern United States made the nearby conflict a matter of personal interest for many. According to the 1870 US Census, Maritimers formed the fourth largest ethnic group in the United States. Another huge topic of conversation around the Maritimes in the late nineteenth century was sports south of the border —mainly cycling, baseball, and prizefighting.[28] Both through family and region, Dixon's connections can be seen as always pointed south.

The Census of Canada 1881 clouds the date for the Dixon family exit from Nova Scotia. In 1893, Dixon wrote, "When about 8 years of age, my parents moved to Boston where I still reside." That would put the date at 1878 or 1879. In 1930, his brother John's obituary in the *Chicago Defender* said he moved to Boston when he was seventeen. That would put the date at 1879 or 1880. As part of his *Black Dynamite* series in 1938, Nat Fleischer said the Dixons left for Boston in 1880. That latter date has been used repeatedly throughout the twentieth century. But, as shown in the Census data, the Dixons were among the counted in 1881. The family definitely does not appear in the Census of Canada 1891. Their exact exit date remains unknown. Nevertheless, the Dixons found a home in Boston—one forever associated with George's career inside the ring. Canada was left behind.

———

Dixon was not a demographic anomaly among his peers. In fact, his journey from Canada to Boston mirrored the experiences of thousands like him over a generation. Caught in a cultural jet stream south, Dixon became part of one of the city's most vigorous and important migrations. The Dixons settled in this major northern American metropolis, featuring a large and diversified economy and an established relationship with the Maritimes. News from Canada, and more specifically from the Maritimes and its major seaport of Halifax, dotted the pages of Boston newspapers almost daily. The city's readers were well versed on the issues, challenges, and, yes, sensational news of the day in Maritime communities some four hundred miles away. The majority of the stories linking the two communities centered on their shared connection to the sea—the dynamics of trade and the dangers of this vital part of both their economies. But when a fire swept through a Halifax asylum in 1882—carried in Boston newspapers under the banner "The Halifax Holocaust"—it was reported with the same intimacy and graphic detail as would be assigned a local story. The reporter spared no details for Boston readers about the fire that caused "terror among the 400 or 500 inmates."[29]

Thanks to a strong Abolitionist movement, Boston embraced few segregated institutions at that time. As well, Boston showcased a widely respected system of free public schools. The city acquired a reputation among Blacks, perhaps overstated, as "the paradise of the Negro," a city of unparalleled freedom and opportunity. Since the Black population was a small percentage of Boston's population, the racial animosities of the white majority did not explode into major race riots similar to those in

New York and Philadelphia during the Civil War. The large Irish and small Black populations lived in an uneasy truce, with the two groups dwelling in proximity in the city's West and South Ends.[30]

Dixon had an advantage. Black Canadian immigrants to Boston were better educated than those who arrived from the southern United States. As a group, those from Canada had a higher rate of literacy—a small advantage for the men, but a huge one for women looking to distinguish themselves in the job market. The Dixons were a literate family; George Dixon often spoke of afternoons and evenings spent reading and writing. Even so, nearly 90 percent of employed Black men and all but a handful of women in Boston were employed in menial labor throughout the 1870s and 1880s. A disproportionate number of Black Canadian immigrants were lighter skinned than their southern counterparts—another point of acceptance into Boston society, as well as sporting circles. Fight fans and observers commented on Dixon's lighter skin throughout his career. In 1877, 40 percent of Black marriages in Boston were to whites, the highest recorded rate of interracial marriage in American history and a trend Dixon later followed. That rate would fluctuate a bit from decade to decade, until it declined sharply after 1909. Among men, the rate of interracial marriage was highest among Blacks born in Massachusetts, followed by those born in northern states and Canada.[31] Not surprisingly, interracial marriage was illegal in the South.

Dixon also arrived in Boston during an important sporting juncture, one that took place between approximately 1870 and 1930. Prizefighting was illegal in the United States for most of the nineteenth century. That did not sway its popularity among certain classes, but it did limit the sport's exposure and greatly shaded how it was perceived among the larger population. Doctors, for instance, were reluctant to become involved in prizefighting. The health of its practitioners was in question. Between 1830 and 1845, *The Lancet*, an influential medical journal to this day, carried several articles and letters that "agonized about the wisdom, dangers and morality of doctors assisting at duels."[32] Such doctors risked charges of aiding and abetting murder or, at least, manslaughter.

While "prizefighting" and "boxing" have morphed into a single term today, the distinction was once key. Some draw a hard line between the definitions. Prizefighting is human combat governed by only a handful of rules with the body as the only weapon. Mixing elements of a variety of martial and combat arts, prizefighting also included less artful elements like eye gouging, hair pulling, choking, even biting and scratching.

Fights were open ended, lasting hours until one man remained standing. It was not so much a test of skill as it was an exercise in endurance and ability to absorb punishment. Out of this grew boxing as a skill-based, rule-governed, regimented sport.[33] Others have defined the terms more simply: prizefighters were professionals who brawled for money—honor and science never entered the equation. Boxers, on the other hand, were amateurs who built character and a better country through their pursuits. This attitude carried well through the First and into the Second World War. A particularly memorable piece on the subject was penned by aging fighter and former Dixon foil Jack Skelly in December 1914. As the First World War was waged on foreign shores, yet more than two years before the United States entered that conflict, Skelly—who described himself as "not a warrior nor a believer in wars"—advocated for widespread training of youth in military tactics and physical fitness. And what better way to accomplish the latter than through boxing? He supported boxing training not only among the military ranks, but also among boys in schools across the country:

> We should become a great nation of athletes, just as ancient Rome and Greece were in their days of glory and fame. Just as progressive as Japan is today.
>
> The wonderful effects of proper training have also been shown by the great German Army that has been battling furiously against such tremendous odds, during the past few moons. By their marvelous endurance and almost irresistible energy, the Kaiser's millions of warriors have not only surprised the world, but all the leading military experts of creation.
>
> Sad as the frightful slaughter may be in Europe, we cannot but admire the gigantic fighting done by the well-trained German soldiers. They are certainly a revelation to us all in this modern warfare. . . .
>
> If Uncle Sam wants us to be a fine, strong, healthy nation of trained athletes, with the grit and physique to shoulder a musket and defend our country at the blow of a horn, let him encourage and foster the manly art.[34]

In the 1870s, a more elite class took to boxing. They ignored the law and the disapproval of sections of the middle class. Amateur boxing, unlike prizefighting, was legal and received a good deal of support from the middle classes, especially schoolmasters and "muscular Christians" such as Thomas Hughes, author of *Tom Brown's Schooldays* and himself a boxer. This wider acceptance slowly transformed opinion—and the law. By this time, however, the irrational, bare-knuckled match of indeterminate length of the past was being gentrified into a rationalized sport of gloves, governed by time and shaped by scientific techniques. These changes helped to make boxing more popular and, in turn, opened its availability to larger and larger crowds by extending its legality.[35] In Boston, for much of the nineteenth century, the sport was widely seen as illegitimate and criminal, a pursuit supported only by the underbelly of society. Although many tried to legitimize it by relating it to the "science of self-defense," the mainstream still viewed it as a disgrace. But John L. Sullivan changed all that. His decade-long reign as heavyweight champion starting in 1882 increased the sport's popularity and changed its perception in the eyes of the public and lawmakers alike.[36]

Historian Stephen Hardy outlined in beautiful detail and context the City of Boston into which Dixon landed.[37] In the United States, sport and recreation thrived within urban environments during the nineteenth century because these activities had a unique ability to build cohesion amid chaos. Primarily due to an explosive influx of immigrants into cities—both those moving from rural communities and from abroad—the distinctions between people sharpened, mainly along economic and ethnic lines, within tight quarters. For many cities, this created major disruptions and strife. However, an emerging national culture of sport and recreation offered a way to begin shaping order, identity, and stability. This was not a unique notion to Boston, but the city's sporting culture at that time was arguably the deepest in the nation. Both native-born, middle-class Bostonians and their working-class counterparts embraced sport and recreation. As industrial and business opportunities grew, in direct proportion to creating more income, a wealthier class of citizen had an opportunity to pursue sport, exercise, and outdoor recreation. For the working class, sport offered release from, if not a balance to, the sedentary routine of office or factory labor. For all classes, the notion of free time and escape—if not the opportunity for—became important.

Sporting clubs started to develop and provide common focus and camaraderie for neighborhoods, ethnic groups, and social classes. While the "ultimate promise of sport," as Hardy described it, rested in its overall ability to bind groups together in a spirit of citywide boosterism, these associations also tended to fragment the population in any number of ways, primarily race, ethnicity, class and gender.

Amid the city's increasingly industrialized cityscape, a growing middle class found communal notions of masculinity antiquated. Toiling in the highly competitive market economy, middle-class male professionals increasingly embraced a self-made model of manhood. With mentally rigorous but largely sedentary work becoming the middle-class norm, many men turned to gymnasia for private physical exercise. By the 1830s, these regimens included the English practice of sparring with boxing gloves to strengthen one's body into a robust, muscular vessel for the mind. Historian Louis Moore called Boston "a hub for health reformers," both white and Black men, who set the stage for what would be one of the greatest city sporting cultures in history.[38] While middle-class whites exercised to protect and prove their manhood, Black gym owners used physical culture to demonstrate their fitness for federal citizenship by offering their healthy bodies as proof that they harbored necessary middle-class values. This culture was the foundation upon which men like Dixon built careers.

The story George Dixon told went like this: as a young boy in Halifax, Nova Scotia, Canada, he often visited with a man named "Bailey" who received newspapers packed with illustrations from the United States. After listening for hours to Bailey recreate the bouts from those pages, Dixon went home with a head full of details to spar with his own imaginary opponents. In school, Dixon's obsession with pugilism drew the attention of a local bully, "Johnson," who challenged "Lil George" to a three-round, bare-knuckle bout in a nearby barn. The fight was a fierce one—Dixon's eyes were nearly closed and his mouth was swollen. Nevertheless, the eventual world champion claimed victory that day. When he returned home, however, his mother did not offer congratulations on his maiden triumph. Instead, she gave him a severe whipping and made him promise to never fight again. He kept that promise until his mother died soon afterward, and his mind again turned to fights.[39]

If every hero needs an origin story, then this is the one George Dixon offered his adopted hometown paper, the *Boston Daily Globe*, in February 1891. The interview served as many readers' personal introduction to a young fighter who, at that moment, stood on the precipice of worldwide fame. But Dixon's story of his love affair with pugilism raises numerous questions. In fact, like many of his early life's details, the varied narratives repeated over the years seem liberally peppered with inconsistencies, embellishments, and downright fabrications. That was to be expected.

By the time he gave that *Globe* interview, Dixon was already a carefully crafted commodity under O'Rourke. So perhaps Dixon should be forgiven for engaging in a bit of pre–championship-bout hype. But, alas, as was often the case with Dixon, this was simply one of a series of stories of how he got into the fight game.

A second origin story, written nearly four years later, during a more dire period for Black Americans, spoke of Dixon growing up and playing marbles "for keeps" on Boston's streets. As that was not allowed by law, or so the story goes, the nine-year-old Dixon was approached by a policeman "who warned him of the error of his ways, and dwelt at length upon the ultimate destination of small boys who failed to knuckle down." Dixon rejected the lecture and, instead, argued with the officer, who then drew his club. In response, Dixon drew back a right hand and sent the officer backward into the grass.[40] In 1894, even though Dixon's popularity was high, this story was more palatable for white audiences. Dixon was no longer engaged in his fistfight against a bully—a somewhat heroic gesture. Now, he had attacked a policeman—a lawless act more in line with what white audiences expected from a Black man.

A decade later, the *National Police Gazette*—purveyor of great stories, if not always well-established fact—offered yet a different version of the boxer's origin. In this story, Dixon made the acquaintance of "a modern Job Trotter[41] while delivering orders, from whom he tried to glean some important information. The negro deceived him and Dixon made up his mind that if he ever met the fellow again, he would give him a thrashing." Fate brought the pair together again soon afterward, and Dixon "kept his word with such dispatch that the negro never deceived anyone else afterward. That success prompted Dixon to take up boxing and before long the colored boy startled the sporting world with his ring achievements."[42] This third narrative was even further from what the *Globe* had originally presented. Penned during Dixon's fading years in 1905 and at Jim Crow's heyday, this tale certainly fulfilled the *Police Gazette*'s proclivity to tinge stories, even positive ones about Blacks, with hints of racism. While Dixon was, ostensibly, celebrated in this version of his origin, he was motivated to greatness not by a mother's love, but by a drive for revenge against a fellow Black man.

This murky, ever-shifting origin reveals the central difficulty in reconstructing Dixon's life. His story remains in the hands of a few.

So much of the legacy of George Dixon today depends upon his primary storyteller—Nat Fleischer.[43] Nathaniel Stanley Fleischer became interested in boxing because his father smoked Sweet Caporal and Murad tobacco. Each tin came with a small cigarette card depicting boxers of the day. He saw his first fight live in 1899—Terry McGovern vs. Pedlar Palmer in Tuckahoe, New York, for the bantamweight championship. He then sat ringside for the next seventy years. Strangely, the only memorable date in history Fleischer was ignorant of was the date of his own birth. Although he was born in 1887 on New York's Lower East Side, the exact date has been lost. He chose November 3. Fleischer, known for his conspicuous nose and compelling, resonant, nonstop delivery, produced perhaps more volumes on the sport of boxing than any other single individual in history. When heavyweight James J. Corbett died in 1933, Nat wrote a thirty-chapter biography in thirty-six hours—in, he confessed, a rambling, nonliterary style. He was also a man rooted in his past. In a 1962 interview with *Sports Illustrated*, Fleischer said, "I've always stuck to the old-timers because I saw them. They are fellows who were far superior to the boys today. In recent years, their equals were Willie Pep, Tony Canzoneri, Lou Ambers, Jimmy McLarnin and fellows like Rocky Marciano on his heavy hitting, not as a boxer. These fellows are more like the old-timers in that they possessed combinations."[44]

Fleischer was an enigma. He was a progenitor of many boxing traditions: he created a monthly magazine (*The Ring* magazine, still in publication today), monthly ratings, a Hall of Fame, biographies. Much of the sport's history depends on his record. Yet his research and record keeping leave much to be desired. His biographies and record books are rife with errors. His publications grew old around him and lost their credibility.

Fleischer's historic rankings of the greatest boxers of all time, within each division, drew the ire of boxers and pundits alike for generations. A first-of-its-kind lightning rod, *Nat Fleischer's All-Time Ring Record Book* was first published in 1942. Then the editor of *The Ring* magazine, he set out to create a definitive source on the sport's history, including a detailed history of title fights for each division and a section listing boxing's record setters. At its peak, the book contained six hundred pages of records and statistics. It was a bible for the sport, but not everyone bought into its gospel. American sportswriting giant Damon Runyon used his nationally syndicated Hearst column to chide Fleischer for his book: "One of these days, I am going to corral my friend, Nat Fleischer, sit him down and give him a severe wigging for his errors of omission." Runyon had a point. In Fleischer's all-time rankings, it was rare to find a man who boxed into the 1940s. Among bantamweights, George Dixon was ranked at the top, followed by Pete Herman, Kid Williams, Joe Lynch, and Bud Taylor. Among them, Taylor boxed the latest into the century, ending his career in 1931. Others echoed Runyon's playful critique as each subsequent edition of the *Record Book* was published. However, Runyon usually laid blame at the feet of the boxers, not Fleischer: "Now, I know it would be utterly impossible for any human being to compile an accurate record of all the pugilists of history. Indeed, I think I can safely challenge the accuracy of the record of any pug that ever lived as set down for publication because most such records are from memory and most fighters have poor memories or are just downright liars.... Chronologically, no individual record is ever perfect because here again the fighters do not remember and, in a majority of the cases, the records are padded with inconsequential feats."[45]

In Runyon's eyes, Fleischer's sin was his steadfast belief that his work was accurate without question. Yet there were too many records, with too many questions, across too many years to back up Fleischer's assumption. This perception of Fleischer continued to grow as the years passed. As boxing became essential programming on television in the 1950s, it created more armchair experts in the sweet science, and this growth made it fashionable for commentators—fight historians, television announcers, and beat reporters—to question old assumptions about the sport. Fleischer was establishment, seen as an old guard who had grown too close to many in the fight game, taken in by charismatic sorts like Tom O'Rourke. Some critics, like fight historian/film archivist Jimmy Jacobs, took his case directly to boxing writers by staging mini-festivals populated with his vast collection of fight films to make his points about a foggy perception of the past. After one such evening, *Los Angeles Mirror* editor Sid Ziff, another Fleischer critic, announced to fellow scribes in attendance that "Nat Fleischer owes it to the public and to the accuracy of boxing history to review these films and revise his rankings in the light of the first real evidence that these men have been shockingly overrated."[46] Ziff had a point. People like Jacobs and Ziff contended that fighters like Bob Fitzsimmons, "Gentleman" Jim Corbett, Stan Ketchel, and George Dixon were nowhere near the fighters Fleischer portrayed. "If some of them were fighting today, they might have trouble getting a license," Jacobs said in 1961. Jacobs once screened a copy of a Dixon exhibition match, most likely a genuine three-round fight between Dixon and journeyman Chester Leon staged by the Biograph Film Company. Unlike other staged fight films of the period, the battle appears legitimate, though the knockdown is not convincing. As fight films became popular at the turn of the twentieth century, it was common for boxers, even in genuine fights, to fake knockdowns to boost the film's appeal. The most famous of these was Jack Johnson's drop to the canvas as he ducked under Ketchel's telegraphed haymaker.[47] In Jacobs's mind, Dixon, famously touted by Fleischer as the top bantamweight of all time, was not worthy of such reverence. Ziff agreed. "The guy is a bum. This is disgusting," he said of the film.[48]

Fleischer encapsulated the problem for Black boxers of the era; their main narratives into the 1900s, including all descriptions of style, body, and temperament, depended on the pens in white hands. It often manifested itself in—at least to modern ears—almost unbelievable ways in print. In October 1913, T. P. Magilligan interviewed Bob "Coffee Cooler" Armstrong about Dixon's legacy. Magilligan was a veteran of sports and entertainment writing, often spotlighting Black athletes and performers. However, white reporters' written remembrances were often so tinged with the expected racist buffoonery of the era that a reader almost forgets the content is meant to pay tribute to a Black champion. Of Dixon, Magilligan quoted Armstrong as saying, in part:

> "Little Chocolate, yessah, he was the greatest fightah of dem all. 'Tain't no use yo all askin' me to name any more de greatest fighters. Little Chocolate, George Dixon, he was in a class by hmself . . .
>
> "Dixon had everything," continued Bob. "He could hit: my, how dat brat could hit! And he could box, and dey never was and never am gwine to be no gamer man dan Gawgie Dixon. . . . Dey's only one man who ever beat up Gawgie, and deh he ain't no man, for he is de debbil, and his name is John Barleycorn. Yessih, Barleycorn got to old Gawgie and he got to him hard. Gawgie was jes' natchly dat good to others dat he was bad to himself. His money was a gift. He gave away moah money to his sparrin' pahtaens dan mos' dese champions gib to they managahs 'nowadays."
>
> When Dixon started, Armstrong remembered him as "no bigger dan a cigar-holder."
>
> "Little Gawgie ne ain't got nottin to say. He's most dumb. Fer a time, I thinks Mr. O'Rourke's been off to some mute asylum and picks up dat little chocolate-colored lad.
>
> "C'ose wen Gawgie gets good, and de money starts rollin' in on him like de water rolls over in Ohio wen one dem banks break, he takes to puttin' on some dawg, and dey ain't no one to discourage him. He spends his money like a sailor on shoah leave, and tain't

no time 'fore Gawgie gets a sparrin' limited wound bounts with old John Barleycorn. Dixon keeps even wid dat Barleycorn pahty for a time, den ole Jawn, he puts one ovah on Gawgie and bam—Lil Chocolate, he's out. He was de best of dem all."[49]

This was the fate of Dixon's story throughout his life, but particularly during his decline and immediately after his death. His powerful legacy of innovation was crushed beneath a powerful racist message, even influencing his opportunity to resurface generations later. While the details of stories like his origins may never be cemented in fact, a clearer picture can be gathered concerning how Dixon's earliest circumstances and opportunities shaped him as a fighter, as well as the social changes going on around him during his career and how those changes impacted the lens through which he was viewed.

CHAPTER 2

Discovery

HE WAS JUST A KID. Seventeen years old. Thin lead weights slid into his shoes, between his bare feet and leather soles, so he could climb above one hundred pounds and legally be allowed to compete. Even in his violent world, he had the body of a boy—thin, gangly, with arms slightly longer than his diminutive frame should have allowed. He would grow into those proportions, a bit, but never taller. Years from becoming a physical marvel, he was already handsome, with oversized features, large brown eyes, a nose not yet pounded flat and pockmarked by alcohol, a noble jaw, ears tucked tight to his temples but a touch too big. He shaved his head smooth every week, a choice that somehow made his skull look bigger and his body smaller. As the hair started to grow back at the end of each week, the dark stubble revealed a recessed hairline that started at his crown. In this moment, it was hard to understand that he would be almost unrecognizable in appearance and personality in only twenty years.

Under the crude electric lights of the theater, his Black skin glowed a shade or two lighter than reality. Make no mistake, he was a Black man in the eyes of the world. Crowds were well aware of that; newspapers rarely missed a reference to it—"colored" and "negro" when they were feeling charitable, a cacophony of other vile terms when not. Illustrations depicting his likeness on their pages could be quite heroic or little more than ink smudges. The fact he had far fairer skin tones than many of his contemporary Black fighters often gave rise to wild rumors about his parentage.

He wore little in the ring: a pair of dark leggings with a sash belt showcasing his colors or white trunks oddly resembling an adult-sized cloth diaper. He wore black leather shoes, no matter if fighting on dirt, sawdust, or wooden planks. Prizefighting was not a glamorous spectacle. It was a dirty, corrupt, exploitive business. No place for a kid. Despite his age, however, he was always the coolest man in the room. Even on nights like this, nights where he was taking a savage beating at the hands of his opponent, the crowd knew Dixon somehow would be standing at the end of the bout. He had already gained a reputation among "the sports" in Boston—the hundreds of gamblers, club owners, fight managers, newspapermen, and fans embracing a sport that was cultivating its first heroes while finding surer footing within proper society. These men all saw the talent, but it was Dixon's steady nerves at such a young age and with limited ring experience that made many take note. The kid was a natural.

Years later, James J. Corbett echoed those sentiments and called Dixon one of "the two coolest fighters that ever stepped into a ring." The former heavyweight champion of the world recounted tales of Dixon in his dressing room, calmly flipping through newspapers or discussing fighters only minutes before his bouts. He marveled when Dixon once called for a bootblack to come and shine his shoes, as he wanted them after the fight to wear to a dinner to be given in his honor by some friends, if he won. "I remember on one occasion the little negro asked for pen and ink. He quietly wrote a letter to a friend in the Middle West. Not the least bit of nervousness was displayed and the letter is today preserved by Dixon's friend as a souvenir of the great little man's nerve," Corbett told the *National Police Gazette*.[1]

One of the earliest appearances of that same coolness was on display on this night—March 21, 1888, in the Tremont Athletic Club. This was only Dixon's seventh career bout—his sixth in Boston—and his opponent was a nobody. Being a local fighter, Dixon was already a large enough draw that he warranted full coverage from the *Boston Daily Globe*. The paper billed Dixon as "colored" and his opponent, Patsey "Paddy" Kelley, as having "little notoriety as a pugilist."[2] The latter was an understatement. Kelley fought a total of three bouts over a decade-long career—two against Dixon in 1888 and 1889, and his last nearly nine years later against a fighter named Young Chase who also never fought again. Newspaper reports pegged Kelley at an age disadvantage, putting him a decade older than Dixon, even though he was later remembered as only fifteen years old at the time.[3] Such was reporting of this fringe sport, populated by so many fringe characters. The era is littered with fighters like Kelley— guys who boasted only three or four fights and then disappeared from the sport forever. These men were necessary to the profession by allowing up- and-comers or down-and-outers to pad their records without much risk.

Unbeknownst to Dixon, among the rowdy crowd that night sat the boisterous Bostonian Tom O'Rourke. Born in Boston on May 13, 1856, O'Rourke did not come from privilege like many of his colleagues in the city's fight game. He was a public-school kid, although not a dedicated one. Despite that lack of interest in academics, he boasted a keen wit and a swift, retentive memory. It served him well. Even later in life, he recited dates and details of long-forgotten baseball games, fights, and rowing matches with ease. That talent was both the envy and the crutch of many sports writers. Simply call across the ring and O'Rourke could provide any fact needed for background. As a manager, he was as opportunistic as he was ruthless. His stable of fighters, Black or white, were little more than livestock—treated well so long as they had value, abandoned once injury or age robbed them of utility. His first fighter was Jack Havlin, whom he backed for $500 versus Ike Weir, the so-called Belfast Spider, on July 20, 1887, in Warwick, Rhode Island.[4] It was a bloody affair, even while fought in the skintight gloves gaining preference in the sport. The bout was stopped in the sixty-first round when the referee, fearing for the lives of both well-punished men, declared a draw.[5] While hooked from that moment on, O'Rourke was not in the fight game full time. In fact, he was still a plasterer in Boston when he happened upon Dixon.

When timekeeper James Colville opened the match, Dixon took an immediate right to his stomach, which he countered with a left across Kelley's face. He scored three more lefts as the round progressed, willingly trading them for damaging rights from Kelley to his ribs. It was not the best strategy. He had tipped his hand—his one good hand. As the fight continued, Dixon over-emphasized his left, an admittedly darting and powerful punch, but it was easily countered as he fought as if his right was withered and useless. Kelley used this obvious weakness against Dixon, working his opponent's body without fear of a counter round after round. With Boston fight icon George Godfrey and up-and-comer Frank Steele in his corner, Dixon stood his ground throughout the bout.

O'Rourke was struck by the young man's raw skill and speed. He turned to fellow fight manager and club owner Dick Blanchard: "Dave, that young colored boy has the makings of a great fighter. If I could get ahold of him, I would make him champion. He's green and don't know a thing about the manly art. But he's game as a bulldog, has a naturally fast and powerful left hand and seems to possess an uncanny fighting instinct. If I can teach him to box, he will be a world beater."[6] In the fifth round, Dixon took damage to one eye from a savage Kelley left hand that stopped the fight so Dixon could rub and clear the eye. Years later, O'Rourke remembered that punch, that injury: "Kelley closed one of Dixon's eyes tight as a proverbial drum. That, incidentally, was the only time anything like that happened to Dixon. From that time on, I never remember a fight in which George's opponent succeeded in closing his eye."[7] At the call of time after fifteen rounds, a draw was declared based solely on Dixon remaining upright, as most in attendance believed it to be Dixon's first loss.[8]

O'Rourke, however, had found his man. He wrote about that night years later: "I noticed in that fight that Dixon used only one hand—his left. He did not try to stop a blow with the right, but how he did slam home that left. I immediately decided that here was a jewel in the rough and I took him under my wings with the result that, ere long, he was one of the greatest attractions in America."[9] The next day, O'Rourke inquired as to where Dixon lived and was pointed toward the "colored quarter" of Boston's West End. The story, as O'Rourke told it hundreds of times, was that he walked the streets of the district, asking about Dixon, but few knew the name. This is the point in the story where O'Rourke's tale veers from probable to laughable under the pen of Nat Fleischer:

> I had almost given up my search. And was about to call it a day. I was standing alongside the curb scratching my head in perplexity when I noticed a big, buxom, full-breasted woman leaning out the window in the house across the street.
>
> To her, I repeated my usual query: "Do you happen to know a colored boy by the name of Dixon around here who is a boxer?"
>
> Imagine my surprise when the woman queried in return: "What do you want with my Gawge? He's my husband."[10]

According to O'Rourke, the woman conveyed the message to Dixon and he met the young fighter at his gym the next day.[11] But like much of Dixon's backstory, this tale is, at best, partial fiction used to promote other agendas. Already entrenched in the prizefighting community—witness his two famous corner men that night—Dixon would not have been difficult to find. Nevertheless, O'Rourke and Dixon connected soon after that bout and would never be truly separated again.

———

As a young man in the city, Dixon lived on Knapp Street in Boston, and often visited the boxing exhibitions given by the city's pugilists. He always made it a point to get a seat close to the stage so he could get a good view of every blow given. Dixon also landed a job as an errand boy in the photo studio of Elmer Chickering, one of the most popular portrait photographers in Boston. In that famed studio, Dixon set down his true pugilism roots. Even years later, he spoke highly of his time there. In fact, he spoke more often of Chickering than of his own family—perhaps a nod to the studio's true influence. That period in his life also offers a more viable origin story than any in the popular press. As the *Boston Daily Globe* wrote in January 1900, after news of Dixon's contemplation of retirement from the ring:

> To the [Chickering] gallery, to have their pictures taken, went many of the pugilists of fame of that day. Naturally, they fell to talking of fight as they waited for their turn to face the glaring camera. George drank in the conversations. The bit of a shaver was shifty on his feet and clever with his hands then, without any training. He grew interested as he heard the tales of the giant heroes of the ring. He coaxed some of the old chaps in the fistic profession to give him a few scientific points. He was chummy at that time with one Elias Hamilton, and their respective merits gloved, were argued until it was necessary to settle the question of superiority in regular man fashion. That was his first fight in Boston.[12]

Chickering's studio was the community hub Dixon needed. He met all the names of the day there—from military men and politicians to stars of theater and opera. Sports luminaries, too, especially baseball players and boxers, were subjects of Chickering's camera. He had learned photography as an adolescent in Grandon, Vermont, went into business for himself in 1870, and relocated to Boston in 1884, establishing a studio at 21 West Street. His first-floor gallery was the best exhibition space in the city apart from a museum; the third-floor studio was equipped with state-of-the-art cameras and lenses, including one of the earliest telephoto setups. He immediately distinguished himself from other professional studios in town by specializing in celebrity portraiture.

Chickering's gentlemanly demeanor won him an institutional clientele. He made a small fortune through the public sale of cabinet cards of actresses and actors. Desiring recognition in the professional community as an artistic portraitist, he regularly exhibited his work around the world. He was also not beyond pushing the boundaries of the burgeoning industry. He once photographed Sandro Botticelli's *The Birth of Venus* and then proceeded to sell copies across the city. Over that incident, in June 1887, Chickering was brought to court to face charges of printing indecent pictures. His counsel argued that "copies of this painting can be found in a prominent New York hotel and in several high-toned saloons of this city . . . if this was to be held to be an improper picture then the owners of every art gallery in Europe and America ought to be punished for putting on such an exhibition, for hundreds more indelicate things were shown in interest of art and science."[13]

A month later, he drew the ire of husbands across the Back Bay when he was arrested by Boston police and charged, once again, with printing and selling indecent photographs—only this time of some of Boston's most prominent society women. It had become the rage among young women to have their photographs taken while they posed like figures in the classic paintings of Paris, as well as more fun figures like nymphs, goddesses, and mermaids, all demonstrating "that the Boston girl today does not fall far below the standard of Greek ideal."[14] Actresses and society women came to Chickering's studio to be photographed in "various striking attitudes" for presentation to their husbands. Of course, what were originally shot as personal photos, soon found a way into the larger community where they were reproduced as "private negatives" and sold. They were taken in various poses, after the famous pictures in the French Salon and in reproduction of Greek ideals. Most of the pictures were arranged that the "features of the subject" were strategically veiled. Chickering was known to say: "As devotees of true art, there can be nothing improper in the exposure of natural beauty"[15] In defense of Chickering, the *Chicago Daily Tribune* argued that "to the truly artistic mind, the nude in nature cannot be repulsive or immodest . . . to the pure all things are pure, and it is only the depraved imagination of the police authorities that discovers anything wrong in their doings."[16] In January 1903, a fire in the Chickering studio caused losses between $60,000 and $70,000, including the destruction of one hundred thousand negatives.[17] Respected within the profession and regarded a civic-minded public man, Chickering died a Boston celebrity in the city's Psychopathic Hospital on May 14, 1915. He had been stricken in his studio three weeks earlier and never recovered.[18] After his death, the studio continued operation under the Chickering name until 1919.[19]

Among the hundreds of prizefighters who found their way into the studio, as Dixon tended door and ran errands for Chickering, was fellow Canadian George Godfrey, whom Dixon met just as the young lad was getting started in the fight game. Long before heavyweight Jack Johnson made his dramatic rise to fame, Black Bostonians adopted several boxers as favorite sons. Primary among them was "Old Chocolate" Godfrey, a native of Charlottetown, Prince Edward Island, Canada, who moved to Boston in his youth and worked as a butcher's apprentice and porter. It was there where he started training to box in the 1880s.

At twenty-six, Godfrey began fighting competitively in the bare-knuckles tour. His fights with local Black stars, like McHenry Johnson, attracted hundreds of fans; his bouts with white men drew even more. He was known for his "courage, generalship and science" inside the ring.[20] In February 1883, with a sixth-round knockout of Charles Hadley, Godfrey claimed the world colored heavyweight championship, sponsored by the *National Police Gazette*. That fight was officiated by then–world heavyweight champion John L. Sullivan. In 1886, Godfrey first fought Joe Lannan, a popular white Canadian heavyweight who called Boston home. The pair clashed four times—a draw, a no decision, another draw and, finally, a Godfrey victory. Those bouts proved popular with audiences and showed to all that Godfrey "had no fear for man or mob" when it came to crossing race lines.[21]

Godfrey held the world colored heavyweight crown for more than five years before losing it in August 1888 to Peter Jackson, the Australian heavyweight champion. Godfrey was a slight favorite heading into that match, held in San Francisco. Jackson eclipsed Godfrey, whose 5-foot-10-inch, 170-pound frame looked small next to the 6-foot-1-inch, 190-pound Jackson. Just before the twelfth round ended, Jackson screamed "I've got you now," a comment that drew the crowd to its feet. But Godfrey survived and fought on. In the middle of the fifteenth, a stinging blow jarred Godfrey to the point where he attempted to take his seat in his corner before the round ended. His seconds—what Eagan, the author of *Boxiana*, called a boxer's "faction" and what modern writers call a box-er's "corner men"—pushed him back into the ring. He survived until the nineteenth round, when he offered his hand in defeat to Jackson mid-round. The Aussie shook Godfrey's "hand heartily and threw both hands up in the air and laughed."[22]

Godfrey never had a chance to vie for a heavyweight world championship against Sullivan. They did get matched in 1880 for a bout in Boston, and were stripped and ready for the fray in Baily's Gym when the police interfered. The accounts of that near-bout slipped into the stuff of legend long ago. The *Chicago Defender* wrote:

> The whole of Boston was divided over Sullivan and Godfrey. One would have thought that two popular candidates were running for alderman. Finally, the chief of police signed a permit for them to box ten rounds in Boston, with the provision that anything that looked like a rough house would cause him to call off the fight. The match drew crowds from Providence, Troy, New York, Brooklyn, and

George Godfrey. Signed, "To My Actor Pupil George Godfrey." Photo
by Elmer Chickering. *Courtesy of Special Collections, Fine Arts Library,
Harvard University.*

Philadelphia. . . . The night of the fight those who had tickets and those who did not rushed to the door and started a rough house just as the men were ready to go into the ring. It took every policeman in Boston to quiet down the gang. This closed any chance of Godfrey meeting Sullivan as he would not have a chance outside of Boston.[23]

This wasn't the only possible bout between the two champions. In 1888, Godfrey surprised Sullivan at a benefit by stepping from the crowd to challenge the champion to a friendly bout—then and there. Godfrey walked to the stage to great applause from the crowd, but the champion dodged the bout by blaming his manager for the unexpected challenge and announcing, quite loudly and publicly, that they were parting ways immediately. Overshadowed in the moment, Godfrey returned to his seat.[24]

Godfrey died in October 1901, after a long battle with numerous diseases, including edema and tuberculosis. He was forty-eight years old. A few weeks before his death, the weathered champion called the Rev. Joseph P. Bixby, dean of the Revere Evangelical Institute, to his bedside. He wished to die a Christian man and wanted to review his life with Bixby. Godfrey confessed his hand never struck an unfair blow in battle, he had always been square and honest with his fellow man, and he had never done anyone wrong. He hoped that was enough to enter God's kingdom.[25] An hour before he died, when told the end was nigh, Godfrey asked to be lifted from his bed to stand on his feet one last time. With great effort, doctors and family raised him. He stood—if only for a moment—and then collapsed onto his bed unconscious. He died in a matter of moments.[26] On October 20, 1901, Bixby delivered a brief eulogy for the champion during a funeral service held in the living room of Godfrey's Beach Street home in Boston. In it, Bixby reminded mourners how the body of the deceased, once "a monument to strength," was now "a monument to weakness." Referring to the former champion's last days on Earth, the reverend said Godfrey had given all the attention to the value of being prepared for "the supreme test," as he always had given great care to being prepared in the ring.[27]

Historian Louis Moore artfully places Godfrey and his generation of athletes as the first to shed the overt racism that hung over the country and who saw sports as a means of employment, empowerment, and manly independence. Although Black boxers had to deal with unscrupulous white managers, financial backers, and athletic club owners, they were also independent artisans who controlled their own labor. Many understood their body as a powerful commodity over which they could start exerting some control. Black America was still forced to use its body as a means of capital, but some were starting to set the price.

This would be the first Black man Dixon embraced who had made a career in the fight game—perhaps why some came to call Godfrey "the grand old man who inspired George Dixon."[28] Even after his best days had passed, Godfrey became a popular boxing instructor in Boston, with men from "the elite" to "the street" calling on him for expertise at his 3 Tremont Row gym that he shared with his brother, James, and son, George Jr. Dixon found his way there, as the place Godfrey centered all his training activities. While training Dixon in those early days, he almost certainly instilled in Dixon thoughts on race and missed opportunity that he already carried with him thanks to his Africville roots. Godfrey advised Dixon to forget about his color; he told Dixon to block out what audiences would say about him while in the ring, and only concentrate on the man in front of him.[29] Race, he said, would be nothing more than a barrier to opportunity—find a way around it. Given the legendary standing of "Old Chocolate" in the business, Dixon may have taken no words more to heart than these. It was advice he heeded his entire career, and perhaps the reason why the white community accepted him so widely.

In November 1886, Dixon made his professional fight debut with a knockout of fellow Nova Scotian, Young Johnson. There are no details about the fight recorded beyond the result; it was the first and only bout of Johnson's career. In September 1887, Dixon made his American debut against Elias Hamilton, a Black fighter, at the Way Street Gymnasium in Boston when Dixon was not yet sixteen. He scored a knockout in the eighth round. Again, there is no record of the bout beyond a brief mention by Dixon in 1890.[30]

Boston readers were first introduced to Dixon—the "colored bantam-weight"—in November 1887.[31] With only two fights under their belt, Dixon and his backer, Young Collins, marched into the *Boston Daily Globe* offices and set down a challenge for any 105-pound fighter, specifically citing Tommy Doherty as a worthy opponent. By way of assurance of the young fighter's readiness, Collins offered: "Dixon has been tried and has proven a game fighter, one who will stand lots of punishment."[32] Two months later, he got a fight, against Johnny Lyman, and then they came in rapid succession. Dixon fought a dozen sanctioned bouts in 1888, mostly against the local landscape of journeymen, including the aforementioned Doherty. Dixon was seventeen years old—and small. He weighed ninety-seven pounds at his first fight, about the weight of "a newborn calf" as newspapers pointed out in a bizarre comparison to livestock, a practice that would be echoed through his career. Massachusetts law said no one under the age of nineteen weighting under one hundred pounds was allowed to fight in the state. At first, Dixon fought "on the sly," an easy task for a young unknown. But as he found success, he needed an additional edge. Dixon often weighed in prior to bouts with those lead plates in his shoes—even forgetting to remove them on several occasions.[33]

He was gaining a reputation as an ambitious soul with the right people behind him—Dr. A. P. Ordway, Dave Blanchard, and Capt. A. W. Cooke, all white promoters, each of whom had big money and ample experience in the fight game.[34] Cooke was a noted matchmaker of foot races and prizefights, a Boston sporting insider with connections to the *National Police Gazette* in New York City, the sport's chief editorial advocate. Ordway made his fortune as a manufacturing chemist, and then as famed head of the firm A. P. Ordway & Co., a nationwide seller of bitters, tonics, sulfur soaps, and cure-alls of various types guaranteeing prolonged vitality and life. His multimillion-dollar fortune was an object of public obsession as newspapers chronicled trips on his yacht, *Jane VI*, up and down the Atlantic Coast.[35] As his fortune fueled matches for decades, he remained a fixture at ringside well into his old age as he found his place among an "old guard . . . a bunch of broad-minded, big businessmen, who conducted fistic affairs in a more upright and sportsmanlike manner."[36] In August 1920, his body ravaged by cancer, Ordway shot himself in the head as his wife worked in the kitchen. She discovered his body, half-dressed, prone across the bed, warm revolver still in his hand, and a note that read: "I have suffered a great deal. This is the best way out of it. Forgive me."[37]

Blanchard was a popular businessman in the city who had a propensity for sport, namely horses, dogs, game fowl, and, particularly, boxers. His substantial wealth fed that passion. Blanchard backed many of the biggest names of the day, including John "Benicia Boy" Heenan and John L. Sullivan, and even refereed when called upon. He was a frequent sight at ringside for bouts large and small. Unlike many of his era, he was an advocate of fair fights, and served as an early champion of the Queensberry Rules that would civilize the sport from its backroom roots. Blanchard often found himself in the company of fellow Boston sports.

He was not a native of the city, a fact largely forgotten in his later years as he became one of the primary faces of the Boston sporting scene. Born in New London, New Hampshire, Blanchard was sent to be raised by family in Canada at two years old when his mother died. At thirteen, he returned to New London with his brother, and they set about finding work to support themselves. There they stayed until three years later, when the pair found a job leading five prized horses nearly one hundred and twenty miles to Boston, which became Blanchard's home for the remainder of his life. At twenty-one, he entered sporting circles by organizing dog races and illegal bare-knuckle brawls. Soon afterward, he joined the lucrative pursuit of organizing trotting races at the Mystic and Beacon parks. With that money, he purchased his own stable of Thoroughbreds, among the fastest in the country.[38]

But nobody could do for Dixon what Tom O'Rourke could.

To understand George Dixon, you must understand Tom O'Rourke. No single person is tied more directly to shaping the eventual champion than the Boston-born manager, a caricature of a nineteenth-century gentleman sport, a wheeler, a dealer, and a showman on par with the greats. He had a knack for making money in the blooming popularity of boxing among a larger segment of the public. The Dixon-O'Rourke relationship, cemented during Dixon's rise, became central to both men's success.

The Irish American quarter of O'Rourke's childhood was chock full of kids and, as such, full of altercations of all sorts almost daily.[39] He was always known as a fighter. As a young man, O'Rourke rowed in Boston-based crews across New England for more than a decade—many newspaper reports painted him as a "champion stroke of his time."[40] He drifted—somewhat unsuccessfully—into business, only to be drawn back into athletics, this time as a manager of pugilists. His keen eye spotted talent quickly, and he moved equally as fast to lock himself in as their representation. The *San Francisco Bulletin* wrote of O'Rourke's formula at perhaps the height of his fame: "After choosing his material, he has been extremely successful in cultivating it. He has gotten out of his men all there is in them. After bringing them to perfection, his excellent judgment manifested itself again in making the matches."[41]

In many ways, managers became what urban sociologist Loïc J. D. Wacquant described as "surrogate fathers" to their fighters, as they devoted inordinate amounts of time and energy to resolving their love affairs, financial difficulties, and other private quandaries. In addition to seeing that their man arrived in top shape on fight night, so too did they have to sort out the pitfalls of day-to-day life. To keep constant surveillance on their fighter, they often employed a "web of relations" to help in this cause: manager, trainer, sparring partners, friends, and spouses.[42]

This is a generous evaluation, as often this relationship centered more on protecting an asset. Fathers rarely abandoned sons when their financial value was exhausted. Likewise, O'Rourke was not an altruistic presence in Dixon's life. He was controlling, demanding, violent, and, when Dixon needed him most, absent. This was no father-son relationship; notions of master-slave are apparent in a relationship fraught with societal and racial overtones that, although it made Dixon a champion, came at a serious cost.

It was that chance discovery of Dixon, along with, later, that of "Barbados" Joe Walcott, that made O'Rourke a much sought-after manager-trainer. As famed referee George Siler said: "The truth is that O'Rourke did not know how to put up his hands when Dixon came upon the arena as a fighter. Many say that O'Rourke stuck closer than sticking plaster to 'Little Chocolate' while he was a winner."[43] Inside pugilistic circles, that sentiment was unchallenged—Dixon made O'Rourke instead of O'Rourke making Dixon. That might have been true inside the ring, but O'Rourke was a master navigator of the world outside it. That is what Dixon needed. As a manager, O'Rourke always believed the axiom "a match well-made is half won." He loved a good scrap—not a fully lopsided one, but one where the numbers favored his man, even if by an extra pound or inch. When O'Rourke hit the road with Dixon and booked theatrical engagements for him, the manager carried along a portable ring specially made to his instructions. At each stop, he personally saw to its assembly on the stage. This ring was quite a bit smaller than the regulation size. After hundreds of bouts inside it, Dixon was accustomed to it; the opponents he faced were not. There were even occasions when promoters permitted O'Rourke to use his favorite ring in club battles. When he signed Dixon to box Tommy White of Chicago, the Syracuse, New York, club insisted on using its own ring. Dixon fought to a draw that night and was outboxed in the eyes of many observers. However, tradition dictated a champion could not lose his title unless stopped or beaten by a large number of points. Dixon and White fought four months later in Denver, Colorado, but this time in O'Rourke's favorite ring. The bout went the distance once again, but Dixon prevailed in the tighter quarters.[44]

While others struggled to open clubs up and down the East Coast, O'Rourke was turning people away from his doors. He ran some of the era's most successful establishments in Boston and, later, New York City—the Delevan Hotel, Coney Island Athletic Club, Lennox Club, National Sporting Club, Broadway Athletic Club, among others. He was a diplomat. Mingling among municipal politicians taught him the trick of navigating obstacles—his "gift for gab" was his biggest weapon. His many connections on city councils never hurt in speeding up a license getting issued or a blind eye being turned during one of his bouts. He was, in the words of one publication, "an aggressive, two-fisted Irish-American who believed in getting what he wanted by the exercise of dominant will-power."[45] Connected and tough, his reputation depended upon who you asked. Some colleagues—and even some of his enemies—considered him a fair man who sought deals that made both sides happy—asking for only an "even break," as he called it. For others, he long operated under a haze of impropriety. He was a frequent guest in courtrooms on two continents. He defended everything from his business practices to his temper in front of countless judges.

For instance, as deputy boxing commissioner of New York later in life, he appeared in court to answer charges that he attacked referee James Edward Forbes at Ebbets Field as Forbes was reporting on a bout for the *Brooklyn Daily Eagle*. Seems O'Rourke was enraged when Forbes refused to give up his ringside seat. Days after that confrontation, Forbes received a letter from the New York State Athletic Commission, which controlled boxing in the state, notifying him that "your license as referee, No. 562, is suspended and you are barred from all licensed clubs in this state."[46] O'Rourke brought suit against the publishers of *Boxing*, a sporting paper published in London, which charged him with making "fraudulent arrangements in contests in New York, San Francisco, and other American cities in order to bring about prearranged results and so win considerable sums of money." During cross-examination, O'Rourke was asked about charges made by the *New York Times* and other American newspapers of "foul play" in fights where O'Rourke operated as a manager or principal backer.[47] He denied all charges and—as he often did—dodged punishment.

Under O'Rourke's control, Dixon's earliest tests were against Hank Brennan—including three consecutive bouts in 1888. In the eyes of century-ago fight observers, these long-forgotten bouts—all draws—were a turning point for Dixon's career:

> There was one husky lad in the Hub whom Dixon could never put
> down for the count . . . [Hank] Brennan hooked up with Dixon in a

twenty-six-round draw before the Parnell Club of Boston. Old-time fight experts who saw these four encounters will tell you if Brennan had been properly trained and handled, he would have been the Featherweight Champion of the World instead of the colored wonder. That was where Dixon's luck first manifested itself . . . [Brennan] worked a trade all day and had neither time nor backing to get in proper condition for his encounters with Dixon.[48]

Displaying the fevered passion of fans during the era, the third Dixon-Brennan bout resulted in a riot inside the arena when Brennan fans protested the referee's ruling of a draw. Supporters of both men pressed into the center of the ring. Jeers, catcalls, and hoots rang out—but no punches were thrown inside the arena. The crowd saved that for when they spilled out of the Athenian Club into the Boston streets. At that point, fists flew, resulting in the arrival of the police riot squad to break up the mass.

Dixon continued to navigate a series of journeymen and novices before suffering his first loss in June 1889. Entering the bout against George Wright, who was making both his debut and finale inside the ring, Dixon boasted a record of eight wins, no losses, and seven draws. Dixon was far better than his record showed. Many of those draws would have been victories if he was matched up in an even setting. Usually, however, Dixon found himself in hostile environments where his opponent was the least of his concerns, as an unruly, often intoxicated, and usually white crowd would press and even attack Dixon as he fought. Some draws were outright robberies; others may have spared him a grave fate from an angry crowd. George Wright was a last-minute replacement for a rematch with Frank Maguire, a fighter Dixon beat three months prior; after dropping out of his meeting with Dixon, Maguire never fought again professionally. During his bout with Wright, Dixon illegally struck his opponent twice after the bell—some sources say in the face, others say in the groin—resulting in Wright pulling off his gloves and leaving the ring while Parnell Athletic Club members cried foul. Wright was coaxed back into the ring and awarded the contest. Dixon wrote briefly of that night a few years later: "At the close of the second round, the referee claimed I struck Wright after the gong had sounded, and for that reason which was unfair, he gave the decision against me. I could not induce Wright to meet me again and he has many times since been beaten by men whom I have easily defeated."[49]

Nevertheless, Dixon refused to fade into obscurity as many of his opponents did after early career losses. In fact, he continued to gain a following, mainly because of his size, his strength, and his unique, unheard of approach to bout preparation.

There was always an air of incredulity surrounding depictions of Dixon—a man so small, yet so perfect. He was "freakish" when it came to reducing weight. He could build himself up or reduce as the occasion required. When he started in the fight game, he was "a mere stripling."[50] At first, he fought at 108 pounds. As the years went by, he developed into a genuine bantamweight and fought at 112 pounds; then he went up to 116 pounds, then to 118, and then to 122, all apparently without suffering any loss of skill. The *Boston Daily Globe* wrote of Dixon before his bout against Eugene Hornbacher in December 1889: "The muscles on his chest, back and arms indicated that he was in perfect trim and he had a confident expression on his face. He is a well-built lad above the waist, but his limbs seemed a trifle too small to be proportionate."[51] That bout was "the first time that Dixon was properly trained. In all his previous battles, his training had consisted of a short walk before going to work in the morning and dumb bell exercises at dinner hour."[52]

Preparations for the Hornbacher fight, however, were more sophisticated. Four or five weeks before a fight, Dixon began. The first day, he was given a physical, and for the next three days he did nothing except take short walks without sweating. During the remainder of the week, he did light work that included short walks, calisthenics, and limited sparring. The next week, he increased his walking distance until he reached five miles a day. When he took a shorter walk, he punched the ball. Every morning he ate an orange, and ten minutes later, had his breakfast, which generally consisted of rolled oats, as many soft-boiled eggs as he felt like eating, bread and butter, and a cup of weak tea. On arrival at the gymnasium, an attendant stripped him and rubbed him down thoroughly with Turkish towels. He then took a bath of lukewarm water, after which he was again rubbed down and taken to his room. There, he received a hand-rubbing of liniment until dry. He then dressed himself in dry clothing and went to his manager's home, where he ate lunch at one o'clock. That afternoon, he punched the light ball for twenty minutes, used the half-pound dumbbell and Indian clubs for the next twenty minutes, and the last twenty minutes he ran around the track. He then went through the same process of rubbing as he did in the morning. At six, he ate supper. At nine, he went to bed and slept "peacefully as if nothing was on his mind."[53] The *Boston Daily Globe* reported of this regimen: "This method of getting a man in condition is much different from that practiced by the majority of trainers. Until Dixon was trained in this city, it was considered an impossibility to train a man in a city. The custom had been to hustle the fighter twenty-five, fifty or one hundred miles into the country and for eight to ten weeks have him train under the watchful eye of two or three trainers. The expenses for such training have been known to exceed $500, and yet the man has been in no better condition than Dixon, who had done his training in the city."[54]

In December 1889, Dixon claimed the American 115-pound title from Hornbacher in a second-floor apartment of a hotel in New London, Connecticut—not much of a challenge for the young Dixon, who knocked the weak champion out in the second round. However, that fight, and a bit of the pre-fight buildup of Dixon, set up the most significant bout of Dixon's career to that point. As Hornbacher still "lay limp and motion-less," Cal McCarthy was the first to jump into the ring after the decision and shake Dixon's hand. Cordially, McCarthy told Dixon he was a won-derful fighter. "You think I'm a good one, eh?" Dixon said after a moment. "Well, you'll think so to a moral certainty when you and me meet."[55] They did just that on February 7, 1890.

More than one hundred and twenty-five years later, Dixon-McCarthy I is considered one of the finest fights of all time. Held in a hall above a bank, only the city's elite were invited to the private contest. Every sports editor in the city, sans one, was notified of the bout. Only the *Boston Record* editor, the head of the anti-sport newspaper crusading against boxing, was excluded. As the fight began, referee Al Smith caught a glimpse of the ignored editor peeking in a window from the roof. Some of the crowd's unruly members rushed the editor and threatened to hurl him to the street below. He talked his way down and even into the fight thanks to O'Rourke granting him admission.[56]

A flashy Irishman, Cal McCarthy was born in McClintockville, Pennsylvania, moved to Jersey City, New Jersey, at an early age, and spent his brief fight life in and around New York City. In 1887, he won the Amateur Championship of America at eighteen, and turned professional the next year. The five-foot-two-inch McCarthy made his pro ring debut in February 1888, and by his fifth bout in September of that same year, he claimed the featherweight championship of America in a twenty-one-round bout against Hornbacher. With that accomplishment, he became the first teenaged world-title holder.[57]

Copyrighted by
John Wood N. Y. 1890.

George Dixon. Collodion print on card. Photo by John Wood, 1890. *Courtesy of Special Collections, Fine Arts Library, Harvard University.*

Cal McCarthy with two unidentified boys in boxing poses. Albumen silver print on card. Photo by Napoleon Sarony. *Courtesy of Special Collections, Fine Arts Library, Harvard University.*

The five hundred men gathered to watch Dixon-McCarthy in Boston's Union Athletic Club—men not only from "The Hub," but Baltimore, Philadelphia, New York, and Washington, DC[58]—had been frenzied from the start. The *Boston Daily Globe* reported, "The stillness of the tomb reigned as the men came up to the scratch. The stillness only lasted for a short time."[59] The fight drew heavy betting interest, although nearly all the "sports" in attendance favored McCarthy. So much so, in fact, that McCarthy supporters drummed up a story for days before the bout that the New York–based boxer wasn't taking his training—and, in turn, Dixon—seriously. It didn't work. The purse was set at $3,000 for the winner; more than $15,000 was wagered. Nearly all of that was on McCarthy to win. When the fight reached the fifteenth round, additional wagers were offered on Dixon. There were still no takers.[60] Ringside reports painted the fight's picture: "Time and again he [McCarthy] had Dixon in Queer Street, but the little colored boy had all the luck with him and by dint of sheer cleverness and physical endurance managed to wriggle out of all unpleasant predicaments."[61] Dixon caught that second wind and parlayed it into an aggressive series of late rounds—the sixty-sixth, sixty-seventh, and sixty-eighth. He was not only pressing the champion during those rounds, but he was beating him. Those who remembered the bout later called it "one of the greatest battles ever fought between Featherweights."[62]

But as the seventieth round of that first battle closed out, it became apparent Dixon would be denied the crown and the overconfident gamblers in attendance would be protected. As the *National Police Gazette* described it, "The referee in the Dixon and McCarthy fight either became sleepy or was tired at looking at the protracted struggle, or else he did not desire to see the battle ended in the way it was ending. I am certain, however, that there were many who had bet heavily on McCarthy's chances of winning, who were jubilant when the referee declared the battle a draw, and probably by so doing save a depletion of their bank roll."[63] The fight lasted four and a half hours, yet the presence it announced would last for the next decade.

Irritated by the obvious theft and knowing full well he had a commodity the public wanted to see, O'Rourke orchestrated much of Dixon's claim to the title to irritate the champion and, perhaps, stoke a future lucrative rematch between the two men.

Days after the McCarthy bout, another odd fallout of the bout took place in Napoleon Sarony's New York City photography studio sometime after the Dixon bout. Sarony might be the most enduring portrait photographers of the era given his iconic images of Gen. William T. Sherman, Sarah Bernhardt, Mark Twain, Oscar Wilde, and Nikola Tesla. His images of McCarthy are not well known, even among boxing historians, as they provide little of interest about the man—sans one. McCarthy was recently embarrassed by his inability to defeat Dixon, who soon spurned him for an immediate rematch. Not one to pass up an opportunity, the ever-flamboyant Sarony bookended a bemused-looking McCarthy between two young Black boys, no more than ten years old, not coincidentally clad like miniature Dixons in black tights and striped sashes. For a photographer such as Sarony, a man drawn to excessive, comedic use of props in his images, to stand McCarthy in front of a stark plain background was not unintentional. The boys were his props—a visual joke for those in on the gag.

Having gained a reputation in his war with McCarthy, a challenge dawned for Dixon across the Atlantic. Nunc Wallace, the English featherweight, had conclusively proven that he was, when in condition, the best man of his weight in England. The *Boston Daily Globe*, among other publications, reasoned if Wallace came to the United States, and had the right kind of backers, what a sensation a match between him and George Dixon or Cal McCarthy would make. A fortune would be wagered on the result. But Dixon and O'Rourke were unwilling to wait on his arrival. The pair headed to London. The world would never be the same.

CHAPTER 3

Rise

DIXON HAD GAINED quite a British following when he stepped into the ring against Nunc Wallace, the British bantam- and featherweight champion, in the New Pelican Club Gym, Soho, England, on June 27, 1890. Sporting only a pair of theatrical trunks, Dixon wore what to modern eyes would appear to be an oversized cloth diaper. The outfit was actually a dawning fashion for the time. Although not an uncommon sight today, combatants performing only in shorts was unconventional in the 1890s; fighters typically wore full-length tights throughout the era. The long pants were simply long underwear, sometimes wool, but usually flannel. Fighters in northern Britain commonly layered "winter" pants over their regular pants for additional warmth. Wearing shorts in the ring—from this "diaper" look to the long, loose shorts worn today—can be traced to a lightweight championship bout between Jack McAuliffe and Jimmy Carroll on March 21, 1890, in San Francisco, when McAuliffe's corner man—Jack "Nonpareil" Dempsey—looked to help his man's dying legs by cutting off McAuliffe's tights just below the hips.

Beyond this "pelvis clothing," as the press branded it, Dixon sported around his waist a white silk handkerchief, with a deep-red, white, and blue border. The top corners were filled with the Massachusetts coat of arms; the bottom corners sported three intertwined horseshoes. In the center was a large bald eagle with extended wings surmounted by two American flags with the words, "George Dixon, champion bantamweight, of America, 1890" beneath it. Many supporters bought these colors from vendors upon entering the arena. Dixon had so many supporters in attendance that the souvenirs sold out quickly.[1]

Leading up to the fight, Dixon trained on the estate of Lord Lonsdale, who provided for the fighter and his attendants. Dixon called him "the finest gentleman I came in contact with"—and what an odd pair they were. Hugh Lowther, the fifth Earl of Lonsdale, was an accidental lord.

As the younger brother, he was not to inherit the title. Instead, he joined a traveling circus for a year, then moved on to America, spending months buffalo hunting. He pawned his birthright to make his fortune cattle ranching in Wyoming and was left practically destitute when the scheme failed. But when his older brother unexpectedly died, Lowther inherited both the title and a vast fortune. Known among certain ranks as one of the British aristocracy's greatest eccentrics, he was a lover of prizefighting, as well as a flamboyant womanizer and gambler, who bet on anything that moved—particularly horses and boxers. As the first president of the National Sporting Club, he donated the first Lord Lonsdale Belt in 1909 for the boxing championship trophy. It was considered the top prize in British Isles boxing until the late 1960s. Among the belt's honors, holders were entitled to a one-pound-per-week pension. Into this man's home, and surrounded by this man's lifestyle, the twenty-year-old Dixon was welcomed to train—what an odd contrast to society at large back home.

A security ring of two hundred members of Scotland Yard circled London's Pelican Club on fight night. Despite rumors circulating the week prior pointing to probable police intervention into the Wallace-Dixon bout, the officers stationed outside the club were there to protect the building from a possible "raid by roughs." That never came to be; in fact, the night was quite the opposite. Inside, few of said roughs were found, and instead the elite of London took seats at ringside, including Lord Lonsdale; Sir Richard Webster, attorney general of the Conservative government; Leopold and Alfred de Rothschild, famed bankers and philanthropists; and Lord Randolph Churchill, who attended that night without his fifteen-year-old son, Winston, at his side. Even years later, Dixon lauded British audiences, and particularly this one, as the fairest body of men he ever saw. For Dixon, used to dodging attacks inside and outside the ring while he tried to ply his trade, finding a place where he could focus only on his gloved opponent made quite an impression. When Wallace struck a low blow in the first round, the referee warned Wallace immediately—not the official reaction a young Black fighter was used to in the United States.

Dixon knew Wallace used both his left and right equally well. He knew the only way to beat him was to work fast, play him at his game of rushing opponents. So, when Dixon started that way, his plan stunned Wallace, who observers noted looked cautious. Little action in the first round was followed by a quickened pace in the second, and while both men were considered equals to this point in the bout, the skill of Dixon soon took over. By the end of the third round, Wallace knew the American outclassed him. Wallace spent the fourth round against the ropes as Dixon punished him with uppercuts and body blows. But Wallace rallied to knock Dixon to his knees. The blow surprised the American. Both men battled to a standstill in the sixth, but the crowd could tell Wallace's reserves were exhausted. The accumulation of blows was too much.[2]

Starting in the seventh round, Wallace was hanging on for life. He was smothering Dixon at every chance, draping himself across the younger opponent. In the ninth round, Wallace abandoned all pugilistic efforts and began to wrestle Dixon, who sidestepped the bear hugs and countered with body blow after body blow. In the tenth round, the once evenly divided crowd turned to Dixon. Wallace resorted to hanging around Dixon's neck with one arm and wildly swinging at him, unsuccessfully, with the other. The actions drew a warning from the referee and an avalanche of boos from the audience. Furious, Dixon flooded Wallace. "The English champion got up bleeding like a stuck pig and staggered like a drunken man," the *National Police Gazette* reported of that moment.[3] Wallace never recovered. He drew murmurs from the crowd each time he rose for the next round. Dixon's treatment of Wallace over these next few rounds was noted in reports from the white press in the days after. As a defenseless and dazed Wallace continued to flail at Dixon, the American slowed his assault. He spared Wallace further beating when he could, a move the white press attributed to him not wanting "to spoil his chances of getting a good name for fairness."[4]

Dixon, a "hurricane fighter," toyed with Wallace through the seventeenth round, and then beat him about the ring in the eighteenth. Finding he could not stand any longer, Wallace threw up his hands, and his corner threw in the sponge, all signaling he was finished. Members of the American delegation, who'd bet heavily on Dixon, hoisted the champion on their shoulders and marched him around the ring. The entire crowd rose and sang "For He's a Jolly Good Fellow" as a badly bruised and bleeding Wallace reclined in his corner. Unmarked, Dixon told the *Boston Daily Globe* that Wallace "did not make such a terrific fight as he expected, but he was a good sport all the same."[5]

Back in Boston, word arrived quickly. Followers from across the city, both Black and white, took a keen interest in the bout. Many of them gathered in the *Daily Globe* offices to hear round-by-round updates. Wallace and his backers made no excuses—in their minds, he was beaten— but that didn't stop the American press from questioning the former champion's credentials. The *National Police Gazette* asked, "The English champion must have been overrated to allow himself to be thoroughly thrashed by Dixon. If Dixon can make such a display, and so easily defeat England's best featherweight, what chance would Wallace have against Collins or McCarthy?"[6] The victory made Dixon "one of the biggest cards in England" as he toured the country with Wallace following their bout.[7]

On August 11, 1890, a small army of friends and fans greeted Dixon and O'Rourke as they stepped off the steamship *Etruria* onto Cunard Pier in New York City after three months in England.[8] Attired in a neat-fitting plaid suit, Dixon looked "bright as a new penny" with his arms full of umbrellas and canes. He handed out the souvenirs as he spoke to the crowd of newspapermen who joined the throng. "They treated me like a prince," he yelled above the well-wishers.[9]

The victory over Wallace gave Dixon a strong claim to the world bantamweight title, but beyond the belt, the Wallace victory signaled the beginning of Dixon as a symbol of something bigger. In the months leading up to the Wallace bout, Dixon was serving as an emerging proof point for those announcing the arrival of Black America. Oklahoma's *Langston City Herald* cited Dixon as one of only two named Black men "getting to the front":

> We are proud of our race despite the persistent, unnatural and unhuman prejudice manifested against us in certain quarters. The aggressive and thoughtful Afro-Americans of these United States are steadily forging to the front; he is giving unmistakable and substantial proof of his superior manhood, his intelligence, as well as high social qualities. He is filling all callings in business, professional, commercial and social life. He is deeply interested in all enterprise tending to the general good of mankind. Since the war of rebellion that resulted in restoring him freedom, he has deported himself in a manner to gain the ungrudged approbation of the best thinkers of the Anglo-Saxon race.[10]

That praise grew exponentially in the months following Dixon's victory. Only days afterward, the *Cleveland Gazette*, a Black-owned newspaper, wrote that Dixon and other Black boxers were "doing much to improve the opinion of the race. Of course, there are better fields of action—not from a financial standpoint perhaps—in which we have men and women who stand very high. However, the oftener Afro-Americans produce the best the quicker our importance as a race grows with all classes of people in this great and peculiar country."[11]

Reports like these would continue into fall 1890, many Black-owned newspapers across the country were abuzz with the news that Clement G. Morgan had been named class orator at Harvard University's commencement. Morgan, a graduate of Harvard College and Harvard Law School, was the first African American elected to the board of aldermen in Cambridge. He was a founder of the Niagara Movement, a predecessor of the National Association for the Advancement of Colored People (NAACP). Morgan graduated from Harvard Law School in 1893. A Republican, he served on the Cambridge Common Council in 1895 and 1896, and on the board of aldermen from 1897 to 1899. In December 1890, William Henry Lewis was named team captain for the Amherst College football team for his senior year. That elevation would be the first of many firsts in Lewis's storied athletic and professional careers, which saw him named the first African American College Football All-American while playing for Harvard University during his law school days, and then later, becoming the first African American appointed a US assistant attorney general (1910) and among the first admitted to the American Bar Association. They were among the highest profile of a series of Black students ascending to the top ranks of their classes across the country. The *New York Age* wrote:

> It is a mighty big feather in the hat of the race to carry off the highest class honors in three of the leading colleges and the leading academy of the country in one and the same year: Our detractors used to insist that we were incapable of higher education; now they have changed their song; and when we carry off the highest class honors in the best colleges in the country, they kick and yell like mad, showing nicely, as Shakespeare says, "What fools these mortals be." It's mighty funny.
>
> These young men show what the size of the race's brain is; while Peter Jackson, the heavyweight hard hitter, George Godfrey, the middleweight, and George Dixon, the daisy bantam pugilist, show what the size of our muscles is. We shall yet convince the Anglo-Saxons that they are not the monopolized salt of the earth and sea. And may the best man win.[12]

More than a fighter, Dixon came to represent hope. For example, newspapers and churches in New York City banded together to form the Fresh Air Fund, an effort to lift the poor out of the city and give these families opportunities to enjoy seaside homes or daily excursions to the Long Island shore. The group also organized picnics with activities for needy kids. The Young Men's Colored Athletic Gymnasium caused a bit of controversy at the 1890 event, when the group wanted to introduce boxing lessons and competitions for kids (winners got a ham). The move was resisted by more traditional elements among the group, but the Athletic Club won its argument by insisting Peter Jackson and George Dixon "were the two greatest colored men that the nineteenth century produced."[13]

Or, as the *New Orleans Crusader* put it: "If [George Dixon] handled a Winchester as well as he does his fists, regulators[14] would be scarce and lynchings rare occurrences."[15]

What a statement—and at a time when the Black body remained in such peril. Brought in chains, the Black body never had a chance to be valued, celebrated, or considered worthy of citizenship until 1863. That was more than three centuries after the first Black slaves had arrived in North America. Blacks were seen as beasts of the land by science and society, not worthy of their own culture or history. Ronald L. Jackson II writes about how this thinking—so deeply rooted in the Colonial-turned-American psyche by generations of white intellectuals who contended Blacks lacked the intellectual, behavioral, interpersonal, and physical traits necessary to be considered more than objects—rots a society. Just a generation before the Dixons arrived in the United States, the Black body was nothing more than a tool of labor, an expensive shovel or plow horse, used and abused by a white master. While members of that generation were still alive, Dixon stood as champion, inspiration, among the wealthiest and best-known men in the country. To so many, that was inconceivable. Perhaps today we read over words like "slave" and "master" too easily, but the mindset that fueled centuries of this thinking did not die with the stroke of the Great Emancipator's pen. It was deeply embedded in American culture. Blacks were owned by whites in every sense of the verb, and, as such, whites came to define themselves by being worthy of this right simply because of their perceived superiority of race. They saw themselves as good, pure, competent masters of Black destiny.

It is easy, then, to see how this strong hand continued as Black freedom grew, how white masters continued to lord over their Black charges even if they were technically free. Whites had always attached a financial value to the Black body, and that continued, especially in the emerging entertainment industry in which Dixon immersed himself. While we focus a lot on the Blacks who found success within these fields, the stories of those who failed are left untold. The paths of athletes like Dixon are littered with unnamed souls, tossed aside. Sick or weak Black bodies were considered ruined or spoiled goods on slave ships and often dumped unceremoniously overboard in the middle of the ocean. No funeral. No notation of name. Just wiped off the face of the earth. The same held true for entertainers once their value faded.[16] Dixon would eventually experience that fate at the hand of his white manager and through the pens and words of these same publications celebrating him on this day in 1890. But in this moment, he was a hero to the world.

Back in Boston with a portion of the world bantamweight title in hand, Dixon set his eyes again on McCarthy. The change in the freshly minted champion's confidence did not go unnoticed by the *Police Gazette*:

> I wonder how it is that nearly every pugilist who goes to England from this country to fight, box, etc., returns with what is termed a big head. It cannot be the foggy weather on London, or Barclay & Perkins,[17] or the Southdown Mutton, that causes the American pugilists to be so afflicted. Probably, it is the fact that wealth and fame, with bushels of flattery, come so fast that they are unable to stand the pressure.... As far as big head is concerned Dixon put [Jake] Kilrain and (Peter) Jackson in the shade. It is true he defeated "Nunc" Wallace and won considerable fame by his prowess, but he has other battles to fight before he can reign as champion, and he should bear his honors meekly.[18]

To be recognized as champion, both Dixon and O'Rourke believed that Dixon had to defeat a trio of fighters who also had a claim to the crown—Wallace, Fred Johnson, and McCarthy. In a breach of protocol, Dixon informed the sitting American champion, McCarthy, that if he wanted a rematch, he would have to put up $5,000, an amount McCarthy's people could not raise. The Pelican Club in London offered a £3,000 purse for the Dixon-McCarthy matchup; the Olympic Club in New Orleans, looking to make a splash in the world of pugilism, considered making an offer as well.

On November 20, 1890, Dixon stood just off stage at Miner's Eighth Avenue Theatre. He could hear the large Thursday night crowd working into a lather. They were excited, as the twenty-year-old Dixon was among the hottest tickets in sports. Tom O'Rourke had booked his fighter in a series of exhibitions in theaters across New York City. Now, on this night, the star attraction was set to spar three demonstration rounds with Englishman Jack Willamena, a faceless sparring partner of no concern.

"Gentlemen, please welcome, the champion featherweight of the world . . . George Dixon." No sooner had the theater's manager made that announcement than a squat man sporting broad shoulders and a stone-wall chest ambled onto the stage with an overcoat thrown across his arm and a scowl upon his face.

"That isn't right!" he shouted, making his way toward the announcer from the opposite wing as Dixon. The crowd quickly recognized the man as featherweight champion of the world Cal McCarthy. A low murmur started to rattle the seats in the theater. "Dixon never won the champi-onship. If you still say he did, please explain how it did it." Then, there was a long, awkward pause. No one spoke. Then, shocked, the theater manager stumbled through an explanation of his introduction. "Dixon fought Nunc Wallace in England for the championship and won it. You never fought for a championship."

"Is that so?" McCarthy shot back. "My dear sir, it becomes plainer and plainer that you are not posted on current boxing history. My first professional match was with Eugene Hornbacher, the then universally recognized American champion, at 114–115 pounds, and that and every subsequent contest that I have engaged in has been for the championship, as expressly stated in the articles of agreement. Why, ask Dixon himself if he didn't meet me for the championship."[19]

Championships were rarely defined along clear lines. While most titles would be settled inside the ring, often the changing of hands was greeted with some confusion, at first. Further complicating matters, many of these same fighters competed against one another for the titles of dif-ferent countries, in multiple weight classes, often fighting those bouts in the same handful of venues. Managers and fighters usually specified what title, if any, was up for grabs in these bouts in the articles of agree-ment signed before the matches. But that rarely silenced disagreements if someone wish to stake a strong enough claim.

While Dixon's defeat of Wallace in June may have given the young American the British bantamweight and featherweight title, McCarthy was not about to allow that claim to extend to the American title he was convinced he still owned after his draw with Dixon just four months before that bout. Dixon had defeated Murphy that October while billing himself "the bantamweight champion of the world." So the claim this night over the featherweight championship of the world was either an oversight or an intentional act of clever promotion, as McCarthy and

Dixon were already headed for a highly anticipated and financially lucrative rematch.

McCarthy continued: "I have never refused to meet a man who offered himself and have never been defeated. Now, could Dixon have contested for the world's championship with Wallace when neither was the champion of America? I stand ready to meet Dixon at any time, with any kind of gloves, for any number of rounds or to the finish, and my money, that has been posted three weeks, says so. Yet, I can get no straight answer from Dixon or his manager."[20]

There was a bit of showmanship at play here. McCarthy and his manager had signed the articles of agreement on October 28, 1890.[21] Although O'Rourke and Dixon were aware of the challenge, they would refuse to sign until December 4, 1890. That would set the match for February 5, 1891.[22]

Silent to this point, the crowd exploded with chants: "Cal McCarthy is the champion!" "That's good, square talk." "Hooray for McCarthy." The noise grew; McCarthy looked somewhat embarrassed by the outpouring of support. When the crowd settled, Dixon stepped forward and announced he could not speak to the issue, as his manager, Tom O'Rourke, was in Boston. The two would be huddled next week and, perhaps, Dixon said, he could offer an answer then. McCarthy then restated his challenge and walked off stage to another round of cheers.

The February bout was not meant to be. As fight day dawned, warrants were issued for both fighters for the illegal match. Nevertheless, a crowd of three thousand would-be spectators surged outside the Puritan Athletic Club in Long Island City. Averting a near riot, management called off the fight under community and police pressure.[23]

A few weeks later, the title fight found a home in Troy, New York.[24] Pre-bout hype resumed immediately. McCarthy's camp attempted to fend off stories about his "indulging in strong beverages" during training.[25] It became more difficult when McCarthy's manager, Joe Early, abandoned him the week prior to the fight, notifying all who would listen to withdraw their money, as McCarthy was in no condition to fight.[26] The eve of the bout was eventful for Dixon. During a morning run down Beacon Street near West Chester Park, Dixon was hailed by a man working on a street paving crew. The workman asked Dixon if he was training for the Six-Day Race, an endurance bicycling competition that was building popularity for its New York City debut in October. When Dixon told the man to "attend to his own business," and turned to head on his way, the workman hurled half a paving stone at Dixon's head. It missed. Several people who witnessed the attack confronted Dixon's assailant, demanding an explanation. None was offered.[27]

As clocks struck midnight across the city on March 31, 1891, McCarthy and Dixon set about fighting in the Troy Bicycle Club, in a ring set up on the infield of a bicycle track. The crowd was well above capacity—thanks to many fans gaining entry via hundreds of counterfeit tickets. The club was freezing—so cold, in fact, O'Rourke "fussed around his pet, fearful lest he should have a chill."[28] The fight went on. Dixon wore white trunks; McCarthy wore blue tights.

The whole room knew it was over the minute they saw Dixon smiling. After an active and even first round, Dixon caught McCarthy with a series of body blows in the second round that left the latter gasping and dazed. Against the ropes, McCarthy hung across Dixon's shoulders before a Dixon right across the jaw sent McCarthy to the ground. Only the bell signaling the end of the round saved him from defeat. In the third, Dixon sent McCarthy flying into the referee with a stiff left. Dixon was laughing as he beat on McCarthy, eventually opening up a slash in McCarthy's right ear and dropping him. Although unreported at the time, Dixon broke the little finger at the first joint in his right hand when a chopping block caught McCarthy at a bad angle. That break caused Dixon to favor his left for the remainder of the fight, and allowed McCarthy to creep back into it.[29]

As the fight wore on, the men traded blows, although Dixon maintained the upper hand throughout. After gaining a second wind in the tenth, and fighting his best round in the eleventh by landing a series on blows on Dixon, McCarthy grew weaker and weaker after winning the fifteenth round. In the twenty-second, he stumbled from his corner—dazed—and Dixon was said to have gone "at his man like an enraged lion liberated from his cage."[30] Left. Right. McCarthy down. McCarthy rose. Left. Right. McCarthy down. Again. He struggled to his feet and looked pleadingly at his seconds as though he wanted to give up the one-sided contest, but they urged him on. Straight left. McCarthy down. He rose from the third knockdown after a seven count. He clung to Dixon to survive the round. Dixon continued to pound McCarthy's ribs in the clinch. Finally, McCarthy collapsed from exhaustion. As he attempted to pull himself up by the post, his seconds spraying water on his face to revitalize him, Dixon sprinted from his corner and knocked McCarthy prostrate with a final left. Beyond a slight swelling of the upper lip, Dixon looked the same as he did before the contest began, but "poor Mac was badly punished and appeared to be broken-hearted."[31] As McCarthy left the building, tears were streaming down his face.

McCarthy never recovered from that bout. He soon retired from the ring, although he fought a handful of meaningless bouts over the next three years, including one against Robert Burns that resulted in a TKO thanks to McCarthy being unable to sober up in time for the fight.[32] It was a disappointing end to a fighter who, many in the press believed, could have been one of the greats. As the *Police Gazette* reported:

> Many who saw the fight [with Dixon] found reason to believe that there was some foundation for the rumor, which had been so freely circulated in regard to the unsatisfactory manner in which McCarthy had trained for this great battle. It was the change of McCarthy's life, and why he threw it away as he did, if reports are true, is more than the American public can understand. McCarthy, however, had always claimed that he could whip the colored lad in a gallop, and scarcely felt it necessary to do any very severe training. He is headstrong and a hard man for a trainer to handle, but now he has ample time to realize his vital error.[33]

McCarthy finished his career by being knocked out by Fred Precious, a British journeyman fighting only his second career bout. McCarthy died of tuberculosis less than five years after that second clash with Dixon. He was twenty-six years old.[34]

In Boston that night, the offices of the *Globe* were packed. Outside on the street, some three hundred more men awaited news of the battle. When reporters announced that Dixon had the best of the first eight rounds, the Black contingent danced on the sidewalk with joy. Later, when the fifteenth round, which was in McCarthy's favor, was posted on the bulletin boards, those same men were crestfallen, while white men took their turn at cheering and dancing. The next bulletin, announcing Dixon had knocked McCarthy out in the twenty-second round, "set the Black crowd nearly crazy."[35]

Not all were impressed with Dixon's victory. Some, who saw through McCarthy's thin faux-sober veneer, said the fight was over before it started: "Dixon's luck was a big factor in the victory scored by him. . . . Little McCarthy, as he sat there waiting for the word to go to his Waterloo, showed the marks of long, hard dissipation. When Jere Dunn, the referee, called Dixon and McCarthy to the center of the ring, competent judges saw quickly that McCarthy was not in form. The New Yorkers who had bet on his chances tried hard to hedge, but it was too late for Dixon had become a strong favorite."[36]

A gathering of New York clergymen on April 8, 1891, saw all but one denounce the Dixon-McCarthy match as brutal and disgraceful, censuring city officials and declaring that similar bouts should not be permitted in the city. Only the Rev. Bulmer of St. Luke's at the Iron Works rose to speak against the measure: "I don't know anything about this fight. I have sent many to the sink in my time. I have had pupils in my classes and gave them instruction in boxing—I am a graduate of Columbia College—and it was not thought disgraceful to put on the gloves."[37]

For ten cents, fight fans across the country relived the action on the pages of the *National Police Gazette*. An illustration of "Dixon's Knock-Out Blow" filled the publication's entire front page on Saturday, April 18, 1891. There, McCarthy sat crumpled, supported only by one of his corner men. Inside the issue, readers viewed an illustration of a folded, kneeling, and defeated McCarthy, who appeared across two pages of newsprint to be genuflecting before the new champion in the final moments of the bout. "George Dixon Is Champion!" the headline read. In both images, as close to a "highlight reel" as nineteenth-century sports fans got, Dixon towered over his opponent. Without cuts or bruises, he was depicted unscathed by battle. His skin tone is noticeably shaded, but not menacingly dark as previous illustrations had captured him.[38]

Make no mistake—although pre-fight buildup did not center on it, this fight spoke to the growing racial divide in the country. The headlines alone were colored by race. *Times-Picayune* in New Orleans: "Dixon Wins: The Clever Colored Bantam Knocks Out McCarthy." *The State* of Columbia, South Carolina: "Defeated by Darkey: A Colored Bruiser, of Boston, Wins the Featherweight Championship." *Weekly Capital* in Topeka, Kansas: "Knocked Out: The Lightweight Championship Won by the Boston Smoked Yankee." *World-Herald* in Omaha, Nebraska: "Neatly Done by Dixon: McCarthy Meets a Crushing Defeat at Hands of the Colored Slugger."

What the Wallace victory started in the minds of Black America, the McCarthy victory solidified. With Dixon's win, at least two Black-owned newspapers saw fit to use him as a symbol for not just Black equality, but Black superiority. This victory signaled not the arrival of a Black fighter, but of a generation of Black fighters to come. This is an important notion never attributed to Dixon due to his weight class. But the fanfare in

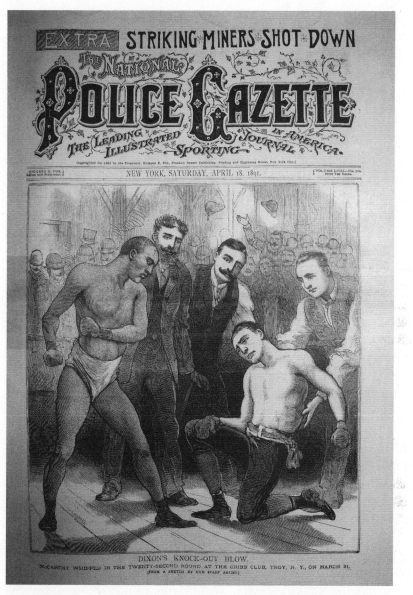

Front page of the *National Police Gazette*, April 18, 1891. *Courtesy of the* National Police Gazette.

support of, and angst against, Dixon's victory signaled a moment equal to that of Jack Johnson's heavyweight championship more than seventeen years later. Dixon—"a thing of beauty and a joy forever"[39]—inspired the *New York Age* editor to boast, "What constitutes superiority in our civilization? Answer this question satisfactorily and many humbugs will be asphyxiated.... Physical toughness and endurance are regarded as among the supreme tests of high mental capacity. It has become common to deny to Afro-Americans possession of these equal to those of white men. These qualities are brought out in the prize ring as nowhere else.... If physical toughness count for anything, we are there, in the prize ring, with both feet.... All along the line, the Afro-American is hitting squarely from the shoulder."[40]

Even Black papers vehemently against boxing took pride in Dixon. The *Leavenworth (Kansas) Advocate* wrote: "While we take no pride in the manly art, yet it is consoling to know that George Dixon is the Bantamweight Champion of the World."[41]

For sixty years after the death of Tom Molineaux, the great Black bare-knuckle champion, in 1818, Blacks participated in sport in relative obscurity. By the mid- to latter stages of the 1870s, a select number of outstanding Black athletes began to distinguish themselves in the ever-expanding and increasingly more structured world of white-organized sport and even to establish national and sometimes international reputations for their athletic exploits.[42] In particular, Black men began to achieve notice in American popular culture. More so than baseball, pedestrianism (race walking), or jockeying, the other three professional sports that had a significant Black presence in the late nineteenth century, boxing was the one sport that could produce an intense (if, in some eyes, vulgar) fame.[43] Now, Dixon's fame was on the rise. Already a star among dedicated fans of the sport, he was honored and feted on a regular basis.

On May 22, 1891, the Full Moon Club took its turn. On this night, Dixon clutched a diamond pin in his hand, presented to him only moments earlier by Full Moon Club vice president Capt. Alexander A. Selden. The young champion stood before an audience composed of mainly young Black men from Boston's West End,[44] an area of the city that, along with Beacon Hill's North Slope, had become a center of the city's Black community earlier in the century. The mostly affluent and white residents of Beacon Hill's South Slope were strong abolitionists, an environment that encouraged middle- and working-class free Blacks to move nearby. After the Civil War, the West End continued to be an important center of Black culture. It was one of the few locations in the United States where Blacks had a political voice, with at least one Black West End resident on Boston's community council every year between 1876 and 1895.[45]

On that May evening, many of those men gathered to honor Dixon, as he and O'Rourke prepared to travel West for a series of bouts—first to Philadelphia, then to Omaha, Nebraska; Denver, Colorado; and across the Rocky Mountains. Selden praised Dixon with a few words. He then turned the room over to Dixon, who said:

> I cannot find the words to express my feelings. I have always tried to do my duty. I have never yet entered the ring but that I was conscious that I was not only fighting the battle for myself alone, but also for the race. I felt that if I won, not only credit would be given to me, but that my race would also rise in the estimation of the public. This token will be incentive to me to do good, fair and square work. Had I not done what was right to myself and friends, I might not tonight be enjoying this reception, which is the first that has been given me since I have come back to Boston.[46]

It must be noted that this moment, among the thousands of mentions of Dixon in the press of the day, is an outlier. Never again in the reporting did he speak about a "duty" to his race. Certainly, his actions in the years that followed were not in line with what Black America expected—or needed—from him as he grew more and more insulated from the realities of the world. Never political or bombastic, rarely confrontational or rebel rousing, Dixon never embraced his race duty more publicly than this moment. Perhaps he felt an obligation to this particular crowd or saw significance in his recent accomplishments that warranted some comment, but never again would Dixon admit so publicly to being "conscious that I was not only fighting the battle for myself alone." In fact, Dixon's language that followed more closely aligned with the advice George Godfrey gave him years earlier to forget about his color and only concentrate on the man in front of him.

White belief in Black inferiority may not entirely root itself in the institution of slavery, but that institution did provide fertile ground for it to grow. Despite Emancipation, this belief lingered throughout the Gilded Age, as the argument switched to a "scientific racism" that purported to root racial inferiority in the increasingly popular notion of Darwinian biology. Black men were not only seen as intellectually inferior to white men, but also viewed as incapable of survival without white men's benevolence. That attitude came straight from Civil War battlefields—pushed by the same men fighting for the freedom of Black citizens. Free Black Northern soldiers were still commanded by white officers. A white Union officer described the reason: "There was as much of a soldier visible in the former slave as there was of an angel in a block of marble awaiting the touch of Michelangelo's chisel."[47] Even as slavery was lifted by the Thirteenth Amendment, harsh new laws limited Black social movement and choice. "Black Codes"—laws directed at newly freed Blacks—established vagrancy, curfew, and other restrictive statutes that trapped Blacks into returning to a life of servitude once convicted of these minor crimes. But these laws were not enough to maintain white superiority. In the eyes of white institutions, Blacks also needed to be separated from whites. Black opportunities to compete with whites disappeared in all but a select few arenas, and even these were well regulated by whites.

Boxing was one of those arenas. Two divergent slaveholder philosophies influenced the opportunities of free Blacks in post–Civil War sports. The first hypothesized that slaves could transcend the horrendous conditions of the institution by participating among themselves in various types of cultural activities, including sports. That concept of escapism continued into Dixon's era and beyond, especially for those fighters who escaped the urban chains of the Industrial Age—poverty, racial oppression, lack of opportunity—through the ring. The second path, however, offered a line of inquiry even more relevant to Dixon's situation. Some of the more physically gifted (and perhaps even more malleable) slaves were involved in their owners' sporting life, for both the owners' and the slaves' mutual benefit. These slaves often had more freedom of movement, special privileges, and closer relationships with their owners. This pattern continued into Dixon's day and beyond: athletically gifted Black men exhibited their physical skills and realized material benefits, yet ultimately were never able to exert any significant individual or institutional control over the activities they participated in.[48]

How does this help define Dixon, born five years and thirteen hundred miles from the end of the US Civil War? Although realizing success by virtue of their outstanding physical talents and work ethic, Black athletes of the late nineteenth century depended on white coaches, managers, and benefactors to negotiate the complex relationship among race, sport, and culture if they wanted to maintain productive careers. Knowing racism could suddenly erupt and jeopardize their careers required Black athletes to cater to the white sport establishment. Their vulnerability did not prevent them from occasionally speaking out about racial discrimination, although many, Dixon included, played a more subservient role. Oftentimes, as with O'Rourke, white benefactors voiced louder complaints about inequitable racial treatment directed at the Black athletes in which they had so much invested.[49]

These words were a direct overlay of the Dixon-O'Rourke relationship. Starting with Dixon's first championship, a power struggle developed between the two men, one that would continue for the rest of their partnership. You can almost see the tension in the lone photo of the two men together squaring off against each other. This photograph is wonderful as it shows how different the two men were outside of a shared Boston background. Dixon: diminutive, defined, darker, even somewhat foreign looking with his shaved head and odd shorts. Maintained like a machine, his body is flawless. O'Rourke: stocky, soft, soapy skinned, perhaps indistinguishable from many other men of his ilk in the era. With the body of an athlete layered somewhere beneath, he is the sort of pudgy that could only come from privilege and excess. Most likely photographed by Chickering in 1890, perhaps even on the same day as previous images, given that Dixon is wearing the same outfit, the interplay between the two men is somewhat comically watered down by the farmland scene the photographer placed behind them.

Sport was becoming a tool for temporary transformation—slave becoming master, powerless becoming powerful, if only briefly. Athletic competition was a "free space where bodies bound and scarred by chains could soar."[50] It was hard to avoid the echoes of the plantation, where sporting competitions were often more significant for the slave. It was an entrance—no matter how fleeting—into a forbidden city.

Dixon maintained the respect of peers throughout his career. As the *Chicago Daily News* wrote of him:

> The best of the lighter division of colored fighters were George Dixon, Joe Gans and Joe Walcott, but as the championships in their respective classes were not considered trust titles, they found opponents galore to try to check their upward careers. Of these, Dixon was the most favored, and had the largest following. This is because he always fought to win, which is more than can be said of the two Joes. It was the shady methods of Gans and Walcott that set the followers of the game against the colored fighters, and as the sport

is not booming, as in its halcyon days, it is only a matter of a short time when the colored fighter will be conspicuous by his absence.[51]

O'Rourke, to his credit, also refused to let his fighter fall victim to a color line, even if only to line his pockets a bit thicker. Yes, there were white pugilists who backed out of battles with Dixon, but not because they drew the color line, as they said, but because they were afraid to fight him. Wherever Dixon went, he was received with popular acclaim. Even in the South, the fighter was seen "only from the viewpoint of the lover of sport and not that of the man prejudiced as to color."[52] It was truly masterful management that allowed this to happen. This does not mean he did not face racial bias within the ring; as mentioned, Dixon often faced unruly crowds, less than neutral referees, even outright theft of wins. As Dixon wrote:

> The colored men who follow pugilism as a means of livelihood have no reason now to complain of not getting a fair show when battling in the ring with a white man. There never was any good reason why those of my color who aspired for pugilistic honors should not have had the same show of winning glory and cash as a white man. No matter whether he was able to or not, it was not until a year or two ago that a colored fighter could win a contest in or outside of a club room anywhere in this country. While I do not wish to throw any discredit on white pugilists, yet it is a positive fact, the best and liberal-minded sporting men of the country will bear me out in my statement, when I say that the colored pugilists have acted more like gentlemen than a great many of the white boxers. You seldom hear of a colored fighter striking people on the street, nor are they boisterous or drunken loafers.[53]

Dixon further poked his audience by applauding Brits. "In England, the colored fighter was never molested while engaged in a battle. I have fought there, and the way I was treated fairly surprised me. The sporting men, wealthy and poor, could not do too much for me, even before I fought their champion, Nunc Wallace. When I was fighting him, no one spoke above a whisper and I was treated as if I was one of their own party."[54]

Hard to imagine a better promotional campaign for an interracial bout than a Black boxer at the height of his popularity calling out fighters from an entire—and opposite—race. And just three months from his key bout against Abe Willis, one fight that would solidify Dixon as the greatest fighter—not just Black fighter—of his division in the world. Never let it be said that O'Rourke and Dixon did not understand his audience.

Nunc Wallace. Photo by
Richard K. Fox. *Courtesy
of Special Collections,
Fine Arts Library,
Harvard University.*

There was no formalized structure for prizefighting—no leagues to organize and accumulate a following. Therefore, more than perhaps any other event, fights needed narrative. Promoters would amplify the most pressing social and political conflicts of the day and drop those opposing forces into the rings—religion, ethnicity, class, and especially race. No issue worked to gin up spectator interest more than Black versus white.

Given that we know more about corner men (thanks to books by Dave Anderson and Ronald K. Fried) than we do about all but one or two promoters, it is no wonder historians Randy Roberts and Andrew R. M. Smith advocated the study of boxing in eras of promotional hegemony—periods of influence that lasted longer than the career of any single boxer. When we see how fights were packaged and sold, they argue, rather than how they were fought and consumed, we get a broader, deeper understanding of the sport and its importance in American history. Take that a step further and apply it to Dixon's era, and you see how promoters—nearly all white—fed racial animosity among all levels of society. The popularity of boxing as a platform provided an incredible stage for their divisive narrative. Most athletic clubs had white ownership and white patrons that created a hostile work environment for Black fighters. White fans called Black fighters racist terms, even threatened to kill Black fighters, especially during interracial contests.

Dixon's unification efforts coincided with a period of extraordinary mobility of Australian boxers—many of whom were former or future national champions—competing in American rings between 1890 and 1895. Thanks to hefty purses, a fight in the United States remained a central aspiration for those plying their trade in the boxing halls of Sydney and Melbourne. Abe Willis was one such boxer.

After he defeated McCarthy, Dixon set Willis—an Australian bantamweight champion who was said to be "full of horseradish and grit"—as his next opponent.[55] A victory would give Dixon the bantamweight championship on three continents—North America, Europe, and Australia. The California Athletic Club in San Francisco initially balked at O'Rourke's demands for a $5,000 purse (plus $500 to O'Rourke for expenses) to host the Willis-Dixon matchup. That dollar figure would have been the largest ever offered for the weight class. The club said no; O'Rourke walked away from the table. Not to worry; a month later, as the dealmaker was closing in on other venues to host the lucrative bout, the club agreed to all of O'Rourke's demands. California sports were not impressed by Dixon—saying he would get a "licking," that Willis would turn him into a "chopping block," and that even Dixon's body type was better suited to being a jockey.

Dixon, however, impressed fellow pugilists in California with his training techniques, which many eastern boxers had already adopted.[56] With wagers from three continents, betting on the bout was as heavy as any pugilistic contest had ever experienced—even perhaps the heaviest of any athletic contest up to that point, according to some observers. Bookmakers in the Bay were "on the jump all day and up to a late hour" keeping up with business for the July 28, 1891, bout.[57]

But the fight did not live up to the hype. From the start, the Australian had difficulty keeping up with the favored Dixon's frantic pace. In the fifth round, Dixon started with back-to-back-to-back lefts to Willis's neck. Dixon worked the head, and then hammered Willis's body, sapping strength from his ribs and stomach. Willis was seemingly defenseless. With a final left to his jaw, Willis was out. That final round proved to be, in the eyes of the *Boston Daily Globe*, "two minutes of the fastest and most destructive work ever seen in the ring room of the club."[58]

Back in Boston, in front of the *Globe*'s offices, a crowd of Black men had gathered for reports from the fight. When the results were announced, a huge cheer went up, and then a rush in different directions to tell the rest of the population the news.

On July 28, 1891, Dixon's wife, Katie, last heard from her husband via a telegram from San Francisco before his bout started, around 10:30 p.m. Boston time. She would not know the results until early the next morning, around 1 a.m., when a friend from the *Boston Daily Globe* came calling to the house announcing Dixon had soundly defeated Willis.

Here is the moment where Dixon's family starts entering the public conversation. Unlike many wives and partners of the era, this relationship is of key importance. Complicating the manager-fighter relationship further, Dixon was a married man—yet his wife was no "dusky belle, nor even what is denominated a 'bright face,' but a pretty white girl."[59] More than that, Catherine "Katie" Dixon was once Catherine "Katie" O'Rourke, a popular Boston North End beauty and sister of Tom O'Rourke. When questioned about her marriage to the Black champion, she often replied, "I married George because I loved him. Let the world think what it may; I will share his joys and sorrows to the last."[60]

Like her brother, Catherine was intelligent, thrifty, and shrewd, a woman who tended exclusively to her husband's wealth, which amounted to $30,000–$40,000 at times. Of course, if not for Dixon's lavish spending, that figure could have been threefold as the 1890s dawned. The *Washington Post* wrote of their relationship: "Plainly, this Othello has reason for the confidence he places in his fair consort. To her, he entrusts all his earnings. Even the receipts of his vaudeville company, which exceeded $20,000, were placed in her care."[61]

On July 29, 1891, Dixon turned twenty-one years old. That afternoon, the *Globe* called upon Katie—most certainly with Tom's blessing—and she offered a glimpse into Dixon's personal life at a moment when the champion was in his prime ability, earning power, and public interest. His domestic life tales were intended to reach a broader audience. It was all about expanding Dixon's appeal, no matter how wildly incongruent to the young champion's well-known nature the stories seemed. None were more absurd than this interview.

Katie O'Rourke—Dixon called her "Kitten"—was described by the reporter as a "buxom young woman, white and fair, with a modesty quite charming." What he did not mention was her relation to Tom O'Rourke. The Dixons shared a Beacon Hill home, No. 19 Blossom Street, front of pressed brick, with an electric doorbell to announce visitors. The home's parlor was handsomely furnished, including lace curtains in the windows adorned with streamers of yellow silk. A visitor would never know it was the home of a prizefighter until his eyes had wandered from engraving to engraving on the walls and, at last, landed upon a full-length portrait of Dixon in his ring costume, stripped to the waist. On this day, in one corner, sitting upon an easel, stood a picture of Dixon done in pencil and crayon and set off by a heavy gilt frame. "George is twenty-one years old today, and I wanted to give him a present, so there it is—the picture," Katie announced. The remainder of the article was a dialogue—stilted, guided and—from a member of a swindler family—almost certainly totally fictional:

> "Are you in love with prize-fighting?"
>
> "No, I don't like it very much, but George does, so I suppose he must fight."
>
> "Likes the money better than the fighting, doesn't he?"
>
> "I suppose so."
>
> "Do you ever go on any pugilistic trips with your husband?"
>
> "No. I did see him spar once or twice here in Boston, but I am afraid if I should go to a real fight I should talk right out in meeting and tell him to come out of the ring. I told George once I should have to accompany him, and he said, 'No, Kitten, you mustn't. It would break me all up.'"
>
> "Dixon gets homesick, I hear."
>
> "Yes, George is a great homebody. When he is in Boston, he stays right here with me, and he doesn't go away. He didn't want to leave for California, but I urged him to go, badly as I felt, in order to brace him up. After he got there, Mr. O'Rourke sent word to me to be very careful what I wrote, else George would want to come home. So I was careful."
>
> "Aren't you afraid he'll get hurt in some fight?"
>
> "No, I never think of such a thing when he is away."
>
> "Your husband has made so much money in the ring!"
>
> "Yes, indeed, and he is careful of it. He looks out for home first, like a good boy. He has saved a considerable sum. Of course, he has many invitations to loan money and many chances to spend it, like any pugilist, but he looks out for it just the same."[62]

Outside the rich irony lost on readers of the time of an O'Rourke commenting on Dixon's love of money—nobody loved a cut of Dixon's money more than Tom and Katie—this interview shows the obsession of presenting Dixon as a domesticated lad. O'Rourke needed to stress that this was not a dangerous Black man, but rather a man who moved easily within white society. Dixon was a commodity in need of packaging. People could not get enough of him—and what better way to deliver the message than via his wife.

Of Dixon's earnings, a full half went to Tom O'Rourke, a man who was not Dixon's financial backer. O'Rourke was Dixon's manager and some-times trainer—meaning Tom O'Rourke had very little of Tom O'Rourke's money invested in George Dixon. Financing the operation fell to New Yorker Edward Nail, who spared no money on facilities for Dixon. And why not? Dixon returned multiple-fold on Nail's investment in him. Nail often boasted of the night he made $10,000 on a single Dixon victory. But the Dixons' home, situated in Malden, Massachusetts, just outside Boston, was worth more than that. Dixon spared no expense on "beautifying it within and without." Newspaper reporters touted how he collected rare works of art, bric-a-brac, and books upon books; how he was an avid reader, a fan of Charles Dickens, whom he considered "a genius"; how he spent many off-training hours reading in his home, accompanied by a good cigar.[63] That report of his life, perhaps off-kilter to the reports that would follow years later, was part of the cultivated image.

He lived a good life, but one where an O'Rourke guided his career and money. As the strongest professional voice in Dixon's life, O'Rourke drove the young boxer to the heights of his profession without yield-ing to distractions. Yes, Dixon faced discrimination along the way, but O'Rourke's skillful hand can be credited with keeping Dixon moving for-ward. The young boxer had now achieved more within his sport than any Black man prior to him, thanks in part to his manager successfully navi-gating societal forces temporarily conducive to Black societal gains. With this success came new pressures to live up to his status as a race hero. And this complex relationship—father-son, master-slave—was fraught with societal and racial overtones that, although it made Dixon a champion, came at a serious cost to be paid later.

Nevertheless, with this victory over Willis, George Dixon became the undisputed world bantamweight champion, the first Black man to earn a world boxing title. And it all happened before his twenty-first birthday. One would think this type of landmark achievement would be celebrated with some volume. It was not. In fact, many newspapers, including prom-inent Black tabloids, viewed the fight only as a victory for America. They

George Dixon and Tom O'Rourke. Cabinet card with handwritten inscription, "Chickering. George Dixon—World's champion FeatherWeight 115# / Born. Halifax. N. Scotia. July 29, 1871." Photo by Elmer Chickering.

attributed no racial tones to it whatsoever. Only years later, as the rights and privileges of Blacks in the United States started to erode, and the grip of Jim Crow tightened, did historians look back on Dixon's victory as the landmark it truly was:

> The negro race in the United States owes a debt of gratitude to the boxing ring, which it should never forget or repudiate. Therein alone it has found that "equality" which is so harped about in political speeches, but is so seldom seen in the ordinary walks and avocations of life, and to George Dixon, the Featherweight Champion, more than to any one other man is due the state of affairs. There were brave men before Agamemnon and there were negro pugilists before Dixon, but none of them ever succeeded in breaking down race prejudice against Black men as he has.[64]

Entering 1892, Dixon's rocky relationship with O'Rourke continued to be troublesome. Dixon would leave, only to have the separations last days.

Disagreements usually stayed behind closed gym doors, where they were seen and settled among close colleagues. But occasionally the clashes were so public that details spilled into the press. During a stop of George Dixon's vaudeville troupe, the George Dixon Specialty Co., at the Miner's Bowery Theatre in New York City, Dixon was facing all comers during a weeklong engagement. One evening, he stepped into the ring against Jim Watson of Paterson, New Jersey. Prior to the exhibition's start, O'Rourke warned the young boxer to throttle back on his efforts. "Don't hit this fellow too hard, Georgie. He is only an amateur, and I don't want him hurt."[65] Dixon went easy on Watson for two rounds, but as the second closed, the challenger pressed, landing heavy blows on Dixon's face and neck. When the round ended, Dixon smiled good-naturedly—but, as the *Boston Daily Globe* reported, it was "not a genuine smile. The colored lad was angry, and he could scarcely wait until the third round was called."[66] When the bell sounded, Dixon sent a left to Watson's throat, followed by an uppercut with the right and a comeback crack on the jaw with a left. The combination practically deposited Watson into a front-row seat. It was over that fast. Moments after the fight was called, O'Rourke rushed Dixon and punched him in the chin. "You're too fresh, Georgie," he said. "And you can take that for your smart trick." Dixon stormed off and "declared that he would get a manager who wouldn't make a punching bag of him. It was agreed that they separate at the conclusion of the engagement."[67]

Boston promoter and manager Joe Pettengill was in line to follow O'Rourke. But it was a separation that never took place. The pair met the following day. "Tom, I don't want to be on the outs with you," Dixon said. "Neither do I with you," O'Rourke replied.[68] But the connection remained one of mutual benefit, perhaps more so than friendship, as Dixon's friends reported a "feeling of coolness and ill-trust" between the two in the immediate aftermath, as well as for the rest of Dixon's life.[69] Those facts were not secrets: "His backer has a goose of the most approved golden variety. It is easy enough to kill the goose, but not easy enough to get another one like it. When Dixon fights, he fights for O'Rourke to just about the same extent that he fights for Dixon. O'Rourke takes half of the profits and none of the blows."[70]

George Dixon needed Tom O'Rourke; Tom O'Rourke needed George Dixon. This partnership was the only marriage that mattered in both lives.

Dixon's claim that he was also world featherweight champion because he had beaten dual title-holders Wallace and McCarthy was not without dispute. His claim to the title was not fully accepted until he fought Fred Johnson, the new British featherweight champion.

He did just that on June 27, 1892, at the Coney Island Athletic Club in Brooklyn, New York. Dixon was fresh off a tour with his theatrical company, one where he took on—and bested—more than a hundred men. But the young champion was not road weary. In fact, many fight reporters of the era point to this bout as the peak of Dixon's physical prime. The *New York Times* wrote of Dixon: "His chocolate-colored skin shone in the electric light like burnished copper, and the free play of his muscles bespoke splendid condition."[71]

The pre-reporting focused on the physical differences between the two men. To many, the match was a mistake, the leap up in weight class too quick for Dixon. Johnson was going to be too much. When he landed in the former Colonies—his first visit—observers noted how Johnson was a remarkably big little man—thick neck, firm jaw, large teeth, broad shoulders. His dark complexion did not go unnoticed either.[72] Johnson stepped into the ring the bigger of the two: ten pounds heavier than Dixon on a much larger frame, and over an inch or two taller. In the minds of reporters, the bout was between "a draught horse and a thoroughbred racer."[73] Although undefeated before entering the ring with Dixon, Johnson stood no chance from the opening bell. Boston's "pride" pounded England's "hope" all over the ring. In the fourteenth round, Dixon ended Johnson's punishment with a left to the chin and a right to the jaw. As soon as Dixon was declared the winner, a "shout went up that could be heard a mile away."[74] Among those voices, a familiar bellow rose from ringside: "Bully for Boston and the United States of America!"[75] That bellow, of course, belonged to John L. Sullivan. Sullivan and Dixon had met while on the road with their respective theater companies, when they happened to cross paths in the lunchroom of a Pennsylvania railroad station, and O'Rourke introduced the two champions.[76]

Many of the fans seated around Sullivan—"some smart alecks who handed me some conversation"—harassed the champion on his way out of the arena. How could Sullivan side with a Black man, they asked. Sullivan responded:

> Dixon's skin may be sunburned, but he comes from my town, and he's defending a title against a foreigner. I've never fought with any color but my own, and I never will, but any man with sporting blood

GEORGE DIXON VANQUISHES FRED JOHNSON.

THE LITTLE COLORED FEATHER-WEIGHT CHAMPION KNOCKS OUT THE ENGLISH CHAMPION IN FOURTEEN ROUNDS, IN THE CONEY ISLAND CLUB, ON JUNE 27.

(FROM SKETCHES BY POLICE GAZETTE SPECIAL ARTISTS.)

Internal spread of the *National Police Gazette*, July 9, 1892. *Courtesy of the* National Police Gazette.

in his skin has got to say Dixon is a great little fighter and deserves all that's coming to him. So long as the white fighters in Dixon's class gave him the chance to climb over them to first place I wouldn't deny him the credit that belonged to him, especially as he was square, even if he was living on the shady side of the street.[77]

George Dixon. Albumen silver print on card. Photo by Elmer Chickering.
Courtesy of Special Collections, Fine Arts Library, Harvard University.

CHAPTER 4

No Hamlet without Hamlet

No matter what your color;
It matters not your size;
If you win in our Olympic Club;
You'll surely get your prize.
There's no such thing as favor shown;
To one man or another;
Not even if he was;
The little president's brother.[1]

JIMMY WISE AND WILLIE BROWN, barely teens, were plucked unsuspecting from the crowd and stripped to the waist. As gloves were hurriedly strapped to their hands, they were shoved beneath the makeshift ropes cordoning off a ring and forced to fight for the entertainment of an all-white audience of South Georgia's finest. Their forum, the Springer Opera House, was conceived amid the fading echoes of the US Civil War when Francis Joseph Springer, a French immigrant grocer, funded its construction in downtown Columbus, Georgia. Since opening in 1871, the theater hosted numerous performances: operas, plays, orations, even appearances by the likes of Oscar Wilde and renowned Shakespearean actor Edwin Booth.[2] The marvelous structure was a sign of the prosperity washing across this corner of eastern Georgia by 1892—an economic growth that had directly benefited many in the Springer Opera House that night. These were men who had reaped the rewards of slavery; these were men who grew even richer under Reconstruction; and these were men who had no qualms about forcing young Black men to fight for their pleasure. Jimmy Wise and Willie Brown knew these men—they had spent their young lives fearing them. And so, they complied with the crowd's demands.

It was Tuesday, September 6, 1892, and the mercury approached ninety degrees on thermometers across the city. Even as evening fell, the three-story opera house held the heat of the day close, as hundreds of white businessmen from across the city gathered inside for news wired in from New Orleans, where the Carnival of Champions had captured imaginations across the country—including those in this South Georgia community. With no ladies present, jackets were removed and white shirtsleeves rolled up. The men were drawn to the idea of "listening" via telegraph to results of the Carnival—three championship fights spread over three nights in the Big Easy, culminating in the John L. Sullivan–James J. "Gentleman Jim" Corbett bout for the heavyweight championship of the world. This scene played out across the country—those who could not make the trip to New Orleans found ways to follow the action in theaters and taverns and newsrooms.

The anticipation was immense, perhaps the most talked-about sporting event in a decade. For weeks, newspapers had milked every detail out of the six featured fighters. The nation, or at least its men, paused. The *American Journal of Politics* snarkily commented, "Everything else was eclipsed by this national event. Even the dread cholera was obliged to take abbreviated notices in the daily papers; and the candidates for the highest office on earth were obliged to pass one day and leave the nation ignorant as to whether they drank tea or coffee for breakfast, in order that the whole front page might be devoted to a description of the brutal contest between sluggers whose only qualities worthy of mention are brute strength and more than ordinary endurance."[3]

In this way, Columbus was no different from anywhere else in the United States. The day before, Monday, September 5, the Georgia gang heard club representatives read wire reports of Jack McAuliffe's knockout of Billy Myer in the fifteenth round of their lightweight championship fight. When they returned for Tuesday night's George Dixon–Jack Skelly bout, the men were greeted by the same setup as the night prior, and as would greet them the next day for Wednesday night's heavyweight main event between John L. Sullivan and James J. Corbett. A table sat at the center of the theater stage where a young man, hand on key, monitored the telegraph for news of the fight. Charlie Springer, son of the opera house's founder, sat in an armchair on one side of the table; Dave Blascoer, whose job it was to announce the incoming dispatches describing the fight, sat on the other.[4]

Against this backdrop, Wise and Brown "continued to hammer on each other with amazing vigor until the warning tick of the telegraph sounded" the end of the impromptu bout and the beginning of the main event, some four hundred miles away. The *Columbus Enquirer* reported the next day: "Dixon being a colored man and Skelly a white one, there was a disposition on the part of the audience to cheer for Skelly. They had little opportunity, however, for any wild display of hilarity, and the news of the frightful punishment that Dixon was inflicting on his antagonist was received without any show of enthusiasm."[5]

When the fight ended in New Orleans, the unsatisfied crowd in Georgia launched an exhausted Willie Brown back into the ring for a second fight—this time against a larger opponent of the same age known only as "Johnson." The crowd passed a hat to collect a small purse for the winner, and then set the young boys against each other. As the fighters clinched and hammered each other over their heads and bodies, the audience went wild with delight. Such was the night; such was how one corner of America greeted news of Dixon's victory. Even on the night the world's first Black champion triumphed on his biggest stage, the world was reminded of the white man's preference for a Black man's place in it.

Have you ever been in New Orleans? If not, you'd better go,
It's a nation of a queer place; day and night a show:
Frenchmen, Spaniards, West Indians, Creoles, Mustees,[6]
Yankees, Kentuckians, Tennesseans, lawyers and trustees,
Clergymen, priests, friars, nuns, women of all stains,
Negroes in purple and fine linen, and slaves in rags and chains,
Ships, arks, steamboats, robbers, pirates, alligators,
Assassins, gamblers, drunkards, and cotton speculators;
Sailors, soldiers, pretty girls, and ugly fortune-tellers,
Pimps, imps, shrimps, and all sorts of dirty fellows;
White men with Black wives, et vice versa too.
A progeny of all colors—an infernal motley crew!

—COL. JAMES R. CREECY, 1860[7]

There has always been a ubiquitous New Orleans scent, something profoundly sensual and suggestive of dampness and decay. The musk is everywhere. The moment you enter the city "something wet and dark leaps on you and starts humping you like a swamp dog in heat."[8] Moisture is a constant companion, especially in the rain-soaked months of March, July, and September. And the humidity—it hangs in the air at its most oppressive in the early evening. That was the designated time for crowds to start gathering for the Carnival of Champions, waiting for combatants to take the ring on three straight nights during the first full week of September 1892. During those evenings, even men of proper breeding had sweat pouring down their backs as they constantly blotted upper lips. What passed for autumn on the bayou had not arrived. To be fair, it rarely did. That far south, cool autumns and freezing winters seemed like stories mothers told summer-sweat-soaked children to induce them to fall back to sleep. In the summer of 1892, that dank heat could not have been a more appropriate metaphor for a season in the city already roiling with racial unrest.

"The South" is not a house built on a single foundation. Those who view it as a unified, unchanging region with defined borders misunderstand its complexity. In fact, the debate over defining its boundaries depends on the ground rules—historical, topographical, cultural, social, political, and perhaps even legal. In pre–Revolutionary War North America, the South was in the Chesapeake Bay Region. Georgia and South Carolina, straddling the Savannah River, emerged as the South in the Colonial Era. The Mason-Dixon Line became the symbolic demarcation for about half of a century after the American Revolution, as every state north of that line sought an end to slavery, while those south of it embraced the barbaric practice. Remnants of that social, legal, and moral line are not hard to find today. Like the country, the South expanded, to Tennessee and Kentucky, then Missouri, Arkansas, Texas, and Florida. By the 1860s, the region included all eleven states that seceded from the Union and joined the Confederacy (Alabama, Arkansas, Florida, Georgia, Louisiana, Mississippi, North Carolina, South Carolina, Tennessee, Texas, and Virginia) as well as the slave states that remained in the Union during the Civil War (Maryland, Delaware, Kentucky, and Missouri).[9] Many lean on this definition of the South, although there are still dangers to this view.

Like the South, New Orleans has defied definition—although that hasn't stopped some from trying. Volumes upon volumes have been filled with various odes to the city. And while most embraced it for its more hedonistic qualities, its port—one of the most important in North America—is not credited enough as another powerful draw. Throughout the 1800s, opportunity led to immigration that, in turn, prompted an explosion in the city's population. New Orleans boasted fewer than ten thousand residents in 1800; by 1900, that number had grown to nearly three hundred thousand.

Two Black communities developed in New Orleans from the time of the Louisiana Purchase in 1803 until the First World War. One comprised French-speaking Catholics who lived mostly in the city's core. Before the Civil War, this group was commonly called Creoles or Black Creoles. They had roots in French, African, and Caribbean cultures. More accurately called Franco-Africans, these people were French-speaking, urban New Orleans dwellers descended from colonial Louisiana slaves and free people of color. They were a relatively young New World community, for slaves were not brought to the Louisiana colony until 1719, one hundred years after being introduced into the English colonies. Hence the new Franco-African community retained a significant amount of their African culture.

The other community of Black residents comprised English-speaking Protestants who lived mostly uptown. This Anglo-African community originated when a few free people of color, plus large numbers of slaves, came—or were brought—to New Orleans from other parts of the South during the decades after the Louisiana Purchase. Mostly from rural backgrounds, they were generally less prosperous and less educated than the Franco-African community. For nearly two hundred years after their ancestors arrived on the shores of the English colonies in 1619, this group had largely assimilated Anglo-American culture and lost much of their African legacy. While most members of the Anglo-African community had darker skins, they also had numerous light-skinned members among them. Similarly, while large numbers of the Franco-African community, perhaps as many as two-thirds, had light complexions resulting from frequent cross-race sexual liaisons in early Louisiana history, many among them had dark coloring. Therefore, physical features were never defining factors for inclusion in, or exclusion from, either group.

By the 1890s, the two groups had grown together—first through their musical traditions and then later by legal definition. Some claim the initial merging of the two groups occurred when they gathered to play music in the bars and whorehouses of Storyville, the celebrated red-light district located in the center of the city, midway between the uptown and downtown communities. Some argue this was the birth of New Orleans jazz.[10]

After nearly a century of growth, the city's "coming-out party" occurred at the 1884–85 World's Industrial and Cotton Centennial Exposition held in Audubon Park and Zoological Gardens. Celebrating southern industry, as well as advertising the newly expanded port, the event marked a century of growth in the cotton trade. Its main building covered thirty-three acres, bigger by two hundred and fifty thousand square feet than the famous Crystal Palace in Great Britain. Its fairgrounds were illuminated by the biggest show of electricity in New Orleans history—four thousand incandescent and eleven hundred arc lamps.[11] The event defined the waning years of the nineteenth century in New Orleans as the city strove to be seen as modern in every aspect. That included shaking off many of the sins of its fellow southern cities. When American essayist and novelist Charles Dudley Warner visited the exposition in 1885, he was surprised that "white and colored people mingled freely, talking and looking at what was of common interest. . . . On 'Louisiana Day' in the exposition, the colored citizens took their full share of the parade and the honors. Their societies marched with the others, and the races mingled on the grounds in unconscious equality of privileges."[12]

As Dixon prepared to take his place at center stage in the South, Homer Plessy, another man who straddled the worlds of Black and white, was preparing to make a statement of his own and make the summer of 1892 event hotter.

Homer Plessy's racial family tapestry reflected New Orleans. His paternal grandfather, Germain Plessy, was born in the Bordeaux region of France. He arrived in Louisiana after fleeing a slave uprising on the island of Sainte Dominguez (Haiti), where he had been working. Soon afterward, this white Frenchman married Catherina Mathieu, called a "free woman of color" in the sometimes contradictory and illogical racial records of the era. Catherina Mathieu's case was further clouded by the fact that her father was also a white Frenchman. In New Orleans throughout the mid-1800s, approximately eleven thousand people were designated as free people of color. These were not outsiders, but integral pieces of middle-class society. Nevertheless, despite the family's mixed-race backgrounds, the Plessy children would be branded as "colored" in state records for decades to come. Although two generations away, the foundation of *Plessy v. Ferguson* began the moment Germain and Catherina give birth to their first child, Ida, in November 1855. Homer Plessy's father,

Joseph Adolphe Plessy, was the seventh of the couple's eight children. Joseph eventually married Rosa Debergue, a free woman of color, listed as "mulatto" by the 1880 Census. Their son, Homer, was born on March 17, 1862. Joseph, who died two months short of Homer's sixth birthday, was a shoemaker; Rosa was a seamstress and housekeeper.[13]

Although Plessy was born less than a year after the first shots of the Civil War, the world in which he came of age was radically different from what he would one day help combat. Following the cessation of fighting in 1865, freed Black men and women were quick to embrace their new rights—they formalized preexisting marriages, established parental rights over their children, bought land, became voters, jurors, and officeholders. War gave rise to Reconstruction, a time when the federal government took a heavy hand in plotting the course of the Confederacy's readmittance into the Union. During that period, Black men held office in every state of the former Confederacy. Between 1870 and 1900, twenty-two Black men were elected to Congress, including two US senators, both from Mississippi. More than one hundred Black men won election or appointment to posts with statewide jurisdiction, almost eight hundred served in state legislatures, and thousands more served at the local level. This was not simply a political revolution, however, as all aspects of society were impacted by a massive influx of new ideas, skills, and creativity from newly freed slaves. The influences of these pioneers during this thirty-year period—on politics, on entertainment, on sport, on the arts—are still felt today.[14]

Louisiana was even more progressive. In 1868, any adult male, regardless of race, could register to vote by paying a $1.50 poll tax (admittedly, a point of concern addressed by the Twenty-Fourth Amendment to the US Constitution nearly a century later). In 1869, Louisiana integrated its school system—the only former Confederate state to do so. In 1870, it legalized interracial marriage. In the last four decades of the nineteenth century, the Black community of New Orleans produced an interim governor, three lieutenant governors, six state officers, thirty-two state senators, and ninety-five state representatives.[15] With the institution of slavery still fresh in many minds, Blacks were entering Louisiana society.

Two years after his father's death, Homer Plessy's mother married Victor Dupart, a politically engaged and connected postal clerk whose family went back generations in New Orleans. Young Plessy was ushered through adolescence with an activist mindset. As an adult, through his stepfather's family, he became active in a number of civic organizations, including the Society of French Friends, Cosmopolitan Mutual Aid Society, Scottish Rite Masons, and the Justice, Protective, Educational, and Social Club. Through the latter organization, Plessy supported education reform for Black children of the city. New Orleans became a model for such reforms under federal occupation during Reconstruction.

Although a place of opportunity, New Orleans was not free of racial strife. Mirroring the activities of the Ku Klux Klan, an organization known as the Democratic White League, a white paramilitary group formed to harass free Black men, conducted a campaign to attack Republicans and Blacks throughout the state. The bloodiest clash occurred in Colfax, Louisiana, on April 13, 1873, when the group killed one hundred members of the state's nearly all-Black militia. Half of those killed had already surrendered. On September 13, 1874, in New Orleans, White League members gathered on Canal Street and urged the crowd to oust Governor William Pitt Kellogg. With the Pickwickian William Behan in charge, the White League clashed with city police, leaving eleven dead and sixty wounded, and took over the city. Federal troops soon restored Kellogg to his office, but resistance continued. Residents of New Orleans commemorated the White League insurrection of 1874 by erecting a monument to the battle in 1891. It was removed in 2017 and placed in storage.[16]

After President Ulysses S. Grant left office in March 1877, however, the trend was clear: the North was backing away from attempts to force Black equality on the South, and the South continued to pass laws and implement rules designed to keep Blacks inferior. National attention turned to taming the frontier, constructing a vast industrial economy, and dealing with immigration. White public opinion was indifferent or hostile to Blacks' quest for freedom, and American presidents from Grant onward, whatever their personal attitudes, were content to follow public opinion rather than lead. During the 1876 campaign, Alfonso Taft, Grant's last attorney general, wrote Republican nominee Rutherford B. Hayes with a warning: "It is a fixed and desperate purpose of the Democratic Party in the South that the negroes shall not vote, and murder is a common means of intimidation to prevent them."[17] Democrat Samuel J. Tilden, governor of New York, seemed to have won the presidency of 1876, after eight years of Republican rule under Grant. But the electoral votes of Florida, Louisiana, and South Carolina were in doubt. Without them, Tilden only had one hundred eighty-four of the necessary one hundred and eighty-five electoral votes. If Hayes carried those three states instead, he would have won.

Each of the states in question sent two sets of electoral voters to Washington, DC, to be counted—one for Tilden, one for Hayes. Congress responded by creating a fifteen-member electoral commission with eight Republicans and seven Democrats to figure out who won. What became known as the Compromise of 1877 was struck. In return for Democrats accepting Hayes's election, Republicans promised to remove occupying federal troops from the South. So, on March 2, 1877, the electoral commission rejected the Democratic returns from the toss-up states and declared Hayes the winner. This all but ended attempts to enforce both the Fourteenth and Fifteenth Amendments. Hayes's belief that southerners would do the right thing in dealing with Blacks was proven quite naïve. Under President Hayes, little was done to prevent the reversal of Reconstruction, even though he campaigned as a friend of the freed slaves. After he left office in March 1881, white supremacy was stronger in the South than before he became president.[18] There followed several decades when most presidents displayed little interest in the matters of race.

When Reconstruction ended in 1877, a crazy-quilt pattern of integration developed. New Orleans public schools returned to segregation, but interracial marriage remained legal. Some hotels, restaurants, bars, theaters, social clubs, and churches remained segregated, while others, indeed most, remained racially mixed until the eve of the First World War.[19] In July 1889, the Louisville, Nashville, and Mississippi Valley railroads added separate cars to their routes designated for Blacks only. Other companies soon followed. Changing attitudes and laws brought about Black disenfranchisement, segregation, and economic hardship. Once again white power structures were sorting society by race. Similar sentiments also echoed in the sporting arena. In the 1870s and 1880s, Blacks participated in integrated baseball and horse racing, but were virtually wiped from white-dominated sports by 1900. Black pugilists, however, were somewhat spared the separate-but-equal fate, especially in lighter weight classes. While fights between Blacks and whites in the lighter classes may have been upsetting to some, size was a mitigating factor. Apparently, lighter fighters did not symbolize the notion of race as did the bigger fighting men—the "heavies" always carried that burden.[20]

In 1888, Homer Plessy married Louise Bordenave. The couple settled in a shotgun-style home in Faubourg Tremé, a multiethnic community north of the New Orleans French Quarter.[21] Home to Creoles since the late 1700s, Faubourg Tremé was rich in what has become known as signature New Orleans culture—jazz musicians, dance halls, festivals.

John L. Sullivan. Albumen silver print on card. Photographer unknown.
Courtesy of Special Collections, Fine Arts Library, Harvard University.

Storyville was just a short walk away. Every night the thick breeze carried the sounds of jazz. In the summer of 1892, Homer Plessy was one of the city's fifteen hundred shoemakers, completely unaware that he would become one of the most recognizable surnames in civil rights history.

On January 9, 1891, John L. Sullivan was drunk. More accurately, John L. Sullivan was still drunk. As his New Year's Eve festivities threatened to spill into a second weekend, his was a drunk so thorough, so public, that newspaper reporters began to chronicle its depths in vivid detail akin to their coverage of Major Samuel Whitside and his US Seventh Cavalry Regiment at Wounded Knee a few weeks earlier. Reports from an early eyewitness in Buffalo, New York, arriving just after New Year's Day, suspected Sullivan and Co.'s "big spree" might last a week.[22] They woefully underestimated the capacity of the Big Man for excess.

Always a man who enjoyed life to its fullest, Sullivan was nonetheless in the midst of an emotional collapse that began a few years earlier. In August 1889, his mother died. A devastating loss, Sullivan attempted to honor her final prayer, offered up moments before death, by giving up his wild ways. That lasted only a matter of weeks. Just a year later, in September 1890, Sullivan's father died. Those two tragic events accelerated his journey down a path of self-destruction, punctuated at one point by his most ill-conceived plan: seriously considering running for political office. "A man who can quiet a crowd in Madison Square Garden, as I have done, can make his presence felt in Congress or anywhere else on Earth," Sullivan wrote.[23] And who knows, perhaps a sober and stable Sullivan might have had a chance—but a life so punctuated by violence and debauchery had no chance of fooling any voter.

Sullivan had not fought a significant bout in nearly a year and a half—a seventy-fifth-round knockout of Jake Kilrain in July 1889 in Marion County, Mississippi, and the last time the world bareknuckle title was on the line. But he had lost interest in the fight game. Never one to enjoying training for bouts, the thought of it now, at a rode-hard thirty-three years old, sent waves of panic through him. While his impact within the ring had been nonexistent, his attitude regarding who was worthy of contending for his title carried more weight than any other figure's in the sport. Through his entire career, Sullivan was clear and consistent on the issue of race: "A white man has nothing to gain by swapping punches with a negro." He lived that credo by ducking opportunities to face Black opponents. When questioned by the press about challenging a Black opponent, Sullivan set his terms with a cry of "White men $10,000; Niggers double the price."[24] His era featured some of the fight game's greatest Black fighters, namely George Godfrey or Peter Jackson. A San Francisco club offered Sullivan $20,000 to meet Jackson, but he demurred. He wrote of that decision: "I was insulted from one end of the country to the other in the attempt to stampede me into that fight and I was angry enough at one time to throw principle to the winds and give Jackson his."[25] Sullivan explained his stand thusly: "When I go to battle with a man, I agree that he is of equal standing. A negro is not the equal of a white man and it is no kindness to the negro to let him think so. Fights between negroes are all right, but the line should be drawn there. . . . I want every negro to do well and my opposition to seeing white boxers meet colored boxers is not based on any petty feelings. But for a white man to meet a negro as an equal doesn't pull the negro up to the white man's level, but rather pulls the blonde down to the brunette's."[26]

When the brightest star in pugilism drew a line like this, its repercussions were extreme. Sullivan dictated the heavyweight division for a generation. That stand resonated not only within the sporting world, but within a larger society still struggling with the entry of newly freed Blacks. Of course, Sullivan was not beyond boasting of unsanctioned bouts against Black men.

Despite months of absence from the ring, and an out-of-control lifestyle, Sullivan was still as big a star as any. And not just among the sporting set. His boisterous nature, explosive temper, and lavish lifestyle made for great theater.[27] Unmoored in life, unchallenged in the ring, Sullivan took to the road around that same time—acting, lecturing, even engaging in a bit of sparring with challengers from the audience. And he also continued to drink tremendously. In an era unafraid of the drink, where tavern culture still survived as a main social center, Sullivan still stood out as a man of excess. As he hopped from city to city to start 1891, his exploits still drew the attention of the masses. On January 8, 1891, in Milwaukee, Wisconsin, Sullivan knocked a newspaper reporter unconscious when the man dared approach the champion for an interview as he stepped off a train from Chicago.[28] This news prompted the Kansas City Star to claim that forty-eight consecutive hours of Sullivan sobriety would serve as a "foundation of sensation" for its reporters. "The only trouble about an appeal for John Drunk to John Sober is that nowadays John never sober," the paper chided the champion.[29]

By January 1892, Sullivan had sworn off drinking—again. Just as his previous binges had, news of his newfound sobriety made headlines across the country. Watching Sullivan mount a platform, a blue-ribbon badge signifying the temperance movement pinned to his broad chest, was an unbelievable sight for most. It made him a target, a source of ridicule. Few believed he would keep his pledge beyond the end of each day, let alone through the end of the year. The *Tacoma Daily News* wrote: "We are sorry. Sullivan drunk is very much funnier than Sullivan sober and he is a bullying brute at all times."[30] But there he stood—arguably the most famous man in the world, and certainly its most famous recovering drunk. He was a major get for the movement as his drawing power remained strong—thanks in large part to the mythmakers within newsrooms across the country who could not stop feeding his mythology. A Louisville, Kentucky, newspaperman made Sullivan the hero of his novel, *Congressman John L.* In it, the fictional Sullivan is elected to Congress where he passes a bill appropriating $100 million for the relief of farmers, as well as making Physical Culture a branch of the War Department. He is nominated for president, but shot while fighting against the syndicates and trusts on the House floor. A revolution follows, and an evil empire nearly rises to power when John L., who has been nursed back to life, rescues liberty and saves the republic.[31] The *Portland Telegram* ran a contest seeking from its readers the best-known man in the world. Great statesmen were named—William Gladstone of Great Britain, Herbert von Bismarck of Germany, US secretary of state James Blaine, and even former president Grover Cleveland. But it was John L. who towered above "any statesman, general, divine or author." Only two other men rivaled his popularity—inventor Thomas Edison and explorer Henry Stanley.[32] Sullivan was also unafraid to feed his own legend, already penning his autobiography, *Reminiscences of a 19th Century Gladiator.*

And there that Sullivan now stood in the early days of 1892, often alongside Francis Murphy, the famed temperance evangelist, in front of the world, a signpost on the journey to sobriety. He was the most striking "horrible example" possible.[33] Like his earlier promise to his mother, that pledge did not last the month. In Ogden, Utah, he began drinking after a theater engagement and had to be carried back to his room.[34] The following night, a drunken Sullivan stormed the stage of the Tabor Grand theater in Denver, Colorado. After fighting his way to the front of the room, he climbed atop the stage and prepared to make a speech before being dragged into the wings by a mob of stagehands.[35] The incident prompted the *Wheeling Register*, a newspaper clear across the country, to announce to its readers the next day: "It may interest the public to know that according to the latest bulletin John L Sullivan was still drunk."[36] In less than a month, he was thrown off a train in Kansas City, Kansas,[37] and then fell off a stage in St. Paul, Minnesota.[38]

This collapse coincided with the tenth anniversary of Sullivan's ascendency to the title with his victory over Paddy Ryan on February 7, 1882. But that seemed so long ago now. Sullivan was a faded quantity who no longer engendered fear in his opponents. While never questioning Sullivan's claim to the title, newspaper reporters wondered what would come of the title should he never enter the ring again. In the eyes of the public, however, he remained their champion. And that would not be taken away until he was defeated within the ring. By March 1892, Sullivan issued a challenge to "any or all bluffers who had been trying to make capital at my expense," stating, in part: "This country has been overrun with a lot of foreign fighters and also American aspirants for fistic fame and championship honors, who have endeavored to seek notoriety and American dollars by challenging me to a fight, knowing full well that my hands were tied by contract and honor. I have been compelled to listen to their bluffs without making reply on account of my obligations. But now my time has come." His challenges called for a fight the first week of September 1892, at the Olympic Club in New Orleans, Louisiana, for a winner-take-all purse of $25,000 and an outside bet of $10,000. "I insist upon the bet of $10,000, to show that they mean business," he further reasoned.

The Olympic Club had only recently joined chartered athletic clubs across the country in promoting boxing events. And thanks to their efforts, New Orleans became the center of prizefighting game, culminating with the Jack "Nonpareil" Dempsey–Robert Fitzsimmons world middleweight title fight on January 14, 1891. These promotions not only flew in the face of the existing anti-prizefight statute of the State of Louisiana, but also the club's own charter and city ordinances.[39] Many predicted disaster early on for the Carnival of Champions.

Sullivan was available to fight in early September—an "inconvenient season" for the Olympic and city alike. The *Daily Picayune* wrote: "Here, the cotton business just begins and a large class upon whom the club depends for patronage has little leisure for sport. Many wealthy people are still sojourning at summer resorts. . . . Some of the best racing of the year is in full blast, and many of the ring's most ardent followers are deeply interested in the daily tests of the thoroughbreds."[40] Instead of backing down, however, Olympic Club members decided to double down on the Sullivan fight—or triple down as the case ultimately ended up being. Unlike previous fights, where fighters, backers, and fans alike had to duck the law, New Orleans was seeing to it that the welcome mat was rolled out.

Sullivan was the first piece of what would become the most important three days in sport for a generation.

―――――――――

New Orleans had a certain civic arrogance. No matter the challenge, the city believed it would rise to the occasion. Its institutions, particularly a cheerleading local press, loved to buoy this notion at every turn. Just a handful of months before the Carnival of Champions, another carnival, one running for more than half a century and far more famous, had just wrapped up. Mardi Gras and all that led up to it was still the biggest party thrown by the city. Balls and social festivals dotted the city map, while celebrations spilled into and continued in the streets for days leading up to Fat Tuesday. Mardi Gras formally ends with the Meeting of the Courts, a ceremony where Rex and His Royal Consort—the King and Queen of Carnival—meet with Comus and His Queen at the ball of the Mistick Krewe of Comus. In 1892, the King of Carnival was marched through the city by a military escort and local dignitaries. After receiving the keys to the city from the mayor, Rex was joined in this citywide street pageant of "gaiety and grotesqueness" by masked revelers. On that night, they marched through the recently electrified lights of the city streets, under a shocking brilliance highlighting the vibrant colors and beauty of the costumes adorning thousands. The *Daily Picayune* marveled as it so often did at its city, one that would offer such "hospitalities and courtesies . . . without regard to any person's social rank or pretensions" for free with expectations of nothing in return and "rewarded only in the consciousness of having given pleasure to others."[41]

The Olympic Club was buoyed by applause for how it had handled the Fitzsimmons-Dempsey bout a year earlier when five thousand men crowded into the great amphitheater with not a single disturbance. The success was credited to the tight regulation of behavior club officials had put in place, and the strong show of force by local law enforcement, even for the class of people now being drawn to the sport. Any disturbance, no matter how minor, would have been reported with glee across the country, but none was to be found—unheard-of behavior for a sport defined and driven by the rowdy. Ever the civic cheerleader, the *Daily Picayune* gushed that "such a state of things could be chronicled of a similar assemblage, gathered for a like purpose, in any other city on the continent. Nowhere in the Union has the art of handling crowds been brought to this perfection as in New Orleans."[42]

This was the moment Olympic Club officials saw a chance to push even further. Change was in the thick air. The city aggressively marketed prizefighting, as well as its openness to a Black boxer fighting a white boxer in the ring. Predictably, religious opponents of the sport attempted to effect its demise, and a resolution in the legislature was proposed for its abolishment. At the same time, "some of the best citizens of New Orleans" came forward to support boxing in the community:

> The Olympic Club has already done much to rescue pugilism from the roughs and toughs who formerly controlled it, and the bad repute into which it had fallen. It hopes to make "gloved contests" as reputable a form of sport and athletics as wrestling, football and other popular games. . . . Under its management, all the rowdyism and disagreeable features of the old "prize ring" have been done away with. The "glove contests," as they are now called, are given under the State of Louisiana, under a special license from the Mayor of New Orleans, with the Chief of Police or other police office, with 50 men or more under him, presiding to see that everything is fairly, honestly and orderly conducted.[43]

Travelers viewed New Orleans as having the "worst streets in America."[44] One of those streets—Royal—led from the central part of the city to the Olympic Club. It was narrow, paved with broad blocks of stone that had become smooth and slippery from constant traffic. The Olympic Club, 2725 Royal Street, squatted across a block between Port and St. Ferdinand streets in the Bywater District. Patrons could enter from Royal or slide around toward the Mississippi River and enter from Chartres Street. Unfortunately for the thousands of visitors, there was no good way to get there. The tramway lines monopolized half of the street, requiring "something of an expert in the driving line to make the journey without losing a wheel or breaking a spring."[45] The tram cars were miserable—hot, crowded, and slow. Anybody who had the means hired a private carriage to carry them to all three nights of the Carnival. Royal Street would be "crowded with carriages, surreys, hansoms and, in fact, anything that had wheels" for all three nights.[46] In advance of the Carnival, the club threw open its doors to the public. Inside was an immense amphitheater laid out like an opera house, with numbered seats for the masses and private boxes with easy chairs for the more elite among them. Three-fourths of the audience each night of the Carnival were guaranteed to be from "the better classes"—lawyers, doctors, bankers, merchants, and men of that kind—and the other quarter were sporting men, mostly from the East.

By September 1892, the United States was two months away from a presidential election, although there were days in the lead-up to the Carnival when that fact would be hard to discern by reading the local newspapers. In a rematch of four years earlier, former president Grover Cleveland, the first Democrat nominated by his party three consecutive times, was matched against the incumbent, Benjamin Harrison—a rare occasion in American politics where both candidates were seeking reelection to the highest office. In 1888, Cleveland, who won the popular vote against Harrison, lost the electoral vote and, therefore, the election. This election, however, felt different. A wave of agrarianism had crested across the country; now, urban concerns were center stage. The presidential campaign of 1892 would elect the first leader of modern America.

Democrats feared defections in the South, not to Republican candidates, but to a wave of third parties, mainly the Populists and Prohibitionists, that dotted the landscape. To secure its base, the party emphasized the threat of a federal-elections bill, popularly known as the Lodge Force Bill, named for its chief sponsor, Republican representative Henry Cabot Lodge of Massachusetts. The Republican platform called for a free and honest popular ballot and laws "enacted and enforced to secure to every citizen, be he rich or poor, native or foreign born, white or Black." Democrats balked at that notion, and the proposed supervision of elections by federal troops, regarded by this plank as the "force bill."[47] In opposition, Democrats echoed the refrain of "negro domination" as often as possible. In a document that unironically warned of the "reviving of race antagonisms, now happily abated" if federal control of elections was allowed, the Democratic Party platform reaffirmed its commitment to states' rights—branded as "home rule"—by noting that a "return to these principles of free popular government, based on home rule and individual liberty, was never more urgent than now, when the tendency to centralize all power at the federal capital has become a menace to the reserved rights of the states that strikes at the very roots of our government under the Constitution as framed by the fathers of the Republic."[48] Newspapers across the South followed suit and decried that "no infamy could be greater" than what Republicans proposed to do to the region:

> Just to think—the negro to be armed; whites and Blacks to mix in the same schools by compulsion and to be brought into close and equal relations . . . and abolition of the laws against intermarriage of whites and Blacks. Let our misguided brethren . . . look this squarely in the face. Their course is virtually constructing a highway over which the infamous measure is to be thrust upon the South. They are accessories in a crime against their own country. Turn back before it is too late. Do not place a weapon in the hands of a foe you cannot take back. Vote for the South and for liberty.[49]

Atlanta was up in arms. An editorial in the *Atlanta Banner* asked, "Are you a Southerner? If so, remember the sacrifices made by our heroes in gray. Did you live in times of Reconstruction? If so, you hardly wish to see them return again. Do you intend voting a third-party ticket? If so, you curse your country and her people with a Republican triumph and force bill. Ponder these things a little and you will find that it will be far better to stand by the old flag."[50] An editorial in the *Atlanta Constitution* followed: "There is not a voter in the country but knows that the Republicans will hasten to turn the Southern States over to negro domination. . . . a result that will follow the election of a Republican candidate for president."[51] Perhaps Tom Watson, a People's Party congressman from Atlanta, summed up the whole argument for history when he declared how the stance of regular Democrats could be "boiled down to one word—Nigger."[52]

In November 1892, Cleveland defeated Harrison, winning both the popular and electoral vote in the rematch, and became the only person in US history to be elected to a second, nonconsecutive presidential term. In the South, the Democrats won clear majorities, although populism was much stronger than anticipated. The People's Party finished second.[53]

The plight of the Black man faded from public concern seemingly overnight. Defeated a month earlier by Cleveland, President Harrison used his final State of the Union address on December 6, 1892, to advocate for "the freedom and purity of the ballot and the equality of the elec- tor," as well as call for federal legislation against lynching.[54] However, civil rights received only sixty-four words in Cleveland's inaugural address on March 4, 1893: "Loyalty to the principles upon which our government rests positively demands that the equality before the law which it guarantees to every citizen should be justly and in good faith conceded in all parts of the land. The enjoyment of this right follows the badge of citizenship where found, and, unimpaired by race or color, it appeals for recognition to American manliness and fairness."[55] After that, Black concerns received little airing from the highest office in the land for, arguably, a generation.

But in September 1892, with an uncertain future still ahead, these issues mattered little to the citizens of New Orleans. Nearing the Carnival's opening, the *Daily Picayune* wrote: "And just now, the most prolific and absorbing subject of conversation in this country—not barring the cholera shadow, the world's fair and the national campaign—is found in the three great fights which are to come off in this city."[56]

The event excited New Orleans as much as Mardi Gras, gave the railroads plenty of business during the dull season, packed the hotels and boarding houses, and caused "general activity all along the line." The railroads especially embraced the spectacle. For the Carnival of Champions, railroad companies bought up $10,000 to $15,000 worth of Carnival tickets at a time—Union Pacific Railroad, headquartered more than a thousand miles away in Washington, DC, bought $3,000 worth of tickets alone. Advertisements spread from coast to coast, offering discount, round-trip fares to the Big Easy. Each ticket had a coupon good for entry into all three nights of the Carnival. Athletic clubs in New York City, Chicago, and Cincinnati ran junkets to the bouts for their members. Though the Olympic Club originally sought a four-night Carnival with a championship in every major weight class of the day—heavy, middle, light, and feather—they managed only three, as no middleweight would take a fight against champion Bob Fitzsimmons, despite the chance at a $13,000 purse. The stage was then set with Jack McAuliffe vs. Billy Myer for the lightweight championship on September 5, George Dixon vs. Jack Skelly for the featherweight championship on September 6, and John L. Sullivan vs. James J. Corbett for the heavyweight championship on September 7. Even with only three bouts, the money at stake was larger than any pugilistic purses ever seen—$45,000 in total prize money, $40,000 in side bets. The only amount matching that was the $80,000 the Olympic Club spent on preparations. The *Wheeling (WV) Register* opined: "It is a big affair, moreover, aside from the money involved, more than ever before dreamed of in pugilism, for it is a new departure in 'the manly art of self-defense,' an effort to make the prize ring refined and respectable—something that gentlemen can patronize."[57]

It was an impressive sight within the Olympic Club. Its parlor featured tan-colored Brussels carpets and rugs of different hues. Four large marble stands, with bronze statues atop them and adorned with silk scarves, stood in each corner. Furniture was covered in a pale blue silk. On the mantel in the parlor sat a marble clock, bookended by a pair of marble vases. A grand Steinway piano sat in the middle of the room. One reporter noted "the whole place ranks with any social resort in the country."[58] Thoughts of completely rebuilding the club's existing arena ended when it was estimated to delay the bouts more than a year. Instead, the Olympic Club enlarged the space, upping capacity from six thousand to ten thousand in just a few weeks. They also added a $25,000 clubhouse. The main room was fashioned after the old Roman Coliseum. The center ring was built of Mississippi River sand packed firm and level. It was surrounded by a platform for police, seconds, and the referee; a barbed wire fence prevented ring jumping "which has spoiled so many fights." The Olympic planned for a press section of more than five hundred journalists, with some northern papers sending contingents that included three or four reporters, an artist, a retired fighter to offer color commentary, a stenographer, and a telegrapher. The club upgraded its telegraph capabilities, allowing papers to send reports straight from ringside to awaiting throngs at home. Behind the press came the private boxes, followed by the parquet, family circle, and gallery. The whole building was lit by electric light, a luxurious novelty at the time. Modern ears would need to get used to the sounds of the fight. Time was marked by an electric clock and gong. Placed in full view of all, the clock not only timed the rounds and intermissions, but also struck the ten count every time a contestant was knocked to the ground. The stage, as they say, was set: "[Olympic Club members] propose to make New Orleans the pugilistic center of the Union—a sort of modern Olympia. . . . It is believed that prizefighting, with the toughs eliminated and the brutality abolished can be made a popular athletic sport in America. This is what the success of the New Orleans pugilistic carnival will mean."[59]

A spectacular twenty-page program, including an ornately illustrated full-color front cover, was produced for the event. The publication served two purposes. First, it celebrated the host city and venue by featuring an overview of the Olympic Club and its executives, as well as a bounty of advertisements for New Orleans businesses, large and small, ranging from Cohen and Ber Fine Furnisher and Clothier to the H&D Folsom Arms Co.; from the American Brewing Company to Jackson Square Cigars;

Cover, Carnival of Champions program, Olympic Club, 1892. *Tulane University Special Collections.*

ARENA.

Arena engraving. By Photo Electric Engraving Co., New Orleans. Carnival of Champions program, Olympic Club, 1892. *Tulane University Special Collections.*

from John F. Markey, funeral director, to W. M. Bartel, an importer and dealer in foreign and domestic birds. The program also included profiles of the fighters, although Corbett's was noticeably missing from the collection. The brief profiles were fairly straightforward with the exception of Sullivan's, the biggest star of the Carnival. Of the heavyweight champion, organizers wrote:

> The champion has stood upon the pinnacle of popular favor; and there are thousands of men today who think there lives no man able to dethrone him. So much has been written about the height of Sullivan, the breadth of chest, the symmetrical outlines of his magnificent frame, the thews and sinews, his style of fighting, hitting power, etc.; all have been so exhaustively treated of by writers, of

GEORGE DIXON.

GEORGE DIXON the colored bantam weight pugilist who comes to New Orleans to fight Jack Skelly, for the bantam weight championship and purse of $7,500, on September 6th, has created a very favorable impression upon those who are anxious to

discover good points in various fighters, and get as near as they can to the "sure thing." Some enthusiastic writer referring to Dixon says: "He (Dixon) is the only real worlds champion pugilist the prize ring ever boasted." Whether this is true or not,

George Dixon bio page, Carnival of Champions program, Olympic Club, 1892. *Tulane University Special Collections.*

JACK SKELLY.

JACK SKELLY the youngster who is to fight George Dixon, September 6th, for the bantam weight championship (and incidentally the valuable trimmings thereto attached) was born in Brooklyn in 1872. He is counted as a game fighter though his record heretofore contains nothing but amateur victories. His style is highly spoken of and the sledge hammer motion and effect of his work has secured for him the cognomen of the "young pile

driver." When able to do any "graft" young Skelly went to work in Palmer's Cooperage, where he had as co-laborers Dempsey, McAuliffe and others who have since turned out to be first-class pugilists.

From all accounts the subject of this writing is what can be called a "model young man." He neither smokes, drinks or chews, keeps good hours and is described as a very exemplary young fellow. Skelly stands 5 feet 6 inches and has a 34 inch chest measurement, 28 inches around the waist and his size in collars is 16½.

Jack Skelly bio page, Carnival of Champions program, Olympic Club, 1892.
Tulane University Special Collections.

more or less consequence, that reiteration now would be wearisome. Poets have sung his prowess, some journalists have been known to become delirious over his marvelous powers of endurance, and even the "divine" has not thought him an unworthy subject for commendatory pulpit address.[60]

George Dixon's mention was smaller: respectful and laudatory, just not quite as lavish in its praises. Of the bantamweight champion, organizers wrote: "All unite in the opinion that for so young a fighter the colored bantam demonstrates superb generalship, and is one of the most careful fighters that ever entered the ring. He never forgets himself, he fights at his man, not for the audience and devotes every second to his work. Despite the fact that he has made such a wonderful record, Dixon is today a modest unassuming boy, rather bashful when being interviewed and has little to say of himself except that he intends to do his best."[61]

Leave it to a Yankee to find humor in the southern way of life. In August 1891, white attorney and novelist Albion Winegar Tourgée began calling attention in his humorous newspaper column to the separate-train-car laws.[62] He thrilled at poking at the irony of the segregation laws, exposing the unintentional hilarity of intended oppression: "No matter how the white cars or compartments may be crowded, the passengers cannot go into the compartments for colored people as long as there is a single colored person in them. As there are ordinarily many more white than colored travelers, the result is that one or two colored people often have half or the whole of a good car to themselves while every seat is doubly laden and men are even standing in the aisles of the white compartments, cussing the niggers for having the best end of the legislation especially intended to degrade and oppress them."[63]

A resident of upstate New York, Tourgée was among the leading white spokesmen for people of color. Although playful in writing, he was smart and serious in his efforts. Following service in the Union Army, he moved to North Carolina and served as a judge. He provided one of the period's most vivid accounts of life as a carpetbagger—a Northerner who settled in the South after the war. In his popular novel, *A Fool's Errand by One of the Fools*, he wrote:

> To the Southern mind it meant a scion of the North, a son of an "abolitionist," a creature of the conqueror, a witness to their defeat, a mark of their degradation: to them he was hateful, because he

recalled all of evil or of shame they had ever known. . . . To the Northern mind, however, the word had no vicarious significance. To their apprehension, the hatred was purely personal, and without regard to race or nativity. They thought (foolish creatures!) that it was meant to apply solely to those, who, without any visible means of support, lingering in the wake of a victorious army, preyed upon the conquered people.[64]

Continuing his legal and literary career after he returned to New York, Tourgée worked to expose the Ku Klux Klan and campaigned for improved conditions for freed Blacks. Convinced the only solution to the race problem in the United States was education, he unsuccessfully campaigned for federal funds to combat illiteracy in Black communities. His high profile caught the attention of the Citizens' Committee of New Orleans (Comité des Citoyens), an activist group composed mainly of Creoles. This group hoped to target the Louisiana Railway Accommodation Act (commonly known as the Separate Car Act), passed by the Louisiana State Legislature in 1890. That law read, in part: "All railway companies carrying passengers in their coaches in this State, shall provide equal but separate accommodations for the white, and colored races, by providing two or more passenger coaches for each passenger train, or by dividing the passenger coaches by a partition so as to secure separate accommodations; provided that this section shall not be construed to apply to street railroads. No person or persons shall be permitted to occupy seats in coaches, other than the ones assigned to them on account of the race they belong to."[65]

On September 1, 1891, the Citizens' Committee gathered at the offices of *The Crusader*, a Black weekly newspaper in New Orleans. The paper's chief contributor, Rodolphe Desdunes, contended that the "law is unconstitutional. It is like a slap in the face of every member of the Black race."[66] The group devised a test case to prove the unconstitutionality of the law and sought to enlist the help of the law's biggest opponent. The committee contacted Tourgée, having raised $1,412.70 to enlist his services. But Tourgée agreed to represent the group for free. His aim, like the committee's, was to get the US Supreme Court to declare segregation laws unconstitutional.

Strangely enough, in 1869, Louisiana had passed a law prohibiting segregation by public carriers—the reverse of the Separate Car Act. A challenge to that law had reached the US Supreme Court in *Hall v. DeCuir*. Josephine DeCuir, a woman of color, boarded the steamboat

Governor Allen for a trip from New Orleans to Hermitage, a landing within Louisiana. The boat master refused to let her ride in a whites-only cabin, and she sued him under the Louisiana anti-segregation law. In 1877 the Supreme Court held the law unconstitutional. While the Louisiana statute outlawed discrimination by common carriers within Louisiana, the Supreme Court struck the law down as a violation of the Commerce Clause by noting that the Mississippi River and its tributaries traverse many states. The court concluded that the statute would force white passengers in a whites-only cabin on a vessel coming from a state that permitted or required segregation to "share the accommodations of that cabin with such colored persons as may come on board afterwards, if the law is enforced."[67]

Tourgée, however, was not going to confront the law head on. His strategy was to have someone of mixed blood violate it, thus allowing Tourgée to challenge the arbitrariness of the definition of "colored" in the eyes of the law. The one-eighth Black Homer Plessy was an ideal candidate, as he often rode in the white car without trouble—his "mixture was not discernible." The legal challenge also received silent support from the railroad companies, which did not like the added expense of providing separate cars.[68]

On June 7, 1892, one block away from that buzzing Olympic Club preparing for its Carnival, Plessy bought a first-class ticket on an East Louisiana Railroad train and sat in the white riders' car. The committee arranged for a private detective with arrest powers to remove Plessy from the train at Press and Royal streets, and to ensure he was charged with violating the state's separate-car law and not some other misdemeanor. Plessy's role "consisted of four tasks: get the ticket, get on the train, get arrested, and get booked."[69] He succeeded on all four counts.

While arguably the most famous, George Dixon was not the first native Nova Scotian to arrive on the banks of the Mississippi River. Acadian immigrants from New Brunswick and Nova Scotia began arriving in New Orleans in 1755 following the "Grand Derangement" of the French and Indian War, when families were cast out of their homes by the British because they refused to take up arms against their French brethren. These were one group of countless immigrant classes welcomed by New Orleans, a city seeded by people who had been "scattered to the wind."[70]

In organizers' minds, Dixon was a given for the Carnival of

Champions. Finding a marquee opponent for him, however, proved a challenge for club officials. Dixon was the only recognized winner of a world-championship title that America could boast, and "to have a champions' carnival without him would have been like the tragedy of *Hamlet* minus the personage about whom the story revolved."[71] But the club was in a dilemma. The recent triumphs of Black boxers were especially unsettling to whites because, to them, those triumphs disrupted the natural social order and challenged the belief in their own racial superiority and true manhood. These Black superheroes offered a new myth of masculine fighting strength to wipe out memories of slavery. They challenged the popular images of lazy, bumbling, simple-minded Blacks propagated in popular media. Any public performance by a Black in popular culture, and especially in sport, had the potential to transform into a political act.[72] Dixon was the most famous of those superheroes. He exhibited the possibilities of his race two decades before Jack Johnson would show their full manifestation. This was also why white boxers were sometimes reluctant to enter the ring against Black opponents, especially in the heavyweight division, which was imbued with far more racial meaning than the lighter divisions because of the fighters' size.[73] Across all weight classes, however, the search for "white hopes" was always on.

Dixon's manager, Tom O'Rourke, initially arranged with the Olympic Club for a fight between Dixon and Johnny "The Birmingham Sparrow" Murphy, a British-born, Boston-based Black boxer who lost to Dixon two years prior in Rhode Island. Southerners were anxious to see Dixon fight, but both managers and fighters refused to travel to the South. They did not fear any "unfair treatment by club officials"; rather, it was outside the club they expected trouble. O'Rourke had assurances, however, from several prominent New Orleans businessmen that Dixon "would not be hampered in the least."[74] The $5,000 purse demanded by O'Rourke, however, proved too rich for Murphy, who ended up as a famed boxing instructor at Harvard University. A new opponent needed to be found.

A week later, after more than five hours of negotiations, Dixon and Jack Skelly were matched up on July 29, 1892. Disagreements centered on the weight at which the men would fight—Skelly backers insisted on 120 pounds, Dixon backers 117 pounds. At one point, O'Rourke and William Reynolds, Skelly's manager, were fighting over a half of a pound. In fact, Skelly and Reynolds had walked out of negotiations and were headed home until a *New York World* reporter advised them to return to the bargaining table. They would settle at 118 pounds. "I have made many a match in my time, but never have I had such work as this," said O'Rourke. "For an amateur, Billy Reynolds is a shrewd matchmaker. I'd rather have three professionals to do business with."[75]

The news of the matchup came as a surprise in Brooklyn. The *Brooklyn Daily Eagle* wrote: "The friends of Jack Skelly on this side of the river will be much surprised at the nerve of the youngster in facing such a cyclone as George Dixon. Those who have seen both boys fight feel pretty well assured that Dixon will have an easy job unless Jack has greatly improved of late in private practice. Skelly is a first-class amateur, but he hardly classes with Dixon's style in the professional ring."[76]

To jump from the amateur ranks and fight for a professional feather-weight championship of the world and $17,500 was less a credit to Skelly than to Reynolds for "surmounting this seeming impossibility."[77] Even photographs of Skelly from that time have an awkward nature to them. One of the few images from Skelly's brief career was taken by Richard K. Fox. Although all the elements of other pugilistic portraits from the era are there—the outfit, the odd backdrop (seemingly set in a similar field as a previous Dixon-O'Rourke image), the classic pose—there is a lack of confidence, an absence of intimidation in his eyes. And that is to be expected, as Skelly was a fresh-faced amateur fighter plucked from regional obscurity to fight who many considered the greatest pound-for-pound boxer of his era. Perhaps we should be forgiving of his thousand-mile stare. Yet Billy Reynolds, of Brooklyn, had faith in the amateur's prowess and was not afraid to risk a small fortune to test it. The twenty-eight-year-old self-made man started out "with less capital than would pay his railroad fare to New Orleans."[78] Many thought him mad for making the match—no matter the amount. "I may be a fool," he told a newspaper reporter in New Orleans. "But perhaps subsequent developments will prove I am right. I believe Jack Skelly to be a fistic marvel and am perfectly willing to wager $5,000 on the result of my opinion, which, happily for me, is not shared by others to any great extent."[79]

At the time the match was made, Skelly was on vacation from the Rochester Lamp Company, where he ran the shipping department. When the contracts were signed on his behalf, his coworkers offered their support: "I naturally suppose that, under the circumstances, he will not come back to work here for a time at least. He can come back whenever he wants to do so; we think a good deal of him here and we shall fill his place only temporarily. He is well-behaved and capable and we have no desire whatever to lose him."[80] Indeed, Skelly did not return to work from vacation, instead headed directly into training for the bout. His friends and coworkers were quoted in newspapers leading up to the bout—none of whom said he would win. "They are not over-confident about the matter . . . but they are by no means hopeless."[81]

His matchup with Dixon also appealed to the romantic in many. If Skelly could manage a victory, the winnings would leave him "comfortably fixed," and he promised to quit the ring forever and marry his "bright little Brooklyn girl" to whom he was engaged.[82] The *Brooklyn Daily Eagle* wrote of the gesture: "'All the world loves a lover,' and Skelly will carry the good wishes and hopes of thousands who read his romantic story. A prizefighter battling for the money, wherewith to marry his waiting sweetheart! Will it require a great deal of imagination to recall the knightly days of old when warriors bold strove for their ladyes faire?"[83]

Skelly arrived in New Orleans to train on August 2, 1892. He pooled training sessions with old friend Jack McAuliffe, who was set to meet Billy Myer on the opening night of the Carnival. The pair lived and trained in Bay St. Louis, Mississippi. Skelly was constantly pressed by reporters about his ability to match up with the champion. In a conversation with his hometown paper, Skelly intoned:

> It isn't as though I were a perfect stranger to Dixon and his ring tactics. I've studied them closely and I know just what I am going up against. Nobody need tell me that I will have my hands full; I know that; but I think you will find that Dixon will be in about the same situation, so far as that is concerned. I have had the advantage of seeing him fight several times, and he is an exceedingly clever man and a hard and scientific hitter. But Dixon has never seen me with my hands up, and that is where I have a slight advantage. . . . This is my first professional battle, and that is the reason why I wanted to go at Dixon, who has bested every man that went before him. I do not need much training, for I have always taken care of myself, never having tasted a drop of liquor nor smoked a cigar or cigarette. The only weight that I want to work off is in the abdominal region, which is not flat enough for me.[84]

In a letter home to friends in Brooklyn, Skelly wrote:

> Even though I see that Dixon has said that he will "try some new tricks with the Brooklyn amateur," you may rely on the fact that, as usual, I will do my best, and I now have every prospect of whipping George, for whom I have great admiration by reason of his wonderful ability. I don't mean to underrate him either in this respect,

simply feeling better than ever, and that I have the chance of a life-time to get comparatively rich and win the championship of the world. The Palmer cooperage graduated two champions ahead of me, Jack McAuliffe and Jack Dempsey, and perhaps we may add another to the list in myself on the night of the coming fight. Give my regards to all the boys, and tell the National Athletic Club fellows that I will give them a chance to get hunk on the Gorman fight if they back me against Dixon. I was never in better condition and confidently expect to win. I see that Tom O'Rourke "expects to win in less than eleven rounds." Well, what do you say to the fact that I expect to be declared the winner in less than that time? It will be a short fight, and the club will see some of the fastest sighting on record. I am certain, for both of us are quick and know what to do. Dixon may defeat me, but it will go on record that his hardest won fight was with "that Brooklyn amateur, Jack Skelly."[85]

Luck, if such a thing can be found in the ring game, did not smile on Skelly during his training. The southern heat crushed the northern lad—he soon contracted fever, which made it impossible for him to get into proper condition. One day before the bout, Reynolds put his man through the paces, turning Skelly loose in a no-holds-barred spar with Johnny Griffin. He wanted to see what the Brooklyn lad had in him. Reynolds told the *Brooklyn Daily Eagle*: "I know of no better boy than Jack. He neither drinks nor uses tobacco in any form. He is modest and sincere and straightforward. He is true as steel, and if I am not sure he is worth all I am doing for him, then I'm not sure I know my own name."[86] Griffin followed instructions and "sailed in hammer and tongs."[87] In the second round of the training session, Griffin hit Skelly so hard that he broke Skelly's nose. He was advised to back out of the Dixon bout, but decided to go ahead.[88]

In advance of Dixon's arrival, O'Rourke penned a letter to Olympic Club president Charles Noel. In it, Dixon was quoted by his manager as saying: "I'll be the first 'nigger' that will have fought in the great Southern club, and I'll give the organization dollar for dollar in the shape of a fight. The oftentimes repeated chestnut that I had better not go down South will receive its quieting, and I am pleased that it is coming so soon."[89] O'Rourke further clarified those remarks with his usual degrading sales pitch: "Our colored friends in the South, we know, will be pleased with George's good behavior, but we will not be there long before George will have his allowance of white admirers. My fighter is black only in color, and even there, he is not very black, so we expect a good time generally down with you."[90]

Hundreds crowded into the depot of the Louisville and Nashville

Railroad at 3:30 p.m. on August 12, 1892, in New Orleans, to see Dixon and his trainers leave for their quarters in Biloxi, Mississippi. When Dixon stepped from the car to board his Pullman sleeper, a roar went up from the crowd. O'Rourke thanked "the kind manner in which they and the colored citizens had treated Dixon." Noel and members of the Olympic Club escorted O'Rourke and Dixon to the depot. The day prior, Dixon visited city hall, police headquarters, and other places of interest.[91] Newspapers owned a vested interest in civic boosting of Dixon and his acceptance by the people of the city. It was proudly reported Dixon was "impressed by all those with whom he came into contact that he was a quiet and nice fellow" and that "the little pugilist thinks New Orleans is more hospitable than Boston, or any other northern city, and he would leave nothing undone to show his appreciation."[92] As the train pulled away, heading east to Mississippi, cheers rose once again as Dixon bowed to the crowd from the back of the coach until the train was out of sight. Later that evening, another large crowd—"composed of both sexes, of all sizes, ages and conditions"[93]—gathered in Biloxi to greet Dixon and company. He planned on staying in a cottage on Magnolia and Water streets. Mississippi newspapers described the first sight of the fighter: "He is a big little man, with broad chest and shoulders, both well-muscled, and while his arms are not large, the muscles are pliable and well massed. Dixon is not Black, but a light mulatto with broad jaws, round head, knowing look and self-confident air. One of his ears looks like it had been through a press, and his face generally gave evidence of having had a hard road to travel."[94]

Despite the initial greeting, widespread interest in the Dixon-Skelly started to fade by mid-August 1892. Ticket sales were sluggish and paled in comparison to the main event. However, Dixon's support among the Black population in New Orleans remained steadfast. They formed an almost immediate ardent admiration for Dixon, and he received the attention of "the best and most representative colored men of this city."[95] As the Black sporting press reported: "It is safe to assert that every Afro-American who can raise a dollar and find a bet will put his money on the little colored fighter from the North."[96]

With a Dixon victory already cemented in the minds of many, before even the first punch was thrown, thoughts turned to the crowd's reception for Dixon, and how that would define a reputation for New Orleans. The city was vested in promoting a tolerant face. As the country still struggled with questions of race, it is not out of line to say the eyes of the country were on New Orleans. The *Tacoma (Washington) Daily News*, a newspaper about as far away from the Big Easy as you could find in the continental United States, wrote: "The Southern people have long wanted to see Dixon, not only because he is known to be a great wonder in his class, but to give him a chance to get out of his head the absurd ideas that he has been represented to have about the Southern injustice to colored fighters."[97] The *Detroit Plain Dealer* wrote:

> The tales [Dixon] has heard of the injustice that would be meted out to him if he ever came south are no doubt as true as the impression that had been formed in the minds of white people here of Dixon's arrogance and ideas of social equality. He has found that the citizens of the South will treat him as kindly and give him as fair a show as if he were white, and the citizens on the other hand have found, instead of the self-inflated colored personage they expected to find, that Dixon is a very modest, unassuming Afro-American, who knows his place, and does not seek to presume in any manner.[98]

Even the New Orleans *Daily Picayune* was cautiously optimistic in the closing days before the fight:

> Dixon's fears about receiving fair treatment here must have, by this time, taken wings eastward. . . . If there is anything Black, or rather dark, about Dixon, it is his skin; in all other matters he is white. A modest talker, he, like some people I know, never puts his foot into his mouth when he opens it. . . . I hope and trust nothing will be done or said to him to wound his feelings, or to smirch the city's well-known name for fairness. I know that the spirit of fair play is the uppermost ingredient in the composition of the New Orleans sporting man, yet a bit of a reminder has often served me well, and this little appeal to your fairness I know will be accepted in the same spirit in which it is written, so of this I shall say no more.[99]

Dixon said little about his upcoming contest. Friends visited his training headquarters the weekend prior to the fight and found him in top form, training to "fight nearly all night, if needed."[100] He was confident in victory, but not certain of a walkover.

Jack Skelly was only one man's idea of a worthy opponent for Dixon—and even he hedged his bets. In April 1888, Skelly was an aspiring, young Eastern District lightweight when he appeared on the undercard of an evening featuring brass bands and boxing, hosted by Brooklyn heavyweight

Jack Skelly. Photo by Richard K. Fox. *Courtesy of Special Collections, Fine Arts Library, Harvard University.*

Joe Denning in the Grand Street Palace in New York City. Like so many of the era's scientific exhibitions of the fistic arts, a police captain sat offstage, screened from the audience, but within full view of the boxers. Throughout the evening, the captain decided when the bout veered from scientific into slugging, and if it did so, his men, situated in premium seats along the front row, sprung into action and arrested all involved. On that night, all operated under the eyes of Capt. George W. Bunce, and so he and his men enjoyed the various contests. The highlight of the evening, for both sworn officers and average Joes, alike, was an appearance by Jack "Nonpareil" Dempsey, who sparred four rounds with Denning. At one point during their exhibition, Dempsey punched his opponent seven or eight times in the stomach, nearly knocking the wind out of him. Despite this obvious slide toward slugging, Bunce did not raise an eyebrow; even then, being the most famous person in the room had its advantages. Earlier in the evening, Skelly fought Joe Ryan, another young name from the Eastern District. The pair "boxed three rounds in dead earnest, without any apparent advantage to either side."[101] Those were the only words recorded about their bout.

Skelly was one of the "Three Fighting Jacks of Brooklyn," along with Dempsey and Jack McAuliffe. The trio met while working together in a cooperage shop in the Brooklyn neighborhood of Williamsburg. They fought through the ranks side by side, becoming fast friends; whenever any of the Jacks was fighting, the other two offered moral support at ringside. Dempsey eventually became a world champion middleweight; McAuliffe became an undefeated lightweight champion.[102]

Of the trio, Dempsey was the eldest and biggest draw. Today, his later namesake overshadows him—the iconic 1920s heavyweight champion known as the "Manassa Mauler." However, fans and officials of his era knew the "original" Jack Dempsey "as great a ring general and as heady a fighter as ever lived."[103] At the peak of his career, he was one of the sport's biggest draws, earning him the nickname "Nonpareil"—or "without equal." He was a handsome man, with a strong chin, dark hair, and light eyes, and captured as such by John Wood in a handful of images during the fighter's peak in 1890–91.

Born December 15, 1862, in Ireland, Dempsey came to New York City as a child. His family quickly set down working-class roots. He turned professional as a lightweight in 1883, at age twenty, and remained unbeaten in his first fourteen fights. In 1884, he knocked out George Fulijames in the twenty-second round to become the American—and some argued the world—middleweight champion. Fighting on both US coasts, Dempsey remained undefeated until 1889 when he fought George LaBlanche in San Francisco. In their first encounter, three years before, Dempsey had knocked out LaBlanche in thirteen rounds. This time, Dempsey battered LaBlanche for thirty-two rounds until the challenger dropped Dempsey with a "pivot punch"—an illegal punch thrown using a backhand motion so that the puncher's elbow, forearm, or fist connected with the victim's head. Dempsey lost the fight, but retained the title due to the illegal blow. On February 18, 1890, Dempsey became undisputed middleweight champion with his victory over Australian Billy McCarthy. In 1891, he faced Hall of Famer Bob Fitzsimmons in New Orleans. Fitzsimmons, who later won the heavyweight championship, dominated the fight by knocking Dempsey down thirteen times in thirteen rounds. Fitzsimmons begged Dempsey to stay down; Dempsey refused, saying, "A champion never quits." He went down a final time thanks to a blow to the throat that affected Dempsey's speech for the remainder of his life.[104]

He was never again himself after that defeat. Though only twenty-eight years old at the time of the Fitzsimmons fight, Dempsey fought only three more times over the next four years. On January 18, 1895, Tommy Ryan soundly beat Dempsey in what would be the latter's final fight. After a lopsided first and second round, Dempsey tried to rally in the third, but his efforts were painful. Cries of "Stop it!" rose from the crowd. Dempsey argued he could continue. The referee stopped the bout in the third round, thus saving Dempsey the indignity of a knockout. As Dempsey continued to protest, police intervened and ordered him out of the ring. Exiting the arena, the last sound Dempsey heard after his last bout was a rising hiss of disapproval from the crowd. As the *Boston Daily Globe* reported the next day: "It was simply a cinch for Ryan to knock the ex-middleweight champion out with a punch, but he was kind-hearted enough to refrain. It was merely a case of youth against old age, and the falling forever of a popular idol."[105]

Dempsey's further decline was dramatic and public. Following the Ryan fight, he brooded and, on several occasions, threatened to kill himself. Following a night out with friends in January 1895, he became violent at the dinner table, stabbing himself repeatedly with a table fork. Doctors pronounced Dempsey "insane" and advised his removal to an asylum. In their mind, he suffered from "melancholia super induced by worry and drink."[106] While hospitalized, he continued to be burdened by fainting spells and seizures. By late summer, he was sent home to family in Oregon. His fame was so great, and condition so visibly dire, he drew the

Jack Dempsey. Albumen silver print on card. Photo by John Wood. *Courtesy of Special Collections, Fine Arts Library, Harvard University.*

attention of fellow passengers on his cross-country trip. On July 12, 1895, in Vancouver, British Columbia, Dempsey and his wife disembarked the train to board a steamer to Portland, Oregon. He was a physical wreck. He fainted numerous times during the journey, and many passengers expressed doubt to porters on board that the former champion would make it to his destination alive.[107] Bedridden at his wife's family home for weeks, his final days were spent in a delirious fever often replaying fights, talking to long-gone fighters whom he saw in his room, calling family members and nurses the names of former compatriots. "I'm at your back, Jim." "Goodbye, May Freeman; I must go." "I'm tired, Jim."

On November 2, 1895, Dempsey died surrounded by family. The evening prior, around midnight, he roused himself one final time and told family and friends: "This is my last day in this world."[108] Years later, on his way back to Brooklyn from a fight in Reno, Jack Skelly detoured to Portland, to visit the last resting place of his friend. There, he made a sad discovery. After Dempsey died, his father-in-law, M. J. Brady, refused to permit the former pugilist's friends, including John L. Sullivan, to raise funds to erect a monument over the grave, though the family believed a four-foot marble shaft was sufficient.[109] Skelly told the *New York Times* upon his return home: "It was with some difficulty that I found The Nonpareil's grave—unmarked, without a 'stone' to tell the brave man who lay beneath the green sod. In England, they have erected handsome monuments over the graves of their fistic heroes, while we Americans seem so quickly to forget our grand gladiators who have passed in."[110]

Of the trio of Brooklyn Jacks, Jack McAuliffe, known widely as the "Napoleon of the Prize Ring," was the most skilled fighter. He remains famed to this day for being one of the few champions to retire undefeated. McAuliffe always said he threw his first punch ten days after his birth on March 24, 1866, in Cork, Ireland, when he landed a small, smooth jab into the eye of his godfather, James O'Quinn, on the way to be baptized by the parish priest. At five, McAuliffe arrived in the United States with his parents, and lived in Bangor, Maine, until the family moved to Williamsburg in 1882.[111] He started working as a telegraph messenger, but soon switched to apprenticing as a cooper with his father.[112] There in the cooperage, he met Dempsey. They became fast friends after the latter walked up to the former at work and asked, "Would you like to spar a bit?"

McAuliffe often recounted the hours they spent working on the "new-fangled idea of footwork and side-slipping—how they aspired to be boxers as well as sluggers."[113] In later years, he remembered:

Hour after hour, Dempsey and I worked to perfect our sidestepping and to learn to roll with a blow. Dempsey used to stand with his back to the wall in the McAuliffe Family kitchen and let me try to nail him with an overhand right while he held his arms at his sides. He got so he could twist his head only three or four inches and make me miss. We lived, talked and slept boxing. We rigged up a pillow for a punching bag. Often, we went without lunch to spend the time boxing behind freight cars. . . . At first, we only whispered to each other about our ideas, because we knew everybody would laugh at us for trying such fancy stuff. We were sparring in the kitchen one night and everything was a mess. The table had been knocked over, one chair was broken and blood was dripping from my nose where Dempsey had landed a left.[114]

By eighteen, McAuliffe was one of the city's best amateur bare-knuckle fighters at 133 pounds. In 1885, he had his first professional fight and soon laid claim to the American lightweight title with victories over Jack Hopper in February 1886 and Bill Frazier in October 1886. McAuliffe claimed the vacant world title by stopping Canadian Harry Gilmore in 1887. That match set up a confrontation against English champion Jem Carney, whom he battled to a seventy-two-round draw. The bout ended in controversy when American fans stormed the ring after McAuliffe was dropped for the third time in the fight. When order was restored, both pugilists claimed they were world champion. In 1889, McAuliffe battled to a sixty-four-round draw with Billy Myer, but then proceeded to defeat Myer in two subsequent bouts.

He was an odd sort, flamboyant, hot-tempered, even somewhat theatrical. Perhaps that is why he was drawn to marry not one, but two actresses in his life. Witness his pleasantly bizarre portrait by Chickering picturing the fighter as crossed with a northern tundra explorer. His fur-trimmed topcoat, gripped crop, and parlor setting put viewers in the mind of the Explorers Club rather than the prize ring.

On October 14, 1890, McAuliffe's wife of only a few months, the actress Kate McAuliffe, died suddenly at the West Side Hotel in New York City. A cast member of the Donnelly and Girard Natural Gas (Theatre) Company, she was known to her theater admirers as "Kate Hart."[115] The couple first met in San Francisco following McAuliffe's knockout of Jim Carroll in the forty-seventh round of their world lightweight title bout.[116] Jack and Kate soon married. Almost immediately after her death, rumors began circulating of McAuliffe's violent temper. The bruised face

Three-quarter length portrait of shirtless man with fists raised in boxing pose, labeled "Jack McAuliffe." Albumen silver print on card. Photo by John Wood. *Courtesy of Special Collections, Fine Arts Library, Harvard University.*

of McAuliffe's deceased wife led to his arrest on October 15, 1890. He was immediately placed in the custody of Detective Hayes, of the New York City Nineteenth Police Precinct, to await the results of her autopsy. By that afternoon, New York City Coroner Hanley reported that the examination of the body showed "vascular disease of the heart, and that the superficial bruises on the face had in no way aided in Kate Hart's death."[117] McAuliffe was immediately released from custody. He would not fight again professionally for almost a year.

In April 1892, word started to spread during training camp in Hot Springs, Arkansas, that McAuliffe might be dying from consumption. A close friend and backer told the *Boston Daily Globe* on April 13, 1892: "The fact will become known soon and there is no harm in giving it away. Jack is almost a goner now. I would not be surprised at any time to hear of his death."[118] The report caused "considerable excitement" in New York. His mother was "almost prostrated when she heard the rumor, and she immediately wired him to learn the truth." Throughout the day, she received telegrams of condolences from across the country. McAuliffe's friend, Dick Roche, wired the champion's camp seeking more information. The response came back loud and clear: "Just my luck. Never felt better in my life. Jack. Hot Springs, April 14."[119]

McAuliffe's health might have been fine, but his temper continued to flare outside the ring for the rest of his life. On February 11, 1894, he again ran afoul of the law when he was arrested in San Francisco for attacking ring rival Young Mitchell. McAuliffe had asked to meet Mitchell to clear the air over past disagreements before the champion headed back East. When the parties came together, McAuliffe, without warning, "struck Mitchell with a terrific blow. The others took a hand in the proceedings, and Mitchell was thrown to the sidewalk, where all of the pugilistic contingent began to beat and kick him." Police arrested all parties involved. McAuliffe appeared in court the following day; Mitchell was unable to attend due to the seriousness of his injuries.[120] On May 16, 1894, McAuliffe sucker-punched fellow pugilist Young Griffo, starting a barroom brawl at the Coleman House.[121]

On July 30, 1894, McAuliffe married another actress, Catherine Rowe, known on the stage as Pearl Inman, one of the famed Inman Sisters dancers.[122] The boxer met the showgirl at a Coney Island, New York, casino run by her mother. Rowe was granted a divorce from McAuliffe on May 6, 1898.[123]

McAuliffe retired the first time after defeating Owen Ziegler on

November 19, 1894. He returned to the ring in April 1896 and fought only five bouts over the next year and a half, ending his career after an "agreed draw" with Tommy Ryan on September 30, 1897. After his second retirement from the ring, McAuliffe had a few more brushes with the law, including one from running an illegal pool room. During the First World War, he traveled overseas as a secretary for the Knights of Columbus, working among the troops of the American Expeditionary Force. Once stateside, he became a familiar figure at horse tracks around New York, where he was known for his ready wit and stories of the prize ring. Although his fighter's physique diminished during his later years, he remained known for elegant yet conservative attire. In 1934, he entered politics as a candidate for the New York General Assembly, representing the Sixth District of Queens. As the *New York Times* pointed out: "His success in the ring found no parallel in politics."[124] McAuliffe died November 4, 1937, after an operation to address an ailment of his throat glands.

And then there was Skelly, the youngest—and least accomplished—of the Brooklyn Jacks. By 1889, Skelly became a local tournament favorite in Brooklyn thanks to his showmanship. During one undercard bout early in his career, a "laugher" by all accounts, Skelly sported a taunting smile on his face throughout. Bored by his opponent, he started to entertain himself—and the audience—as some of "his antics" drew huge laughs from the crowd.[125] Skelly won the National Association of Amateur Athletes of America championship in the 155-pound class, defeating three men in one night; triumphed in the Park Athletic Club tourney, defeating Frank Neager while giving away eleven pounds; and prevailed in the Newburgh Athletic Club tourney in April 1890 to become state champion in the 188-pound class.[126]

Skelly was a punishing fighter—a "dignified and showy sparrer"[127]— who often saw opponents attempt to withdraw from their bouts mid-round, or be knocked around so viciously they often failed to answer the call of the next round.[128] His reputation grew and soon Skelly commanded newspaper headlines by the time the amateur champion became the main event on July 31, 1890, in an "uncomfortably packed" National Athletic Club in New York City, filled with men sporting wilted collars and cuffs, all while sweat trickled down their faces. It was a cranky crowd. Hot. Twice the announced number of preliminary bouts delayed Skelly's entrance into the ring, which finally came around 10:30 p.m. In the tenth round, Skelly dropped John McTiernan twice—once with a shot to the neck, once with a swinging right. Each time, McTiernan rose and clenched. Skelly, however, fought on, despite calls from the referee to break in accordance with the rules of a scientific exhibition. The referee succeeded in separating the men just as Police Capt. Martin stepped onto the stage and stopped the fight. Skelly was announced as the winner and presented with a gold watch.[129] The National Athletic Club also witnessed his only defeat as an amateur, at the hands of Johnny Gorman. Skelly nursed a broken hand throughout the bout, leading to a more cautious approach for the usually exciting champion. He toyed with Gorman in the first three rounds, and then hammered him all over the ring in the fourth and final round. The bout closed with Gorman on the ropes—all but out. Yet Skelly was as surprised as the crowd when referee Jack Adler declared Gorman the winner.[130]

Although not an official fight, Skelly made his professional debut in a four-round bout with Fred Johnson for the latter's benefit at the Academy of Music in New York City. The evening featured a lineup of entertainment, which included twenty exhibition bouts and a battle royal between twelve "culled gentlemen." Also on the bill that night was the featherweight champion, George Dixon.[131]

There had not been a major prizefight anywhere in the country in more than a decade without "One-Eyed" Connelly in attendance. For years, Connelly was as much an attraction at championship fights as the action inside the ring. The former fighter turned vagabond fan made jumps across the country by hopping freight cars. He was always admitted to a ringside seat because of his raw nerve and reputation—and never because he paid the price of admission. There was a rumored "power" in that glass eye—one Connelly used sparingly to curse, as he claimed, those who crossed him. Sullivan once kicked Connelly, who was working in the corner of the Boston Strong Boy's opponent, when he confronted the champion before the fight. For years afterward, the more superstitious among the boxing set believed Sullivan was marked after that moment with some "evil eye hoodoo."[132]

The popular conman, gambler, and raconteur arrived in New Orleans from Boston on the morning of September 4, 1892, and immediately set about talking up the desk clerk of his hotel about the recent arrivals of fellow sporting men. While casually speaking with the clerk, Connelly removed his glass eye and began spinning it about the marble countertop. At some point in the conversation, Connelly offered to spar the clerk over a four-day hotel bill. The clerk declined. Connelly then drifted off toward the bar and began to air his opinions on the forthcoming fights. He regarded Sullivan as a counterfeit; Billy Myer as a sure winner; and, "with his one good eye, he could not see how [George] Dixon could possibly lose."[133] Connelly was not alone. Jack Skelly was a bit of a mystery to gamblers and the sporting press alike, especially to those outside of Brooklyn, which the challenger called home and where he made a career. The possibility of a long shot did not entice wagering; bets fell heavily on Dixon's side of the ledger.

However, this fight was not simply about money. For those living the moment, this fight was about a city. Tears were starting to show along poorly hemmed racial seams and its reputation in the eyes of the country. This fight was about something more than civic pride; it was yet another pressure point in debate over resealing the subservient place of Black residents of New Orleans—and, in turn, a nation—for generations to come. On the eve of the Dixon-Skelly bout, September 5, 1892, the *Boston Daily Globe* announced, "this fight will test the color line at New Orleans, as it will be the first time a colored pugilist ever sparred in that city."[134] In its defense, the city had preached restraint to its citizens for weeks. The *Daily Picayune* cautioned:

> The city is full of strangers, who have come from all States of the Union to witness these events. They have been made welcome, and in return they have a duty to perform. They must conform strictly to the rules of the club. . . . [They] will not be allowed to annoy the contestants, nor in any way disturb the audience. Good behavior is absolutely required of every person who is admitted to the amphitheater where the contests occur. . . . The audience will be as orderly as any in an opera house, and the strangers will see what they came here to see, safely, comfortably and with no fear of accident.[135]

Not all of Black America was happy about Dixon's journey south. The *Plaindealer* called on Dixon to use his stature to take a stand against the Olympic Club's rebuff of heavyweight Peter Jackson. The paper wrote: "[Dixon] could just now make himself a greater reputation for manhood than he can ever within the ring. He should unqualifiedly, and at once, refuse to fight before the Olympic Club."[136] But that was not Dixon's style. To Dixon, his celebrity belonged to him alone. Not to a race. Or a country. Demands on him like those of the *Plaindealer* to use that celebrity for something other than himself, something political, were not worth the risk to his reputation and standing. Dixon not only took the fight in New

Orleans, but also never stood down for a fight anywhere, regardless of the politics of the region or establishment.

On the first night of the Carnival, the rabble entered off Chartresse Street, where they were greeted by a horse-drawn chemical truck and patrol wagon, just in case the crowd got out of hand and needed a "squirt" to tame it before being hauled off to jail for the night. That proved unnecessary, however, as a natural downpour sent the crowd in search of cover rather than confrontation. That left the large police presence of both uniformed and special officers recruited for the occasion with little to do; they instead gathered in hallways and under verandas, swinging their clubs and talking about what the next three nights held for them. Those attendees holding tickets for boxes or reserved seats, as well as members of the press, were to be ushered in first, although most were slow to arrive due to the reserved nature of their tickets. The idea of not fighting for a space at ringside was unique and appreciated. It was a vast improvement over the old way of pushing forward and packing tight, making for not only uncomfortable viewing, but also easy targeting for pickpockets.

The Olympic Club roof was not entirely tight and, as such, rain trickled down the backs of some spectators who drew damp seats. One member of the club staff slipped a coffee bag over the gong at ringside "to keep it from catching a cold." Eight coal-oil lamps spread across the room reinforced the electric light—a precaution as the burgeoning technology had failed in previous events across the country, leaving all in the dark. Ropes running between four stakes, all freshly painted red, marked off the ring. Some spectators brought sandwiches and liquor in anticipation of a protracted bout. For those less prepared, peanut and fan vendors started working the crowd well before the fight began.

Inside the Olympic clubhouse, men stood six deep for a drink. Sporting men flush with cash lined every available wall. Mingled among them were fighters from darker days of the sport. Tom Allen, the British-born former bare-knuckle champion of America, was there. Now of St. Louis, the fifty-two-year-old held court over an audience of men telling of his ring battles against the likes of Sherman Thurston, Dan Ryan, and John Tooney. Allen was a conspicuous figure among the predominantly refined elements of the Olympic Club. In his fighting days, every ring encounter with Allen meant a riot among the roughest elements of the sporting fraternity. While attending a fight between Tommy Kelly and

Billy Parkinson in 1868, Allen pulled a pistol on a referee, demanding he rule in favor of Kelly. As the fighters were rushed to safety, a riot started among the audience. The following year, Allen was denied a victory after he beat Mike McCool unconscious when backers of McCool stormed the ring with clubs and pistols and prevented a decision being rendered in the fight.

Little had been heard of Allen since his final fight in 1876. This night, Allen was dressed in a sack coat—a jacket of manual laborers, soldiers and trade unionists—and a tall silk hat. The whole package hinted further at the oddity of his presence. Along with a handful of others, Allen reminded those in attendance of the evolving nature of the sport. The bare-knuckler brawlers were dying out, but still lurking about. Allen would make headlines only once more before his death in 1903. In February 1899, Allen shot Tom Confoy, a theater stagehand, and a bartender following a barroom quarrel in St. Louis. The bartender, shot through his head, somehow survived. Confoy died instantly. Allen was later acquitted of the killing on grounds of self-defense.[137]

The Carnival of Champions was a decidedly male affair where "gentlemen and toughs sat side by side." Former Dodge City lawman turned gambler Bat Masterson was one of the first men seated, but, finding himself alone in the area for some time, found his way into the clubhouse. Thomas L. Harris of Louisville, Kentucky, presented himself at the clubhouse door with two slimly built companions. Harris handed the doorman three tickets, and the trio headed toward their seats, only to be stopped by officers. Turned out, only Harris was a man. His two companions were poorly disguised women in men's clothes. They were arrested and escorted outside. Harris spent the fight alone bookended by two empty seats. However, another woman—"young and passably good looking"—found her way into the clubhouse and hid behind the blinds. Two years prior, she had attempted to sneak into the Jack Dempsey–Robert Fitzsimmons fight in January 1890 in New Orleans by dressing as a man. Although dozens of women were reported to have snuck into that bout, she was denied admission. However, on this night, this nameless woman from Colorado saw her fight.[138]

Dressed in a soft hat and plain business suit that hung funny off his skinny build, Jack Skelly entered the room to huge applause. While Black men would witness the fight the next evening—for the first time in club history, upon Dixon's insistence—only one was in attendance this night. George Dixon walked in after Skelly and was welcomed with a riotous cheer.

Jack McAuliffe's confidence might have been best indicated by the multiple bottles of champagne he had chilling at ringside to pop upon his victory. From the opening bell in New Orleans, the audience could tell history would not repeat itself. The bout was never in doubt—McAuliffe could have ended the whole thing in the second round when he rained rights upon the overmatched Myer, but instead, the champion opted to carry his challenger across another thirteen rounds. Boxing fans and journalists had been critical of McAuliffe, saying he did not have the stamina or the stomach to fight a twenty-round bout. And so, when a pair of devastating knockdowns in the fifteenth round ended any thoughts of a Myer miracle, McAuliffe was feeling particularly feisty in victory. After finishing a bottle of champagne in the immediate aftermath, he grabbed a second and walked over to reporters at ringside, where he shouted: "A great many people will doubt my words when I say I could have licked Myer in three rounds, but that is an absolute fact. He didn't hurt me the least during the fight and couldn't possibly have licked me if we had stayed there a week. . . . From time to time, Myer said some harsh things about me and I decided to make him pay. I think I have paid the score."[139]

On the second day of the Carnival, the arena did not fill up as rapidly as the night before. Among the earliest arrivals for the Skelly-Dixon bout were Black spectators for whom a large section on one of the upper general admissions stands had been set apart. It was a first for the club—an amazing sight in the heart of the former Confederacy. Among the crowd of two hundred Black men were prominent politicians and regular men lucky enough to snag a ticket.[140] Down below, an all-Black waitstaff maneuvered through the crowd serving ice water. Those patrons who desired something stronger went into the clubhouse, where "the most fastidious found everything that could be desired."[141] It was apparent to some that the crowd did not care to see a white man knocked out by a Black man, a moment many expected. The *Boston Daily Globe* wrote: "The effect of such a result would make the negro simply unbearable. It would be a local calamity."[142] The stifling heat of the night before was relived slightly by club officials raising the roof four feet to offer some open space at the top of the immense amphitheater. Skelly's backer, William Reynolds, took his seat at ringside, directly behind Dixon's corner. He wore a conspicuous red shirt in a sea of black and white, and on his lap sat a small monkey—a good luck charm, at least to his mind. By 9 p.m., five thousand people had filled the arena. The crowd behaved, in the words of one observer, "magnificently." The *Times Picayune* reported: "Dixon was given a welcome which convinced him from the start that in New Orleans and before the Olympic Club fair play must rule."[143]

Dwarfed by the burly men who made up his ringside team, Dixon entered the ring wearing a white sweater that dropped just below his knees. The reception to his entrance was mixed. The *Boston Daily Globe* wrote "the colored spectators in the gallery were of every hue, from pale canary yellow to deepest ebony. They all showed their ivories and clapped their hands when Dixon appeared."[144] The remainder of the crowd greeted him with polite applause. City councilman Charles Dickson, a prominent member of the Olympic Club, welcomed Dixon into the ring and then warned the crowd that the upcoming contest was between a Black man and a white man, "in which fair play would govern and the best man win." The ringside media yelled questions to the champion, asking if Dixon expected a long fight. "I hardly think that's a fair question," he said with a wink of his left eye.[145]

Skelly's entrance was delayed. Seems the challenger forgot his trunks and was required to borrow the ones worn by Jack McAuliffe the night before. Once he entered, the room erupted, so loud that Dickson abandoned the rest of his speech and exited the ring, but not before handing the $7,500 purse to the referee, Professor Duffy. In the center of the ring, Skelly and Dixon shook hands and, while surrounded by their seconds, received instructions from the referee. Skelly was a head taller than Dixon and looked every bit as strong as him, except about the chest and shoulders. There, he "seemed to be no match for the dusky champion."[146]

Both men sprang to the center of the ring as the gong sounded for the first round, but the early action was cautious as the combatants felt one another out. Once the second round started, however, the fighting became "fast and furious" with Dixon as the obvious aggressor. Every time Skelly feinted—whether he landed or not—the crowd went wild. Every time Dixon landed a blow, there was a loud roar from the small section of Black spectators, who yelled in support of Dixon throughout the bout. As early as the end of the second round, the Brooklynite appeared in distress. Skelly attempted to push the action as the third round opened, but was greeted with a heavy left hand that floored him for the first time in the bout. The men traded blows until Dixon planted a right to Skelly's jaw that newly floored the challenger a second time.

At the start of the fourth round, blood erupted from Skelly's nose, the result of a wound he had suffered during training.[147] Dixon, of course, knew all about his opponent's plight, so the featherweight champion simply jabbed with his long left until he had Skelly's nose spread all over his face.[148] The *Boston Daily Globe* wrote of the moment, "There were thousands of long faces among the whites in the crowd when the blood showed on Skelly's face."[149] The *Chicago Daily Tribune* offered even more graphic detail: "The little darky pelted him in the nose until that organ swelled as big as a corncob and a welt came over his eye the size of a California egg plum. . . . The colored boy went at his opponent and wore him out, welting him in the right side—'cachug,' 'cachug'—until the wind was knocked out of the white boy. Dixon got some blood on him from a little cut, but the white fellow was as bloody as a butcher from his forehead to his waist. He was game, but the little darky had the science."[150]

Back in Boston, fight fans gathered outside newspaper buildings across the city and awaited word from the bout. The *Boston Post*—a paper that proudly boasted being "second in morning circulation"—printed intricate directions in that morning's newspaper for a series of light signals they would use to communicate the bout in progress from the roof of their building. The newspaper boasted: "The *Post* will flash the code of signals, a reflex in the Heavens of the smaller ring in New Orleans." Five flashes of light, five seconds in duration, signaled the start of the fifth round. Plans were for varying arcs of light across the sky to signal both a winner of the round and, ultimately, a winner of the bout. Thus far, only the Dixon signal—a light beam brought from the zenith above down to the horizon—was offered up to the appreciative crowd.

By the end of the fifth, Skelly's face was covered in his own blood. Dixon looked untouched. After a "fearful exchange" of blows from Dixon in the sixth round, "the white boy looked as if he could not last through another round." Skelly was dropped to the floor twice in the seventh round, the final knockdown looking to finish the lad off, if not for the gong. Once in his corner, Skelly was showing the obvious signs of his punishment.[151] His wind was gone; his knees trembled beneath him; he reeled about the ring and presented "a pitiable sight—bruised, disfigured and bathed in blood."[152]

As the eighth round began, the crowd showed obvious signs of discomfort. At the opening gong, Dixon forced Skelly into the corner, where a right-left combination by the champion drew gasps from the crowd. The crowd was astonished at how Skelly stood the punishment. He was gone, however, and in a heavy exchange Skelly was beaten to the ground with terrible right- and left-handed swings. Try as he might, the challenger could not get up before the ten seconds elapsed.[153] Back in Boston, the light above the *Post* building shined from horizon to horizon for five minutes, signaling a victory for their hometown hero.

Skelly was despondent following the bout. Tears streamed down his face as he left the ring, and when he reached his dressing room, he burst out crying. Two policemen were stationed outside the door of his dressing room. Nobody was allowed in except Skelly's closest friends and two doctors who were witness to the terrible beating the challenger's body took. Red welts rose as his body rested; his nose was swollen to twice its normal size with its bridge fractured and still bleeding. Through the tears, Skelly held forth: "I would never have entered this fight if it had not been that I wanted to get enough money to start in shape, as I am to marry, but now I don't know what I will do. I shall never forgive myself for making this match, not because I was whipped, as that does not bother me a bit. As far as the pain and that sort of thing goes, I can stand that very well, but I know friends in Brooklyn who could not well afford to risk their dollars, backed me for friendship's sake. That is a bitter pill to swallow."[154]

As a whole, spectators were "disposed to be fair, and there were no remarks tending to show race prejudice. Dixon was doing such pretty work that even the most prejudiced could say nothing."[155]

Immediately after the bout, Black members of the community swelled with pride on the streets of New Orleans, where "the colored men did not make themselves objectionable, except that they congregated in bright-eyed, excited groups. Their pale-skinned brothers glared at them and, when possible, crowded them from the corners."[156] Journalists prepared for a night where they expected the "killing of a dozen or more negroes."[157] Some among their ranks considered Dixon lucky to get away from New Orleans "with a whole skin, for some of the hot-headed Southern sports actually wanted to shoot Dixon in the ring for 'whipping a decent white boy.'"[158]

Nevertheless, no actual violence against Dixon personally was ever recorded. The streets of New Orleans "were filled with happy Afro-Americans on one side and sullen whites on the other."[159] When a Black Dixon supporter "was imprudently talking too loud of Dixon's victory . . . he was knocked down by an indignant white man."[160] It looked like serious trouble for a moment, but a quick-witted policeman hustled the assailant out of the hotel and then drove the Black man out of another entrance. The *Detroit Plaindealer* reported: "The feeling is actually very bitter, and it would have been better for the peace of the community if there had been no prizefight this evening."[161]

On day three of the Carnival of Champions, September 7, 1892, Sullivan and Corbett entered the ring. In New York City, thirteen hundred miles away, a red beacon was readied to light up on top of the Pulitzer Building if Sullivan won, a white one for a Corbett victory.

As early as the third round, Corbett's dominance was undeniable, although he carried the visibly aging Sullivan along until the twenty-first round, when he finished the great champion off. By the fifth round, Sullivan's face was a blur of his own blood, gushing from a freshly broken nose and mixing into his ample chest hair. Every charge of his was met with a powerful right by Corbett. First to the nose. And then the ears. And then the lips. Sullivan remained game, chasing the challenger around the ring, but he had no answer for the technical skill of Corbett. The frustration became visible on Sullivan's face as he failed round after round to land his famous right and finish this match once and for all. By the end of the eighteenth round, he flopped into his corner, unable to breathe, barely able to sit upright. By the twentieth round, Corbett banged mercilessly on Sullivan as he lay across the rope. As the twenty-first opened, even the champion's most ardent supporters knew the end was near. Sullivan opened at the center of the ring, as Corbett circled, and then the big man offered one last charge at the challenger. Bang went Corbett's left into Sullivan's jaw, then a right, and then a flurry of undefended combinations eventually toppled Sullivan backwards.

Until his dying day, Sullivan tried to redefine this moment in the eyes of the public. But the felling of a giant was news around the world—every paper across the country had a description of Sullivan's final moments as champion. Taking one final combination across his jaw, Sullivan toppled backward, obviously unconscious from the punishment, as he made no effort to brace himself against the fall. Loose limbed, he fell flat on his back. A mighty thud echoed across the stunned room as his head hit flush against the compacted sand floor. For a moment, the world thought John. L. Sullivan was dead.[162] He rose to a sitting position, but fell back, struggled up again, fell back full length, then rose to his hands and knees before again falling back and rolling over onto his side. Sullivan's seconds tried to lift him back to his corner, but struggled. Instead, Corbett leaned over to help lift his fallen foe up off the ground and guide him to a chair. As Corbett joined his own celebration, Sullivan slowly showed signs of returning to consciousness. He unsteadily stood, shook hands with

James J. Corbett.
Photo by Elmer
Chickering.
Courtesy of
Special Collections,
Fine Arts Library,
Harvard University.

Corbett, and held up his hand to silence the room: "Gentlemen, all I've got to say is, I stayed once too long."[163] He then muttered something about if he had to be whipped, that at least he was "licked" by an American.[164] He then shuffled off the stage one last time.

Sullivan and his seconds didn't leave the Olympic Club to head back to their hotel until after 2 a.m. following his fight. The now former champion was still drinking freely after his bout when the club doctor arrived to tend to his wounds. Sullivan remained on his cot, with a glass of wine in his hand, as the doctor examined the wounds inflicted upon him by Corbett in the closing act of the Carnival. Sullivan sported pronounced dents on his nose and face, along with cuts across his lip and forehead, requiring three and two stiches, respectively. Once the doctor finished his work, Sullivan limped to his hotel where the somber party continued deep into the morning. The only person allowed into the Sullivan suite was a hotel bellboy, who came armed with several more bottles.[165]

———

The Carnival represented a major transition for boxing; what happened on day three was perhaps the most significant moment in the sport's history. Sullivan's decade-long reign as heavyweight champion came to an end that night at the hands of Corbett in the first heavyweight title fight held under the Marquess of Queensberry Rules. That night ended the era of bare-knuckled brawlers and began one of "sweet scientists"—or, as the *New York Times* not so subtly described it, "the dethronement of a mean and cowardly bully as the idol of the barrooms is a public good that is a fit subject for public congratulations."[166] This fight has been parsed perhaps more than any other—especially by Sullivan, who reflected bitterly upon for years afterward.

One day prior, the *Cleveland Gazette*, another anti-boxing publication, applauded Dixon's victory: "He had and is doing much to elevate the race in the opinion of a large class of Americans, and therefore, is a credit to his race."[167] Going on to state, "Dixon has given a favorite Dixie prejudice a terrible Black eye. . . . It is all right to see one white man whip another in the south, but to pay one's dollars and a number of them, too, to see a Hamite 'whip the stuffing out of' a white man, even if he is a northerner, and then give the former an ovation, is something more than the average southerner can or will stand."[168]

But the editor was also quick to point out that, perhaps, Sullivan's loss the next evening was a greater win for Black America: "The defeat of that bully, braggart and brute, John L. Sullivan, is another cause for congratulation. He it was who refused to fight Peter Jackson, the colored pugilist and champion, referring to him as a 'nigger.' The dirty whelp Sullivan has received his just deserts at last and we believe a great majority of the people in America, as well as abroad, are heartily glad. There is especial cause for congratulation as far as Afro-Americans are concerned, because Corbett's whipping Sullivan virtually makes Peter Jackson champion heavyweight."[169]

The fight haunted Sullivan the rest of his life. Arguably once the most famous man in America, Sullivan was a "has-been" by 1905. More than a decade removed from the ring, he had been earning a living as a monologist, a career move that lasted until 1907. It was a rather unsuccessful lecture circuit run—"a string of talk that lasted like a cheese sandwich that had been a long time dead,"[170] as he once described it. This was due mainly to his unease in front of an audience, terrible stage presence, and growing girth (now nearly 350 pounds), which often winded him during presentations. His nationally syndicated newspaper column, "Jolts from 'John L.,'" was a natural offshoot of these performances.[171]

No longer the ideal specimen of masculinity he was throughout the 1880s, Sullivan was now a bloated, fading star, broke from years of excess. Yet his deep well of bloviation remained full after a career built on such banter. Yes, some of his prose was dedicated to prizefighting and score-settling from his career. But he also offered more than enough insights into diagnosing modern America's ailments and offering a few prescriptions for her better health. There were also more personal notes—moments when real thoughtfulness, even lament, snuck into the prose. Sober for less than a year prior to his column's launch, Sullivan occasionally spoke with the authority of a born-again temperance man: "My advice to the men who are on either side of the bar is to cut the whole thing, and change their luck while they have a chance. Don't I know? Why, to be able to give the above advice I've paid out bundles of money, and wasted years of learning the lesson. And this advice is worth a bank account to any young man who will follow it."[172] He also looked back with a broken heart and scarred ego on days gone by: "All who remember that I am the undefeated champion of the world under the London Prize Rules will please stand up. I don't see many to count. Yes, indeedy, I am still the champion of the world in that class, the toughest kind of fighting that has been known in a long time."[173] As part of those remembrances, Sullivan also wrote of the Carnival of Champions week and his friendship with Dixon. The words must be viewed through the lens of Sullivan's natural exaggerations; nevertheless, they provide a rare look into the fighter's interaction with his colleagues outside the ring. Sullivan wrote:

> Some of the Southerners objected to Dixon chumming along with some of us white trash, and, to avoid getting us in bad, Little Chocolate tried to give us the shake. I wouldn't stand for this, and told him he was to remember he was in our party.
>
> On the day when we went out to the ring, me to get my finish and Dixon to cop a $17,500 purse, me and Tom O'Rourke, Dixon's manager, climbed into an open hack tied to several horses. We

looked around for Dixon, but he was hanging back. O'Rourke yelled to him to get aboard.

"You just go along by yourselves, and I'll take a horse car out there," says Dixon. "This is down South and they don't like niggers, so it'll save a heap of friction if I ain't quite so public."

"You're going out with us as part of the show, and anybody who don't like it can see me about it," says I. With that, I grabbed him by the collar and snaked him into the cart. And we rode out together without the least of trouble.

Dixon had an easy thing of it with Skelly, for Jack was in no condition to fight, getting a fever on him and also getting injured in training. When Dixon licked him, some of the spectators who couldn't stand a negro knocking out a white boy made bluffs about filling Dixon full of lead right in the ring, but it was all bluff.

Dixon was whiter than a lot of white men I've seen. He never picked up any of the dirty tricks that some of the more gentlemanly white fighters saddled onto the ring.[174]

Immediately after the Dixon-Skelly bout, Olympic Club members regretted pairing the two, as testified by club president Charles Noel following the bout: "The fight has shown one thing, however, that events in which colored men figure are distasteful to the membership of the club. After the fight, so many of the members took a stand against the admission of colored men into the ring as contestants against white pugilists that we have pretty well arrived at the conclusion not to give any more such battles. No, there will be no more colored men fighting before our club. That is a settled fact."[175]

Later that month, the Olympic Club opted against offering a purse for the lucrative Peter Jackson vs. Joe Goddard bout "because the Southern people do not like to see contests in which a white man is opposed by a negro."[176] Those sentiments carried over into the final night and its marquee event.

Weeks after Dixon-Skelly, southern papers were still up in arms over the bout. Dixon-Skelly opened eyes to the "inherent sinfulness of such contests," the *New Orleans States* declared, saying that "thousands of vicious and ignorant negroes regard the victory of Dixon over Skelly as ample proof that the negro is equal, and superior to the white man." The religiously focused *Independent* used Dixon-Skelly to further push Black men out of society applauding the "Olympic Club's shutting its doors to at least one kind of prizefights; and nothing would please us more now than to have the liquor saloons of New Orleans follow the example and refuse to admit negroes within their doors."[177] The *American Journal of Politics* used the bout to critique the sport, the society and press that enabled it, and every fan who dared enjoyed it:

> An event that tends to sustain the theory that man has descended from the monkey, and, in fact, that he is still descending in some respects was the recent pugilistic combat in New Orleans. . . .
>
> It is not surprising that men are willing to engage as principals in this demoralizing business; for men in all times have been willing to undertake anything, no matter how dangerous or degrading, how painful or loathsome, where money and applause are the reward. It does seem remarkable, however, that there are in every large city thousands of men more or less intelligent who are willing to pay from $10–$15 to witness so brutal a spectacle, and thus encourage and lend their sanction to the demoralizing practice.
>
> For all this interest and ferment over a fight, and for the demoralizing effects it is universally admitted to have, the press must shoulder a large share of the responsibility. When the papers of the country devote column after column and page upon page to the description of an event in all its details, it is but natural for the public to infer that such event must be one of importance and one on which the people should be informed. The public doesn't stop to consider that the motive of the publisher is a sordid one, and that he is simply taking advantage of the public foolishness to make money by printing what nobody ought to read, but what nearly everybody will read when an opportunity is offered. Publishers should not "lead us into temptation."[178]

But the *Detroit Plaindealer*, one of the country's trailblazing Black newspapers, covered the racial fallout from the fight better than many—not surprising, given the publication's history. Founded in 1883 by the brothers Benjamin and Robert Pelham Jr., along with Walter H. Stowers and W. H. Anderson, the *Plaindealer* covered social issues, providing sympathetic coverage to progressive elements in the emerging labor movement and documenting the abuses of Jim Crow in the South and in its less overt local guises: "The idea of an Afro-American[179] besting a white man is too much. These journals are advising the superior whites, whose prestige is menaced by this fight, to rise in their might and vindicate their title to superiority by killing a few Afro-Americans on general principles. Every Black man who looks cross-eyed now is guilty of brutal insolence that is worthy of death. Such is the nature of the bourbon brood."[180]

It was a sentiment echoed broadly by Black newspapers across the country. The *Cleveland Gazette* wrote, "We thought the sight of one of our race pummeling the face and body of even a northern white pugilist would be more than they could stand, and our readers can now see how correct our estimate was."[181]

Violence persisted throughout the fall. The press reported isolated clashes stemming from the fight. In Boston, John Liston, a Black man, stabbed "Spider" Ike Weir, a white man, in the face after the two got into a fight over the Dixon-Skelly match fought a month earlier.[182] Around the country, Dixon's bout served as a reminder of the disintegrating race relations of the time, and foreshadowed other events on the horizon.

Dixon returned to Boston soon afterward to spar with Jack Havlin at the Howard Athenaeum. Speaking of his recent bout with Skelly, Dixon called it "one of the easiest he ever engaged in . . . He was treated finely by the people at Biloxi and the members of the Olympic Club, he said, but he would not care to fight again in the South, as the feeling against the colored people in that section is very bitter."[183]

Following the fight, Skelly traveled back to Brooklyn in McAuliffe's private train car. By then, he had recovered from the beating Dixon delivered to him. Among the rumors circulating was the fact that his loss would prevent his marriage to the Brooklyn girl awaiting his return. Yet his main regret continued to be his wish to have made a better showing of himself. The *Brooklyn Daily Eagle* wrote: "He hasn't an excuse to offer; he takes no refuge in the plea that he was out of condition or that there was any unfairness in the fight." Skelly told the paper, "The less said about my fight the better. It wasn't a fight at all." Reynolds, however, was not heartbroken—he won on McAuliffe and Corbett and more than covered his losses on Skelly. He cleared $4,000 over the three-day event. (More than $100,000 in current money.) "If Skelly had won, I would have taken a small fortune out of New Orleans," he shouted from his passing carriage to reporters.[184]

Big fights, like Dixon-Skelly, were invariably followed by exhibitions and benefits. As a rule, the beneficiary was the man who sustained defeat. Skelly arranged the date of his exhibition benefit so Dixon could attend. Neatly attired, Skelly also sported a souvenir bandage across the bridge of his nose. But when he looked at the audience, he must have felt that something had gone wrong. "They can't fool me on the box office tonight," he told the sparse crowd. "I can count every man in the house in five minutes." The night was capped by a "rematch" of Dixon and Skelly. The crowd stirred, and then crushed toward the entrance, as Dixon entered the theater. He stepped almost immediately into the ring. Skelly found himself once more face to face with Dixon. Neither man wanted to take things easily. They warmed up at once and it was give-and-take from start to finish. Skelly surprised everybody. He held his own throughout and sometimes gave a little more that Dixon. When it was all over, the spectators asked each other how on earth Dixon had managed to make such short work of Skelly in the Crescent City. At the end of the evening, Skelly carried off a floral horseshoe.[185]

––––––

In November 1892, five months after his arrest, Homer Plessy came before a Louisiana District Court presided over by Justice John Howard Ferguson. A native of Massachusetts, Ferguson was a carpetbagger. He rooted himself in the South after marrying the daughter of a prominent New Orleans attorney. Between Plessy's arrest and trial, Ferguson ruled on another test case of the separate car law. This case involved Daniel F. Desdunes, a Black man who could pass for white, arrested for traveling in a white car on an interstate train. Desdunes, twenty-one, was the son of Rodolphe Desdunes, one of the leaders of the New Orleans citizens' committee challenging the law. Ferguson ruled the law was unconstitutional when applied to interstate trains, as only the federal government had the power to regulate interstate commerce. The committee celebrated the victory, but it was short lived: unlike Desdunes, Plessy had traveled on an intrastate train. Therefore, the judge upheld the law, ruling the state had the power to regulate railroad companies operating solely within its borders. With that ruling, the constitutional challenge that both sides desired was on. The Plessy decision was appealed to the Louisiana Supreme Court, where it was upheld. The issue was headed to the US Supreme Court.[186]

Albion Tourgée, Plessy's attorney, delayed the case's moving forward, hoping for changes in the political climate of the country. That, however, did not occur.

In February 1890, at the National Convention of Colored Men in Washington, DC, former Louisiana governor P. B. S. Pinchback, the organization's president, delivered a stirring call to action for Blacks.

Pinchback was already a bit of a celebrity. After the Louisiana legislature impeached incumbent Governor Henry Clay Warmoth in 1872, over certifying returns of a disputed gubernatorial election, Pinchback became acting governor on December 9, 1872, and served until January 13, 1873. This elevation made him the first Black governor in the history of the republic. Despite unsuccessful runs at both the US House and Senate, he maintained his standing as a powerful voice advocating for anti-lynching legislation. At that convention, he outlined the plight of the Black man in America: "We are compelled to obey laws that we have no voice in making; we are subject to taxation without representation; we are obligated in many localities to submit to the verdicts of juries and the decisions of courts in the creation of which we are not allowed to participate."[187]

Between June 1892 and April 1896, southern lawlessness was gaining attention across the country. "Judge Lynch" was on the march—not a who, but a what, a personification of "lynch law" sweeping the southern states. Not found in statute, lynch law is, simply stated, mob justice. Organized bands of men seized other men charged with or suspected of crimes, often from custody with little or no resistance from law enforcement (though occasionally with their assistance), and inflicted punishment upon them without any authority of law. The accused were beaten, shot, hanged; their bodies were often mutilated and left hanging from trees and telephone poles. Few survived lynch-law justice.

Northern papers were shocked by the actions, saying "it seems almost too whimsical and wild for belief that terrorism of this kind could be successfully practiced upon the people in any part of the country." The New York papers used every opportunity to decry the mob violence and to shame the South—Louisiana was often a favorite target. The *New York Advertiser* wrote that "the people have become so bloodthirsty that they will lynch a man simply because he happens to look like a criminal of whom they are in pursuit." The *New York Mail* expressed amazement that a race war had not already erupted, writing, "In striking contrast is this spirit of moderation exhibited by the colored people of Louisiana with the rancor, violence, and lawlessness of the white element now disgracing their state and outraging every instinct of honor, magnanimity, and justice." The *New York Tribune* placed blame at the feet of a silent majority when it wrote that "the very worst feature of it is that the newspapers which represent public opinion at The South so generally palliate the widespread lawlessness."[188]

In July 1892, Frederick Douglass used his final published essay to absolve the "ignorant mob"—he brushed them aside as "simply the hangmen"—and excoriated those who had stood idly by as lynch law gripped the South:

> The men who break open jails and with bloody hands destroy human life are not alone responsible. These are not the men who make public sentiment. They are simply the hangmen, not the court, judge, or jury. They simply obey the public sentiment of the South, the sentiment created by wealth and respectability, by the press and the pulpit. A change in public sentiment can be easily affected by these forces whenever they shall elect to make the effort. Let the press and the pulpit of the South unite their power against the cruelty, disgrace and shame that is settling like a mantle of fire upon these lynch law states, and lynch law itself will soon cease to exist.[189]

Lynchings took place with increasing regularity. Although no reliable statistics of lynchings exist prior to 1892, shortly thereafter, the Tuskegee Institute began to gather the numbers. According to that organization's figures, 4,730 people were lynched between 1882 and 1951 in the United States—3,437 Black and 1,293 white. The largest number of lynchings occurred in 1892, with 230 that year—161 Blacks and 69 whites. Those numbers continued as the Plessy case awaited its day before the Supreme Court—118 Black men lynched in 1892, 134 in 1894, 113 in 1895.[190] In 1892, one out of every three lynchings took place in Louisiana.[191]

The *Chicago Daily Tribune* published a powerful article that simply listed the names and race of every lynching victim in the United States in 1891. Of the 195 victims, 121 were Black, 69 white, 2 Native American, 2 Asian, and 1 Hispanic. "That one hundred and sixty-nine were lynched in the South and twenty-six in the North furnishes its own comment on Southern justice and its weak condition," the paper wrote. A staggering twenty-nine victims were lynched in Louisiana, by far the most in the nation. In March alone, eleven men were murdered by a mob on a single day—although every one of them was white.[192] Following the acquittal of a group of Italian Americans charged with the assassination of the New Orleans chief of police, an outraged mob of two hundred soldiers, businessmen, and "a better class of citizens," armed with axes and guns, surrounded the courthouse, stormed the jail, and killed the accused. Eleven men—all accused members of the "New Orleans Mafia"—died that day, nine shot to death, two lynched.[193] The actions, however, were not met with universal condemnation. The *Indianapolis Journal* wrote that "if lynch law could ever be justified it would be in breaking up such an organization as the Mafia. If the bloody events of yesterday shall have that result, the cause of justice will not have suffered."[194] It was a theme that would continue as southern newspapers pushed back on the critique of lynch law, offering up the mobs as a more efficient justice system than a court they saw as too lenient. In June 1892, the *Atlanta Constitution* argued that "it is easy to see why we have these lynchings. It is because . . . it is safer to commit murder than any other crime in America. The people know that they have no right to take the law into their own hands, but they are not going to stand for one hundred and twenty-three legal executions for six thousand murders. Such a state of affairs is deplorable; but, until justice is swifter and more certain in the courts, lynch law will continue to do its terrible work."[195]

Stories of white victims were used to deflect the racial element of the practice. In June 1895, a gang of six white men, including John Frey, son of prominent Big Easy doctor John Frey, were determined to lynch Frances Woodsen, a Black woman who lived in Gretna, Louisiana, just outside New Orleans. Catching word of the group's intent, Woodsen fled. Finding her home empty, the mob demolished its contents and burned the structure to the ground. Later that evening, the gang came across a Black man on the street and beat him nearly to death. So outraged was the community, a group of white citizens organized with the goal of lynching the gang, a task they followed through on when Frey was arrested later that evening. The crowd took Frey in hand from the arresting officer and hanged the lad from a telephone pole.[196] The circumstances were unique enough for the *New York Times* to call the evening's events a "novelty."

Overall, those murders were secretive affairs, conducted silently by small groups of white men in dark woods, particularly in the Deep South. Some acts of vigilante violence, however, became public events. White men, women, and children filled town squares and ate picnics as they waited for "the show." Following the violent hangings, the audience often bought morbid souvenirs as they dispersed—among those, photographs of Black bodies hanging from trees.[197] Philosopher William James wrote a widely circulated letter to the editor of the *Springfield Republican* warning that the lynching of Blacks across the country signaled an end to civilized man and an unleashing of something more sinister, more savage within the population. Civilization, he argued, was not designed to encourage such behavior; instead it sought to suppress the "aboriginal capacity for murderous excitement which lies sleeping even in his own bosom."[198]

He drew a bold line connecting lynching bloodlust and the rapid rise over the previous few years—and acceptance—of popular "masculine" pursuits like prizefighting:

> One or two real fanatics there may be in every lynching, actuated by a maniacal sense of punitive justice. They are a kind of reversion, which civilization particularly requires to extirpate. The other accomplices are only average men, victims, at the moment when the greatest atrocities are committed, of nothing but irresponsible mob contagion, but invited to become part of the mob and predisposed to the peculiar sort of contagion, by the diabolical education which the incessant examples of the custom and of its continued impunity are spreading with fearful rapidity throughout our population. Was ever such a privilege offered! Dog fights, prizefights, bull fights, what are they to a man-hunt and a negro burning? The illiterate whites everywhere, always fretting in their monotonous lives for some drastic excitement, are feeding their imaginations in advance on this new possibility. The hoodlums in our cities are being turned by the newspapers into as knowing critics of the lynching game as they long have been of prize-fight and football.[199]

Lynchings perpetuated a climate of unchecked lawlessness whose near-sole focus was the Black population. But by the latter half of the decade, to color this crime beyond race would be a disservice. Whites may have been occasional victims, but Blacks lived under a constant fear. And Dixon felt that threat—neither fame nor wealth could protect him from a motivated mob. He read the papers up and down the East Coast. He knew Douglass's words, perhaps by heart, that "the negro meets no resistance when on a downward course. It is only when he rises in wealth, intelligence, and manly character that he brings upon himself the heavy hand of persecution. . . . When the negro is degraded and ignorant, he conforms to a popular standard of what a negro should be. When he shakes off his rags and wretchedness and presumes to be a man, and a man among men, he contradicts this popular standard and becomes an offence to his surroundings."[200]

Tourgée's strategy to wait for the country's race mood to come around was not working. Even an event celebrating Black accomplishment, the Atlanta Exposition in 1895, turned against Plessy. Booker T. Washington, one of the leading Black voices in the nation, stood before the crowd and offered these words: "In all things that are purely social, we can be separate as the fingers, yet one as the hand in all things essential to mutual progress." Although not a personal backer of separate-but-equal, his words became a ringing endorsement for segregation.[201]

The US Supreme Court heard oral arguments in *Plessy v. Ferguson* on April 13, 1896. Tourgée built his case on the fact that segregated facilities violated the Equal Protection Clause. As the Thirteenth Amendment prohibited slavery, and the Fourteenth Amendment guaranteed the same rights and protections to all citizens, then the Louisiana rail law was depriving of life, liberty, or property without due process of law. As a fully participating citizen, Plessy should not be required to give up any public rights or access. The Louisiana law violated the Equal Protection Clause and was, therefore, unconstitutional. The State of Louisiana, on the other hand, argued that each state may make rules to protect public safety. As segregated facilities reflected public will in Louisiana, a separate-but-equal facility protected the provisions of the Equal Protection Clause.[202]

Justice Henry B. Brown of Massachusetts delivered the 7–1 majority decision of the court that upheld the Louisiana law requiring segregation. Brown noted the Thirteenth Amendment applied only to slavery, and the Fourteenth Amendment was intended to give Blacks only political and civil equality—not social equality. The court's reasoning resounded over across the next sixty years of political debate. As Brown wrote, "Legislation is powerless to eradicate racial instincts or to abolish distinctions based upon physical differences." The court declared that the Louisiana law was a reasonable exercise of the state's "police power," enacted for the promotion of the public good. In the key passage of the opinion, the court stated that segregation was legal and constitutional as long as "facilities were equal." Hence, the separate-but-equal doctrine was codified into national law. The ruling read, in part:

> We consider the underlying fallacy of the plaintiff's argument to consist in the assumption that the enforced separation of the two races stamps the colored race with a badge of inferiority. If this be so, it is not by reason of anything found in the act, but solely because the colored race chooses to put that construction upon it. . . .
>
> The argument also assumes that social prejudices may be overcome by legislation, and that equal rights cannot be secured to the negro except by an enforced co-mingling of the two races. We cannot accept this proposition. If the two races are to meet upon

terms of social equality, it must be the result of natural affinities, a mutual appreciation of each other's merits and a voluntary consent of individuals. . . .

Legislation is powerless to eradicate racial instincts or to abolish distinctions based upon physical differences, and the attempt to do so can only result in accentuating the difficulties of the present situation. If the civil and political rights of both races be equal one cannot be inferior to the other civilly or politically. If one race be inferior to the other socially, the Constitution of the United States cannot put them upon the same plane.[203]

The court paused in its majority opinion in *Plessy v. Ferguson* to remark about Plessy, a man with a smidgen of African ancestry, that it might be a "question of importance whether, under the laws of Louisiana, the petitioner belongs to the white or colored race."[204]

Among the seven upholding the Louisiana law, only one was from the former Confederacy—Justice Edward White. White, who eventually became chief justice of the United States in 1910, served in both the Louisiana State Senate and the US Senate, until tapped for the nation's highest bench by President Grover Cleveland in 1894. White carried the baggage of the Confederacy to the highest bench in the land, as a member of both the New Orleans Pickwick Club and the Crescent City White League, both elitist organizations with deep-set racist roots. Named in honor of the Charles Dickens novel, the Pickwick Club was launched in 1857, when members of the Mistick Krewe of Comus, the first parading organization of Mardi Gras, decided to start an elite gentlemen's club. Several Pickwick members were elected to the Louisiana state convention that voted to secede from the Union on January 26, 1861. About two weeks later, members of the organization rode in the Mardi Gras parade wearing blackface and carrying an effigy of Abraham Lincoln. Following the Civil War, Harry Hays, a former Confederate general, became the new president of the Pickwick Club. Postwar tensions in New Orleans exploded on July 30, 1866, when a white mob attacked participants attending a convention on Black suffrage, killing forty people. The group was inflamed by Reconstruction policies of integration, as well as state-level efforts that granted voting rights to Black men and integrated schools and public accommodations. In response, Pickwick members joined other residents to form the Crescent City White League, a volunteer militia that promised to reverse "the most absurd inversion of the relations of race."

The *Plessy v. Ferguson* ruling was also interesting from the point of view that a Northerner from Massachusetts wrote the majority opinion and a Southerner from Kentucky wrote the dissent. Born in Boyle County, Kentucky, John Marshall Harlan was a former slave owner who fought for the North in the Civil War, freeing his own slaves before the end of the war. Dissatisfied with both the Republican and Democratic parties, he joined the Know-Nothing Party, which boasted strong anti-immigrant, anti-Catholic stances. His views evolved, however, and eventually turned to supporting the need to protect the freed slaves. When Rutherford B. Hayes became president in March 1877, he sent Harlan and four other special commissioners to Louisiana to mediate a dispute over the state's 1876 elections. Thereafter, Hayes appointed Harlan to the Supreme Court, where he was often at odds with the majority, becoming known as the "Great Dissenter." He was the lone dissenter in *Plessy*. In his opinion, he wrote:

> The white race deems itself to be the dominant race in this country. And so it is, in prestige, in achievements, in education, in wealth, and in power. So, I doubt not, it will continue to be for all time, if it remains true to its great heritage and holds fast to the principles of constitutional liberty. But in the view of the Constitution, in the eye of the law, there is in this country no superior, dominant, ruling class of citizens. There is no caste here. Our Constitution is color-blind and neither knows nor tolerates classes among citizens. In respect of civil rights, all citizens are equal before the law. The humblest is the peer of the most powerful. The law regards man as man and takes no account of his surroundings or of his color when his civil rights as guaranteed by the supreme law of the land are involved. . . .
>
> The arbitrary separation of citizens, on the basis of race, while they are on a public highway, is a badge of servitude wholly inconsistent with the civil freedom and the equality before the law established by the Constitution. It cannot be justified upon any legal grounds.[205]

For all his "moral courage and rhetorical power, for all its insistence that the law be color-blind," Harlan was bound by his own time and culture.[206] Witness his actions in 1899, three years after *Plessy*, when the court heard its first challenge to racially separate schools. In Richmond County, Georgia, separate high schools functioned for Blacks, white girls, and white boys. When the district's buildings became overcrowded, the Black high school was converted into an elementary school, leaving Black high school students with no public school to attend. Relying on the majority opinion in *Plessy*, parents of the Black children sued, claiming they were entitled to "separate but equal" schools. In *Cumming v. County Board of Education*, the Supreme Court rejected their claim in a unanimous opinion written by Harlan, who offered "no hint of candor or moral outrage. It is a whitewash job well worthy of the Plessy majority."[207]

Opinions on *Plessy* were plentiful across the country, as one might guess. The *Daily Picayune* opined on the ruling the following day: "Equality of rights does not mean community of rights. The laws must recognize and uphold this distinction; otherwise, if all rights were common as well as equal, there would be practically no such thing as private property, private life, or social distinctions, but all would belong to everybody who might choose to use it. This would be absolute socialism, in which the individual would be extinguished in the vast mass of human being, a condition repugnant to every principle of enlightened democracy."[208]

North of the Mason-Dixon Line, the *Republican* of Springfield, Massachusetts, wrote: "The law may now be expected to spread like the measles in those commonwealths where white supremacy is thought to be in peril. Did the Southerners ever pause to indict the Almighty for allowing negroes to be born on the same Earth with white men? We fear it was the one great mistake in creation not to provide every race and every class with its own Earth."[209]

Following the *Plessy* ruling, segregation became the law of the land as southern states and municipalities were flooded with so-called Jim Crow laws. Although the origin of the term is hazy, it may have arisen from "Jump Jim Crow," a song and dance that became the signature of T. D. "Daddy" Rice, a white comedian who first performed in blackface in 1828. As the song's popularity grew, so did demand for Rice, who later changed his stage name to Daddy Jim Crow. There is no definitive version of the song; the lyrics evolved and expanded over time, with some published versions featuring more than 150 verses. "Jump Jim Crow" is one of the earliest examples of "Black imitation" by white performers.

When Jim Crow finally became embedded in New Orleans, it drew rigid segregation lines through the population. The city's long tradition of easy interaction crumbled. Even the famed New Orleans jazz scene, far from prospering in the newly segregated society, almost died. Full segregation arrived in New Orleans not in the 1890s, but only around the time of the First World War. Starting with Louisiana's adoption of a new constitution in 1898, 95 percent of Blacks and a quarter of poor whites were struck from the voter rolls. A long series of Jim Crow laws and local ordinances were enacted, each calling for segregation across society—not just hotels, theaters, bars, and restrooms, but whorehouses and churches, insane asylums and cemeteries.[210]

And across the country, "separate but equal" was simply a baseline. White lawmakers saw an opportunity not only to separate Blacks from whites, but also to disenfranchise them. At its heart, the post-*Plessy* era of Jim Crow was defined by accelerated expulsion of Blacks from every process—the voting booth, the jury box, the classroom. Blacks, like Dixon, had grabbed too much political and economic power in too short a time. Jim Crow became the last stand by a white power structure losing its foothold. In 1899, US representative George H. White, a Black man, saw the changes coming and offered up his thoughts in an address:

> We seem, as a race, to be going through just now a crucible, a crisis—a peculiar crisis. Possibly more than by any one thing, it has been brought about by the fact that, despite all the oppression which has fallen upon our shoulders, we have been rising, steadily rising, and in some instances we hope ere long to be able to measure our achievements with those of all other men and women of the land. This tendency on the part of some of us to rise and assert out manhood along all lines is, I fear, what has brought about this changed condition.[211]

White, who was the last Black man to represent North Carolina in Congress for seventy years, saw Jim Crow as more than "separate but equal." He saw "the limitations and humiliations" of Jim Crow as the rapid re-elevation of the white man over the Black man, a re-establishment of the Black man's "place" in the world. It was a denial of commonality written into law. In the South, masculinity was power, and, as such, translated itself into economic, political, or physical power. George Dixon's victory over Skelly drew ire because it challenged deep-set notions of superiority upon which southern society was based.

As Black Americans entered the twentieth century, their fortunes had changed considerably in a few short decades. They had gone from a state of slavery, to a state progressing toward political equality with whites, to a state of semi-citizenship, all in less than two generations.[212] In fact, the timing for Blacks could not have been worse, as the country was just starting to pull itself away from the economic roller coaster of the 1890s. The appearance of massive department stores fed a burgeoning consumerism characterized by world's fairs, hotels, museums, films, magazines, and tourism. The pace of turn-of-the-century industrialization accelerated, notably in the rapid spread of mass production, oil refineries, pipelines, retail chains, bigger and faster railroads, and emerging telephone systems. Within one generation, the average white standard of living jumped nearly two-thirds. But that was for only one portion of America. For the other portion, the doors to opportunity were not only shut, but slammed shut. The *Plessy* ruling had enormous consequences, none more devastating than its economic impact on the Black community. It not only created second-class citizenship, but it "effectively cut off Blacks from the era's exhilarating possibilities."[213] One small corner of the Black population flourished—entertainers, from comedians and singers to sport stars. Each found success within admittedly reduced space. In their popularity was power.

After the high-court ruling, Homer Plessy returned to everyday family life and worked as an insurance salesman. In both 1900 and 1910, census takers in New Orleans recorded "M"—"mulatto"—next to the names of Plessy and his wife. In 1920, the couple was recorded as "W"—"white." When he died in 1925, Plessy was buried in St. Louis Cemetery No. 1, in Tomb 619, just off Conti Street, in New Orleans. This was a segregated facility, although not by race; he was buried in the Catholic section of the cemetery. Though he did not live long enough to see the culmination of his influence, he did witness its genesis. Ten years after the *Plessy v. Ferguson* ruling, a group inspired by the case convened delegates from fourteen states and formed the Niagara Movement. That movement led to the formation of the National Association for the Advancement of Colored People (NAACP), which played a central role in the fight for federal civil rights legislation in the 1950s and 1960s. Leading a team of NAACP lawyers, Thurgood Marshall, who eventually became the first Black US Supreme Court Justice, successfully used *Plessy*'s Fourteenth Amendment arguments before the US Supreme Court in the landmark *Brown vs. Board of Education* decision of 1954, which overruled the separate-but-equal doctrine. And on June 7, 2005, Homer A. Plessy Day was established in New Orleans through the combined impetus of the Crescent City Peace Alliance, former Louisiana governor Kathleen Blanco, the Louisiana House of Representatives, and the New Orleans City Council. His distinguished memory is carried on by members of the Plessy and Ferguson families through the Plessy & Ferguson Foundation, an organization that provides civil rights education, preservation, and outreach.[214]

From the start, Olympic Club president Charles Noel never wanted the spotlight. When lauded with the rapid rise of the club, the New Orleans native often pushed credit toward his colleagues, his assistants, or various committee members. Just as happy casting a public shadow as thin as his actual one, the second-generation lumber baron was an indefatigable worker not yet thirty years old. But when public opinion turned against the mixed-race fight, Noel became the face of the decision. It was indeed a gamble that Noel and the Olympic Club took on the people of New Orleans and their city being ready for mixed-race fights. Turns out, the city was not ready.

In the weeks after the Carnival, the Olympic Club was tearing itself apart from the inside. Old guard members balked at the massive expense of the event and at rumored corruption among club officials. Receipts from the Carnival totaled $101,557.89 with expenses of $58,937.88. Of that amount, $42,000 went to purses for the fighters, and the rest was spent in a number of ways. It was that remaining $16,000-plus in expenses that raised the ire of membership. A member of the Contest Committee accounted for a few of those expenses, including $6,500 to enlarge the arena; $1,000 paid to the Police Charity Fund for permits; $2,300 in police services during the event; $2,500 in posters and advertising; $1,000 in lights and tarpaulins; and $2,607 for carriages for fighters, extra help, and miscellaneous expenses.

These were all legitimate expenses, Noel argued. Williams made several lengthy and costly trips on the club's dime, but, it was argued, his matchmaking made the entire event possible.[215] One such trip had Williams paying *Police Gazette* sporting editor William E. Harding $1,500 to publish the pictures of Olympic Club officers in the popular publication in order to gin up excitement. Despite publishing the requested lavish, extensively illustrated spread, Harding pushed back against the rumors, saying, "I never asked for any money, never got any, and the club are under no obligations to me." That was technically true—Harding never received payment because stockholders refused to pay the bill when it was put forward to them as part of the expenses.[216] As part of the event's autopsy, members demanded an account for every expense, no matter how minor, and for each complimentary ticket issued. That last point had merit. On the first night, 651 reserved seats were sold for Myer-McAuliffe, while club officials handed out 660 complimentary tickets. The trend continued the second and third nights when 602 reserved tickets were sold versus 821 given away for Dixon-Skelly, and 1,031 reserved tickets sold versus

884 given away for Sullivan-Corbett. That is a huge number of free tickets to issue, if they were truly given away. Or perhaps, as some accused, they were sold by club officials for their own gain.

On October 3, 1892, a meeting of club stockholders erupted in violence numerous times; on more than one occasion, a full-scale riot nearly broke out among the membership. During the three-hour affair, Noel was peppered with questions from the floor about the Carnival's finances. Wildly unprepared for such a barrage, Noel deferred detailed answers until the next day when he would issue a detailed report from the event. That did not satisfy the crowd, resulting in multiple, lengthy speeches questioning the honesty of the officials and demanding a full accounting to the stockholders.[217]

By October 30, 1892, Noel was creating quite the stir, this time in New York City. With fresh wounds from battling the Olympic Club Board of Directors, he found himself negotiating the rights to some of the biggest fights on the horizon, now under a new flag. The Crescent City Athletic Club was an unfamiliar name to all, as it had just formed under the leadership of Noel and his loyalists. Noel was, in fact, its sole officer—no official of any type had been named. There was no physical club, either, only a proposed plot in New Orleans where, Noel assured would-be investors, he would build a peer institution to any club in the world. Before taking off for New York, Noel had written out his resignation and handed it to the board chairman.[218] It would not be formally accepted until three weeks later, when the board officially replaced Noel as president with Charles Dickson, a member of the old board of directors who, while a rival and deeply opposed to the Dixon-Skelly fight, otherwise helped Noel stave off opposition to the Carnival within the organization.[219]

The Carnival of Champions represented the high-water point for boxing in New Orleans. What followed the mega-event was the sport's rapid slide toward irrelevance in the city. Attendance fell off for fights in 1893. The new Louisiana governor, Murphy J. Foster, was hostile toward the sport and ordered the state attorney general to file an injunction to stop any future bouts at the Olympic Club on the grounds that, while the fights were legal, the paying of prizes to the winners was illegal. In *State v. Olympic Club* (1894), Louisiana brought suit against the Olympic, seeking to revoke its charter on the grounds it had hosted prize-fighting exhibitions contrary to state laws. It also sought an injunction to restrain and prohibit the Olympic Club from further promoting such events. The case centered on an anti-prizefighting act passed by the state's general assembly on June 25, 1890, that banned the state's citizens from, among other items, promoting, advertising, or participating in any form in prize-fighting within or outside the state.[220] The act called for penalties of up to six months in the parish jail and fines up to $500. An additional proviso, however, said the act did "not apply to exhibitions and glove contests between human beings which may take place within the rooms of regularly chartered athletic clubs." The statute owed much of its construction to Ordinance No. 4336 of the City of New Orleans, adopted by the New Orleans City Council on March 5, 1890. It read, in part:

> That exhibitions and glove contests between human beings for the development of muscular strength be and the same are hereby permitted to take place within rooms of all regularly chartered athletic clubs in the City of New Orleans, provided that at the time when said exhibitions and glove contests shall take place that the side or giving of spirituous liquors in said club rooms is hereby prohibited; and provided further, that all such exhibitions and glove contests shall be under the suspension of the police authorities of the City of New Orleans; and provided further, that a glove weighing not less than five ounces shall be used in such exhibitions or contests; but under no circumstances shall this ordinance be construed as permitting any sparring contests in such club or clubs on Sunday; provided further, that for each exhibition the parties shall be required to donate $50 for fund of public charities of New Orleans; and that a good and solvent bond of $500 cash shall be given, to be forfeited in case of any violation of said ordinance, the proceeds of said forfeited bond to go to the said fund of public charities.[221]

In April 1894, the case rose to the Louisiana Supreme Court. The ensuing court action pitted, among others, New Orleans mayor John Fitzpatrick, testifying for the Olympic Club, against former mayor Joseph Shakespeare testifying against the club. At trial, the judge's decision hinged on "the distinction that is taken in the statute and ordinance between a glove contest and what is commonly called a prize-fight; for upon this distinction depends the criminality *vel non* [or not] of the contests which took place between the combatants." The state's case seemed clear cut in the definition of what had transpired at the club—two men fought often to a finish; blood was drawn; championships changed hands; victor and vanquished were rewarded monetarily. In addition, the state noted that between September 1890 and October 1893, a period including the Carnival of Champions, seventeen bouts of that kind took place with prize money totaling $95,200, of which $86,050 went to the winners and $9,150 to the losers. The Olympic Club hid behind the argument they hosted "scientific and skillful" exhibitions only. In its defense, the club contrasted the bloodiness of the Sullivan vs. Ryan and Sullivan vs. Kilrain title bouts fought under the London Prizefighting Rules, with the Sullivan vs. Corbett bout fought under the Queensberry Rules. The defense convinced the jury that neither the club's charter nor any ordinances were violated.[222] Justice Watkins observed:

> These contests were but trials of the skill and powers of physical endurance between well-equipped athletes, and that, being trained in this so-called "manly art of self-defense," it was a matter next to impossibility for one of the contestants to administer, above the belt of the other, any serious physical punishment—fighting, as they did, with five-ounce gloves. That a nose was occasionally made to bleed, that now and then a lip was left in a swollen condition, or the face somewhat bruised and disfigured, does not alter the case, as like occurrences are apt to take place in boxing, fencing or football . . . If, indeed, such contests are violative of good morals and sound public policy, the matter comes plainly within the prerogative of the legislative department of the government, which alone can be looked to for relief.[223]

The court, however, found that due to irregularities in testimony, the state could resubmit its case. Until that time, the club was free to conduct bouts as it had.

However, the fatal blow for boxing in the city came on December 14, 1894, during a fight between Andy Bowen and George Lavigne at the Auditorium Club. Bowen was a mixed-race fighter. Although his light complexion lend credence to his claims of being Irish Spanish, the New Orleans fighter was more than likely a mix of white and Black ancestors. In the eighteenth round, Lavigne landed a right to Bowen's jaw, knocking the southern lightweight champion backward where he struck the wooden platform at full force. Bowen was carried "limp and senseless from the ring," where doctors tended to him.[224] He never regained consciousness and died the following morning. Lavigne and his team, including his manager, seconds, and timekeeper, were arrested along with club officials and charged with manslaughter. In the aftermath, Fitzpatrick declared: "I do not know what effect the death of Bowen will have on pugilism in the future. . . . If death was caused by the blow which Lavigne struck, then boxing is dead, but if death resulted from Bowen's head striking the floor, then the death was attributed to circumstances and could be avoided in the future."[225] James Corbett also responded to Bowen's death by telling the *Chicago Daily Tribune* that "[the death] will hurt pugilism, and makes me more eager than ever to get out of the business."[226] On December 27, 1894, the coroner ruled the concussion causing death was a result of hitting the floor. Charges against Lavigne and his team were dropped immediately.[227] Further, it was later discovered that Bowen had requested padding be removed from the ring because "he could not move with agility on a padded surface."[228]

None of that redemption mattered for the sport in New Orleans, however. The mayor, pressured by state officials, revoked fight permits for the next scheduled match in the city. The second hearing of *State v. Olympic Club* went against the club. In the leading opinion, Justice McEnery said glove contests, when the object was only for the display of the art and skills of boxing, were permissible and could continue to be held in the Olympic Club, but that the fights described by the state authorities, which were invariably fought to a bloody finish, were unlicensed and illegal prizefights.[229] With this reversal of its previous judgment, the state Supreme Court essentially pronounced fighting for a purse illegal in Louisiana.[230]

The Olympic Club was not alone. Similar decisions clamping down on the scope of boxing exhibitions popped up across the country. For a short time, professional prizefighting found refuge in the more relaxed legal climate of the West. For example, the California Athletic Club established a reputation for prizefighting in San Francisco in the 1880s and 1890s, while Carson City, Nevada, was the host for the celebrated Bob Fitzsimmons–James J. Corbett heavyweight title fight on St Patrick's Day 1897. Notwithstanding these developments, professional prizefighters knew the "real" money was in the East and, more specifically, in New York, which had a massive, concentrated, and interested population willing to embrace the sport. It was the home of the national sporting press and the city had venues as diverse as Coney Island and Madison Square Garden. Most importantly, New York's infrastructure better facilitated the arrangement and promotion of international bouts. At the turn of the twentieth century, authorities in New York initiated several legislative schemes to become a model of boxing administration, with its adoption of definitive weight divisions, greater medical supervision, and the licensing of referees and promoters. This was mimicked across the United States as boxing entered the new century on sounder legal footing.[231]

Despite what followed, all that transpired in the ring between George Dixon and Jack Skelly took on a somewhat mythical quality over the years—most of it rather apocryphal in nature. Dixon has often been credited with "knocking out" Jim Crow that evening, but nothing could be further from the truth.

One night after Dixon defeated Skelly—just down the street from the Olympic Club—Louis LeSoire saw the lifeless body of Henry Dixon hanging from the oak tree outside his home. The Jefferson Parish Police Jury member first summoned his white neighbors together to bear witness, and only after they had their fill did he call the coroner to remove the body. Several Black residents had seen the body earlier that day, but said nothing. Seems a local mob mistook Henry Dixon for the would-be assassin of Judge Henry Long, who three months earlier had been fired upon outside his home by someone hidden behind a tree outside the train depot. Two bullets struck the judge, who survived the attack after several grueling weeks of recovery. As he fought for his life, police investigators became convinced that Black conspirators were meeting and planning a series of assassinations, starting with Long. Found on the streets on New Orleans, Dixon was one of the men rounded up by authorities and charged with the attack. About 2 a.m. Wednesday, white masked men raided the jail in Kennerville, Louisiana. As many prisoners fell to their knees in fear and prayer, the leader of the masked men called out for Dixon. Finding him among the crowd of prisoners, they dragged him away, then carefully nailed the jail door they had kicked in back into place. Silence followed. Then, a volley of gunshots. Jim Crow, it seems, was alive and well.[232]

In 1988, Halifax playwright George Elroy Boyd staged *Shine Boy*, a wildly fictional account of George Dixon's rise as champion. Boyd, a well-regarded chronicler of the Canadian Black experience, mentioned the Skelly-Dixon bout prominently in the short production. The scene included portrayals of real people or real names applied to fictional characters, as well as outright fictional characters. The conversation took place between Tommy O'Rourke, Dixon's manager; Geoff McGeough, a fictional former boxer; Elmer Chickering, a fifty-year-old shoeshine boy (although named for the real-life photographer/mentor of Dixon's youth); and various other shoeshine boys:

> Leonard: Skelly never had a chance.
> Elmer: He was no match for Little Chocolate.

Troy: New Orleans was eight rounds of living hell for George.

Geoff: A crowd of men circled the ring.

Elmer: White men, with Billy clubs and freshly lit cigars.

Geoff: They beat Little Chocolate each time he ventured near the ropes. His back became a mass of welts and bruises.

All: All nigger-boys should know better than to beat a white man in Dixie!

Tommy: There was nothing we could do, but watch as they crushed their cigars into his flesh.

Geoff: Each time he came near the ropes, they would burn him with a cigar or smack him with a club.

All: All nigger-boys should know better than to beat a white man in Dixie!

Tommy: George Dixon retained his World Featherweight Title by knocking out Jack Skelly in the middle of the ring . . . in the middle of the ring.

Geoff: It was a consummate display of fistic prowess and stamina.

Tommy: Then the Klan decided to extend its good cheer.

Geoff: A lynch mob entered the ring. Demanding George, they strung a rope. We tried to push them back—keep them away from George.

Tommy: But they bound us and dragged George into the center of the ring. Then John L. Sullivan leaped between the ropes with a shotgun in hand and they released us.

Wright married elements of real-world experiences (Dixon often fought in places where he could not venture too close to the ropes) with elements of pure fantasy. Nothing in this scene happened in New Orleans. And while the dramatic license is clear, this is a popular vision of Dixon's actual experience. Perhaps this need to mythologize an already significant moment is a testament to the significance of the Dixon-Skelly matchup in the minds of many.

Following the Carnival bout, Skelly fought, officially, only fourteen more times professionally after meeting Dixon. But it wasn't the last time they crossed paths as professionals. In March 1893, Skelly withdrew from a fight with George Siddons at the Coney Island Athletic Club, after contracting malaria. Dixon offered to take his former foe's place.[233] While Dixon slid into Skelly's slot, he offered little to the crowd, who amused themselves by singing "Home Sweet Home" and yelling, "Fake! Fake!

Fake!" throughout the twelve-round bout. The fight ended in a draw. At no stage did Siddons attempt to fight. Although Dixon worked heroically, he failed to do any damage to his opponent who "kept prancing around the ring like a dancing master."[234]

Fewer than two months after losing to Dixon in New Orleans, and three weeks after his failed benefit, Skelly served as referee for a benefit bout in Springfield, Ohio. His style of refereeing did not suit the Springfield sports and they "thumped and kicked the ex-amateur champion until he was badly bruised."[235] He tried his hand outside the ring, as well. In October 1893, Skelly found himself stranded in Saratoga, New York, with a fifteen-person theater troupe, in which he was a featured attraction. He was with the company for its performance, *A Winning Hand*, on Saturday night, only to see it fold on Sunday night with seventy-nine cents in the treasury. Skelly and nine others attempted to escape their bills at the Noonan House, but they were caught and arrested. Once the situation was resolved, the troupe was dropped at the train station with tickets home, offered to them by "sympathetic locals." It was at the station where Skelly saw a young girl, who later claimed to be sixteen, but looked nowhere near it, being ushered away briskly by three men. As the troupe boarded the train for New York City, Skelly stayed behind and traced the girl to a local boarding house where the men took her and drugged her. The men fled when Skelly arrived. The young girl required medical treatment to be revived. Skelly escorted her home to New York City and took her to her mother.[236]

Skelly's greatest beating took place outside the ring. In October 1894, he was dangerously ill in hospital from wounds in the neck and head inflicted with a dinner fork during a street fight in the early morning hours of October 18.[237] During his testimony against the accused, he said: "My religion will not permit me to hold a grudge. Every night when I hit my knees and say my prayers, I forgive my enemies."[238] In May 1896, he joined a theater company in its performance of *O'Grady's First Lesson*, which, perhaps rather strangely, concluded the play with three rounds of a scientific boxing exhibition.[239] Only thirty-one people attended the performance—"Sit closer together and perhaps we can see you," remarked one of the show's stars from the stage on opening night.[240] Reviews were not kind: "It is flattery to say that the show was very, very poor, and before it was over, a majority of the audience had departed."[241] By time the scientific exhibition had come around at show's end, there was one lone soul in the orchestra seats. The police had no call to interfere in the mild sparring affair and couldn't if they had wanted to. Like much of the audience, officers had grown tired of the show and went home. During a part of the performance, there were more people on stage than on the other side of the footlights, and "both actors and audience appeared to be very sorry that they were there."[242]

Tommy White ended Skelly's professional career with a fifth-round knockout on January 23, 1897. Skelly finished his career with six wins, five losses, and four draws. He then tried his hand at managing fighters. On March 21, 1898, Henry Braun jumped into the ring for the first time in his career. His opponent, Jack Smith, was managed by Skelly. Smith landed punches at will throughout the six-round contest. Braun was floored twice in the fifth—both by blows to the jaw—and then again in the sixth. At the close of the bout, Braun, a New Jersey featherweight, was carried to his dressing room and then ushered off to the hospital. He died the next morning as a result of a hemorrhage on the brain. He was twenty-nine years old. The medical examiner determined death "might have been produced either by a blow or a fall"—both of which he experienced the night prior. Smith was charged with manslaughter. Skelly, along with referee Sam C. Austin, was held for questioning.[243] On March 24, 1898, the Mercer County Grand Jury refused to indict Smith, Skelly, or Austin in the case.[244]

Skelly's boxing career looked positively elite when measured against his time on the stage. A performance of his ill-fated vaudeville show came to an abrupt end when stagehands refused to raise the curtain until they were paid back wages owed to them—amounting to $25.20. Skelly, manager of the show, said he would pay the men in a few days, if only this performance could get off. The previous performance had only brought in $19. The electric company had already demanded $6 in back payment before they turned the power back on earlier that evening. After a brief huddle, the stagehands refused Skelly and walked out—with the audience soon to follow. It was perhaps all the better. Many of the actors had been refusing to perform for days, as they had not been paid. Amateur understudies took their places.[245]

In the years that followed, Skelly ran a tavern in Yonkers, New York, and became a well-respected referee and a member of the New York State Athletic Commission.[246] John L. Sullivan reflected on Skelly years after the bout with Dixon:

> In the same ring that Corbett won the championship from me was held a fight that never got the notice it deserved because the whole world was so busy talking about my defeat . . . It's the Dixon-Skelly battle I refer to as the one that never got what it deserved.
>
> When the fight ended, Skelly told his friends at the ringside to

telegraph his friends in New York that he didn't know how to fight. But he did know how, and he had the courage of a lion, but Dixon was Dixon, and that's all there was to it. I've always had a soft memory for Skelly, because his defeat was to him as great a surprise as mine was to me, and he got his where I got mine. Gentleman Jack Skelly is now running a hotel in Yonkers, and he's so far out of the fighting game that he won't even fight a hotel beat, preferring the easy life.[247]

Skelly's "last hurrah" near the ropes came as an alternate referee of the Jess Willard–Jack Dempsey heavyweight championship fight on July 4, 1919. Dempsey knocked Willard out in that bout, taking the title and setting the stage for one of the most famous heavyweight champion reigns in history.[248] Skelly died May 25, 1956, after a long illness, at the age of eighty-three. His fight with Dixon dominated the text of his obituary.

———

Dixon rarely ventured into the south again, limited to only three trips to Louisville, Kentucky, in three separate years, with the last coming in July 1899. Nevertheless, it was his first visit south in 1892 when we start to see societal forces shift somewhat against him.

More than any other, the journey to fight this bout showcased Dixon as a figure of transition, not only in boxing, but also in the societal landscapes of the late nineteenth and early twentieth centuries. At the Carnival, Dixon arrived at the right place, in the right time, under the right circumstances to spark a discussion among fight fans about the changing face of America. In doing so, Dixon also changed the trajectory of his career. Until that moment in New Orleans in September 1892, Dixon was an insulated fighter. Then he landed in the middle of forces already in motion, forces still lingering from the aftereffects of slavery and the Civil War, forces challenged in New Orleans by Homer Plessy, forces codified into law by the US Supreme Court. All of those forces would gain strength that summer and continue through Dixon's lifetime. Like Plessy's challenge to his place on the train, Dixon's challenge to his place in the ring would be referenced as societal forces shifted to a more aggressive approach toward limiting Black opportunity. Shielded from those forces for years, Dixon would soon experience them head on without the protection of the white world in which he inhabited. The Carnival of Champions was not a moment when George Dixon changed the world; it was the moment when Dixon left his sheltered existence and became part of it.

George Dixon. Albumen silver print on card. Photo by Elmer Chickering.
Courtesy of Special Collections, Fine Arts Library, Harvard University.

CHAPTER 5

Perfect Man in Miniature

Box me a tune, "Little Chocolate"
come box me a boxer's tune
So box me a hook;
then box me a jab;
now box me a hook-off-of-a-jab.
Go biff go bam, go buff, go bam,
go biff-bam-bam-bam!

Box me a tune, "Little Chocolate"
come box me a fighter's tune.
So box me a lead;
then box me a feint;
now box me a lead-off-of-a-feint.
Go biff, go bam, go biff, go bam,
go biff-bam-biff-bam-bam!

Box me a tune, "Little Chocolate"
come box me a fistic tune.
So box me a cross;
then box me a slip;
now box me a cross-off-of-a-slip.
Go biff, go bam, go biff, go bam,
go biff-bam-biff-bam-bam!

Box me a tune, "Little Chocolate"
come box me a Queensbury tune.
So box me a counter;

then box me a block;
now box me a counter-off-of-a-block.
Go biff, go bam, go biff, go bam,
go biff-bam-biff-bam-bam!

The winner and new World Champion . . . [three times]
George "Little Chocolate" Dixon!!! [1]

THERE IS THAT NAME. If they know him at all, modern readers know Dixon, almost reflexively, as "Little Chocolate." However, in terms of Dixon's career, the nickname was a late addition. Early in Dixon's career, race was used as a frequent descriptor in press reports. Through the mid-1890s, the term "colored" was used widely by newspapers to describe Dixon. For instance, stories often referred to "George Dixon, colored" or "George Dixon, the colored bantamweight" as a first reference, and then as "Dixon" throughout the remainder of the text. It was not an uncommon site on other pages of the paper, either, as race remained at the forefront of reader concerns. Rarely, however, was race the dominating descriptor, although passing references, slights, and terms crept into coverage depending upon the author. That started to change in 1896.

The origin of the word "chocolate" dates back to the 1600s from Nahuatl (Aztecan) "xocolatl," a combination of "xocolia," meaning "to make bitter," and "atl," meaning "water." Nearly three centuries later, it took on a new, loaded meaning. Both *Green's Dictionary of Slang* and *The New Partridge Dictionary of Slang and Unconventional English* put the origin around 1905–06 of "chocolate" as both a noun and adjective referring to Blacks. Obviously, as fans of Dixon can attest, the term was in heavy rotation nearly two decades prior to that. Throughout 1889–90, the *Chicago Daily Tribune* ran a comedy feature entitled *Old Chocolate*, where the author—billed only as "Judge"—penned a poem in exaggerated Black dialect. An example, titled *Old Chocolate's Jocoserlous Chat*, read, in part: "When yo' hungry de dinnah ah late. De cowshus huntah gits a shawt range. Old Dinah kin darnse, but dar's no fun in hit. Do biggah de boss do proudah de hiah'd man."[2]

George Godfrey, Dixon's mentor, was already being billed as "Old Chocolate" when, in 1891, the *Boston Daily Globe* described Dixon's blood as "streaming down his chocolate-colored flesh."[3] The following year, the *New York Times* referenced how Dixon's "chocolate-colored skin shone in the electric light like burnished copper."[4] Always using a lowercase letter, denoting an adjective and not a nickname, reporters used "chocolate" to describe Dixon for several years, often adoringly. It is difficult to pinpoint the exact moment when "Little Chocolate" become his official moniker; sometimes it was as subtle as a lowercase letter. In January 1896, the *Los Angeles Times* wrote that one particular boxer was "asked to fight a man who gave George Dixon forty rounds of the toughest grueling that ever culminated in a victory for 'Little Chocolate.'"[5] In February 1896, the *Washington Post* wrote that "[Pedlar Palmer] slipped in and out on Dixon, prodding little Chocolate in the face."[6] And when describing the weigh-in prior to his bout against Jerry Marshall in March 1896, *The State*, of Columbia, South Carolina, wrote that Marshall looked "as if he would give little Chocolate the toughest battle of his ring career."

By September 1896, the term was no longer used as a descriptor of Dixon's skin, but as a popularly accepted nickname appearing in both the body of stories and in headlines. "Little Chocolate" was born—and it is difficult to ignore the timing. As the country, including the US Supreme Court, pushed back on Black progress, so too did newspapers and promoters push back on the lone Black champion in the sport by branding him with a demeaning nickname. There was a notable exception: the *Boston Daily Globe*, Dixon's hometown newspaper. The paper rarely embraced the nickname, instead referring to Dixon as a "little man" or "little champion" instead of the loaded term "Little Chocolate."

While certainly used during Dixon's career, the nickname was not popularized until after his death. In fact, it is an enduring moniker thanks to its perpetuation by Fleischer in his *Black Dynamite* series, and then carried on over the decades as Dixon biographies essentially traced those words exactly.[7]

While fighter nicknames were a highlight of the times, many hinged on physical traits or ethnicity. Dixon's particular nickname signaled a fascination with the fighter he could never escape. Be it his skin, his physique, or his style, George Dixon was a physical obsession of his era—transcending his size and race in the process.

———

Buying another human being was surprisingly easy until 1865. In fact, the American economy had become ruthlessly efficient at the process of pedaling flesh through public markets or private sales. Interested buyers budgeted accordingly by following the prices of recent transactions in newspapers. People were products and, like any commodity, were fit into categories for buyers to understand the differences in quality and prices. Slave traders sorted and tagged their lots according to gender, age, height, weight, skin color, strength, and skill. With a monetary value attached to their flesh, people not only could be bought and sold, but also rented out for work or breeding, or perhaps even used as collateral for mortgages. Owners insured slaves. States assessed property tax against them. And professional appraisers, when hired to probate wills of deceased plantation owners and distribute their estates among heirs, assigned value to slaves along with buildings, land, and livestock. These people were property in every sense. This backdrop taints any discussions of Dixon's body, and marveling over a Black man's dimensions requires a willing disregard of this backdrop. It does not matter if we are talking about pre-fight promotion during Dixon's heyday, or the wall-to-wall coverage of a modern NFL Combine—these obsessions carry over from a dark time.

In the moment, Dixon did not discourage this behavior. In fact, his unique characteristics, mixed with a ruthless manager willing to exploit them, may have propagated the obsessions somewhat. We are allowed to appreciate the man today because of the pages and pages of newsprint and surprising number of photographs dedicated to his physical form. In Dixon, perhaps more than any previous fighter, we see the dawning of an obsession not simply rooted in physical ownership, but also in an appreciation for how his body, combined with his skills and intelligence, could in many respects make him a man worthy of emulation. That would not have happened at any time before Dixon and would not happen again for years after. But he arose in a moment where a society was turning to the body, a sport was maturing, and the media was perfecting mythmaking.

Pugilism is, as urban sociologist Loïc J. D. Wacquant described it, "a body-centered universe" where the boxer's body is "the template and epicenter of their life, at once the site, the instrument and the object of their daily work, the medium and outcome of their occupational exertion." He continued, "The fighter's body is simultaneously his means of production, the raw material he and his handlers (trainer and manager) have to work with and on, and, for the good part, the somatized product of his past training and extant mode of living."[8] The public viewed Dixon's universe, despite his short stature, as one of a physical specimen and innovator in the "science" of boxing training, a particularly relevant consideration held in high regard at a time when "The Prizefighter" was becoming a tangible icon of desired masculinity.

The sporting public was obsessed with Dixon's body. Such obsession also meshed with a sport developing ever-more stringent body classifications. Attention to his form was not without its pitfalls, however, as his representation often slipped from admiring descriptions into racial caricatures, at times edging into depictions that failed to shake a haunting similarity to obsessions with the bodies of African American slaves scarcely a decade before. This was also a time of pseudoscience and wild biological theories rationalizing human differences, of phrenologists determining intelligence by measuring the bumps on the human skull or the circumference and weight of the brain. This was an era of wrongheaded social Darwinists drawing sport into the debate over difference, centering on race and physical abilities.

Countless scholars have covered how men grew disconnected from their bodies in the late 1800s, pointing primarily to the all-encompassing fallout of industrialization and urbanization as culprits. Many of those same scholars, in fact, pointed to prizefighting, and its related pursuits of bodybuilding and wrestling, as evidence of their views. It is important to understand how much those urban environments gave rise to the fascination surrounding Dixon's body.

From 1835 to 1900, Massachusetts underwent a radical shift in its population. Not only did the commonwealth add more than two million residents in those years, but the majority also descended on its urban areas. In just half a century, Massachusetts went from a population that was 81 percent rural to 76 percent urban.[9] These people were no longer engaged in a self-sufficient economy, like agriculture; instead, they became dependent on the growing industrial machine located in cities. Now tethered to an economy beyond their direct control, workers' livelihoods (and the families they supported) were far more sensitive to the radical swings in the economy during this period.

The fallout of this economic environment cannot be stressed enough, although it has often been overlooked by sport historians as a major influence on the rise in popularity of the era's great fighters. Despite newfound freedoms for African Americans, violence remained a way of life in Black communities across the country. To fortify themselves against this threat, Blacks depended heavily upon their growing institutions, namely the church and a maturing middle class. In Boston, as in Philadelphia and New York City, many Black families had begun to accumulate wealth— not on the scale of the Rockefellers, Carnegies, or Vanderbilts, but still quite substantial within their communities. In Boston, for example, three generations of the Ruffin family held sway over Black society. Down south, a Black aristocracy was rising in cities like Charleston, South Carolina, and New Orleans. Lawyers, doctors, and politicians headed these families who were increasingly vital parts of the entire community.

Although not politically conscious as a group, many Black athletes felt an obligation to help less fortunate members of their race. The more successful, the more sealed off into a white world they became, the more they reached out to the less fortunate in the Black community in order to maintain some connection.[10] Dixon was a perfect example of this strange distancing. His struggling working-class admirers looked to him as both a great athlete and a great hope—he was a man who "made it," by his own hands through the use of his body, in the most trying of circumstances. People often sought him—and his wealth—out for assistance. Among hundreds of anecdotes, one story involved Harry Banks, a Boston boot-black known for his quick wit, who passed away following an asthma attack at his Chelsea home. It was at the height of Dixon's championship reign. Banks, unfortunately, left his widow with nothing; his friends, knowing the family was quite poor, sent word to his brother, a well-off landlord in Providence, Rhode Island, seeking help. In the meantime, they collected a small sum of money from friends to bury Franks, but not nearly enough. When the brother arrived, he arranged with the undertaker for the interment of his brother; but when the day of the funeral arrived, and the bill came due, Harry Banks's brother was nowhere to be found.

Following the pre-burial funeral service, the undertaker demanded his money before he would move the body. Everybody present, thinking the brother would be responsible, had stopped raising funds; the sum already collected was barely $10. Some of Harry Banks's friends then rushed to the barbershop and told this story to the deceased's former employer—who happened to be shaving George Dixon at the time. Banks and Dixon often met at a Cambridge Street barbershop where Dixon was regularly shaved when in the city.

"Well," Dixon said, "Harry will get buried, and buried decently." He left the shop and went straight to the family home, arriving just as the undertaker was about to drive away. "I want you to bury that man, who is a friend of mine, at my expense," Dixon said. He pulled out a roll of bills, drew from it a $100 bill, and threw it at the undertaker to cover his $47 charge. Dixon then served as a pallbearer at the burial.[11]

Dozens of similar stories appeared in newspapers of his era. The

Boston Daily Globe often wrote of Dixon's well-known generosity: "Many a man of this city has touched the generous heart and the pocket book of the scrappy lad, when finding himself stranded away from home, and the colored boy has provided pantaloons, furnished food and paid the cab fare back to the Hub."[12]

The era's fluctuating economy created daunting challenges, not only for working-class men, but also for white middle-class men, who felt additional pressures. Beyond the economic challenges these men faced, middle-class women, as well as working-class immigrants and newly freed Blacks, were gaining more stature. Middle-class white men responded by celebrating "all things male." They flocked to fraternal orders; focused on the next generation by making "boys into men" through organizations like the Boy Scouts and YMCA; and glorified muscular sports like college football, bodybuilding, and prizefighting. For white middle-class men, the body became the platform upon which they measured manhood among themselves and against other classes and races in the city.[13] In this environment, the popular imagery of the perfect male body evolved. In the 1860s, middle-class men viewed "lean and wiry" as an ideal frame. But by the 1890s, bulk and well-defined muscles became the rage.

The German bodybuilder Friedrich Wilhelm Müller—known to the world as Eugen Sandow—ushered in that mindset. This "father of modern bodybuilding" made his New York City debut in 1893, then traveled throughout the United States for more than a decade, repeatedly burning his image into the minds of millions. His appearance shattered the prevailing image of the strongman as a thickset, barrel-chested circus performer. Following his Broadway debut and continued run on the "Great White Way," Sandow won the applause of elite theatergoers before demanding the attention of middle- and working-class men. To all, he represented a new standard of excellence—fitness, beauty, strength, and potency. He became a hypermasculine icon who embodied the very characteristics that men and women believed were eroding in the modern world.

When the curtain rose on his show, Sandow often appeared wearing only a loincloth and Roman sandals. Aside from posing, he offered examples of his dexterity, often done with a piano accompaniment. He performed backflips holding dumbbells—then executed the same trick with bound ankles—or lifted men hanging from opposite sides of a large barbell. For the finale of his two-hour show, Sandow performed the "Tomb of Hercules," which involved shaping his body into an arch with his chest thrust upward, hands and feet anchored to the floor. Once

Eugen Sandow. Albumen silver print on card. Photo by Napoleon Sarony.
Courtesy of Special Collections, Fine Arts Library, Harvard University.

in position, three horses, at an advertised total weight of 2,600 pounds, walked across a plank of wood supported only by Sandow's chest.

It was hard not to be impressed; spectators viewed Sandow's body as an attraction and a challenge, a model of strength and an object of desire, an inspiration, a rebuke, and a seduction. He simultaneously incited superlatives and stirred controversies and ambiguities. He was touted as the "strongest man in the world" and "the perfect man," yet he was pursued by challengers, imitators, and impostors who claimed they could duplicate or better his feats.[14]

Thanks in part to Sandow, the country could hardly avoid turning its eyes toward the physical form of "The Heavyweight," James J. Jeffries.[15] More so than the overexposed John L. Sullivan, Jeffries lived the idea behind the ideal more than any public figure in his era. Many fight historians regard Jeffries as the single greatest heavyweight in history. Even though his loss to Jack Johnson, after a six-year layoff from boxing, remains the most memorable moment of his career, Jeffries fought nine future International Boxing Hall of Fame pugilists and made seven title defenses in his twenty-one career professional bouts. He embodied the "rugged, two-fisted hulk of brawn that people at the turn of the century wanted their champion to be."[16]

Blessed with a daunting, natural physique, Jeffries worked as a boiler-maker outside the ring, driving their massive rivets by hand. That action, repeated day after day, honed his hulk and added further power and muscle definition to his shoulders, arms, and chest. He was an outspo-ken advocate of physical health and training. In July 1909, the Rev. G. L. Morrill, a local preacher, met with Jeffries during an amusement park appearance the champion was making in Minneapolis, Minnesota. When the minister introduced himself, the fighter replied: "You are welcome, but not anymore, because you are a minister. . . . Why in thunder don't you preachers say something about a man's body as well as his soul? How is a man going to save his soul when his liver is out of order?"[17]

The legends surrounding Jeffries were expectedly Bunyan-esque. A lover of hunting, Jeffries was said to have once killed a large deer and carried it on his shoulders nine miles to camp without stopping to rest. Friends who accompanied him had difficulty keeping up with him on the jaunt home. Or, on another occasion, when he caught pneumonia, he supposedly combated the illness by downing a gallon of whiskey. What is true, however, is the fact that Jeffries took training for each bout seriously.

He took five months to prepare for his championship match against Bob Fitzsimmons. He explained his training to the *Atlanta Constitution*:

> I trained two months on the road in the ordinary way. Then I put in three months of the hardest kind of work, running, boxing and above all, dieting for the fight. I weighed two hundred and forty-seven pounds stripped when I began the real work of conditioning, and that was my normal weight—not fat. For three months, I ate hardly anything. You'd be amazed to know how little a big man really needs to eat and how much stronger a man becomes if he doesn't eat too much. It's no joke that people dig their graves with their teeth. I would eat two small lamb chops for my dinner, with all the fat trimmed off. That made about two small bites to each chop. I had a little fruit and toast. I had dry toast for months—very little. All through that hard training, I ate as little as I could and drank nothing at all but a little cool water with lemon juice in it.[18]

Across the street from his Burbank, California, ranch, Jeffries owned a barn that served as a makeshift boxing gym and fight arena. There he trained for his bouts and held weekly amateur matches. Both events grew in popularity. Soon, film stars turned out to watch the champion train or referee a bout or two; celebrities and their admirers swelled the crowds even more. In 1954, the California Historical Society put the Jeffries Barn on its list of historical buildings. Later, it was moved to Knotts Berry Farm and used as a boxing museum complete with an historian to discuss boxing. In the late 1960s, the historian died and the museum was removed. Today, the Jeffries Barn hosts a collection of china dolls. Hidden on a wall in the back is a small brass plaque that reads: "Jeffries Barn—Historical Landmark."

Beyond the participants themselves, the evolution of prizefighting's rules during this time also focused more attention on the body. In 1865, Welsh sportsman John Graham Chambers developed a new boxing code, one that in 1867 would be published as "the Queensberry Rules for the sport of boxing." Chambers's code became popularly known as the Marquess of Queensberry Rules, named for Scottish nobleman John Douglas, ninth Marquess of Queensberry.

Douglas, who publicly endorsed the code,[19] was a brash, brutish sort—strangely fitting, then, that he should lend his name to civilizing a similarly brash, brutish sport. The outspoken atheist and secular humanist, whose deathbed profession of a love of Christ ushered him into the Catholic Church before his passing, is perhaps most famously remembered for his confrontations with Irish author, playwright, and poet Oscar Wilde. Wilde was romantically involved with Queensberry's son, Lord Alfred Douglas, a reckless lad who, along with Wilde, frequented the Victorian underground of gay prostitution. Queensberry often confronted the pair about their relationship, most notably in June 1894, when he visited Wilde's home unannounced. Queensberry threatened Wilde, "I do not say that you are it, but you look it, and pose at it, which is just as bad. And if I catch you and my son again in any public restaurant, I will thrash you." Wilde responded, "I don't know what the Queensberry Rules are, but the Oscar Wilde Rule is to shoot on sight."

In February 1895, the still-seething father left a calling card for Wilde at the author's club, the Albemarle. It read: "For Oscar, posing somdomite [*sic*]." Against the wishes of friends and advisors, Wilde sued Queensberry for libel and had him arrested on the charge. Queensberry, to avoid conviction by demonstrating his accusation was rooted in truth, hired a team of lawyers and private detectives to unearth evidence of Wilde's homosexual liaisons. They did not have to dig too deep into the record, as Queensberry was aware of their numbers. The libel trial became an event of epic proportions—a celebrity trial, if you will—that would make modern fame-seekers blush. Salacious details of Wilde's private life were put on public display. Queensberry was found not guilty, as the court declared his accusation that Wilde was "posing as a Sodomite" was justified. Under the rules of the court, Wilde was legally liable for Queensberry's considerable expenses, which left the author bankrupt.[20]

With this background in tow, the now-named Marquess of Queensberry Rules replaced the *Revised London Prizefighting Ring Rules* (1853), which, in themselves, were the first update of prizefighting's rulebook in more than a century. The *Revised London* rules replaced the *London Prize Ring Rules* (1743), a loose set of standards penned by English bare-knuckle boxer Jack Broughton, the first person to set down rules for such contests.[21] Used intermittently for a decade or two, the Queensberry Rules were popularized in the United States and Canada in 1889. The new code set down twelve defined rules, addressing many of the problems that had arisen in wilder matches over the years.[22]

To men struggling with defining their masculinity in a changing social climate, these were welcome changes to the sport's structure. The ring was becoming "a true democracy, in which men succeeded or failed under conditions of perfect equality of opportunity."[23] The most attractive regulation for the middle class was the mandated weight classes.[24] An early sanctioning body, the National Sporting Club of London, amended the Queensberry Rules in the early years of the twentieth century, with an additional nine specific criteria, such as designating the role of officials, devising a system of scoring bouts, and enabling the referee to determine a winner.

In 1909, National Sporting Club members officially recognized eight traditional weight classes, or divisions: heavyweight, lighter or light heavyweight, middleweight, welterweight, lightweight, featherweight, bantamweight, and flyweight. Those divisions went into effect in 1910.[25]

This is the point where pugilism, designed as a battle of equals, entered its modern era. Boxing, unlike the boom-and-bust capitalism of the time, was now regulated. At a time when big businesses and corporate cartels unscrupulously destroyed competitors, weight classes offered competition among equals. Every man now had a fair chance to prove himself against an adversary who was approximately his own size.[26]

Weight divisions slowly codified during Dixon's prime, although instead of being defined by official sanctioning bodies as seen today, they were determined by tradition and outlined specifically by each combatant's manager in advance of the match, with weigh-ins coming right before the bout. The ceremony surrounding the weigh-in was akin to slave auctions of the past—naked men put on display for consideration of a mainly white crowd willing to gamble on them. Of course, these weigh-in rules only applied to sanctioned bouts, where a title might change hands.

These strictly defined weight classes offered hope for fair play; they also focused the public's attention more intently onto the bodies of the pugilists.

The detailed evaluations of top pugilists—standard fare for newspaper, magazine, and, later, television reporting on fights—always include separate objective measurements of body parts, hands, arms, and feet. There were also subjective ratings for different physical attributes, like stamina and the ability to take or deliver a punch. Muscular-skeletal structure was also discussed as it was often used to define the style of fighter standing before the observer. Thin and lanky stylists who used reach, speed, and technique to outpoint an opponent were usually called "boxers," while short and stubby stylists who used short, powerful blows in close to wear down and knock out an opponent tended to be called "fighters." The news was valuable information for gamblers seeking an edge.

But as the new rules gained popularity, readers were treated to long descriptions of fighters' bodies and their regimens. The *Boston Daily Globe* wrote of Dixon during his championship run: "He also stands today as one of the finest developed men in the country, and a number of prominent men who are interested in physical culture have been examining him daily at the gymnasium where he has been training. He has surprised them all by his remarkable 'build.'"[27]

Dixon's physique was often viewed with curiosity. He displayed a bottomless font of energy and, perhaps most obviously, he was a Black man finding unbounded success in a white world. The *New York Herald* wrote of Dixon's domination: "[Dixon] seems to be drawing the color line with great distinctness by thrashing all white pugilists he meets in the ring. Africa will soon want more room on the world's map, with her Peter Jackson, her George Dixon and a colored lad chosen as the orator of a graduating class at Harvard."[28]

The public fascination with both aspects filled the pages of newspapers and the pockets of those entourage members surrounding the champion for more than a decade. Dixon was special. And people could not get enough of the "how and why" behind that fact.

There was a recognition of beauty among the brutality, as the movement within the ring of more than one practitioner of the craft has been compared to that of a dancer. As Wacquant further wrote, a fighter "must constantly monitor every part of his body and synchronize a large number of movements, the placement, orientation and spacing of his feet, his balance and muscular tension, and the course, height, speed and position of his hands, elbows and chin, all while visualizing an opponent firing punches at him in rapid-fire succession of offensive and defensive moves."[29]

That still holds true. Nearly a century later, author and journalist Norman Mailer obsessed over the fighter's form. Every great fighter had a particularly significant part of the body Mailer remembered. He wrote of Joe Frazier: "It was his legs. They were not even like tree trunks, more like truncated gorillas pushing forward, working uphill, pushing forward."[30] Of George Foreman: "[He] had something like Samson's arms—he could pull down the pillars of the temple."[31] Of Muhammad Ali: "He had a face, and the arms to punish anyone who came near that face. He had fast feet. He would play ping-pong better."[32] If Mailer had the opportunity to comment upon Dixon, he surely would have zeroed in one of two areas: Dixon's left hand or his feet.

A handful of years prior to Dixon's passing, Tom O'Rourke approached *The Ring* magazine editor Nat Fleischer seeking his assistance in recording the veteran manager's reminiscences. Fleischer spent many hours with O'Rourke listening to tales of his charges, including Tom Sharkey, Joe Walcott, and especially George Dixon. Those interviews never found their way into a published book. What pieces of those conversations that did eventually emerge (mainly on the pages of Fleischer's *The Ring* magazine) are colorful and sentimental. However, they are not always accurate, perhaps the result of O'Rourke's memory and Fleischer's penchant for mythmaking.

In those remembrances, O'Rourke spoke often of Dixon as a sharpshooter with both hands. But, O'Rourke contended, it was Dixon's left hand that made him special. Dixon boasted the best left O'Rourke had ever seen. His feet were also perfection. Combined with timing and an ability to judge distances, his superb footwork allowed him to feint, duck, and drive forward with a smoothness unseen in the ring at that time.

Dixon was forever known as an innovator in the gym as he perfected those earlier workout regimens, ever more finely tuning his workout. In preparation for a later bout with Solly Smith, Dixon converted a long shed, usually a dining hall for picnickers, at Coney Island, New York, into a makeshift gymnasium for his daily practice. Halfway down the hall, a number of boards were nailed on the cross-joists overheard so that they formed a platform about ten feet in the air. From the center of that platform, a big, leather ball was suspended, which was used in an exercise known as "punching the bag." He had invented the heavy bag, a training device still commonly used in gyms and garages today. Around the gym were scattered dumbbells, Indian clubs, and boxing gloves.

When the Coney Island Athletic Club representative visited the training headquarters, he saw Dixon in mid-routine wearing a close-fitting gym suit, over which he wore a heavy, white sweater. He picked up a pair of dumbbells and began a short march up and down the length of the place. At each step, he threw his hands out in combinations and counters, as if meeting an imaginary foe, and then took the next step. As he finished that exercise, his seconds took down the leather ball and replaced it with an even larger one, pumped up and laced tight. Dixon donned gloves and proceeded to bang the ball with all his might. No matter how quickly the ball rebounded, Dixon met it again. "Faster and more furiously did he strike and the ball, in turn, struck the platform with a noise which could be heard half a mile away," wrote a *Brooklyn Eagle* reporter of what he witnessed. After the ball, he again took the dumbbells in hand and began to go through "the motions of running, though he stood in the same spot on the floor at all times. This was intended to strengthen the legs, and it is practically as good as running in open air. Almost as much physical effort is required, for though one is not advancing, he steps higher than would be necessary in real running." He then repeated the circuit.[33]

These techniques were among the earliest uses of the most common training methods used today—heavy bag, speed bag, and "shadow boxing." All of these innovations were developed by Dixon and O'Rourke. With such revolutionary ideas in training, Dixon was a man in demand. And he did not mind filling it.

Boxing or "self-defense" manuals first appeared in the mid-seventeenth century, but did not take off until the eighteenth and nineteenth centuries, when notions of science entered into pugilistic thinking. Some historians place popular acceptance of the manuals around the time of *A Treatise upon the Useful Science of Defense*, by Capt. John Godfrey, who included a section on boxing in his 1747 book. Although light on details, the work signaled the start of these coaching and training guides in the skills—even in the "science"—of boxing. As they traveled from city to city, professional fighters often provided live boxing instruction to paying local men. Their printed manuals were an additional source of significant income—a "leave-behind" for clients who wished to continue their study.[34] For modern researchers, the manuals provide a detailed record of these boxers' techniques and training practices.

Written during leisure moments and evenings leading up to his Solly Smith bout in September 1893, Dixon's self-published manual, *A Lesson in Boxing*, released that November, was his response to a growing demand. By this time, Dixon had been traveling the country with his vaudeville company for years. At each stop, men approached Dixon and requested private instruction in the art of boxing. But as his company stayed in each city no more than a week, Dixon saw no use in taking on clients as "it would be useless for me to attempt such a thing, as it requires fully a month to obtain even a fair idea of the many points and tricks which one must learn to [illegible] and evade in a set-to with gloves."[35] *Lesson* served as Dixon's solution for training—examples shown through a dozen photos and short descriptions of everything from "The Proper Position" and "A Straight Counter" to the "Pivot" and "Knock Out" blows. Dixon wrote: "I believe every young man should know enough about boxing to protect himself in case of emergency. It is also a splendid exercise and will strengthen and develop the muscles and improve your health, in general, when not practiced to excess."[36]

Dixon's fight stance was studied with religious sincerity—standing erect, head and shoulders slightly back, right hand directly over the heart, left arm extended, cocked at the elbow, fist turned half round. That right was key. He looked as if pledging allegiance to some unseen flag. But while the left attacked, the right protected. Positioned halfway between his head and his waist, Dixon could block an opponent's attempt at a left-hand blow to either the face of the stomach with his well-positioned right. And his heart was always safe.[37]

His arsenal was varied. On the attack, however, he relied on his "three terrible blows": a direct punch to the jugular, a punch to the jaw, and—perhaps his signature blow—a direct shot over the heart.

The heart shot. Dixon considered that his "most effective as well as most dangerous of all body blows,"[38] even if it didn't bring a crowd to its feet like a solid head shot. He tried to draw an opponent to lead with his left hand. Once his opponent was fully extended, Dixon used his left arm to block his opponent's attack, thus exposing an open side. Dixon called it creating "the letter V turned upside down." Once the cross counter was completed, Dixon then countered with a compact right hand just under the heart. It was as painful a blow as any to the body.[39] In that move, Dixon was causing *commotio cordis* (Latin for "agitation of the heart") nearly half a century before researchers identified it as a risk in sport. Although a rare occurrence in boxing, due to the larger surface area of the fist versus, say, a cricket ball or baseball (for which the risk is truly serious), commotio cordis was a stronger possibility in Dixon's era and weight class. Smaller fists, combined with near-nonexistent gloves, could land during the split second in the pumping cycle when the heart was relaxed, a vulnerable moment when a blow to the chest could trigger an irregular heartbeat.[40] In theory, such a blow could have been fatal; although Dixon never struck a lethal one, the heart shot did drop several of his opponents.

Dixon was a master of technique, but of no single school of thought outside his own. His jab was a weapon. He looked for that opening—one that came often, "nine cases out of ten"—when his opponent was so anxious about landing his own left that he forgot to guard his face with his right.[41] As a small but speedy man, Dixon also feasted on body blows, usually delivered with his left. Admittedly the trickiest for him to deliver, he targeted a small circle exactly in the pit of the stomach. He wanted to take an opponent's wind and this was the best place to snatch it. One

shot there reduces mobility, drains endurance, makes it incredibly difficult to breathe or move. That pain, that soreness your opponent cannot
shake off between rounds and nags them throughout the bout. In an era
where bouts could last hours, the body blow was potent, even deadly if
inflicted repeatedly. A relatively unprotected area, the abdomen has no
bony protection, only soft tissue in the form of the abdominal wall, fas-
cial layers, and skin. That is all that stands between your nearly bare fist
and a number of your opponent's vital organs. The most common and
damaging body-blow injury is blow to the solar plexus, that moment
when your opponent gets "the wind" knocked out of them via paralysis
of the diaphragm. At the moment of impact, they feel substantial pain
and acute shortness of breath. Often panic follows because they cannot
breathe normally. That is when you know you have them.

But the most dangerous potential abdominal injury from a body
blow is severe organ damage. A punch to the abdomen could cause fatal
internal bleeding or organ failure. This type of trauma can be deceiving,
even today, as it may start as only mild tenderness. Organs, however, can
hemorrhage slowly for days or weeks before symptoms of dysfunction
or failure show. A blow to the lower back can result in a contused or
ruptured kidney. Blunt trauma to the high abdomen, especially the right
side, can damage the liver. With enough force to the abdomen, intestinal
damage and even bowel perforation can occur. Splenic ruptures are likewise serious and a real possibility.[42]

Reporters noticed Dixon's body blow right away; in numerous stories
they pointed to that driving left into the stomach.[43] When delivering it,
however, Dixon was careful to stand upright, for if he stooped too low or
leaned too far forward with his head, the opponent could land a devastating right to the back of his head.

Dixon never minded a little "give and take." Often, in order to land a
right straight into his opponent's jaw, he opened a crease for his opponent
to return the same blow only with a left. This seemingly even exchange
worked in Dixon's favor not because of his strength, but because of his
speed. The fighter who struck the first blow in this exchange broke the
force of the fighter throwing the second as it stopped the second body's
momentum from coming toward the first.

Although fighting has been fighting for centuries, rule changes have
eliminated some punches from the modern arsenal. For instance, the
"pivot blow" would come as a surprise to modern fighters. Long outlawed,
the blow was controversial even during Dixon's era. To land a pivot, Dixon

waited until his opponent led with his left, aiming at Dixon's face. Dixon then countered by placing his left against the outside of his opponent's attacking left, locking it into place. Then, the instant the arms met and locked, he lifted his right foot and forced his opponent's body to spin around using their own momentum. At that point, Dixon would attack the jaw now sitting wide open due to the locked and twisted body on the man in front of him. Too many things could go wrong with the blow—a missed connect with the left, an opponent jumping back, ducking, or even stepping with the spin. But if it landed, against the odds, it was an effective punch, if slightly dirty by today's standards.

Dixon also relished the beauty of his oddest blow, a comedic, even somewhat improbable swinging trick shot behind the back. He saw it as the prettiest, most scientific counter-blow in his arsenal. It was a punch that, if landed, an opponent scarcely knew how it materialized. To land it, Dixon used the forward momentum of an opponent landing a left to his body. When the opponent ducked Dixon's countering left by moving to their right, they often found themselves with their head too far forward. Dixon then attacked by swinging a right hand behind his back and catching the face of his opponent square from seemingly nowhere.[44]

While the world watched George Dixon, George Dixon locked on his opponent's eyes—not as a form of intimidation, but as a method for divining intent. Some men shifted their eyes sideways or frequently looked down. Dixon knew this was because they were weak and needed a moment's rest. Other fighters used eye movement as a decoy to draw their opponent to the same spot on the floor, thus setting up an opening for a free punch. Dixon never bit at such ploys. Other men shifted their eyes out of pure fear. That was the look Dixon wanted to see—"a dangerous practice, and almost sure to bring the chap who plays it to grief."[45] He used the eyes as the proverbial window into the soul. Or the heart. Or weakening knees.

Dixon thought deeply about his craft. His success mirrored the qualities he saw within himself—heart, endurance, controlled temper, a Spartan fortitude to endure and inflict punishment, the patience of Job combined with the impetuosity of a war horse, speed through "cat-like activity of the foot," and unerring ability to judge distance.

While hard work and training sharpened skills, to Dixon's mind, boxing was an inborn talent. And his was singular. As he wrote of his work:

A fighter, like a poet, is born and not made. Every man can and should learn to box well. But every man, no matter what skill he may acquire, cannot become a premier pugilist any more than he can become a star actor, leading lawyer or eminent physician. The ability to fight, like that of acting, is a natural gift. The ambitious candidate for fistic honors can, of course, improve wonderfully under the tuition of a scientific preceptor, but to become a great fighter, he must possess what actors call that "vital spark" which animates the whole being and impels its possessor, be he author, artist or what not, to constant and diversified thought and action.[46]

These words did not stop men by the thousands from marveling at the ring master, seeking his instruction, guidance, and training to achieve his level of physical perfection.

As his championship reign continued, the scientific aspects of Dixon's body—weight, muscle measurements, lung capacity, movement, endurance—became the subject of intense study for medical practitioners, researchers, and amateur scientists. When he arrived in a city, Dixon was pored over, every detail recorded. (One can imagine O'Rourke saw to it that he received a healthy honorarium for the use of his charge's time.) Always drawn to Dixon, especially on the eve of major fights, journalists chronicled Dixon's training and, occasionally, captured the flavor of some of these research sessions as well. Their presentation to the public was one of awe—marveling at the diminutive but defined champion.

As Dixon became a more advanced fighter, his training became more sophisticated—more scientific—drawing the interests of scholars and researchers. In June 1892, a physician examined Dixon in the presence of researchers "who are making physical culture a special study." A Dr. Brown commenced by testing the strength of Dixon's pectoral muscles with a hand dynamometer. The result was a surprise. The indicator registered 132 pounds. "There's where he gets his hitting power," said the doctor. "The strength of his muscles is wonderful, and they have as much power as a man weighing one hundred and seventy-five or one hundred and eighty pounds." O'Rourke, who weighed close to 200 pounds, tried the dynamometer and registered only ninety-nine pounds. The doctor then tested the traction of Dixon's muscles and another remarkable result was recorded. The register indicated eighty-eight pounds. With the leg dynamometer, he tested the adduction muscles, and the test was equally surprising. He also had a strong grip with both his left and right hands. The test showed them equal at ninety-nine pounds. His lung power was excellent, being 190 pounds. Without inhaling, his chest measured thirty-four and a half inches, and when drawn in it measured thirty-one and a half inches. The depth of his chest was seven and three-quarters inches, and the depth of his abdomen seven and a half inches. His waist was twenty-eight inches; biceps, eleven and a half inches; thigh, nineteen inches; calf, twelve inches. In measuring the forearms, the doctor found that the right was ten inches, and left ten and a half inches. The action of his heart, the doctor reported, showed he was not "an excitable lad." The doctor also examined Dixon's lungs and the muscles of his arms and body and pronounced them in fine shape.[47]

But there was something more to this attention. Yes, the bodies of other boxers were explored on the pages of these publications—just not to the extent or frequency of Dixon's. And admittedly, Dixon was a physical marvel for his size, but certainly not an overly unique or even sideshow oddity that commanded the public's attention during this era. So why the particular, and peculiar, obsession by researchers, newspapers, and the public with Dixon's dimensions over those of his fellow pugilists? To answer that question, look to the roots of these late-nineteenth-century men of science. In their training lies the root of their obsession.

"The body" played a central role in American slavery. Presbyterian minister James W. C. Pennington, a fugitive slave, once argued that the "being of slavery, its soul and body, lives and moves in the chattel principle, the property principle, the bill of sale principle."[48] This reduction of man to merchandise exerted a powerful force that shaped medical encounters between doctors and slaves, and went far in the selection of subjects for experiment, dissection, and specimen harvest.[49] Across the South, slave cadavers were crucial to the development of anatomical teaching and research. Early in the nineteenth century, the South had few medical schools, but by midcentury that started to change. Within these institutions, an understanding of anatomy was conveyed through hands-on dissection. Human remains prepared and preserved as specimens by students and faculty during their education and research formed the nucleus of established college museum collections. Southern medical journals indicate a large portion of the specimens and preparations deposited in the region's medical museums were derived from enslaved subjects. Examining specimen collection and circulation in key locations across the Deep South reveals both the urge to collect and the focus on slave bodies. As was the case with autopsies and surgical experiments, southern physicians faced less public opposition in their appropriation and use of Black bodies as specimens than of white bodies. Already inscribed with the mark of servile status, Black bodies became further targeted and marked by medicine's practice of racializing anatomy and pathology.[50] The Black body carried with it a fascination.

Dixon was more than a mere body—he was a free, Black body in a world still coming to grips with what that meant. Dixon always drew huge audiences to his bouts, performances, or other public appearances. Yet most of his admirers never saw him in person and, instead, counted on the descriptions of press reports to form in their mind the image of a hero. There were pitfalls to that reliance. As Frederick Douglass once said, "Negroes can never have impartial portraits at the hands of white artists," and perhaps that was never truer than when considering Dixon's image in the hands of the era's press, namely the sport's most influential publication, the *National Police Gazette*.

Founded in 1845, the *National Police Gazette* became one of the nation's most popular tabloid magazines of the nineteenth and early twentieth century. With an obvious bias toward scandal and sex, the New York City–based publication targeted male readers wherever they congregated—taverns, barbershops, gambling halls—with bright prose and splashy images in the form of full-page woodcuts. Printed weekly on pink-tinted paper—to stand out from its competitors—the *Police Gazette* became the era's leading "chronicler of debauchery."[51] As with all tabloids, its excessive nature came at someone's expense. Given its main audience, the *Police Gazette* looked to define clear lines between the (predominantly) white men reading the publication and "the others" who were threatening them. Gender and race became its chief lines of delineation. Racism and anti-Semitism abounded in *Gazette* columns, but its treatment of Blacks was particularly ugly. *Police Gazette* publisher Richard K. Fox, who took over the publication in 1876, has been described as a racist, sexist, sensationalist, even a "good hater."[52] Yes, the publication called for the prosecution of those who lynched Black men. But it often covered those same lynchings in a dispassionate voice. The formula worked: during the 1880s and 1890s, the *Police Gazette*'s weekly circulation was one hundred fifty thousand copies.

This figure rose dramatically under Fox's promotion of certain boxing matches. Fox first noticed this in 1880 when coverage of the Paddy Ryan–Joe Goss heavyweight championship bout boosted circulation to more than four hundred thousand copies. Soon afterward, the self-professed "Leading Illustrated Sporting Journal in America" began actively promoting mainstream sports like baseball, rowing, running, and walking, but also focused on contests of aerial jumping, shin kicking, oyster eating, and all manner of other competitions that emerged in the late nineteenth century's brand of masculine competitiveness.

And then there was prizefighting. Nearly thirty percent of the headlines from 1879 to 1906 dealt with boxing, peaking in 1889 at about 60 percent. Fox knew a good thing and was not afraid to exploit it. For George Dixon, this meant massive amounts of exposure not afforded any fighter before him. There were times he could not avoid racist portrayals, such as being rendered as little more than a Black smudge on the page, as in his July 1896 bout with Albert Griffiths, better known as Young Griffo, who fought the champion to a draw in a scientific exhibition of the sport. Illustrations accompanying the article show a shadowy figure, with little definition, fighting a white figure.[53] Simply stated, Dixon was reduced to an ink stain. But then there were the lavish treatments for his championship bouts with equal fanfare for his triumphs, as well as his defeats. There was a genuine, seemingly mismatched, appreciation for the Black champion on the pages of the tabloid. *Police Gazette* sports editor Sam Austin branded Dixon as the "fighter without flaw,"[54] further framing him as "the greatest fighter—big or little—the prize ring has ever known."[55] Dixon's embrace by the publication remains a mystery. It did provide cover from critics who often accused the publication of race baiting and inflaming tensions in cities. How could the publication be viewed as racist if it was so willing to embrace the Black champion?

Perhaps it is important to note that while Dixon was an admired marvel, he was not a threat. Much of his widespread acceptance hinged on his smaller-than-normal stature. He was manageable. As the ideal man grew bulkier in the eyes of the era, a man of Dixon's stature was an oddity, a sideshow, not seen as a challenge to the newly agreed-upon image of the perfect man. That was what he became; that was what he embraced. And it worked for him. Interracial bouts among lower weight classes were widely accepted long after the "color line" was drawn in the heavyweight division. Later, writers who attempted to shame their era's pugilists into crossing the color line often latched onto this nugget. They claimed Dixon, among a handful of his contemporaries, bolstered an argument that the "color line is only a myth."[56] As the *Los Angeles Times* wrote: "Notwithstanding the claims of some prejudiced writers, and weak-kneed dubs who masquerade as fighters, events in the world of sport prove almost conclusively that the famous 'color line' which needs must [*sic*] be drawn to make itself felt, is practically—of course we except the case of Jack Johnson—is practically [*sic*], if not purely, a myth. For the quasi-athlete, who requires an excuse for avoiding an encounter with a worthy foe, the color line comes in handy, but with a big preponderance of the public, this bugaboo does not exist."[57]

Without this acceptance, Dixon's finest moments never would have been possible.

———————

Even for Dixon's contemporaries, few knew what the man looked like; the era and its technology afforded few opportunities to be exposed to the physical boxer beyond what was conjured in the mind. While their work inside the ring, and even on the stage, placed them in front of thousands, what of the tens of thousands of other loyal followers—many of whom, by racial or financial limitations, could not see them perform live? How did they come to understand the physical athlete beyond the printed word? Commercial photography was introduced a half century before Dixon threw his first professional punch. But photographic images remained almost nonexistent in newspapers throughout his career. Enterprising photography studios, like Chickering's, gladly filled that void.

To understand a bit of the motivation for capturing these images, one needs to understand the format the images took. Surviving images of Dixon, as well as many of the fighters of his era, are captured keepsakes like tobacco and cabinet cards, the dominant photographic format of the 1880s and 1890s.

In 1890, Dixon was one of thirty cards portraying top boxers of the era, including John L. Sullivan and James Corbett, issued by the P. H. Mayo & Brother Tobacco Company of Richmond, Virginia. Produced throughout the decade, the small cards, measuring one and a half inches by three inches, were inserted into large tins of loose tobacco. Mayo's Cut Plug Boxers are one of the earliest and rarest of all boxing issues. Along with sets issued by the company for baseball and college football, these cards represent the dawn of sport card collecting. A significant note about this set is its inclusion of four Black men among their white contemporaries, with George Godfrey, Peter Jackson, and Joe Walcott joining Dixon in being immortalized on cheap cardboard. Although Mayo only lasted the decade producing cards, the American Tobacco Company built on the idea and produced higher-quality cards well into the new century. Though rare, these cards survive in collections and form the legacy of many fighters who otherwise would have been forgotten.

The cabinet card has also provided lasting value. The format was brought from England to the United States to buoy a waning public interest in photography after the Civil War. Once studios and patrons embraced them, the cards created a booming collector market. Cabinet cards were generally albumen print photographs from wet-plate collodion negatives that measured four inches by five and a half inches. The images were then mounted on firm cardstock measuring four and a quarter inches by six and a half inches. The extra space created a frame for handling the card without touching the image. The backs of these cards were often blank, but advertising slowly appeared over time. These cards were lucrative commercial ventures, as studios often sold cards depicting royalty, stage and sport celebrities, even erotica, alongside family portraits. But the genius of the format was its universality. Whether produced in Yokohama, Japan, or London, England, or Boston, Massachusetts, the cards fit with similar ease into specially designed albums—yet another revenue stream for a studio. The albums ranged in style from simple velvet covers to elaborate leather-bound versions with music boxes that played when the album was opened. Some featured elaborately hand-painted pages on which cards would be displayed.

Beyond its profit potential, the format allowed for a new style to develop. No longer limited by the diminutive *carte de visite* format of the previous generation, photographers embraced the opportunity to move beyond the simple head-and-shoulders image. Backdrops and props became an important element, often creating seemingly incongruent scenes of people captured in front of an Egyptian desert or icy North Pole, posed beside suits of armor, stuffed birds, even Russian sleighs. Photo studios quickly became dumping grounds for "the dealers of unsaleable idols, tattered tapestry, and indigent crocodiles."[58] Card photos were odd, deeply personal displays, yet what we know of—and infer about—boxers of that era stems directly from these cards.

This was not the typical depiction of Black men to the general public. These images are not far removed from the slave daguerreotypes of Louis Agassiz, a series of fifteen highly detailed images on silver daguerreotype plates showing front and side views of seven southern slaves, men and women, largely naked, taken in Columbia, South Carolina in 1850. These images were designed to analyze the physical differences between European whites and African Blacks, but at the same time they were meant to prove the superiority of the white race. Agassiz hoped to use the photographs as evidence to prove his theory of "separate creation," the idea that the various races of mankind were in fact distinct species.[59]

While Agassiz's images were clothed as science, other images of Black men taken at the same time as Dixon's were nothing more than souvenirs of pain and hatred. Incomplete in itself, the souvenir required "an accompanying narrative," as scholar Harvey Young defined it. For example, a seashell, removed from a beach, can represent a beach vacation. Although the shell carries no real meaning in and of itself, it assumes a symbolic value when a narrative is attached to it. Young wrote: "The souvenir saves the past and represents it in the present."[60] Young later recounts his interview with James Allen, a collector of a series of lynching postcards, who acquired his first images by attending antique fairs and flea markets in the 1970s. Within those spaces, he was then approached by individuals who, in a whisper, would offer to show and sell him various images of lynched figures. Allen remembers, "A trader pulled me aside and in conspiratorial tones offered to sell me a real photo postcard." While it is remarkable that Allen was able to obtain the various images that fill his collection, what fascinated Young, within the context of the accessibility of lynching narratives, are not the pictures on the postcards but the few lines of text that appear on the back of them. Although these words were written in a relatively public forum (a postcard), they signal the types of conversations and exchanges people would have held within a private space. On one card, a son, referring to the image of the burnt body of William Stanley, who was murdered in August 1915, writes to his mother: "This is the Barbecue we had last night, My picture is to the left with a cross over it, Your son." On another, a postcard depicting the March 1910 murder of Allen Brooks, an unidentified author notes: "Well John—This is a token of a great day we had in Dallas, March 3, a negro was hung for an assault on a three-year-old girl. I saw this on my noon hour. I was very much in the bunch. You can see the negro on a telephone pole." These photographs joined the ranks of more troubling souvenirs from these events: pieces of the murdered man, including fingers, toes, genitals, even fragments of bone.

When looking at cabinet cards of Black boxers, however, one quickly notices the even-handed nature of their presentation when compared to their white counterparts. There is no sense of mocking or buffoonery prevalent in other forms of media. Compare these card images of Black boxers to the cartoons and illustrations that appeared in newspapers, ones often depicting Black fighters as animals or mere ink smudges.

Peter Jackson. Albumen silver print on card. Photo by W. M. Morrison, Haymarket Theatre, Chicago. *Courtesy of Special Collections, Fine Arts Library, Harvard University.*

For instance, one popular image of George Godfrey, photographed by Chickering around 1890, shows him in the classic fighter stance, a standard for images of this type, with fists at the ready, a stern countenance, and adorned nattily in white tights, striped belt, and thin loafers. He looks every bit the gentleman boxer of his day. Given Godfrey's popularity, and the respect for the subject with which the image is composed, Chickering would have sold hundreds of these to white and Black fans alike. Photographed by W. M. Morrison around 1890, Jackson, however, was portrayed in another classic pose, a waist-up shot, shirt removed, arms folded, confident glare. What easily could have been loaded with slave subtext instead comes across as respectful, noble in presentation.

This is how many fans came to know their heroes. This was a moment where the image of the fighter—his look, his size—became part of the obsession for the larger public. And in the 1890s, there were few images more obsessed over than Dixon.

CHAPTER 6

Lost in Excess

"BLACK BOHEMIA" DID GEORGE DIXON NO FAVORS. A man increasingly bending to his many weaknesses was unable to resist the smorgasbord of temptations that one of the nation's most notorious hot spots offered nightly. When it came to New York City at the turn of the twentieth century, Manhattan's Black Bohemia differed radically from white-dominated areas of the city. Unlike Brooklyn and lower Manhattan, this area "embodied the newer and more daring phases of negro life."[1] On these streets, visitors found a lively mix of vice and vitality, with clubs packed nightly with free-spending sporting and theatrical people, as well as those hoping to catch a glimpse of those famous patrons.

The neighborhood constituted a part of the famous Tenderloin District and retained the old vices present when whites were its main residents. The Tenderloin was branded as such by the quick wit of one man—New York Police Department Capt. Alexander Williams. The Nova Scotia–born police officer—known less than affectionately as "Clubber"—fully embraced the protection money solicited by police officers from local business folks, including all the unsavory sorts who did not want to draw police attention, across his East Thirty-Fifth Street precinct. "I've been having chuck steak ever since I've been on the force," Williams said, "and now I'm going to have a bit of tenderloin."[2] Also known as "Satan's Circus," the area become a national symbol of urban depravity, noted mainly for its gambling houses, saloons, brothels, shady hotels, and dance halls that stayed open all night. However, beyond vice, a Black entertainment class flourished in the neighborhood—writers, musicians, and entertainers. These individuals were the seeds of the Harlem Renaissance to come as they moved north in the city.

Among the seemingly infinite row of clubs, Ike Hines owned perhaps the best-known cabaret in the city, an institution so iconic it slipped into popular works of the day like Paul Laurence Dunbar's 1902 *Sport of the*

Gods and James Weldon Johnson's 1912 *Autobiography of an Ex-Colored Man*. The club was opulence on a scale rarely seen in Black America. The main floor of the three-story building featured two large rooms: a carpeted parlor and a square back room into which the parlor opened. Small tables and chairs were neatly arranged around the back room. The windows were draped with lace curtains and the walls were covered in photographs of seemingly every Black person in America who had "done anything." There were pictures of politicians and race men, like Frederick Douglass, as well as famed pugilists, like George Dixon, and lesser lights of the prize ring, along with jockeys, stage celebrities, all the way down to the latest song-and-dance teams. In that same back room sat a piano and a bare floor with its center left vacant for singers, dancers, and others who wished to entertain the crowd with their talents. It was a place to see—and to be seen. Literature of the day embraced it as well. As Johnson painted one scene in *Autobiography*:

> These notables of the ring, the turf and the stage, drew to the place crowds of admirers, both white and colored. Whenever one of them came in there were awe-inspired whispers from those who knew him by sight, in which they enlightened those around them as to his identity, and hinted darkly at their great intimacy with the noted one. Those who were on terms of approach immediately showed their privilege over others less fortunate by gathering around their divinity. I was, at first, among those who dwelt in darkness. Most of these celebrities I had never heard of. This made me an object of pity among many of my new associates. I, however, soon learned to fake a knowledge for the benefit of those who were greener than I; and, finally, I became personally acquainted with the majority of the famous personages who came to the "Club."[3]

Many of the men who frequented Black Bohemia earned large sums of money—"easily and spasmodically."[4] One of the popular figures of the scene was the jockey Isaac Murphy, the "Black Archer," whose appearances in New York always caused a stir. Hailed as "America's greatest rider," he won the Kentucky Derby three times—1884, 1890, and 1891—a feat not duplicated until forty years later by Earle Sande, a white jockey. Most riders were from the South, where horse racing began and where Blacks of the servant class were the first stable boys, trainers, and jockeys. To them, Black Bohemia was "the negro metropolis."[5] In time, these men developed into horsemen without peers. When the first Kentucky Derby was run in 1875, there were thirteen Black jockeys in a field of fourteen. Over the next quarter century, seven Black riders won the race eleven times. When the center of racing moved from the South to the East, and Jim Crow laws started to tighten, Black riders were elbowed out. The last Black winner of the Kentucky Derby was Jimmy Winkfield in 1902.

This reflected a larger trend in society—a hysteria over Black gains triggered a radical reaction among white power structures governing sport. Branded the "Jockey Syndrome" by some, this method of disenfranchisement was to simply change the rules of the game when unwanted competition began to gain ground, taking away previously granted rights and diluting access through power, force, and intimidation. Although the term has sporting roots in the systematic elimination of Black men from horseracing, every corner of the nation was seeing a similar effort post-*Plessy*.[6] The Jockey Syndrome shaved years off careers and lives. It created stress and frustration among Black elites in knowing whatever heights and rights they attained could be taken away—in knowing whatever heights and rights one attained could have been higher, if not for artificial barriers erected because of their race.[7]

Many of the Black jockeys threw away incredible sums of money; many were merely small-town boys heady with success, seeking amusement in "the big city." As Johnson wrote:

> I remember one night a dapper little brown-skinned fellow was pointed out to me, and I was told that he was the most popular jockey of the day, and that he earned $12,000 a year. This latter statement I couldn't doubt, for with my own eyes I saw him spending at about that rate. For his friends and those who were introduced to him, he bought nothing but wine; in the sporting circle, "wine" means champagne and paid for it at five dollars a quart. He sent a quart to every table in the place with his compliments; and on the table at which he and his party were seated there were more than a dozen bottles. It was the custom at the "Club" for the waiter not to remove the bottles when champagne was being drunk until the party had finished. There were reasons for this; it advertised the brand of wine, it advertised that the party was drinking wine, and advertised how much they had bought. This jockey had won a great race that day, and he was rewarding his admirers for the homage they paid him, all of which he accepted with a fine air of condescension.[8]

By the turn of the century, jockeys were fading as the big spenders at Ike Hines. While the baseball players were performing in a segregated

league, the Black boxer was flourishing in competition with white opponents and earning great sums. And while few boxers of this period were
residents of New York City, they all found their way to Black Bohemia.
George Dixon was among the most popular fighting visitors—no small
wonder, the *National Police Gazette* reported:[9] "During his career as a
fighter, little George has annexed himself to many a huge bundle of cur-
rency, but unfortunately none of it seemed to have the sticking consis-
tency of an Allcock's plaster, and the result was he separated himself from
it almost as quickly as he got his hands on it. He used to say that a roll of
money in his pocket spoiled the shape of his trousers, and he never used
to carry a checkbook."[10]

Dixon found himself among an elite level of earners during a period
of economic uncertainty for most of the United States. As such, his wealth
was the subject of numerous articles, including some where wire services
estimated the tax bills for famous fighters. In 1895, Jim Corbett topped
the tax list for pugilists with an (admittedly broad) estimated income
ranging between $50,000 to $200,000. Dixon—"doing well, being a business sort of a fellow"—had his income placed at $10,000 for that same
year. His tax bill then, based on paying 2 percent on his income over
$4,000, was $120.[11]

Dixon was also still finding success in the ring, reeling off thirteen
wins, five draws, and three no-decisions before defeating Eddie Pierce on
August 7, 1893, at Coney Island, New York. He was at his peak earning
power. So much so, Dixon took pen in hand to assure his fans that "my
hat fits me as easily now as it ever did." He wrote:

> In my humble opinion, a fighter should confine all his arguments
> to the 24-foot limit accorded him by the usage of the ring. Of late,
> however, it has become the practice of the champions to fight their
> battles in print, as well as in the roped arena. I am not anxious to
> emulate their example, but in the present instance, I am constrained
> to follow them, first, because a legion of friends have requested me
> to make known my true physical condition, and, second, because a
> suspicion has arisen that I have become afflicted with a dangerous
> disease known as "swelled head."[12]

Rumors, however, were already circulating about the champion's condition. And there was substance to them. Dixon blamed this on his "theatrical life." His shows were successful, but that success on the stage was
forcing him to compress his championship fighting into a narrower and
narrower window in order to be on the road as much as possible during

the theatrical season of September to June. As Dixon advised others in an August 1893 article:

> Aside from the social dissipation a successful pugilist is likely to indulge in, the wear and tear of travel, the loss of sleep and the constant strain on the mind and body caused by rehearsals and one or two daily performances are sure to have a deleterious effect upon a fighter's physical resources. Even if he is the strictest kind of a temperance man, he is sure to become weak, inactive and unenduring by the end of the season's arrangements. Should he dissipate even in a minor degree, he will, of course, still further impair his powers and finally become a physical wreck.[13]

What that Eddie Pierce fight lacked in sporting significance and drama, it made up for in its historical timing. The fight took place in the heart of the Panic of 1893—a time when unemployment skyrocketed across the United States. It was one of several panics during the Gilded Age that dragged the country deeper into an economic malaise. Even so, it would have been difficult to understand the depth of the crisis simply by looking at those at ringside. As the *New York Times* reported:

> If the financial men of the country, who have been ill at ease of late over the scarcity of small bills, had paid a visit to the [Coney Island Athletic Club] last night, they would have witnessed a sight calculated to send a thrill of joy to their innermost souls. Bills of all denominations, from the modest single to the crisp hundred, were there in profusion.... Currency may be scarce with bankers, merchants and mechanics, but the sporting men can always find the price to witness a prizefight, and incidentally fish out enough to make a good-sized wager, if called upon to back their judgment.
>
> It was thought some of the sporting men last night were under the impression that the war was not over, judging from the manner in which they flashed fifties, hundreds, five hundreds and thousands, looking for wagers. To say the least, it was a pleasant spectacle and worth a journey to the island even to sit next to the man able to handle thousands like free tickets for a political barbecue.[14]

Unlike previous bouts during better financial times, Dixon-Pierce drew a more mixed, motley crowd—bankers, bunko men, merchants, jockeys, brokers, ball players, mechanics, aldermen, real estate men, trainers, railroad men, horse owners, steamboat captains, bookmakers, lawyers, pickpockets, doctors, green-goods men, journalists, and "men whose methods of eking out an existence even puzzle the police sat shoulder to shoulder and tested their lung power at the least provocation."[15] Dixon's skill remained sharp—"he fights like a piece of machinery"[16]—although the low quality of the opponent had much to do with that. The crowd offered up its loudest cheer, not for Dixon, but for James Corbett and John L. Sullivan, who attended the bout at ringside.

Once protected by his championship status, Dixon was beginning to experience a creeping disdain that other Black fighters had experienced for some time. To say race never colored fights in the North would be unfair. Reporting on the Dixon-Pierce fight was sure to mention the community fallout from the Dixon win: "After the fight, nobody cared to go home on the tally-hos. They were almost empty and went up the Coney Island road like a funeral procession. Several enterprising Fourth Ward gin-sellers bought fireworks to celebrate Pierce's victory. They were not used last night. 'De Fourth'll be in mournin', remarked one of Timothy D. Sullivan's constituents. 'Yes,' answered his companion, 'worse'n dat, De Fourth Ward'll be broke for some time to come, and the niggers'll be playn' policy wid our money. It's tough, ain't it?'"[17]

Just two weeks later, the Dixon Era experienced its first real fissure when the "Napoleon of the prize ring for the past half dozen years, met his Waterloo in Madison Square Garden."[18] On August 22, 1893, Billy Plimmer, a bright-faced chap from Birmingham, England, hammered the champion in a four-round, non-title-fight exhibition. Dixon was not in his usual superb condition, while his opponent was trained to perfection.[19]

Although the race issue always hovered, Dixon encountered increasing agitation as time went by. His fears were no longer limited to the South. Unlike his earlier career, where race appeared only in a description of Dixon, newspapers started reporting how race was a factor in the bouts, not just among the crowds, but the officials as well. The *New York Times* wrote, "It was plainly evident that the race prejudice was very strong. Plimmer is a foreigner, but nine-tenths of those present wanted to see him win."[20] Following the bout, it was a minute before the master of ceremonies rendered addressed the crowd. Cries of "Plimmer! Plimmer!" resounded. Finally, when order was restored and the decision was announced, the Englishman went over to Dixon's corner and shook the conquered gladiator's hand. This was the signal for another outburst. A mob surrounded Plimmer, picked him up, threw him from one to another, patted him, hugged him, kissed him on the forehead, and told him he was "the greatest little man in the world." The men were frantic with joy. Twenty-five policemen pounded and prodded a lane through the throng, and Plimmer was carried downstairs from the ring to the main floor. Some two hundred enthusiasts left in the ring tore down the stout, wooden posts, six inches thick, in joy. Dixon got to his dressing room after much difficulty.[21]

Dixon's work ethic was immediately called into public question. As the *National Police Gazette* reported: "A champion who has been successful and never met defeat is very foolish to attempt to win on time, for he believes he can fight four rounds without training, and when he enters the ring, he meets his opponent in the best condition, and in spite of his superiority as a boxer, he is handicapped and, in my opinion, this was Dixon's case when he fought Plimmer. Dixon supposed he did not have to train very hard to defeat Plimmer in four rounds, and when he toed the scratch, he discovered his mistake."[22]

Even following victories, questions of desire dogged Dixon for the remainder of his career. Despite some uneven performances, however, he maintained his winning ways. His bouts continued to feature action, as well as the oddities of turn-of-the-century pugilism—random arrests, strange endings, and general chaos. For instance, Dixon started slowly against "Solly" Smith on September 25, 1893, sleepwalking through six rounds, until the seventh, when he splayed Smith across the canvas. Ringside observers said Dixon pulled a "Doctor Jekyll and Mr. Hyde act. From a most passive colored youth, he changed to a demon bent on doing mischief. His eyes flashed and he stood in front of the pugilistic member of the Smith family like a conquering hero."[23] A beaten and bruised Smith was then arrested following the bout while changing into his street clothes—not on charges of the fight that closed moments before, but for a previous bout he had fought in Roby, Indiana. Later, Dixon's fight against Billy Murphy on January 5, 1896, nearly ended in a riot after Murphy punched the referee who stepped between the two clenched fighters to pry them apart. Enraged, the referee then threw a right-left combination to Murphy's face, who was knocked back into the ropes. The crowd was sent into an uproar, only to have the fight ended by police who entered the ring to separate referee and boxer. Amid "wild disorder," Dixon was awarded a knockout on a punch he did not even deliver.[24]

Were one looking for an opponent against whom Dixon's stature seemed to erode, his invincibility seemed in question—even his standing among the best of the Black fighters of his size went unchallenged—then look no further than Walter "Kentucky Rosebud" Egerton. The North Carolina–born, Philadelphia-based boxer with the Bluegrass

State nickname had numerous battles with Dixon, exciting exhibitions of a handful of rounds. Egerton earned a certain amount of fame from a March 1894 bout with Dixon, as reports from it were carried around the world because of a rare—and incorrectly billed as "the first"—Dixon knockdown.

Dixon had been knocked down in previous bouts. That is not in question. The only debate was over definition. In order to maintain maximum drawing power, O'Rourke and Dixon would shrug off each knockdown as a stumble, a fall, a slip, a tumble—never a knockdown. But it was more bluster and reputation preservation than fact. Egerton knocked Dixon down more than once before that 1894 bout. Rosebud first dropped Dixon in the third round of a four-round exhibition on October 29, 1892 at the Ariel Club in Philadelphia.[25] The challenger's performance was so celebrated by the crowd of four hundred that night, that he was carried from ringside on the his supporters' shoulders. Then Rosebud repeated the knockdown feat on November 11, when he landed a right to Dixon's heart in the second round and sent the champion to the ground again during their bout at the Lyceum Theater in Philadelphia.[26] The Dixon myth was shattering—and it was coming at the hands of an extremely skilled Black fighter. That first pitched battle between two Black men after the Carnival led more than one ringside report to say Rosebud would have made a far more interesting Carnival opponent than Skelly.[27] Dixon raged against the reports of his knockdown. "He never knocked me down. Whenever I rushed him, he ducked and I fell over him on the floor from the force of my lead. I can lick that fellow any day. I'll admit, however, that he is a very clever lad."[28]

While the March 1894 bout did not feature Dixon's first knockdown, Rosebud's blow was Dixon's first recorded knockout. Although the exhibition had no official decision, reports show Dixon was out cold for up to five minutes after taking a punch from Rosebud. The blow sent Dixon backward, where he struck his head on the floorboards. When the champion did not move, the referee dragged Dixon's body to the corner, where O'Rourke lifted him onto a chair. He was not simply dazed, but unconscious for a full two minutes before he opened his eyes. O'Rourke sprinkled a sponge soaked in ammonia over Dixon's head to revive him. Dixon required five minutes between the second and final round of the exhibition before he could continue.[29] Despite all ringside reporting to the contrary, Dixon and his team tried to make the difficult argument that this again was not a fair knockout, O'Rourke claiming that "Dixon started to rush, and that the Rosebud held up his elbow, and Dixon ran his chin against it. Dixon does not claim that Dixon was not knocked out, and he said: 'I am glad it happened, although it was an accident.' It may be the best thing that happened to George."[30]

Rosebud's stock would never be higher. He boasted about the knockout at public appearances for weeks afterward and even traveled to Boston for a series of exhibition appearances billed as "The Man Who Knocked Out Dixon." A *Boston Daily Globe* ad proclaimed, "The unqualified champion of his class and the cleverest fighter living at one hundred and eighteen pounds; the plucky and clever boxer who knocked out the featherweight champion of the world—George Dixon—who was compelled to lower his colors to the redoubtable Rosebud in the hottest fight on record and who stands ready to meet any man (Dixon preferred) at his weight in a finish fight."[31] He played to sold-out houses for two weeks. For years, he made a series of public challenges of Dixon to a fight-to-the-finish bout.[32] No more exhibitions for Rosebud; he wanted a shot at the title. He would never get that shot. While they fought five exhibitions over three years, Dixon repeatedly dodged Rosebud's calls for an official bout.

But those Rosebud fights amplified murmurs about Dixon's "staleness" as a fighter.[33] Macon McCormick of the *Wheeling (West Virginia) Register* wrote: "It begins to look as though that wonderful little boxer, George Dixon, is 'going back' a bit.... The Rosebud is the most conceited coon in the ring, and I don't wish his opponent would half knock his head off for his monkey shines. He can fight, though, and he is as tricky as a snake."[34]

It was not that Dixon was handling too many official bouts, or even entirely the hard living, but the number of exhibitions as part of his traveling show that was exacting a terrible wear and tear on his body, in the name of capitalizing upon his highest level of fame following the Carnival. The papers were noticing: "Dixon is meeting too many lads in his variety show act of 'meeting all comers.' His hands cannot certainly be kept in good condition with such work, and some nights he is likely to go up against some tough nut who may do him with a punch or two. Stranger things than that have happened in the ring, and all newspaper men of experience know that it is the impossible that is always coming to pass."[35] Or reported again: "I don't think Dixon's hands would stand a long fight. He has used them so much in these four-round bouts that they are no longer the weapons they were."[36]

Dixon's vaudeville-and-specialty company was a major attraction during the champion's decade-long reign and is primarily responsible for the seemingly impossible figure of one thousand career bouts. In advance of the troupe arriving in town, a notice was posted that $50 would be given to any person who could stand up before Dixon for four rounds. That appeal to masculinity and racial superiority consequently attracted large crowds to his nightly events. At the close of the show, Tom O'Rourke introduced Dixon, who boxed four rounds with one of several traveling pugilists, as well as accepting numerous challenges from the audience. During these engagements, Dixon fought hundreds of men whose names will never again be known. He met all comers and agreed to forfeit substantial sums if he failed to save a knockout, or at least soundly defeat his opponent. Dixon often fought fifteen men irrespective of size in the same night—an immeasurable toll on his small frame.[37]

One young man, plucked from the crowd in Springfield, Connecticut, ran from the stage after Dixon's landed his first punch. More often than not, the crowd exited before the final round was finished.[38] Another night, local pugilist Patrick Hennessey took the challenge at the Lawrence Opera House in New York City. Like so many before him, and so many after, he proved no match for the skilled Dixon. Hennessey took a sound beating—dropped to the floor by an uppercut, and then nearly knocked unconscious, in the first round. He stumbled into the second round, where Dixon bloodied his nose and mouth and unleashed further damage, prompting the theater's manager to step in and stop the fight. Hennessey was carried from the ring to a dressing room, where it took him nearly an hour to recover. The beating was so vicious, even the law could no longer turn its usual blind eye and accept what took place on stage as merely an exhibition; warrants were issued for both Dixon and Hennessey on charges of assault. Both men were found guilty and fined in police court the following day. Ever the showman, Dixon's appearance before the judge caused great excitement and packed the courtroom with spectators. These stage performances did not always end in victories for Dixon. On one occasion, Martin Morarity of Lowell, Massachusetts, lasted four rounds with the champion. Dixon willingly awarded his $50 to the local pugilist.[39]

In addition to boxing exhibitions, the Dixon road show included a singing duo who worked with a trained dog, sketch comedy, burlesque, acrobatics, and comedians. Admittedly, song-and-dance was the strength of the playbill, as the boxing exhibitions were often one-sided or uninspired. The biggest draw, however, was not the champion—it was "The Human Frog."[40] William Delhauer, the greatest contortionist of his day, built his fame as a member of the team Guyer and Delhauer and toured the world in the late 1880s as the "Clown and the Frog." Delhauer's "suppleness of limbs and his apparent absence of a backbone made his frog specialities seem like fabled metamorphoses."[41] His act was so popular, and so often imitated, that he required a name change to "The Original Human Frog" during his later Dixon tour. In January 1897, Delhauer was found dead in his Chicago hotel room. He had been in poor health for some time, yet continued to tour. His death was attributed to a sudden hemorrhage in his lungs caused by violent coughing.[42]

Dixon's theater troupe landed for extended stays in cities across the country, gracing the same stages and performing for the same audiences as minstrel shows and vaudeville acts. The fact that these latter performances were heavily tinged with race was no coincidence. Blacks have been depicted through caricature since the seventeenth century, but the popularity of these distorted representations grew wildly through the 1800s. Developed in the North, these shows reflected the fear of Black progress in the post-Reconstruction period. American audiences were obsessed with the blackface minstrelsy that dominated these shows. For many white theatergoers, who had few to no day-to-day interactions with other races, these dangerous and degrading characterizations broadly came to represent Black Americans. White actors dressed in wild costumes, painted on exaggerated features, acted with buffoonery. Presented notions of a lazy, oversexed race took root in the minds of white America. All these images and stereotypes were used to evoke notions of Blacks as hopelessly unfit for the normal society to which they sought entrance.[43] Among minstrel characters, the most popular were Rastus, Tom, Buck, Zip Coon, Sambo, and, of course, Jim Crow.

With the rise of mass production, stereotyped imagery appeared everywhere from newspaper pages to song sheets to food labels, making the blackfaced minstrel a permanent part of the American landscape. This imagery further reflected and reinforced white supremacy while causing Black America immeasurable pain.

This was not an exclusively white craft. Shortly after the Civil War, Black performers capitalized on white America's desire for minstrel shows, marketing themselves as "authentic darkies" and "Ethiopian delineators." Historian Karen Sotiropoulos speaks of a cohort of Black artists who came of age during the rise of Jim Crow in the 1890s. They brought Black music and dance to America cities at the same time that intellectuals and activists like Ida B. Wells and W. E. B. Du Bois were developing new strategies in the struggle for the citizenship rights that Emancipation and Reconstruction had failed to bring. These performances were the price of participation in public life—a careful monitoring and appeasing of white audiences. Black artists thus conformed to white expectations by using the conventions of the newly popular vaudeville stage—including blackface makeup—in their productions. While "blacking up" was arguably dangerous in its implications, these Black artists played to the white desire for racist stereotypes in order to participate in the theater. Always conscious that they were performing stage types, however, they manipulated the stage mask in innovative ways that helped them forge a space for dialogue with their Black audiences—dialogue that included both assertions of Black nationhood and critique of the racism that perpetuated stereotyped imagery.[44]

Such was the price Dixon paid. While not required to make up his face, his body was sacrificed to the audience night after night, diminishing a career in the name of participation. How strange a sight—the greatest Black boxer of his generation reduced to sharing a stage designed to degrade his race.

On August 19, 1895, a "boxing and bag-punching tournament" was broken up at the Academy of Music in New York City when Mike Leonard got a bit overzealous in his exhibition match with Dixon, charging the champion and throwing him to the floor twice. In mid-bout, police on site arrested Leonard, Dixon, O'Rourke, and three others. Magistrate Kudlich of the Yorkville Police Court discharged Dixon and fined Leonard $10 on a charge of disorderly conduct. Leonard appeared in court, but Dixon sent word from a hotel that a large crowd had gathered and was planning to follow him all the way into court. The magistrate sent back word that Dixon should remain in his hotel to await the decision.[45] The case demonstrated the inconsistencies—and sheer dark comedy—associated with policing fighting in the era:

> The examination was conspicuous for the admitted ignorance of the police official and his subordinates. The former swore that he had never attended a prizefight, but had witnessed several sparring matches; he did not know that gloved contests were permissible under the law; nor was he cognizant of the fact that the Amateur Athletic Union holds boxing tournaments annually, in which gloves, similar to those worn by Dixon and Leonard, are used. He claimed

to be unable to tell where scientific boxing ends and when "slugging" begins, and admitted his inability to tell the difference between a cross-counter and uppercut and yet this individual, a product of the reform agitation which is now shaking the Metropolis to its very core, and disgusting the people who made it possible for such a condition of affairs to exist, presumed to the extent of arresting two alleged offenders upon no other excuse than he "thought the law was being violated."[46]

Admittedly, Leonard was known for his overzealousness. During his next fight, Baltimore police stopped the bout after he resorted to fouling his opponent. Newspapers called for Leonard to be blacklisted from every reputable club in the country.[47]

Noticeable cracks in Dixon's once spotless technique were developing. Buffalo, New York–based boxer Frank Erne threw Dixon a "surprise party" during a scientific exhibition bout on December 5, 1895, in New York City's New Manhattan Athletic Club. Dixon's speed was waning; his punches were no longer beating his opponent's attempts to block; his grunts were louder and more emphatic as blows that would once find empty space were now landing squarely on his face. The bout was a draw. Dixon's followers were stunned.[48]

Throughout this run of events, race was a growing specter for Dixon. While it was viewed as a novelty in his early days, public sentiment was shifting. Under O'Rourke's heavy hand, Dixon had always "known his place" in society, and his manager was quick to make mention of that fact in the press. As the *National Police Gazette* reported: "Nearly every time Dixon has been pitted against a champion, no matter whether foreign or native, the majority has named Dixon for the loser, probably through prejudice, owing to his color, and yet, he has won. There was a transaction between Dixon and his white audience—Dixon minded his temper, never boasted, played the 'Uncle Tom' expected of him, and his white backers and fans would sing his praises. But step out of line, and he would be roasted. His high-profile contemporaries felt similar pressures, namely the heavyweight Peter Jackson, who often found himself in Dixon's corner."[49]

Always a lover of a good time, Dixon increasingly celebrated his victories with or drowned his troubles in alcohol. That led to numerous confrontations with police. Troubling for Dixon was the fact that his personal demons—drinking, gambling, violence—were clashing with public sentiment toward Blacks in the wider society. His celebrity—and an increasingly frustrated O'Rourke—no longer shielded him. He was locked up in New York City's Grand Central Station police substation at 1:15 p.m. on May 18, 1895, and charged with being drunk and disorderly after purchasing tickets back to Boston. Dixon and a friend had spent most of their pre-boarding time in a saloon, which resulted in Dixon becoming aggressive and insulting.[50] The champion entered the train's parlor car and took his seat next to an older white man, who then protested "he would not ride in a car with a nigger. Another passenger echoed this sentiment, and Dixon resented it. Loud words were entered into, and as Dixon had been drinking a little, he showed the excitement plainly under which he labored."[51] An officer soon intervened, but not on Dixon's side. Dixon and company were removed from the train for continued aggressive behavior and profanity. Once back in the station, Dixon insulted a police officer and was removed by force from the premises. The *National Police Gazette* reported: "Dixon is not a quarrelsome lad, even after indulging in a glass or two more than his tankage capacity warrants. He has ever been peaceful and gentlemanly. That he lost his temper when publicly insulted is not to be wondered at, but that he gave vent to his feelings in language that could be construed as ungentlemanly is deplored."[52] This would not be his last clash with police. As John L. Sullivan said of his friend: "I'd give a good deal to have hooked Dixon up with me to the water wagon, but he was too far along the road when I tried to get him to make the swift change—poor fellow."[53]

Reporting on Dixon's decline continued in 1895, when his compounding failure of betting on and buying up Thoroughbreds was widely ridiculed.[54] By the next year, his drinking had become a source of public concern. His on-again-off-again relationship with O'Rourke did not help either. The two men were often at odds—verbally, physically. Dan Saunders, another Boston sporting man, occasionally stepped in to manage Dixon during extended separations from O'Rourke. He pressed for Dixon to reform his behavior, but to no avail.[55] Saunders joined a chorus of voices begging Dixon to slow down. In July 1898, John L. Sullivan urged Dixon "to quit, before, like myself, he is a 'has-been.'"[56]

But Dixon did not slow. After a few years of success, Dixon began to frequent Black Bohemia and, by the time he became a regular, he was bleeding money into the district's many establishments. The ponies got some; George couldn't resist craps; and then there was booze to be bought at high prices for everybody.[57] And he drank—"the poor boy can hardly be blamed for this, because in the circles in which he moved, to open wine, that is, to buy and drink large quantities of champagne is considered the only real manner of the gentleman."[58] Dixon would tear off $5,000 as his share of a win and it would disappear, one way or another, in a few days. "Dixon got rid of his money faster than any fighter I ever knew, except myself," Sullivan wrote. "They used to call him the John L. of his class, and the name fitted him more ways than one."[59] Dixon's exploits outside the ring were gaining far more notoriety than those inside it.

No longer an inspiration, he became a cautionary tale for Black America. As the *National Police Gazette* warned: "There is a great and constantly growing class of athletic men in this country who will find that it pays to study the case of little George Dixon. These are the fellows who for a few years are noted amateur boxers, runners, jumpers, football or rowing men in universities, colleges, schools and athletic clubs. There are, in all this country, at least a million young or middle-aged amateur athletes who will find that it pays to study the history of poor George Dixon."[60] He was a champion on the decline. But, as Dixon pointed out often in defense of himself, he was a champion nevertheless. He and his many benefactors still basked in the benefits of that standing.

––––––––––

Dixon was now a fading star. He did not score a victory in the latter half of 1896—two draws were followed by a twenty-round decision loss to Frank Erne at the Broadway Athletic Club, New York, on November 27, 1896. Erne stood up to Dixon's fierce rushes "like a man and was not afraid to mix things up."[61] Even so, ringside observers pointed to the fact Dixon had undoubtedly declined in strength, for Erne was able to stop his rushes with hard clinches and straight lefts that almost always landed on the face. By fight's end, Dixon was badly used up. Both eyes were almost closed while his nose and ear were all puffed. Erne, on the other hand, did not bear a mark or a bruise and retired from the ring almost as fresh as he entered it. John Boden of the *New York Press* summed up Dixon thusly: "Dixon showed his old-time aggressiveness from the start, but he was not the springing wildcat of other days. It was the old story of the pitcher going to the well once too often. . . . He was certainly not the wonder of old."

Many were not surprised, then, when on October 4, 1897, Solly Smith outpointed Dixon in a twenty-round bout in San Francisco. Smith weighed 120 pounds—two pounds over the featherweight limit—but O'Rourke and Dixon agreed to put the title on the line anyway. After

Smith was announced as the winner, O'Rourke walked Dixon back to his dressing room, only to spin around once he reached the door, and rush back to ringside to corner Smith's manager. O'Rourke explained: "Ed, Dixon did not lose the championship tonight because Smith came in over the Featherweight limit."

Ed Smith looked O'Rourke in the face and roared with laughter: "That's my boy, Tom, always playing the corners, never missing a trick."

"I'm not joking, Ed. I mean what I say. I'm going to claim the title."

"You'll never get away with it."

In the next day's newspaper, O'Rourke bought space for an advertisement that read, in all capital letters: "George Dixon is still champion. The fight last night was fought at catchweights[62] and the challenger was three pounds over the weight."[63] But despite O'Rourke's bluster—and expense—the press was already hailing the American as the new featherweight champion. Smith's reign did not last long, as he lost the title a year later when he broke his arm in a bout against Dan Sullivan. Dixon then regained it by knocking Sullivan out in ten rounds on November 11, 1898, in New York City. The bout did not signal the return of Dixon, as Sullivan lost the bout not by his own hand—or even Dixon's—but because of his brother, Jack Sullivan. Dan warned his brother away, as he felt like he was coming back in the fight, but Jack—believing time was up in the tenth round—jumped into the ring, forcing the referee's hand to disqualify Sullivan. With that victory however, Dixon, set another first for his sport by becoming the first champion of any weight class to lose and then regain his title.[64]

Nevertheless, Dixon's decline was becoming more and more apparent, even to those outside boxing's inner circles. His public appearances were starting to suffer. He was no longer dispatching inferior fighters with ease; now they lingered, forcing the champion into later and later rounds, even dealing out physical punishment Dixon had seldom experienced. Good bouts were followed by terrible showings.

On January 17, 1899, Australian Black featherweight William Dudley Brown, bearing the nickname "Young Pluto," made his American debut against Dixon at the O'Rourke-run Lenox Athletic Club in New York City. The South African–born Brown was the first native of that country to fight for a world title. Dixon-Brown was also the first title match between a Black champion and a Black challenger.[65] Fight observers warned Dixon that Brown was a "very clever boxer up, up to many new tricks"—a defensive specialist who fought off Dixon's aggressive advances until a left to the stomach dropped Brown for good in the tenth round. It took him nearly half a minute to regain consciousness from the blow.[66] The headlines read the next day: "Kangaroo Colored Man Drops Like a Hard-Hit Bird." Adding insult to injury, Brown's trainers, William Akers and Williams Shannon, both of San Francisco, stole their boxer's $325 purse. When Brown confronted them about his share, they knocked him down, beat him, kicked him, and threw him out of the room. When he took his complaint to O'Rourke, manager and operator of the venue, he was told that nothing could be done for him; the money had been given to his trainers. Brown later appeared at police headquarters and was accompanied back to the venue with a detective. The following day, Brown appeared in New York City Police Court and was granted a summons against his two trainers.[67] The papers did not follow the results of that case. Brown went on to lose his next six bouts in the United States and United Kingdom. He retired from the sport in 1911 to run a poultry farm in Australia.

On August 11, 1899, Dixon barely earned a draw over Eddie Santry of Chicago at O'Rourke's Broadway Athletic Club. During pre-fight introductions, John L. Sullivan was called through the ropes to thunderous applause. The house shook as "the grizzled bruiser clambered through the ropes and displayed a paunch which eloquently declared that he had turned his back on 'the boxing business.'"[68] Sullivan had only recently opened an uptown saloon, so the venerable showman and tireless self-promoter took the opportunity to advertise the fledgling establishment. "Gentlemen, when I was in the boxing business, I tried to do the best I could," he said. "However, I'm in a new business, and I've quit the arena, and if you'll come up to my place and drink some o' the booze I sell there, I'll guarantee it'll knock ye clean out."[69] As for the fight, however, it was an unpopular affair. Not a single spectator felt Dixon won— and "hundreds of them put their opinions into vigorous language." The announcement of the draw was made as "groans and hisses resounded over the house, and shouts of 'Robber! Robber!' freely arose."[70]

The fight was a savage affair. Dixon's eye was cut badly in the fourth round, and his opponent continued to target the wound for the remainder of the bout. Damage to the eye was so severe, in fact, doctors were forced into patching up the injury on site, warning Dixon if he didn't take the best of care of himself during the time he would need to undergo treatment, he could lose sight in the eye.[71] The crowd was already irritated when the originally scheduled twenty-five-round bout was shaved down to twenty rounds. There were cries of "Fake!" when the announcement was made about the decision that ultimately favored the waning Dixon.

As this fight, and many others, were starting to expose, Dixon's career was hitting uneven patches, and his personal demons were taking over. With an increasingly frustrated O'Rourke at his side, Dixon was slowly being exposed to the fate many Blacks had been experiencing for years across the country. His popularity no longer shielded him from social reality. But so long as he was still a champion, and therefore a box office draw, there was money to be made and utility left in him for those driving his career.

CHAPTER 7

In Common Sorrow

TERRY MCGOVERN NEVER enjoyed being called a "star in the constellation of burlesque queens."[1] Yet, he was. He was the headliner on a popular show, drawing in a large female following. He was a matinee idol of some standing, a popular figure in New York for his talent and charm. Nevertheless, he was happy to receive word in October 1899 that he was matched to meet George Dixon for the featherweight championship of the world.

A Pennsylvania-born, Brooklyn-raised featherweight, McGovern was the oldest of three fighting brothers. He was a feared puncher who recorded thirty-eight knockouts in his first sixty-two fights. He was ferocious, not fancy, more brawler than ballroom dancer. As a laborer in a lumberyard, McGovern's boss encouraged him to become a fighter. He turned pro in 1897 at the age of seventeen. Within two years, he was a contender for the vacant world bantamweight title. He faced British bantamweight champ Pedlar Palmer for the crown in September 1899. Though previously unbeaten, Palmer could not last one round with the solid-punching McGovern, who knocked him out in less than two minutes.[2] Beaten mercilessly by McGovern, Palmer fought back against claims he took a dive, instead maintaining he lost sight of his opponent in the newly installed lights at ringside. And he may have had a point: filmmaking was becoming commonplace—and a distraction—in and around the ring.

Almost as soon as motion pictures were invented, filmmakers were drawn into the ring. The sport offered combat in confined space, drama within a single frame. It was the same love affair television producers would have with boxing a generation later. Based in Thomas Edison's Black Maria Studio in West Orange, New Jersey, W. K. L. Dickson's Kinetoscope Pictures brought in professional fighters to spar five or six rounds while technicians recorded their actions in ninety-second installments. Those

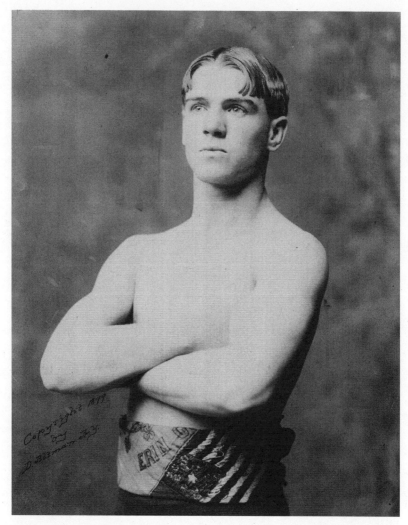

Terry McGovern. Photo by D. Altman. *Courtesy of Special Collections, Fine Arts Library, Harvard University.*

films were sold to owners of "peep-hole" parlors, popular in the mid-1890s, where patrons paid a quarter to see five rounds of boxing displayed on five separate Kinetoscope machines.[3] The popularity of these films exploded; seemingly any recording of a prizefight between figures of even passable significance promised substantial profits.

However, like the corruption that defined prizefighting at the time, by the turn of the century cinematographers had gained a dubious reputation—and O'Rourke was at the heart of it. The issue boiled down, as it always did, to money. Control of the distribution—be it to the parlors or private hands—meant control of the money. It also depended on how fast you could get the film to market. There was a direct financial correlation between showing a film in the weeks immediately after a fight, while interest was still high, instead of months later. Seeing opportunity, O'Rourke dabbled in films from the start. He co-presented the Jim Jeffries–Tom Sharkey fight in November 1899—the first indoor fight ever successfully filmed. The mounted lights for filming were so close to the ring and so hot that the fighters' hair was singed.

Harnessing McGovern's popularity, the American Sportagraph Company made plans to capture the McGovern-Palmer fight using the most advanced technology of the time. Cameras, printers, and projections were specially commissioned; a unique, wide-gauge film stock was employed; a proprietary machine for reproduction was designed and built. Plans called for the fight film to serve as the main event of a three-hour show playing in opera houses across the country, alongside footage of yacht races, wrestling matches, foot races, and other sporting spectacles, accompanied by live vaudeville acts. What was captured on film was "superior in technical quality to a previous fight film."[4] Yet when the fight lasted less than a round, the footage was deemed nearly unusable. The company had film of the fighters preparing for battle, the coin toss for corners, the donning of the gloves, and the introduction of dignitaries and the referee, but so little actual fighting that the film was a financial boondoggle.[5] Nevertheless, McGovern found his way under the klieg lights again soon afterward.

On the eve of the McGovern fight, Dixon was confident. He had heard the grumbling about his decline—and saw it manifested in two-to-one odds offered in favor of his opponent. He admitted McGovern was "young and strong and clever. But I'm not an old man myself."[6] Dixon told the press, "This is not meant for bragging, but I simply want to cheer up my friends who may be scared half to death by all the talk about betting two-to-one on McGovern. I have been taking care of myself for a year now, so that when I began to train hard a month ago I was in good shape right at the start."[7] The bout was scheduled for twenty-five rounds on January 9, 1900, at the Broadway Athletic Club in New York City in what would be the first championship battle ever fought on Manhattan Island with the sanction of law.[8]

Four hours before the fight, men clamored outside the club for any kind of seat. A month earlier, Dixon announced he would retire following the fight, in order to become the proprietor of a "swell boozing den in the heart of the Tenderloin."[9] That thought only drove interest higher in perhaps seeing the ring great's final bout. Originally to be sold at $5, $8, $10, $15, and $20, ticket prices skyrocketed, with some going as high as $75 each. A pair of $15 seats sold for $120 on the sidewalk in front of the club, while another would-be spectator paid $250 for three seats that originally cost $60. "The crowd seemed money mad," the *New York Times* wrote.[10] Eventually, forty-eight hundred people wedged into the four-thousand-seat room; it was the largest crowd ever to witness a boxing match in New York City.[11] Spectators from Wall Street had snapped up the box seats immediately, leading many VIPs to sit in the back of the room. John L. Sullivan was in attendance, but had a seat in the rear, along with other former greats who expected better treatment.

From the opening bell, the Brooklyn fighter was by far the better man. The *Washington Post* described the scene as the moment when "age bent the tottering knee of surrender to youth's bloom and vigor when the little mulatto gladiator fell to his doom."[12] Starting in the first round, McGovern landed blow after blow on Dixon's midsection. He dedicated most of his efforts to battering Dixon's abdomen and ribs, smashing him over the kidneys during the clinches—the hardest blows he'd ever taken, he later attested.

After three rounds, Dixon's strength started to wane. He moved slower and slower. The champion was completely puzzled by McGovern in close and unable to counter in any way. Dixon must have known after the fifth round he had no chance to win. Nevertheless, he faced certain defeat with "a gameness and persistence to which no amount of praise can do justice."[13] "That was George Dixon," O'Rourke said years later, "the little man with the chocolate-colored skin and the heart as white as the undriven snow."[14]

Now heading into the sixth round, O'Rourke had been asking for several rounds to signal the fight's end by throwing in the sponge. But Dixon did not allow it. "Don't, Tom. Don't stop it," he begged. "Haven't you even seen me knocked off my pins before? Leave me alone and give me a chance. I'll get him."[15] Down again in the sixth, Dixon knew it was over, yet he was determined to take his punishment. Just then, he heard McGovern say in a low voice, "Get up, George, I won't hurt you." Dixon's mind flashed on the many times he had opponents in similar helpless conditions, and he knew the importance of those words. From that moment, Dixon acknowledged later, he admired McGovern perhaps more than any other man he had ever met or seen in the ring.[16]

When Dixon returned to his corner after the sixth, he began to vomit blood. "What's the matter, George? Has he hurt you inside?" O'Rourke asked.

"No," Dixon said. "I'm all right. That tooth I had this morning bled steadily almost up to ring time. The first sock Terry hit me started my jaw bleeding again. I've been swallowing blood so that he wouldn't think he has hurt me."[17]

He survived the seventh round, and then training, muscle memory, and pride brought Dixon from his corner in the eighth. Dixon had recovered "a little of his jaunty air, but only a little."[18] His legs were mush as he walked flat-footed across the ring. McGovern boasted a "studious, keen, anxious expression on his face, and started after him like a hungry creditor."[19] Dixon's punches found only air. As the *Washington Post* described it:

> The scene of pugilistic death was so deeply pathetic that the stout heart of his conqueror felt, almost wept, for him. For prize-fighters have hearts, even though they be sometimes termed human brutes. It was plain to every feverish throbbing soul on the "mountain" and "plain" around the ring that Dixon was in for the last stroke when he walked to his fate in the eighth round, a brave game effort at a swagger and strut and a heave of the shoulder, his last defiant attempt to smother the gnawing of his inwards. Slowly, almost painfully, he passed his left arm for a swing, and missed a mile.[20]

A McGovern right to the jaw draped the champion over the ropes in his opponent's corner. He rose—dazed—with a "pleading expression on his honest, battered dark face."[21] McGovern lifted him up by his arms, helped him to his feet and walked him back to the center of the ring. Dixon could no longer mount an attack, and instead, he aimed to hang on the challenge.

McGovern took a step back; Dixon staggered forward and greeted another right—this one to the ribs. He dropped to all fours. Without a moment's hesitation, McGovern grabbed Dixon again under the arms and lifted him to his feet. Another rush from Dixon. Another blow to the stomach. Dixon was now flat on his belly. His corner motioned for him to stay down. But at the count of six, he rose. McGovern chased Dixon around the ring and dropped the champion a fourth time in the round with a right to the jaw. This time, Dixon looked up and saw McGovern smiling down at him. It was "a ghastly sight—the champion on the verge of collapse, and his rugged young rival, smiling, happy and only waiting for the chance to finish him."[22]

Dixon rose and fell three more times. His eyelids were drooping and his legs were shaking, but he made a vicious rush at McGovern and swung his left fiercely for the jaw. McGovern, laughing, ducked it and clinched. For the first time, he drew back his body so as to get distance, then rammed home his right on Dixon's sorely battered ribs. Dixon fell flat on his face. He remained on the floor four seconds, then got up on all fours and looked around for his opponent. He was weakly gathering his strength and striving to raise himself from the floor when a big white sponge sailed through the air and landed in the middle of the ring.[23]

Dixon would want it mentioned here that he was not knocked out; he reminded people of that fact until the end of his life. He surrendered his crown for the final time while still on his feet. Instead, his seconds saved him the indignity of a knockout blow by throwing the sponge, signaling their surrender to the punishment their man was taking. Dixon turned when he saw the sponge fly toward the center of the ring and heard the soaked thud of it hitting ground. He ran, laughing a somewhat delirious cackle, back to his corner—a "last effort of a brave heart, assumed to show the vast crowd that though beaten, he took his defeat lightly."[24] Upon reaching his awaiting seconds, Dixon spun and crossed the ring to shake McGovern's hand. The new champion bent forward and kissed Dixon on the forehead. Dixon then returned to his corner, leaned his head onto the ropes, and sobbed while his seconds removed his gloves.[25]

O'Rourke rushed to gather the champion. He sponged off Dixon's bruised and bleeding face and patted him on the back. Dixon asked, "You won't think much of me now I've been beaten, will you, Tom?"

"Don't you worry, George, I'll take care of you the rest of your natural life. You don't need to fight again."[26]

Joe Walcott, Dixon's friend and companion for years, followed the fallen champion across the ring as Dixon slowly made his way over to shake hands with McGovern and his corner men. The crowd had seen an era pass before their eyes. Walcott, a short, broad-shouldered Black man, hung his head and swung both his fists into empty air. Tears streamed down his face. His display of emotion was so overwhelming that three policemen jumped into the ring to subdue him. He gasped and hurled explanation; they released him. Still weeping, Walcott went over and shook McGovern's hand. "I'd rather you had killed me, Mr. McGovern," Walcott told the new champion. "But you won fair; you won fair."[27]

Dixon left immediately for the Hotel Delaven, owned by O'Rourke, where he refused comfort from any supporters. His cries were anguished, and there was not a dry eye among his friends who filled the hotel room. Dixon reclined on the bed and covered his face with a pillow. He wept for hours[28] and remained in bed until noon the following day. He was bruised blue, badly injured and, perhaps, bleeding internally. For his efforts, he made 25 percent of the gate—$2,983.50. In speaking of his defeat, the former champion said, "I was outfought by McGovern from the end of the third round. The blows to my stomach and over my kidneys were harder than any I ever received. . . . I entered the ring as confident as ever, but after going a short distance, I discovered that I was not the Dixon of old. My blows, although landing flush on my opponent, had no effect."[29] O'Rourke echoed those remarks: "McGovern's victory can be attributed to youth and superior strength. He was too young and too strong for Dixon. George became exhausted from the hot pace he set. This, I think, was more responsible for his defeat than were McGovern's punches."

Some came to Dixon's defense following his loss. *National Police Gazette* sports editor Sam C. Austin argued in print that Dixon was not knocked out: "Those who bet on the knock-out will argue that if the sponge had not been thrown up, he would have been. That is only a supposition, however, and not a fact. The sponge was thrown up to save him from being knocked out, and there is no line of argument which justifies the disposition of a bet on supposition or theory. The fact is, that he was not knocked out."[30]

But most celebrated the loss. Long a thorn in the side of Jim Crow philosophy, the lone Black boxing champion was finally defeated. Reporting on the McGovern-Dixon bout dripped with racist glee: "From black to white, from the cloud-capped cupola of the son of Ham[31] to the alabaster skyline of the fiery Brian Boru from Brooklyn, Terry McGovern. That was the change in complexion of the Featherweight Championship last week. 'It was a kind of roulette switch, and whites were trumps,' remarked McGovern's manager Sammy Harris."[32]

McGovern was held up not only for skill, but for lifestyle: a demon in the ring, but a gentleman, husband, and father outside it—a stark contrast to Dixon's well-publicized dissipation. White-run papers called McGovern's victory a revolution for the sport. The *Chicago Daily Tribune* proudly announced, "He has shown a prizefighter can lead the life of a puritan. He does not drink, smoke or swear; he is religious and devoted to his family."[33] Dixon, on the other hand, was reduced in many papers to a Black ink smudge in illustrations of the fight—his face no longer visible to readers. In defeat, Dixon was no longer viewed as a Black ideal; he became a cautionary tale again used by editorial writers across the country to warn of the damage caused by hubris and fast living.

Black-run newspapers were the most pointed in their remarks. Perhaps this is not surprising given what they had to lose compared to what white newspapers gained. The *Plaindealer* of Topeka, Kansas, opined:

> In later years, George Dixon had begun to brag and "blow" as much as Sullivan . . . and when a man begins to blow a great deal, he fights little. When Dixon was modest, he was invincible, never losing a battle; but lately he had accumulated a great desire to talk and drink, and neglected himself, and got licked. . . . He now quits with nothing save a saloon, which he will probably drink up, and afterward die a pauper, neglected and friendless. . . . The race has no gladiator now to represent it. . . . We are in darkness, for Dixon's light has been put out.[34]

In the words of even his Black supporters, Dixon had "enlisted in that vast army of fighters who went into the ring once too often."[35] But still others saw hope in Dixon's success; as the *Colored American* noted, they saw the possibility of rising and making a name for themselves against an increasingly stacked deck:

> Why was Dixon followed, admired, feted and given a man's consideration? It was a matter of business, pure and simple. He had something that somebody wanted. Somebody could benefit themselves by dealing with him, and they came to him. When the Negro can put up the best fight, build the best steamship, make the best wagon, raise the best cotton and corn, turn out the best butter, write the best book, design the best house, perform necessary service in a better and quicker manner than any other class . . . his hour of recognition will come. Money will come with it. Other privileges now denied will follow in its wake. . . . The Caucasian race owes us nothing but fair play.[36]

Despite his fragile condition, less than a week after the fight, the fallen champion set out on one of the oddest sidebars of his career. On January 13, 1900, Dixon, along with heavyweight challenger Bob "Coffee

Cooler" Armstrong, walked unannounced into the White House in Washington, DC. The unlikely visitors strolled about the East Room and created a "panic among White House employees" unaccustomed to seeing Black men walk about the building.[37] The vision of the two—one a withering drunk, one a powerful Black heavyweight of menacing size and visage—walking into the White House is quite amusing, especially given the history of that structure and the struggle with accommodating Blacks as visitors. Once staffed by slaves, the White House opened its doors during the latter half of the nineteenth century to Black entertainers, like diva Marie "Selika" Williams, and political leaders, including Frederick Douglass and Sojourner Truth.[38] A White House dinner between President Theodore Roosevelt and Booker T. Washington on October 16, 1901, created a firestorm across the country, and mainly in the southern press, resulting in no other Black man or woman being invited to dinner for almost thirty years.[39] The *Atlanta Journal* said the president "blundered without excuse"[40]; the *New Orleans Times-Democrat* asked, "White men of the South, how do you like it? White women of the South, how do you like it?"[41]; and the *New Orleans Picayune*, among the loudest critics of Dixon in 1892, reminded readers that "the president is a very peculiar man, and has in many instances, showed little regard for official, routine or social and political convention."[42] But to understand the pure bile that existed between the white power structure of the nation, and the entire Black race, the angry, hateful words of an unnamed congressman should be consulted:

> I have no hesitation in saying that I believe I voice the sentiment of every intelligent Southern-born white man and white woman when I say that they can never take President Roosevelt or any other publicman to their hearts who sits at the table and eats with a "nigger." I confess, Booker Washington is a smart nigger and above the average, but at the same time, he is a nigger just the same, and we people of the South have been born and raised so that we cannot accept the negro as our social equal and we cannot respect any man who does. If President Roosevelt expects to build up a respectable white man's party in the South, he can never succeed by inviting niggers to the White House for dinner.[43]

Still, ten months before Washington's White House visit, Dixon, who still bore fresh cuts and bruises from his loss, walked into the White House and asked permission to see President William McKinley. The request was taken upstairs to the president's secretary.[44] Unfortunately for them, Dixon and Armstrong were told the president was busy consulting with a Cabinet officer. The men left without incident. "I am going to retire. I have some money and that, with the benefit to be given me, will probably place me in comfortable circumstances," Dixon told White House staff.[45] In the press, the incident was treated as comedic, not with contempt.

The Boston sporting public did not linger on the loss. Dixon news faded in days as the city's attention soon turned to the tragic tale of Boston Beaneaters catcher Marty Bergen. At some point during the evening of January 18, 1900, Bergen slaughtered his family. First he attacked his wife in the bedroom, hitting her multiple times in the head with the blunt side of an axe. She fell dying on one of the beds. Bergen then attacked his son, who died in the other bed after a single blow from the sharp side of the axe. In the kitchen, Bergen killed his daughter. When finished, Bergen retrieved a razor, stood in front of a mirror in the kitchen, and sliced his own throat, nearly severing his head. He fell beside his daughter. The event caused a stir among the sporting world. Doctors had previously called Bergen "insane" and a "maniac" and believed the condition was far out of his control. The *Boston Globe*'s Tim Murnane wrote that Bergen "was entitled to the undivided sympathy of the baseball public, as well as players and directors."[46]

As Dixon deteriorated, the United States appeared to be doing the same to itself. The specter of a potential Black heavyweight champion in Jack Johnson sparked further tightening of racial restrictions in the sport. Many athletic clubs closed their doors to Black fighters, even in former havens like Chicago and Detroit. One club, The Badger in Milwaukee, Wisconsin, banned Black men from serving as corner men, let alone fighters. Fight reporters blamed some of this on a string of questionable bouts involving Black fighters. Yes, major pugilistic draws like Joe Gans and Joe Walcott admittedly threw fights. Yet whenever questions of a "fix" arose in print, Dixon was fondly remembered as a man who never threw a bout. As the *Los Angeles Times* wrote, "The game and honest negroes have passed away and a generation of Africans come in of a different pattern. A few years ago, the negro was on the top notch of popularity. Whenever a colored man was billed, there went crowds sure of seeing a gallant contest and a fair, honest battle. These days have passed away."[47]

To be fair, Dixon was not totally forgotten, although perhaps at times he wished he was. The sporting public sustained its obsession with Dixon's body throughout his life. Even in darker times, as his skills eroded and he faded into semi-obscurity, the obsession remained, although its focus shifted to the ravages of his bad decisions. As his vulnerabilities became highly visible, the sporting public was exposed to the destruction of a body it once held as a physical ideal. In ancient Greece, it was considered a sign of the greatest skill in a boxer to conquer without receiving any wounds. In some ancient vase paintings of boxers, vulnerability is key— representations of blood are seen streaming from their noses, and teeth are missing. And then there were the ears. Given they were exposed to the greatest abuse, they were often mutilated and broken on frequent pugilists. Hence, ancient artists often depicted the ears beaten flat and swollen.[48] Dixon eventually saw his own vulnerabilities on full display. When Tom Callahan out-pointed Dixon in June 1900, the *National Police Gazette* wrote: "It was not the Dixon of old, however, and while there is still a pretty good fight in the little colored man, he has lost that aggressiveness for which he was once so famous. Dixon had the appearance of having trained for the bout, but he carried something of a belly, and the body punches which Callahan continually drove into him had their effect."[49]

His personal life also became of concern to Black newspaper editors: "Black newspapers that were prone to talk so enthusiastically and admiringly about 'George Dixon and his white wife' ought to say something now about them. Mrs. Dixon and her brother, Mr. Tom O'Rourke, the manager of Dixon, have succeeded in getting rich from the young pugilist's labor, and are preparing to 'drop' him altogether, Dixon's wife already having secured a divorce from him on the ground of cruelty. The young pugilist probably blew his breath in his wife's face, and she fell down."[50]

Most agreed the sun had set on Dixon's marvelous career as a fighter. Friends banded together almost immediately to start a fund for Dixon, and raised $2,100 in a matter of days, a total that included a $250 donation from McGovern.[51]

There was a look of sadness upon Dixon's face as he entered the Broadway Athletic Club's arena on February 21, 1900, and saw a conspicuous number of vacant seats. It was the night of the Dixon testimonial, a celebration of the now-former champion. His friends were certain the place would be packed. Dixon had always been foremost in giving his services in time of need and many a worthy charity had benefitted through his efforts. The press reported: "His hand was always open to a distressed friend or professional rival. . . . One can therefore imagine how the game little hero of eight hundred battles must have felt when he noticed the absence of those whom he had himself befriended in the halcyon days of his career."[52]

Nevertheless, boxing exhibitions were put on by his pugilistic colleagues Joe Gans, Frank Erne, Eddie Sharkey, even McGovern, who staged a three-round sparring exhibition with Dixon. When introduced, a loud roar rose from the crowd for both warriors. Before their bout, McGovern handed Dixon a check for $300. Dixon, through the master of ceremonies Joe Humphreys, thanked all those who had contributed to his benefit by their presence as well as by their subscriptions, and also thanked his brother boxers for their kindness in appearing in the bouts. He also announced that while he had defended the featherweight championship for years against all comers, he was "glad that when he met his Waterloo, it was handed to him by an American."[53] In addition to McGovern's check, Sam Harris, McGovern's manager, handed Dixon $2,500, and Bob Armstrong presented Dixon with a $50 bill.

With $8,000 raised that night, and another $2,000 from a previous benefit in Denver, there was plenty of money for Dixon to open his bar. The initiative—a drunk opening a bar—drew attention: "Maybe that is why he stops boxing to conduct a saloon in the metropolis of the Empire State, hoping to lay up treasure in the bank for the days to come when youth has fled, when the eye ceases to measure distances accurately and the good right has lost its power in a lead for the solar plexus."[54]

On March 30, 1900, Dixon opened the White Elephant saloon to a capacity crowd. The bar was located at 511 Sixth Avenue, right in the heart of the Tenderloin District. The place was a mecca for the "swell sports of the metropolis."[55] As his establishment was in its infancy, Dixon was still on the town. That same week, Charles "Kid" McCoy—the light heavyweight credited as the namesake origin of the saying "the real McCoy"—opened a bar a few blocks away from the White Elephant, on the corner of Broadway and Fourteenth Street. Dixon was among those of the "sporting elite" who stood in front of the McCoy rail from "early morning till dewy eve, and an hour or two after buying White Seal and other brands of 'grape' until the supply threatened to be exhausted."[56]

Predictably, Dixon's days behind the bar, and outside the ring, did not last long. As the *National Police Gazette* chided the former champion: "You can drop your pen, quit thinking up things to say about him and put the unfinished biography away on the top shelf. George Dixon's hasn't retired from the ring . . . He found the 'job' of lubricating the tonsils of the colored sports of the Tenderloin anything but a congenial one, so the first 'live one' who came along on purchase bent got the café, and Little Chocolate stepped down and out."[57] Out from behind the bar, Dixon was set on regaining his title. In less than two weeks, he fought two warm-up bouts—a loss to Tim Callahan and a draw with Benny Yanger. Then, at Tattersall's in Chicago, on June 23, 1900, he entered the ring against McGovern a second time.

The fight was "fast and furious, from beginning to end, with Terry on top of his man all the time."[58] Dixon tried every conceivable tactic to gain the advantage, but his blows could not equal those of his younger opponent. McGovern started slowly, and perhaps offered a glimmer of hope to the fading champion of once again wearing the belt. Why not—he had lost and regained before. Dixon staggered McGovern midway through the second round with a blow to the jaw. However, the champion woke up at that point and began to press the fight. McGovern worked Dixon's soft body, forcing Dixon to clinch as much as possible to survive. Although not knocked out, Dixon was in distress and holding on for dear life.

In the sixth and final round, Dixon was reduced to collaring McGovern around the neck at every opportunity to avoid the champion's two-handed punishment. Still, Dixon took a severe beating in the round and was weak-kneed at bout's end. This fight, perhaps more than the first McGovern bout, wrote the death notice of Dixon's career as a championship-caliber fighter. What hope remained died that night in front of four thousand spectators.

After defeating Dixon, McGovern successfully defended his featherweight title several times in 1900 and 1901. He also scored a third-round knockout over the world lightweight champion Frank Erne in a non-title bout and beat Joe Gans in two rounds in 1900—although Gans later admitted to throwing the fight. McGovern lost his title to Young Corbett in 1901, and was unsuccessful in their 1903 rematch, getting knocked out both times. He fought infrequently for the next five years, never regaining his earlier skill. In the latter stages of his career, his behavior became erratic, and he spent time in various sanitariums. He collapsed while serving as a referee at an Army camp during the First World War and died soon after on February 22, 1918.

For years after the bout, O'Rourke—a "heartless mercenary" in the minds of some for putting a diminished Dixon in the ring—took the blame for sending Dixon into a fight his manager knew he could not win.[59] As the *Washington Post* reflected years later: "While his manager was satisfied with a few glasses of beer after a victory, Dixon would get a pocketful of money and start opening wine and buying drinks for everybody like a millionaire out on a lark. The colored fighter had a big heart and slipped many a five or ten spot to broken down boxers and old friends. . . . In view of his weakened condition, he should never been allowed to enter the ring with the South Brooklyn boy."[60]

Few have explored why O'Rourke risked the reputation, and perhaps even the life, of his once-proud charge in putting him in the ring with McGovern in the first place. One interesting explanation can be found not among fights, but films. O'Rourke and Sam Harris partnered on the film for McGovern-Dixon. Harris, a gifted producer/promoter, looked for a way to showcase his man. Although plans for the one-minute McGovern–Pedlar Palmer film three months earlier had gone awry, the undefeated "Brooklyn Terror" remained the most-watched of the pugilists in the lower weight classes and a popular boxing celebrity in New York. Lights and cameras were installed for McGovern-Dixon I; Biograph cinematographers captured the eight-round bout on film. Dixon was no stranger to the camera; he had been filmed a year earlier when, in 1899, Dixon sparred Black journeyman Sam Bolen while Biograph conducted camera tests for the Jeffries-Sharkey Contest.[61] Dixon's only other film performance came just before his final retirement in February 1906 when filmmaker Billy Bitzer recorded Dixon and journeyman Casper Leon in a three-round boxing exhibition. Unlike other sparring films, Dixon-Leon showed two boxers going at it in earnest. The production, then, was something of an oddity, showing the first above-board fight between prizefighters performing solely for the camera. Nevertheless, the backdrop the men fought in front of replicated earlier studio reenactments and used the same set that appears in *Mr. Butt-in*, Bitzer's fictional film shot a few days earlier. Sadly, the Leon film is the lone moving picture of Dixon to survive this period.

The spectacle of a controlled, physical struggle between Black and white athletes no doubt carried significant dramatic tension for audiences who were aware of racially motivated violence on an almost daily basis. The popularity of the interracial films is reflected in the number produced. Despite the heavyweight color line and the legal prohibition of interracial bouts in New York, California, Pennsylvania, and Wisconsin, nearly half of all the fight films produced between 1900 and 1915 depicted Blacks battling whites. Furthermore, the Edison Company's film burlesque *A Scrap in Black and White* from 1903, in which white adults laughingly coax a young Black and a young white child to spar with each other in a miniature boxing ring, laid bare the true motivation for the interest in the boxing film.[62]

Few details about the filming of McGovern-Dixon I were reported. Even the identity of the crew is unknown. The films, sold broadly, indicate that 35 mm equipment was used, but print advertisements mentioned no brand name. With O'Rourke and Harris acting as "the sole managers and proprietors," the McGovern-Dixon I film defined the category of "independent" production better than any other of its era—the men advertised prints for sale and handled orders from their rooms in a Manhattan hotel. But working outside the established film-handling process created problems. Technical difficulties arose during the development of negatives and prints. Announcements of the films did not appear until a month after the bout, when O'Rourke and Harris solicited bids for rights to exploit pictures that would "be ready in two weeks." To keep interest alive, the promoters prompted their men to stage a live exhibition on February 21, 1900, in New York City. Belatedly, in late March 1900, the film was shown as a special feature at scattered theaters.[63]

The delay created an odd space in the marketplace. Soon after McGovern-Dixon, German American filmmaker Siegmund Lubin hired actors and filmed reenactments of three popular recent fights (a five-round bout between Kid McCoy and Peter Meher from January 1, 1900; a three-round bout between McGovern and Oscar Gardner from March 9, 1900; and McGovern-Dixon) and packaged them as a single presentation, given that all three bouts were of relatively short duration. What Lubin lacked in authenticity, he made up for in speed. Films of the reenacted bouts were in front of audiences within weeks, thus beating O'Rourke and Harris to market by months, a fact that did not sit well with either. O'Rourke called Lubin's films "spurious," "counterfeit," the work of an "irresponsible pirate." [64] And he wasn't far off; in many ways the first film pirate, Lubin later went on to copy and distribute feature films from other filmmakers, too. Nevertheless, Lubin's work remained popular for years; when his company went out of business immediately after the First World War, Lubin returned to work as an optometrist.

The first ad for *The Genuine Pictures of the McGovern-Dixon Championship Fight* appeared on April 7, 1900. The three-month marketing delay necessitated a rethinking of exhibition strategy. Instead of a theatrical tour, O'Rourke and Harris suggested that "these pictures can be engaged as a Special Feature for Parks, Summer Resorts, and to

Strengthen Road Companies." Interest was low, and by June the promoters were forced to pair their fighters against one another for the third time in six months—this time without cameras.[65]

That this transpired cannot be argued, but where gray might exist is questioning the motivation of O'Rourke. He appeared to be putting his burgeoning film operation before the wellbeing of his fighter, forcing Dixon into the ring three times against a far-superior opponent in a matter of months to attempt to recoup a struggling investment.

Nevertheless, immediately after the second McGovern loss, Dixon suffered a truly embarrassing defeat on July 31, 1900, at the hands of Tommy Sullivan, who broke Dixon's arm in the sixth round. For the first time in his career, Dixon was resoundingly booed by the crowd. When not ridiculing his effort, newspapers begged him to quit the ring for good:

> Dixon's pugilistic sun has set and the twilight finds him without the competency and means for an independent living, which he unquestionably earned during his long, energetic and profitable connection with the ring. When a comparative novice like Tommy Sullivan can "trim" the famous champion of all champions so effectively as he did in six rounds it is time for Little Chocolate to pass out of the game.
>
> Some time ago, I advocated a scheme to organize a fund large enough to give Dixon an annuity for life and establish him a business. Part of the sum realized was invested in a café in the Tenderloin of New York City. George attended to business for a while, but after the novelty of the thing wore off, he abandoned the place and it was sold to satisfy the claims of an exacting mortgage. As honest as the sun, brave, fearless, courageous in the ring, he was well entitled to the admiration of every true sporting man in the country and it is to be hoped that some means will be devised to provide him with an occupation that will keep him from fighting again.[66]

Dixon was bottoming out with nowhere to turn. He wrote: "I lost my money gambling, playing the races, leading a fast life and by lending my money to friends. When I think of how much money I went through, it gives me chills. . . . If I had my life to live over again, I bet I wouldn't spend my money as recklessly as I did."[67]

Throughout 1901, he fought skilled and unskilled men without preference, and with only indifferent amounts of success. There were sad moments. In Denver, O'Rourke showed "his true hand here, for the man who made a fortune out of George Dixon, and who declared with a flourish that the great little fighter would never want for anything while he was alive, has attached Dixon's paltry share of the gate receipts from his recent fight with Young Corbett II," a ten-round loss on August 16, 1901.[68] This left Dixon stranded in the Mile High City with no funds with which to return to New York City. If you need to find a singular point when the white world turned its back on Dixon, there is a strong actual and symbolic moment to be had here. O'Rourke no longer saw Dixon as an investment to be protected; in this moment, Dixon had become a burden no longer worthy of consideration. O'Rourke took his substantial cut—and left Dixon behind.

When Eddie Lenny pounded the former champion to the boards on January 24, 1902, a groggy-headed Dixon attempted to stand, but his corner men threw in the sponge.[69] Lenny had almost beaten Dixon for the championship on November 21, 1899, but lost on points. That fight served as a harbinger of Dixon's future, as he lost to McGovern in his next bout.[70] Dixon lost or drew fourteen straight bouts over the two-plus years between his narrow victory over Lenny in 1899 and his loss to Lenny in 1902. After a draw against Tim Callahan on June 30, 1902, Dixon knew it was time for a change of scenery as his options stateside evaporated. John L. Sullivan often reflected on this period of Dixon's career—perhaps mindful of his own decline. He wrote:

> After McGovern took his title, and the money came in smaller rolls, it went ten times as fast, and the poor little coon ran into all kinds of hard luck. When he had money, he couldn't pinch any of it for the rainy days ahead, and when it began to rain for him, it never let up. When I think of the square little fellow who had been champion so long, and after all the easy living he'd had, going hungry, cold and sometimes without a place to bunk at night, it makes me swearing mad, for he didn't deserve to go down so low. Some of the coin he squandered on bum friends ought to have come back when he needed a meal, but there were only a few that remained.[71]

Black America experienced its own crisis simultaneous to Dixon's. But unlike Dixon's decline, there were glimmers of hope. After the assassination of President William McKinley in September 1901, just six months into his second term, Theodore Roosevelt assumed the highest office in the land. By all accounts an activist president, Roosevelt was a populist hero who sided with the Everyman against the financial barons and corporate giants that had grown up amid the rapidly industrializing nation. That progressive nature, however, did not fully extend to Black America. Roosevelt believed in white superiority, rooted in what he claimed to be history and science. He believed European whites had proven themselves as the dominant race on the planet through successes in science, war, and the arts from the age of the explorers until his present day. As he wrote to author Owen Wister, the "father of Western fiction," in 1901: "I agree entirely that as a race, and in the mass, [Blacks] are altogether inferior to whites. . . . I do not believe that the average negro in the United States is as yet in any way fit to take care of himself and others as the average white man—for if he were, there would be no negro problem."

This did not mean Roosevelt ignored the problems of race. He puzzled over it somewhat. He was troubled by southern resistance to the advances of Blacks. While he opposed special government programs to assist Blacks specifically, Roosevelt liked to say he judged individuals on their merits. He publicly condemned lynchings, especially the mob violence that had taken hold of certain swaths of the country. He wrote: "I have not been able to think out any solution of the terrible problem offered by the presence of the negro in this continent, but one thing I am sure, and that is that in as much as he is here and can neither be killed nor driven away, the only wise and honorable and Christian thing to do is to treat each Black man and each white man strictly on his merits as a man." He also chided the "indifference of the great masses of people [in the North] to whom the wrongdoing in the South is a matter afar off and of little immediate consequence, and who are impatient of any attempt to make things better in any way."

Despite this, however, political realities took hold. Not wanting to risk his reelection bid in 1904 by provoking the South, Roosevelt pivoted from discussing race and lynching and toward other issues. "I have nothing to gain and everything to lose by any agitation of the race questions," he said, also declaring during the campaign, "If I am to be blamed by anyone for any failure in my duty, active or passive, toward the South, it must be for the failure to take action as regards the nullification of the Fourteenth and Fifteenth Amendments in The South." After his election, he was uncertain how to proceed on the race question—a main obstacle was a "partially successful movement to bring back slavery." Ultimately he retreated from attempts to heal, deciding the issue was intractable.[72]

Often, the story of Black America at the turn of the century focuses on violence and the loss of opportunity. And that is understandable. Political power for Blacks had all but evaporated. Between 1890 and 1908, ten southern state legislatures, mainly controlled by Democrats, passed new state constitutions with explicit provisions restricting voter registration. Millions of Black men were purged from the voting rolls. Literacy tests to vote debuted and, although literacy rates had risen dramatically among Blacks since 1850, southern Blacks continued to lag behind and were blocked from voting by this change. In 1901, George H. White of North Carolina left office, becoming the last Black congressman elected to federal office for the next twenty-eight years—and the last Black man to represent a southern state for seventy-two years.

Outside the halls of power, violence continued to be a part of everyday life for many Blacks. Two famous uprisings characterized this period. On July 23, 1900, the New Orleans Race Riot (also known as the Robert Charles Riot) erupted after a Black activist shot and killed a white police officer. White mobs terrorized Blacks on the streets of the city for four days. Twelve Blacks and seven whites were killed. On September 22, 1906, a white mob of ten thousand men flooded the streets of Atlanta searching for Black men after four alleged sexual attacks on white women by Black men were reported in the local white press. The mob surged through Black neighborhoods, destroying businesses and assaulting hundreds of Black men. Officially, twenty-five Blacks and one white died, but, unofficially, more than one hundred from both races may have died.

Yet all was not lost. The gains of the previous decades were not completely forgotten. Powerful voices—both familiar and new—would shape the movement known as civil rights for the next century by influencing the great names in that crusade. In 1901, Booker T. Washington published his ghostwritten autobiography, *Up From Slavery*, chronicling his life and philosophical position on racial advancement. As he proclaimed at his Atlanta Exposition speech six years earlier, Washington remained accommodating of the white power structure and begged patience and perseverance from Black America. He wrote, "The wisest among my race understand that agitations of social equality is the extremist folly, and that progress in the enjoyment of all privileges that will come to us must be the result of severe and constant struggle rather than of artificial forcing."[73] Two years later, Washington was challenged by a young Black scholar from Atlanta University. In *The Souls of Black Folks*, W. E. B. Du Bois rejected Washington's gradual approach and called for agitation on behalf of Black rights as he saw that the "problem of the twentieth century is the problem of the color line." He wrote:

> They do not expect that the free right to vote, to enjoy civic rights, and to be educated, will come in a moment; they do not expect to see the bias and prejudices of years disappear at the blast of a trumpet; but they are absolutely certain that the way for a people to gain their reasonable rights is not by voluntarily throwing them away and insisting that they do not want them; that the way for a people to gain respect is not by continually belittling and ridiculing themselves; that, on the contrary, Negroes must insist continually, in season and out of season, that voting is necessary to modern manhood, that color discrimination is barbarism, and that Black boys need education as well as white boys.[74]

These two men, Washington and Du Bois, formed the centerpiece of the era's debate. However, lesser-known voices were having a huge impact. In 1896, Nannie Helen Burroughs was among a group of women who founded the National Association of Colored Women. Four years later, at the annual conference of the National Baptist Convention in Richmond, Virginia, she delivered a speech, "How the Sisters Are Hindered from Helping," that gave voice to Black women within the powerful Baptist Church. Her words inspired the formation of the Women's Convention Auxiliary, a group that boasted more than one and a half million members by 1907. In February 1900, brothers James and John Johnson witnessed the debut performance of their song "Lift Every Voice and Sing." In Jacksonville, Florida, a choir of five hundred children in their segregated Sunday school sang the song in celebration of Abraham Lincoln's birthday. A staple of the American civil rights movement of the 1950s and 1960s, the song has often been referred to as the Black National Anthem:

> Sing a song full of the faith that the dark past has taught us,
> Sing a song full of the hope that the present has brought us;
> Facing the rising sun of our new day begun,
> Let us march on 'til victory is won.

In 1905, Du Bois and William Monroe Trotter gathered a group of Black intellectuals and activists to form the Niagara Movement. Named for the location of its first meeting, the group met on the Canadian side of the falls when the American side refused them accommodations. The movement furthered echoed Du Bois's sentiments against Washington's policy of conciliation. The group's manifesto read, in part: "We claim for ourselves every single right that belongs to a freeborn American, political, civil and social; and until we get these rights we will never cease to protest and assail the ears of America. The battle we wage is not for ourselves alone but for all true Americans. It is a fight for ideals, lest this, our common fatherland, false to its founding, become in truth the land of the thief and the home of the slave—a byword and a hissing among the nations for its sounding pretensions and pitiful accomplishment."

Although it ultimately failed in its goals, the Movement set the stage for the foundation of the National Association for the Advancement of Colored People (NAACP).

The early twentieth century erased numerous borders, including providing Black fighters with a never-before-seen level of success. In Paris, Black fighters were superstars, owning the stage for themselves before the influx of entertainers, artists, and soldiers arrived at the beginning on the First World War. Names like Joe Jeannette, Sam Langford, Sam McVey, and others relocated to France. Dixon, guided by a manager more familiar with the British Empire, never traveled that path. In September 1902, Dixon headed to Great Britain, although under far different circumstances than a dozen years earlier when he traveled there to unify the crown. Across the United Kingdom, the fading champion's fame still carried weight with audiences, even though his skills no longer did. He did not return to fight in the United States for three years.

Dixon fought thirty-nine official bouts abroad and countless others in exhibitions and challenges. All those bouts took place in Great Britain save one: a draw in Copenhagen, Denmark, against Richard Longhi Monnefeldt (or Monefeldt) Christensen—known as Dick Nelson—on May 28, 1905. The Danish-born, New York City–based Nelson was making his debut against Dixon. Nelson went on to fight 209 professional bouts in his career, often against some of the top men in the welterweight and middleweight classes in the United States and Denmark. Among others he met in the ring were Young Corbett II and Dixie Kid. Although he holds the record for most professional fights by any Danish boxer, he never fought for a title. He retired from the ring in 1921; he died in 1922.

Dixon's exploits continued to be reported stateside, although the flowery narratives were now gone, replaced by bare-bones basics of the bout, often only a paragraph or two in length. He even faded from the pages of the National Police Gazette and Boston Daily Globe, arguably

Dixon's biggest boosters. He was fighting, he was winning, but he was having difficulty surviving. Jack "Twin" Sullivan, the New England welterweight champion, sent a letter home from England advising his fellow boxers to stay away, as purses for bouts had dried up. George Dixon, according to Sullivan, received only $50 for losing his last fight.[75]

Dixon reached the high point of his exile on November 9, 1903, when he outpointed Pedlar Palmer in a battle for the 120-pound championship of England. Fans in the United States welcomed news of the victory, as it offered hopes of a comeback. The *National Police Gazette* reported:

> To many lovers of boxing, the cable never conveyed more pleasing intelligence than it did the other day when there flashed over it the news that George Dixon, the former featherweight champion, had cleverly outpointed Pedlar Palmer in a battle for the one hundred and twenty-pound championship of England. Dixon showed something of his old-time form, and had no trouble in whipping the Englishman. . . . He lost no speed and his cleverness was marvelous. . . . According to experts in things pugilistic, Dixon has a good chance to "come back" and regain some of the old fame that was his before he went down in defeat before Terry McGovern. All he has to do is to live regularly and keep his present form.[76]

That did not happen. Most observers acknowledged Palmer gave a disappointing performance, and in addressing the house at the close, he admitted as much. "I held the old man too cheaply, and I have been well beaten," he said at ringside following his defeat.[77] As his slide continued, Dixon again announced his retirement in December 1903. "Little George Dixon is out of it at last," the *National Police Gazette* wrote.[78] Again, his retirement lasted less than a month.

Dixon's messages home were always positive. His friends were surely gratified to know that, according to Dixon's speaking to the *National Police Gazette*, since he went to England a year ago he had made $7,000. He said he has saved the bulk of his money and intended to hold onto it: "I used to be a fool when I was younger and careless. I never used to know the value of money. It was like nothing to me. But I have tasted the bitter pangs of poverty and know what it is to be hungry. I must have earned over $300,000 in my day, but I have little of this money left. I'm taking excellent care of myself and continue to do so. . . . I will return to America, but not permanently. I have been well treated in England and expect to finish the rest of my days here."[79]

Dixon was living with Frank Craig, the "Harlem Coffee Cooler," and "through his guidance, the wonderful negro is coming back to his own again. Craig is very rich and thinks Dixon has another chance to accumulate a fortune."[80] Even as late as March 1904, Dixon found himself, once again, in the championship debate thanks to his perceived success abroad.[81] But the windfall was short lived—if ever true in the first place. By May 1905, the sporting press reported Dixon was broke and unable to raise enough money to get back to the United States. Owen Moran, an English bantamweight, said Dixon was receiving $25 or $50 per fight, when he was paid at all.[82]

After he lost his title, Dixon rarely had more than a few hundred dollars in the bank. His only asset was his Boston home, for which he paid $6,000 several years earlier. He was never shy about his shortcomings and what led him into financial ruin from such lofty heights. In response to questions from the *Philadelphia Inquirer*, Dixon estimated his share of career earnings at $97,000. Given O'Rourke's take, and subtracting for various expenses, his total earnings amounted to more than $300,000 in just over a decade. (In 2019 dollars, that represents more than $8.5 million.) That number made Dixon one of the wealthiest Black men in America.[83]

In August 1905, Dixon arrived home on the steamship *Campania*, which also brought back Congressman Tim Sullivan. "Big Tim" not only paid for the former champion's passage, but also fitted him in suits for the trip. Unlike his last return from abroad, where he was hailed as a champion and a hero, Dixon returned to no fanfare. He had little to show for three years and forty-six bouts overseas. "I am really ashamed to tell you the money I made in England," Dixon said upon arriving home. "I got such a small amount that I am sure I could go into any crap game and, with a little luck with the bones one evening, I could come out of the place with more money than I got out of all the fights I had in England."[84]

Abandoned by his long-time manager and protector, Dixon was now naked and exposed to an unfamiliar world, as the changing atmosphere of America forced him into a life he was never prepared to lead. With no title and no manager, his end accelerated. It would be too simplistic to say Dixon was falling victim to the Jim Crow era, when in fact he fell victim to his own shortcomings and vices. Without the support of his backers, who had all but left him by this point, Dixon continued to slide into irrelevance. As the *National Police Gazette* explained: "Dissipation killed Dixon, the fighter, and left in his place Dixon, the jaded, wrinkled, incompetent little old man. It is useless to use the example to point a moral for professional fighters, for as a class, they all seem bound to dash themselves to pieces in the same way. . . . As a rule, the greater the fighter, the surer he is to throw away his strength in riotous living. To such men warning is useless."[85]

George Dixon's end was foretold by a man who wrote more words about him than anyone else in the sport. Taking his seat at ringside for an unnamed bout in the fall of 1905, Samuel Austin recognized right away the shuffling corpse of Dixon, now a wrinkled and jaded soul at only thirty-five years old, consumed by a dissipated lifestyle yet still famil- iar to the long-time sports editor of the *National Police Gazette*.[86] "Say," Dixon asked, "have you got one of those old books you wrote about Black champions?"

"Yes," Austin replied. "What do you want it for?"[87]

Dixon responded, "Oh, I just want to read about what a fighter I used to be. From the way I've been doing lately, I find it difficult to believe that I ever knew anything about it."[88]

The changes to Dixon's physicality were shocking. Once a proud specimen, he started to show a hard life's toll. Few photos remain of Dixon overall; those surviving cluster around a few years during his prime fighting days. Given the era's practice of placing fighters in simi- lar poses for their portraits, Dixon's few photos look remarkably similar to one another. Images outside Dixon's career are even more scarce, but they do exist, and one such image illustrates perfectly the toll life took on Dixon's body. Look at the face in his earliest known photograph— noble, handsome—and compare it to one of his last. Only two decades have elapsed, yet the face staring back in his latter images looks aged well beyond its years—scarred, drawn, pockmarked. The eyes are dead; the ears, always pronounced, are tattered. It is a face that has taken a beating in the ring and beyond. Even the studio image, once known for its flat- tering portrayal of these gladiators, was no longer kind to Dixon. Unlike earlier photographers, the unknown who snapped this one did not set out to create any mystique about the fighter—the drab background, seem- ingly disheveled and unkempt, reflected Dixon perfectly. Unlike previous photographs, lit to define the champion as a physical specimen, this shot explores all that has gone wrong with his body. Note the withered legs, the dawn of a paunch, the arms' sagging strength. And the face. For those who knew Dixon as a fresh-faced lad, it was difficult to see the mileage tracked across it.

Despite his fading form, Dixon was still a magnet among newspapermen and the public. No longer known for his skill, he was a tragic spectacle that engendered a lot of respect, as well as sympathy, in print and in public. Ordinarily the boxing world had little consideration for has-beens. The moment a pugilistic star—or public man, or great warrior, or brilliant statesman—shook hands in defeat, his usefulness faded and he disappeared from public view. Only in two instances—John L. Sullivan and George Dixon—did fading stars of this era never lose their ability to draw attention. As the *Chicago Daily Tribune* wrote: "No man is utterly without friends, and 'has-beens' do not seek sympathy in vain. But the cases in which the great mass of the people, that heterogeneous aggregation known as 'the public,' still clings to a beaten and disgraced pugilist are so rare as to be worthy of being specially recorded. [Dixon] has fallen from the high plane he once occupied, but many a hand will be thrust out to help him, and many hearts will beat in sympathy."[89]

That did not mean the world was not cruel to Dixon. In advance of his bout against Tommy Murphy on September 20, 1905, one reporter wrote that "someone rolled the stone away and George Dixon ambled out of his tomb of retirement not far from New Dorp, Staten Island."[90] Memories of what he once was were mixed with what he was now. Even for sympathetic publications, Dixon's rapid decline was difficult to ignore. The *National Police Gazette* wrote: "[Dixon was] four times as strong and able as the average boy of his years, and at least twice as able as the average well-trained amateur boxer in his class. He did not fear white men; he did not fear anybody. He was a game, honest, clever fighter.... Ring followers are not sentimentalists, but many hardened old followers of the game turned aside so that he might not look at this poor, faded, flabby shadow of Dixon being beaten down."[91]

Matchmakers were also still interested—although at drastically reduced prices. In Philadelphia, fight organizers offered Dixon $350 for every bout he could survive. The Apple Blossom Athletic Club of St. Joseph, Michigan, offered Dixon $1,500 for a ten-round bout with Johnny Morrison, a Michigan featherweight. Even as late as June 1906, the *Police Gazette* was trumpeting Dixon as flashing "his old-time form."[92] But that was simple hype.

Dixon's last victory in the ring came on January 4, 1906, when he outpointed Harry Shea in the latter's only professional fight. Although he won, Dixon failed to summon his "old-time punch" to knock his opponent out.[93] A pair of draws followed over the next two months and then, on December 10, 1906, Dixon and Harry "Monk the Newsboy" Kronski fought fifteen rounds at the Standard Athletic Club in Lymansville, Rhode Island. Monk earned the decision—the fourth and final victory of his thirteen-bout career. Newspaper reports were brief. Descriptions of Dixon's withering condition far outweighed reports on his actual bouts. Those once flowery expositions on his escapades were now reduced to only two or three sentences. Only five paragraphs signaled what would ultimately be the last bout of a brilliant career. The *Boston Daily Globe* wrote: "The Dixon of last night was not the Dixon of old. He showed that he had lost much of his cleverness, and was exceptionally poor at judging distance. . . . [Monk] got away from Dixon's leads with great agility and then would dash in and wallop before George could recover himself."[94] And that was it.

The disposal of Dixon is maddening. As the weeks passed, Dixon grew angry, bitter, and isolated. He started to see the world for what his friend John L. Sullivan warned him it was all along. Dixon was quoted as saying: "It isn't what you used to be, it's what you are today. The men who followed me in the days of prosperity can't see me when I am close enough to speak to them. John L. Sullivan is the only man in the world that never turned me down when I was in trouble. . . . Tom [O'Rourke] was always broke when I needed money and could not earn it with my fists. Once, he threw me out of his saloon, almost breaking my arm."[95]

Lightweight Joe Gans drew a lot of attention to himself by offering Dixon a job as the head bartender at the Goldfield, Gans's hotel in Baltimore, Maryland. The offer, however, was nothing more than a publicity stunt. There was no job for Dixon.[96] "I never heard anything from Joe about going to Baltimore," Dixon said. "I guess he was advertising his show when he said that. But his hotel would sure look good to me right now."[97] As Christmas 1907 neared, George Dixon made his final public appearance in the ring. Three former champions—James J. Corbett, Terry McGovern, and Dixon—sparred on December 12, 1907, at Hurtig & Seamon's Music Hall. Newspapers pulled no punches in describing the purpose of the event: "The object in bringing the former champions together at this time is to raise a little ready cash for Dixon, who is 'down and out' financially."[98]

The next three weeks were the most silent of Dixon's career. What must they have been like for the former champion? In his *Sporting Notes* column on December 30, 1907, J. Ed Grillo made a passing mention of Dixon, "now broke while O'Rourke has plenty of this world's goods."[99] In another article a week later, a writer claimed to have spotted "a second George Dixon" during a bout in Great Britain.[100] And then there was the obituary of "Hannibal," a "quaint old negro candy man" on January 1, 1908. Billed as a "mascot" of Yale students, Hannibal was a familiar figure on campus selling molasses candy accompanied with a clever verbal patter. Said to be more than a hundred years old when he died in the fall of 1907, he also taught students sleight of hand, sang and danced, made speeches, and gave boxing lessons. As his obituary explained:

> Early in his life, he was an instructor in boxing in the Yale gymnasium. He was one of the quickest pugilists in action whoever struck a blow, and he met George Dixon in several bouts without the former negro world's champion getting the decision. He was thrown into a room with John L. Sullivan when that champion was at the height of his popularity. John L. at that time weighed more than two hundred and fifty pounds, and when Hannibal was asked if he wished to meet the champion, he answered: Hannibal is not Mahomet, and must refuse to mix it up with the mountain.[101]

Although it sounded like fiction, Dixon and Hannibal did indeed meet in the ring, although not officially. During a stop of Dixon's theatrical company in New Haven, Connecticut, Dixon challenged any in the audience to take him on. Hannibal, then in his seventies, accepted the champion's call. Initially, Dixon laughed off the challenge and sought another opponent. But, Hannibal insisted, and entered the ring. Hannibal was frail and light yet still quick and agile. Dixon did not give a full effort—and both men parted with a draw.[102] It was a story Hannibal told for the remainder of his life, as well as a story that found its way into his obituary—meeting the most important Black athlete of his era meant something to him. And now, at Dixon's darkest hour, readers were reminded of that meaning once again.

But no one spoke louder and more eloquently in Dixon's final days than Sullivan. During Dixon's decline, O'Rourke justly shouldered much criticism in the eyes of many who hinted that the "fighter's erstwhile mentor had neglected his once protégé."[103] Sullivan, more than anyone, spoke of the injustices that Dixon was getting from those around him. In his "Jolts from 'John L.'" column, he wrote:

> When I advertised the fact a short time ago that Tom O'Rourke ought to do something for George Dixon I got a swift call by some people who said O'Rourke had done all the law allowed for the Little Chocolate. Well, let that go, to save an argument. At the time, my facts came out about Dixon being on his uppers, Joe Gans declared himself in for some free advertising by wiring for Dixon's address, promising to make the little fellow who held the featherweight championship for 10 years the head bartender in the Gans hotel.
>
> Up to the present, I haven't heard that Gans has made good the bluff by giving up the job he offered, and the little fellow is not likely to get the chance to handle the kinds of suds that he trained on for his last fight when Tommy Murphy put him out in one punch. Probably Gans meant the job offer just as much as he did the one he made a while ago to retire from the ring, a stall that I called.
>
> Between the white and black bluffers, Dixon is getting the con good and strong, and it isn't putting any meals under his belt nor any overcoats on his back. Pretty raw lines for the bronze fighting machine that led the whole world in his class for 10 years, and even went beyond the feathers to tackle the best men in the lightweight line.
>
> If Dixon had even the interest on the stacks of stuff he put into the pockets of some of his "friends" he wouldn't be wondering today where his next highball is coming from.[104]

Perhaps signaling what was to come, Sullivan also wrote of the games being played between the reigning heavyweight champion and his top challenger: "Jack Johnson says he will be waiting at the dock when Tommy Burns comes home from England, and the dark man swears he will force Burns to fight him. Before Burns sailed away, he swore he would fight Johnson when he got back. That looks like they would get together right away, perhaps right there on the gangplank, don't it? But I don't think they have any intention of disturbing the peace."[105]

———

On January 4, 1908, accompanied by an unknown white man and Black man, George Dixon was carried into Bellevue Hospital in New York

City suffering from apparent alcoholism.[106] He was wasted and worn. To the doctors, he famously said he had "fought his last fight with John Barleycorn, and had been beaten." He told physicians he had no friends except for John L. Sullivan.[107]

His condition became worse on Sunday and continued sinking until he died at 2 p.m. Monday, January 6, 1908.[108] He was thirty-seven years old. It was afterward discovered Dixon was the victim of an acute attack of inflammatory rheumatism, a type of autoimmune disease whereby the joints all over the body are inflamed and infected for a long period.[109] Signed by Henry C. Sears, a twenty-seven-year-old doctor, Dixon's death certificate lists him as "a single, colored boxing professor." His father, four brothers, and a sister survived him. A fitting, if unsigned, piece in the *Augusta (Georgia) Herald* captured the seemingly unavoidable trap that Dixon's celebrity forced him into over the previous decade. It read, in part:

> The finish of George Dixon is a lesson. I'm sorry that I was almost a prophet of his death. I saw him to the alcoholic ward at Bellevue and sprung the story of his final count. I didn't think he would cash in so soon, but death had him marked and it happened.
>
> Some men can drink and get away with it, but a fighter can't. A poet may dally with the bubbling bowl and still keep the job. Edgar Allan Poe could keep up a souse and write *The Purloined Letter*, but Arthur Duffy couldn't run a hundred yards inside of 10 flat with a hangover from the night before.
>
> There's procession that rum has downed. Beginning with my own recollection, Cal McCarthy, the featherweight champion, thought that he was always there, and took to the jovial thing. He forgot that another boy might come along, clean living, strong and unaccustomed to the hurrah of misplaced applause, who would take it away from him.
>
> George Dixon was the boy who did. Cal laughed at the little coon when he first met him in the ring. What chance had this unknown against him, the champion? And the newcomer made it a draw. It was a surprise. Had Cal been wise, he would have known why. Then the second try, and the champion went down in defeat.
>
> The boy who had never been soused beat the one who knew what it was to be thirsty in the morning.
>
> Then the cheers and the halo and the admiring "come and have one with me" for Dixon. He, too, fell for the foolish thing. He went along, popping them over, and between victories celebrated. Then he got his. . . . Again rum tolled the bell on its patron.[110]

By notable coincidence, Dixon and "Pike" Barnes, the jockey, two of the greatest Black athletes known to the sporting world of their era, died on the same day. Both were the same age, were intimate friends, and earned thousands of dollars in their primes but died penniless. Barnes made more than $100,000, but fast living dissipated both his fortunes and health. When Barnes retired, he had considerably more money than Dixon, as he invested it in the Keystone Café in Chicago. However, that endeavor faded and Barnes ended up spending his final days working as a bartender in Columbus, Ohio.[111]

Dixon's body was taken to the morgue and embalmed. In the event that none of his Boston friends claimed it, members of the Longacre Athletic Club in New York City agreed to defray the expenses of burial and offered its club rooms on West Twenty-Ninth Street for funeral services.[112] In the end, Dixon's brother John arranged to have the body sent to Boston.[113] But before that journey home, the body of George Dixon lay under the brilliant lights of the Longacre Club.

On Tuesday, January 7, 1908, hundreds filed past for one last look at the former champion who died broken in health, penniless and stripped of all honors won in the ring. In the main room of the club, the coffin rested under "the lights which were wont to shine on boxing bouts held for the amusement of those who a few years ago cheered to the echo the very appearance of the fighter whose dead face the lights illuminated."[114] Black men by the score, and more than a few Black women, also paid their respects, leaving small floral tributes. Some went to gaze at the dead gladiator out of curiosity, but they were the minority among the masses. "Genuine grief and sorrow" filled the room.[115] There was a generational divide among the worshippers, as is often seen when a hero of the past passes. Many of the young fighters who filed past did not know of Dixon as a champion. However, their elders were deeply disturbed by the Dixon in front of them versus the one they remembered from just fifteen years earlier.

Dixon's body arrived in Boston from New York at 7 p.m. Wednesday, January 8, 1908. Originally, the body was to be delivered to his brother's house, but plans were changed due to the outpouring of grief across the city. Dixon laid in repose in the chapel attached to the undertaker's business. He rested in a drop-side casket of steel gray embossed with silver extension bars, a gift provided by the city's sporting men, many of whom had earned handsome profits on Dixon's bouts over the years. Around the casket were a dozen floral designs, four bouquets, and a host of cut flowers, all sent by his New York friends. It was there that the family viewed the body.[116]

On Thursday, January 9, 1908, the Charles Street African Methodist Episcopal (AME) Church in Boston brimmed with two thousand people, white and Black, men and women. Another three thousand gathered outside, unable to gain admittance.[117] In the years leading up to the Civil War, the Charles Street congregation served as a gathering place for abolitionists and activists, including the likes of William Lloyd Garrison, Frederick Douglass, and Sojourner Truth.[118] The church led the fight against the 1850 Fugitive Slave Law and other forms of oppression against the city's Black population. It was a haven for former slaves and a transit point on the freedom trail for runaway slaves fleeing to Canada. With each succeeding pastor, the church rose in political and civic prominence as it grew into the city's largest Black congregation. In 1876, the church purchased the Charles Street Meeting House, a red brick structure topped by a white stone steeple, hunkered down at the foot of Beacon Hill. And thirty-two years later, the Dixon funeral would be the biggest event in its esteemed history.

Waves of humanity ushered the funeral procession as it wound slowly through the city, then escorted the body to the church steps, arriving shortly after 2 p.m. Beethoven's "Funeral March" echoed down the church's center aisle and out into the cold winter afternoon air as the casket, met at the door by the Rev. T. W. Henderson, was carried to the front of the church by six pallbearers, including Dixon's old friend Joe Walcott.[119] Newspapers made note of the fact that no color line was drawn that day—"white and Black mingled in a common sorrow."[120] The *Los Angeles Times* said "Dixon's death was a stimulus for a great display of esteem the public had for him. Men who were supposed to be overwhelmed by racial prejudices literally fell all over themselves to contribute a mite to the fund which provided a decent burial of this boy, who was undoubtedly one of the most popular fighters that ever faced a crowd."[121]

After a hymn by a women's quartet, the Rev. Henry J. Callis read the words of Job 14: "But a man dies and is laid low; he breathes his last and is no more. As the water of a lake dries up or a riverbed becomes parched and dry, so he lies down and does not rise; till the heavens are no more, people will not awake or be roused from their sleep." A prayer followed; a solo was performed. Then, Rev. Henderson rose to address the largest funeral gathering for a Black man in the history of the city (a distinction not overlooked by newspapers of the day).[122] He spoke from Hebrews

9:27: "It is appointed unto man once to die, but after this the judgment." At the close of the sermon, Henderson eulogized the former champion. Following the service, some five thousand people filed past to see Dixon one final time. It was close to 4 p.m. before the lid was closed.

The delay was such that darkness fell on the funeral procession as the hearse, followed by ten carriages, arrived at Mt. Hope Cemetery in Boston. Burial was performed by lantern light. Few, however, missed the irony of the outpouring for a man who died alone:

> Many of these [friends and followers] were among the men, who, after Dixon's career had ended, smothered his casket with floral tokens, but who wished not to give the little Negro the price of food to keep him alive. There are many who will say he came to his end by his own hand—that he drank himself to death. Whatever truth there may be in this can be taken as it will, but the question is: Where were the friends who shared the shekels he made in his fights, after he became useless as a ring idol? Not one of them offered him aid and before his death Dixon said he had only one friend in the world and that was John L. Sullivan, who, strangely enough, ended his fighting career long ago. It seems strange that one who had helped so many others to succeed could claim but one friend at the end and on every hand the comment was free: Where was Tom O'Rourke?[123]

Dixon was initially buried in an unmarked grave. However, New York boxing promoter Mike Newman took charge of creating a monument. Working with the local undertaker, Newman arranged for a final resting place elsewhere in Mt. Hope. A single plot was insufficient for a monument, so Newman campaigned to purchase four plots for Dixon and his monument.[124] Originally, plans called for a six-foot-square base of dark granite with a full-body bronze statue of Dixon atop it standing six feet, six inches—a full foot higher than Dixon's true height. It would show Dixon clad in boxing attire with his right hand resting on his hip and the left hand hanging by his side. The cost was $1,500.[125]

Those ambitious memorial plans changed. Instead, a granite memorial was purchased for, and still marks, the grave in Mt. Hope Cemetery. The polished, oval Westerly granite panel stands four feet high. Its face features a bust of Dixon in his prime. It cost $300. Only a few friends were present when the stone was placed in position on May 24, 1909.

This was the second memorial to Dixon purchased with funds collected nationwide by Joe Humphreys, Terry McGovern, and Young Corbett.[126] On April 14, 1908, in New York City, two hundred miles down the Atlantic Coast, the Art Commission of New York approved a $1,500 design for a Dixon Memorial Fountain, a memorial with a peculiar rounded basin and an ornate spiked light pole projecting out of it.[127] That design was later changed to a less ornate, but similarly grand fountain, featuring a horse trough fed from a lion's mouth on the street side and a smaller human water fountain on the sidewalk side.

The fountain was ultimately installed at the intersection of Eighth and Horatio Streets. Set within an ethically and racially diverse West Village neighborhood, dominated by the Irish, the memorial basin celebrated Dixon's achievements and his memory as "an ideal of class and interethnic solidarity grounded on mutual admiration for heroism in sport."[128] Fountains in that era served both commemorative and utilitarian purposes. A fountain was cheaper, less controversial, and easier to get approved than a statue. Like monuments, fountains were also good vehicles for what in today's parlance would be "donor recognition." Hence, many horse troughs became memorials by incorporating inscriptions. Their popularity was short lived, however. Animal drinking fountains generated disputes between advocates of tradition and modernity over what amenities and how many should the Greater New York City streets and sidewalks accommodate. Moreover, automobiles and trucks were beginning to supplant horses and horse carts. These new vehicles constantly bashed into the troughs and fountains, many of which subsequently had to be removed—unceremoniously—as traffic obstructions.

Dixon's fountain, too, was removed at a later date, presumably for reconstruction of a traffic triangle, but there is no record of when this occurred. Two black-and-white photos of the Dixon fountain are all that remain.[129] Yet when it had been installed, newspapers across the country took note of this final gesture to remember Dixon:

> It is rather unusual for a monument to be erected in a public thoroughfare in honor of a pugilist. But that is what has been done in a street in New York. And the monument takes the form of a fountain from which flows nothing stronger than water. The pugilist was not one of the amateur, or millionaire kind either, but was a plain professional fighter and a colored man at that. In short, he was George Dixon, the late negro boxer and one-time champion featherweight of the world. . . . The fountain is of a simple and beautiful design. The side facing the sidewalk provides water for thirsty human beings who may be passing by and the opposite side that facing the street contains a watering trough for horses.[130]

George Dixon Memorial Fountain, rear view, dedicated on August 28, 1908, at the corner of Thompson and Broome Streets in New York City. *Courtesy of the Library of Congress Prints and Photographs Division.*

George Dixon Memorial Fountain, front view, dedicated on August 28, 1908, at the corner of Thompson and Broome Streets in New York City. *Courtesy of the Library of Congress Prints and Photographs Division.*

An inscription on its base read: "In Memory of George Dixon Erected by His Friends."

Seen as "the dealmaker" in his early days, O'Rourke's public image changed in his later years. "Prizefighting" had been criminalized in the State of New York in 1859: all prizefighting activities became misdemeanors, including arranging, engaging in, or training for a prizefight. The law endured until September 1896, when the Horton Law legalized boxing in the state. The new law expanded the definition of this misdemeanor to include: "public or private sparring exhibition(s), with or without gloves, within the state, at which an admission fee is charged or received . . . provided, however, that sparring exhibitions with gloves of not less than five ounces each in weight may be held by a domestic incorporated athletic association in a building leased by it for athletic purposes only for at least one year, or in a building owned and occupied by such association."[131]

The loophole created by that latter provision ushered the sport into prominence, mainly by giving rise to athletic associations that promoted sparring exhibitions. But the Horton Law was short-lived. In September 1900, the Lewis Law replaced it and made boxing, once again, illegal in New York. However, the sport continued in the state until 1911 on a club-membership basis. There were always ways around the laws, like by charging admission fees as membership dues and conducting bouts judged to be non-decisions, even having sportswriters provide judgments on winners and allow members to settle gambling bets.

O'Rourke did not hide his feelings on the decision to repeal the Horton Law. He blamed a "hayseed faction" of New York legislators for the repeal and more than insinuated that bribery was involved: "I will not say that the question of the almighty dollar cut any figure in this repeal. Whether it was the itching palm or not is a question that some lobbyists at Albany might answer. They are pretty good judges in palmistry." Of course, O'Rourke's protests were compromised by the fact that he was part of the festering problem lawmakers sought to address. Boxing in the early 1900s was rife with fixed bouts. As newspapers later reflected, "Managers of pugilists and promoters of pugilistic bouts so befouled the city and the sport that men with even very liberal consciences could endure their inequities no longer."[132] Lawmakers—troubled by the "series and succession of fakes, frauds, double-crosses, 'barneys,' flops, grafts, etc."—ended the whole sport instead of dealing with its widespread corruption.

Charles Harvey, "Tex" Rickard, Les Darcy, Tom O'Rourke, and E. T. O'Sullivan at New York Harbor, December 1916. Glass negative. Photo by Bain News Service. *Courtesy of the Library of Congress Prints and Photographs Division.*

Money—and lots of it—sat at the root of the corruption. As O'Rourke explained, "Many of the wealthiest merchants and bankers of New York were regular patrons of the big contests and several well-known and wealthy sportsmen have come to me and expressed their keen disappointment at the victory of the Lewis anti-boxing bill. The endorsement of boxing by the better class, by responsible businessmen, by the wealthiest sportsmen in New York, has placed boxing on a higher level than it ever before obtained. The Horton Law will soon be a dead letter, but that doesn't mean that boxing is dead."[133]

Lawmakers and reporters cited the Kid McCoy–James J. Corbett bout on August 30, 1900, in Madison Square Garden, as the final bell for the sport in the state. The bout was the last one conducted under the Horton Law, and was found so corrupt that lawmakers changed the law the next day. Both men had a long track record of corruption. Two years earlier, Corbett's match against Tom Sharkey, under O'Rourke's management, ended when Corbett's second entered the ring to protest a foul. At that point, referee "Honest" John Kelly declared the fight over and all bets off. A near riot followed.

Soon afterward, New York state senator Timothy D. Sullivan convened all parties to investigate the possibility that Corbett's second had been paid off to interrupt the match. O'Rourke, of course, saw the controversy as a reason for a rematch.[134] The McCoy-Corbett bout was the third fight card in three days at the Garden. Only days earlier, in the eleventh round against Tommy West, the crowd violently booed Joe Walcott out of the building after he quit the fight by sitting on his stool, claiming an arm injury. Already wary, the McCoy-Corbett crowd processed rumors that McCoy would take a dive in the fifth round—and it didn't help perceptions of the fight when Corbett knocked him out in the prescribed round.[135]

The game, in many ways, simply passed beyond O'Rourke. Although he had moments of success—including Walcott winning the welterweight championship in 1901—his feud with *Los Angeles Times* sports columnist Harry Carr typified his relationship with boxing after the turn of the century. Carr outlined O'Rourke's oafishness in print, calling the veteran manager "typical of a phase of the sporting world that is passing. [He] was considered rather a good sample of a 'smart' manager of the old, rough days of the prize ring."[136] Carr wrote of a visit O'Rourke paid to a training demonstration that Carr was covering: "He didn't belong. He was from a different class of life. A tedious old 'sport' who didn't fit in, who dimly realized the fact and was filled with chagrin and rage in consequence. . . . Before we had been in the training camp twelve hours, O'Rourke attempted to influence *The Times* to hold back the true report of [heavyweight Al] Palzer's condition and degree of boxing skill in order to help out some betting scheme."[137]

Carr continued that if O'Rourke employed the same methods with modern boxers he "would kill a boy." O'Rourke, never one to walk away from a fight, fired off a letter to Carr, which was printed in the newspaper in February 1913. The jilted manager wrote, in part:

> I'm not in the habit of noticing scurrility, even though it emanates from the brain of a brilliant sporting writer like yourself. What? Lie down there, Fido. A sporting writer who can command a weekly salary of perhaps $30 and "grabbings" is not to be sniffed at, let me tell you. It's almost as much of an achievement as managing a fat-headed prizefighter.
>
> But I'm straying from the subject. While I've never gone about with a chip on my shoulder looking for a fight, I've sometimes felt the necessity of kicking a mangy mongrel out of my way in order to

avoid contagion and this seems to be another case in point—and, mind you, I like the dog and dislike reflecting on his loyal and noble nature by making odious comparisons.[138]

But Carr was correct. O'Rourke got greedy, lazy, and even more corrupt in his later years. He often passed up a better matchup for his man at a competing club in favor of a lessor one at his own establishment. He became a bloated caricature of himself; even his physical appearance started to slide. Although an athlete in his earliest days, the image of O'Rourke that dominates his later years is one shaped after he fully embraced his success. His once barrel chest had settled into a rather prominent belly; an admittedly round chin of his youth dropped and spread; his eyes were dark and wide set. He parted his hair, neatly slicked, just off-center, down toward his ears and then back. He was aggressively mustachioed, yet cleanly shaven elsewhere on his face, as many of the men of his day were. He was a formal, tidy dresser of some renown. His strong, unwavering nose hinted at a man who spent more time outside the ring than in it.

Negative headlines dogged O'Rourke. In May 1911, heavyweight Al Palzer, the "most promising of the white hopes," had a falling out with O'Rourke. He had grown tired of "acting as a meal ticket" for his manager.[139] Like Dixon, and his numerous falling outs with O'Rourke, Palzer returned—and for the same reason. Say what they did about O'Rourke, he was a man who could make a deal.

Featherweight champion Abe Attell accused O'Rourke and his National Sporting Club physician of doping him with cocaine in order to tilt his bout with "Knockout" Brown. O'Rourke did not deny the act, only the motivation, instead claiming they were trying to numb Attell's injured hand: "The physician did the same thing to Al Palzer before he fought both Kennedy and Kaufman. It's funny this little treatment should put Palzer into the championship class and affect Attell in the opposite way."[140]

When O'Rourke resigned as boxing commissioner in August 1922, he spoke—without intended irony—of his efforts at cleaning up the game: "I've put in the most strenuous year of my life settling the differences between managers, promoters and boxers. I thought I knew the ins and outs of the game, but I had to join the State Athletic Commission to be taught the intricacies and methods used by present-day managers and promoters against the boxers."[141] Two months later, O'Rourke formed an agency to promote fighters for international bouts, in direct competition against fellow promoter Tex Rickard. O'Rourke obtained a lease to the Polo Grounds in New York and promoted several championship bouts there. During his management of Irish heavyweight Pat Redman, O'Rourke sued several New York papers as a result of statements made by sportswriters about Redman, but scored no "legal knockouts." In February 1924, he charged that Rickard, a man with whom he served as a fellow pallbearer at the funeral of legendary Old West figure Bat Masterson,[142] had turned over $135,000 worth of Jack Dempsey–Luis Angel Firpo tickets to a ticket speculator. A legislative inquiry into the action was sought, but nothing ever came of the claim. Subsequently, the State Athletic Commission warned Rickard that "the evil of ticket speculation must be wiped out" or the commissions would close Madison Square Garden off as a venue for fights.[143]

In his final years, O'Rourke called the Pioneer Gymnasium his home. Located at West Forty-Fourth Street in New York City, he operated that facility with long-time friend Charlie Doesserick. There, he lived among memories of brighter days than he would never know again, such as opening the National Sporting Club, the "swankiest fight club in the country," in that same building a quarter century earlier.[144]

For his last trip to a prominent public stage, O'Rourke served as Max Schmeling's trainer when the German heavyweight made his first trip to America and fought his way up to a heavyweight title fight with Boston's Jack Sharkey. Schmeling won that bout on a disqualification, then lost the title in a rematch with "the Boston Sailor" two years later in a controversial decision. In June 1936, Schmeling was matched against Joe Louis, the most prominent Black boxer since Jack Johnson. The bout was heavy with international political tensions. While the world predicted a speedy win for Louis, O'Rourke—billed by the press as "the oldest referee and fight manager in the world"—was standing up for Schmeling.[145] A few hours prior to the bout, O'Rourke raged at the refusal of the Boxing Commission to restore him to his post as a judge of fights, a response based on the commission's reluctance to believe the arguments of the eighty-four-year-old O'Rourke that his vision was clear and judgment unimpaired.[146] His last words to the press, delivered in the German's dressing room just before the fight, were, "Schmeling is slow. He is not a great boxer, but he has plenty of moxie. That German can take it. If there is no hitch and the fight goes through, you can quote me as being one fellow who says Schmeling will stand up under Louis's earlier attacks and then come through to batter his way to victory. And I will be right in Schmeling's dressing room to congratulate him."[147]

He was only half correct. O'Rourke collapsed and died immediately after he grasped the German's hand and wished him good luck. His last expression, so said those at his side, was "one of surprise—he couldn't believe death had overtaken him."[148] Schmeling's handlers tried to convince him that O'Rourke had merely passed out. Some American writers on hand attempted to use the moment to paint the German as "cold" and "heartless" as "he watched a man die without a flicker of emotion."[149] Medical assistance was called, but O'Rourke was dead before any attempts to revive him began. Police initially misidentified O'Rourke as a thirty-five-year-old man—an odd bit of police work given the veteran fight manager and promoter was an octogenarian at the time. After a business card was discovered in O'Rourke's pocket, and the number on it called, a positive identification was made.[150] Schmeling went on to an unexpected victory over Louis, unaware he had said goodbye forever to his friend.[151]

Despite a career that continued nearly three decades after Dixon's death, O'Rourke never shook the connection. Often called upon to reflect on Dixon's life and career, he never spoke an ill word about his former charge. However, his actions—and absence—during Dixon's darkest days spoke volumes. Many called Dixon's needs to O'Rourke's attention. As only the big man could do, Sullivan made it clear what the manager needed to do: what "[O'Rourke] ought to have done long ago—put Dixon in the front room of the first house on Easy Street."[152]

O'Rourke's legacy is a complicated one. His dealings with Black fighters, and particularly Dixon, granted his charges previously unseen opportunities and wealth. The man could make a deal. And without that talent in his corner, Dixon never would have become a world champion. O'Rourke was a visionary, blazing trails across the country and across the pond to Great Britain, which eventually turned into a favorite destination for American boxers. But there was the dark, controlling O'Rourke, who bullied and financially bled fighters and business associates alike. He had no use for anyone he saw as having no use to him. The complicated epitaph of Tom O'Rourke, as the saying goes, would require both sides of the tombstone. In his pamphlet, *A Lesson in Boxing*, Dixon included a photograph of O'Rourke, and these words written at the height of both men's fame:

> The accompanying cut is an excellent likeness of Mr. Thomas O'Rourke, my Manager and Backer. . . . He has brought before the public many successful boxers, and as well as being a thorough

sporting man, is a careful and shrewd businessman. He is a sociable and pleasant fellow and his disposition is always the same. In every contest of note in which I have figured, Mr. O'Rourke has superintended my affairs and I owe my success to his good engineering. Pugilists, as a rule, make very poor managers. It is a combination rarely found in one person. Any person who has ever transacted business with him will agree with me when I say that he is an honest, straightforward businessman, and I am indeed proud to claim him as my manager.[153]

At the time of Dixon's death, the United States was a country at odds with itself. In the minds of some, 1908 represented the moment America matured into modernity. The events and innovations that occurred within that twelve-month frame marked the country's entry into the modern world as its citizens started discovering a "sense of what was possible." Henry Ford launched the Model T. The Wright Brothers revealed flight to the world. American warships steamed around the globe. Six automobiles set out on a twenty-thousand-mile race from New York City to Paris via the frozen Bering Strait. Buoyed by these achievements, from sensational to the sentimental to the silly, the country felt confident enough in its genius, resourcefulness, and military might to begin playing a dominant role in global affairs.[154] Yet within this same year, even as playwright Israel Zangwill coined the phrase "melting pot" to denote the nation's capacity to absorb and assimilate different ethnicities, the "color line" between Black and white continued to thicken.

As short-sighted as it seems in retrospect, many around the fight game thought George Dixon might signal the end of an era. Opportunities for Black fighters were narrowing as racial divisions widened. Folks like John L. Sullivan rejoiced at the fading of Black boxers among the ranks of championship-caliber challengers. He wrote: "[Joe] Gans is out, and so is Dixon and [Joe] Walcott. There isn't any other clever dark meat in sight and I am guessing it will be a long time before white men will allow the sun-burned brother to get back to terms of equality in the ring."[155]

Drawn around more than sport, that color line touched every corner of society. As a result, violence continued to erupt frequently between the races, most notably in August 1908 when whites in Springfield, Illinois, the hometown and resting place of Abraham Lincoln, tried to drive Black citizens from the city. White mobs burned Black businesses and homes and lynched two Black men, in reaction to multiple reports that a white woman had been assaulted in her home by a Black man. Springfield Police took into custody a vagrant, Joe James, for one of the assaults; George Richardson, a local factory worker, was arrested for the second. The mob assembled at the Sangamon County Courthouse to lynch both men. Unable to reach the accused, the mob turned its wrath to two other Black men who were in the area and quickly lynched them. The mob then vented its fury on the homes of Black families in Springfield. Some fought in self-defense, shooting back when fired upon, and the first victim of the lynch mob, Scott Burton, used his shotgun in an attempt to save his life and home. The second victim was an eighty-four-year-old cobbler named William Donegan, whose reputation had been tainted in the eyes of the mob by his having been married to a white woman for more than thirty years. When the carnage finally ended, six Black people had been shot and killed, two lynched, and hundreds of thousands of dollars' worth of property destroyed. About two thousand Black people were driven out of Springfield as a result of the riot.[156]

Much of this violence was inflamed by newspapers that populated headlines with racial sensation and violence. Readers wanted tales of murders, lynchings, suicides, divorces, and the like, and newspapers gave them what they demanded. They also became more racially accusatory: "Negro Kidnaps a Boy." "Negro Who Attacked Seven-Year-Old White Girl Given the Limit." "Fatal Fight over Negress." "War Office Bars Negro." "Northern Negroes Barred as Teachers." "Must Draw the Color Line, Says Gov. Hoke Smith." "Asbury Park Now Has Negro Bugaboo." "Hoke Smith Says Slavery Was Boon." "Negro Accused of Attack on Child." In an article for *McGrit's Magazine* in 1908, Richard Wright Jr. was one of the first scholars to take issue with the press and its portrayal of Black Americans. While admitting there "is not particular demand for the good side of negro life," Wright exposed the rampant pessimism shown toward the race by the press of the day. Son of famed civil rights activist Richard Wright Sr., he was a powerful voice in this growing movement. He received the first baccalaureate degree ever awarded by Georgia State Industrial College in June 1898. Later, he became the first Black man to earn a PhD from the University of Pennsylvania. He went on to be a professor and president of Wilberforce University in Ohio. In his article, Wright deduced:

> Now the great mass of people gets their ideas of the negroes from what they read in the daily papers. Can it be wondered at there has been a growth of hostility toward the negroes; that many of the former friends are becoming indifferent, if not indeed hostile? The

cause is not so much the undue increase of crime but the undue emphasis on crime by the newspapers. All who study the subject carefully are agreed that the negroes are making much progress against severe odds. But all are not students; the majority of the people are busy men and women, with no time for statistics. It is to them, as well as to the negroes, that the injustice is done by the undue display of the vice and crime of the race.[157]

Consider the "angry Black man"—an ugly, enduring American stereotype with roots running well deeper than the nation's founding. The image of this Black man, one full of violence and hate, goes back at least to Nat Turner and the revolt of Virginian slaves in 1831. Fear of rebellious slaves has haunted the dreams of white masters since they first brought them ashore. But the thought of a Black man not only on equal footing with a white man, but also with a fighting chance to beat him, defeat him, maybe even kill him, was too much to bear. Even inside the ring. George Dixon was not seen as this stereotype. He was hailed as a man who "knew his place." Yet as far back as the Carnival of Champions in 1892, white response to Dixon victories over white men was excessive, and even this only served as only a small taste of what was to come.[158]

Perhaps the ultimate breaking point for race relations in the United States didn't even happen on domestic soil. On December 26, 1908, in Sydney, Australia, a thirty-year-old Jack Johnson stepped into the ring to fight Tommy Burns, the heavyweight champion of the world. Like every titleholder before him, Burns drew a hard color line. But Johnson pursued Burns, who agreed to a match on terms that he received $30,000 of a $35,000 purse. Johnson destroyed Burns before twenty-five thousand spectators. Blood was pouring from Burns when police stopped the fight in the fourteenth round. Johnson remained the heavyweight champion for seven years, fending off a series of "Great White Hopes."

After Johnson's victory, Dixon was used as a counterbalance. With time and distance, Dixon's standing as an honorable, forthright boxer was restored—but not without a motive. Dixon was presented as the Black man who succeeded because he knew his place, a perfect counter to Johnson's "bad nigger" archetype. As New York City's Black sports celebrated their newly crowned champion in Johnson—brass bands, cakewalks, automobiles, lofty speeches—Dixon was remembered fondly by those longing for a different type of champion:

> Only a few days ago, the same daily papers that spoke of how the colored people appreciate the negro World's Heavyweight Champion

told to the world how the first Black man that ever held a championship died in Bellview [sic] Hospital without a home or friend in the same New York where colored sports went wild over Johnson.

The man who died was George Dixon, once the champion of champions of the whole world, the man that put the negro on the fighting map, the man that made the lovers of the sport take notice to little men. . . .

Could these gallant sports overlook all of these good things this little negro has done? Did they forget him so soon? Some sports, who haven't a good word for anyone, say that he spent his money among the white men, which is only partly true. Dixon spent his money freely among all races, but made it off the white people. Prize-fighting that amounts to anything is solely supported by the white man. He makes the negro champion and pays him for his work.[159]

Soon after Dixon's death, a forgotten photograph of a young Dixon, no more than seventeen years old, still working as an errand boy for Elmer Chickering, was presented to the *Boston Daily Globe* by a man who worked alongside Dixon in the photo studio years earlier. He uncovered the photograph while cleaning out his attic. Most believed it to be the earliest photo of the young pugilist. The unnamed man regaled the newsroom with tales of Dixon's early days in Boston, as well as blow-by-blow detail of what he believed to be Dixon's earliest bouts in the United States. No details were recorded, except for one brief paragraph: "I saw him fight the first five battles. After he won from a little Hebrew named Cohen, for which he received $40, he went to a clothing store and spent all the money for clothes. He had a black eye the next Sunday, but he was the warmest colored man in the West End."

George Dixon. Collodion print on card. Photo by Richard K. Fox. *Courtesy of Special Collections, Fine Arts Library, Harvard University.*

Forgotten Legacy

HE DOES NOT EXACTLY LOOK LIKE DIXON. He is bigger, thicker, tattooed, including one reading "Dixon" on his right forearm. But there is something special about Trevor Silver's portrayal of George Dixon. Not an actor by trade, Silver was cast because of a family connection—billed by producers as a "distant relative of George Dixon." His representation was a moment of pride, a chance to tell his family's story.

In February 2015, Black Halifax put together this three-minute video celebrating Dixon's accomplishments. Written by Valerie Mason-John and performed by Silver, the video, while presenting no new information, is a wonderful visual representation of the man—the first screen depiction of the fighter. *Black Halifax: Stories from Here* was an interactive project celebrating the personalities, sites, and events of historic significance to the African Nova Scotian community. They were presented by local performance poets and professional actors through storytelling, and are still widely available on YouTube.[1] Mason-John, who also served as co-producer and artistic director for the project, spoke of Dixon's vital inclusion: "Dixon has almost been erased from our history and not just by white people. Our Black history has been forgotten. How is he not on our five-dollar bill? The best creative ideas come when you are rejected, when you are not welcome. He found another way in. He was a genius."[2]

It was an imperfect representation, but George Dixon lived again.

———

What is left of George Dixon's legacy today? Until recently, the next century brought only momentary flashes of Dixon. One press report had Los Angeles as the site of a "second coming" of George Dixon in 1921. *New York Evening World* sports editor Robert Edgren spotted Danny Edwards, a twenty-three-year-old Black fighter from Oakland, California. He was small—five-foot-two, 118 pounds—but coiled with power. Edgren could not help but make the connection as he wrote: "If Tom O'Rourke had this boy he'd make another Little Chocolate of him, with all of Little Chocolate's popularity."[3] In 1955, when Dr. Joyce Brothers hit the $32,000 level on the CBS program *The $64,000 Question*, she successfully named George Dixon as the man who defeated Jack Skelly in the Carnival of Champions.[4] And as recently as November 2015, when Tyson Cave of Halifax won a title fight, the CBC reported the event this way: "Boxing history was made Saturday night at the Dartmouth Sportsplex as home-town favorite Tyson Cave beat Walter Rojas of Argentina in less than two rounds to claim the World Boxing Union super bantamweight title. Cave, thirty-four, was the first Nova Scotia-born boxer to win a world title on home soil. . . . [However] Cave is not the first Nova Scotian-born boxer to win a world title. George Dixon has that honor after being crowned world bantamweight champion in 1888."[5]

In recent years, his home community has reclaimed his legacy. Perhaps inspired by the Black Halifax series, an awakening has happened across Nova Scotia. In 2018, Halifax Parks and Recreation and the African Nova Scotian Affairs Office hung a large portrait of Dixon at the George Dixon Community Centre on Brunswick Street in Halifax.[6] That same year, the Nova Scotia Sports Hall of Fame named Dixon, somewhat anti-climactically, the sixth greatest athlete in Nova Scotia history—falling immediately behind fellow fighter Sam Langford, and along with two hockey players, a swimmer and a curler.[7] In summer 2020, a new mural depicting Dixon was unveiled near the Africville Museum. The mural was painted on the sides of a shipping container the museum used for stor-age. Dixon's name even arose in relation to the ring as Nova Scotia boxer Custio Clayton fought for the international welterweight title in October 2020, seeking to become the first Black Nova Scotian boxer since Dixon to win an international title.[8]

Beyond these hometown asides, however, Dixon has remained hidden from view to the wider world. Even when he was inducted into the *Ring Magazine* Hall of Fame in 1956, the International Boxing Hall of Fame in 1990, and the Canadian Sports Hall of Fame in 1955,[9] his testimonials were little more than rewrites of attempts at biographies. His inductions inspired no new scholarship. Outside of some isolated examples, sport history and Canadian history—indeed, Black history—rarely celebrate his accomplishments. There is an odd silence in his isolation.

When one considers Dixon in context, you see he suffered the same fate as many from his era. His legacy was unfortunately cemented in memory during a period of white rebellion against the idea of rising Black influence, a period more focused on white hopes than on historic Black accomplishments. The grip of Jim Crow was continuing to tighten—and a willing press helped fuel strife between the races.

He also did not plead his case as loudly as others. Dixon did not serve the movement; he was never an outspoken "race man." Scholar Mark Anthony Neal defines that somewhat loaded term as one of a group of "Black men of stature and integrity who represented the best that African Americans had to offer in the face of Jim Crow segregation. . . . Race men inspire pride; their work, their actions and their speech represent excellence instead of evoking shame and embarrassment."[10] Born of oppression, the term's origin is cloudy, although some argue that W. E. B. Du Bois popularized its twentieth-century use. In a 1945 study of the Chicago South Side, *Black Metropolis* sociologist St. Clair Drake and researcher Horace Cayton Jr. described "race men" as those Black men who felt "impelled to prove to themselves continually that they [were] not the inferior creatures which their minority status implie[d]."[11] They also defined a particular kind of race man—the race hero—who felt this need intensely: "If a man 'fights for The Race,' if he seems to be 'all for The Race,' if he is 'fearless in his approach to white people,' he becomes a Race Hero. Similarly, any Negro becomes a hero if he beats the white man at his own game and forces the white world to recognize his talent or service or achievement."[12]

By this definition, George Dixon was certainly a "race hero," as his drive to complete and defeat white opponents was obvious. He was hailed among the Black community as a sign of progress. However, to call Dixon a traditional race man is a stretch. Scholar Sheryll D. Cashin set down two main values for twentieth-century race men or women: First, that race men are strivers who achieve, often in the realm of higher education, and their achievements flow from a confidence in their own innate abilities and that of their brethren. Second, that race men are agitators who are committed to uplifting their people.[13] Cashin again cited Du Bois, a political organizer not content to stay within his ivory tower of Harvard, who used his prestige to help the race. Both of these measures of a man—the striving and the agitating—are necessary to be defined as a race man.

Jack Johnson was the first such Black boxer, and he paved the way for the greats of the mid-1900s, who found vast financial and cultural opportunities unheard of in Dixon's era. By contrast, when Dixon's personal demons eroded any opportunity at long-term security for himself, or future financial opportunity for his backers, he became an exhibit for hire and then a broken man. It is no wonder, then, that mid-twentieth-century civil rights leaders were restrained from resurrecting the legacy of Dixon. Dixon thus missed his biggest opportunity to be revived in the popular consciousness. He sat somewhere in the past, somewhat lost, almost forgotten, a trivia answer.

It did not need to be that way. To see another way forward, historians need to resist the temptation to tease out lessons from George Dixon by comparing him to Jack Johnson. While both men were Black boxing champions, their experiences and existences were far too different. Their sizes, eras, personalities, social structures—there are too many variables to equate these men and draw any significant lessons from them.

When I think back over Dixon's short life, the words that resonate most to me about his missed possibilities were spoken just days after his death. On a Sunday evening, January 12, 1908, the Rev. Henry J. Callis[14] climbed into the pulpit with St. Paul on his mind: "I have fought a good fight; I have finished my course; I have kept the faith." The Columbus Avenue AME Church was filled this evening to hear his message. A staunch Republican, Mason, and Odd Fellow, Callis was known as an exceptional orator. Just days before his January 12 sermon, he assisted in Dixon's funeral services at the Charles Street AME Church. He was inspired by the fallen champion, and on this night, he reflected on lessons from the boxer's life for his assembled congregation:

> The thousands of dollars won by him leave no lasting benefit. Can it be true that what the world craves, what humanity is willing to make any sacrifice to obtain, will do us no good when we come to die? Money, money, money; sport, sport, sport; a good time, a good time, a good time. That is what George Dixon had; that is what the large majority of young people today are looking for.
>
> George Dixon died away from home and from friends, without money, simply down and out. St. Paul died away from home, away from kindred and in prison, but he was not down, he was not out. He was up on the wings of faith; he was in the arms of a loving savior for whom he had fought a good fight and won a crown of never-fading glory. Which one of these men are you going to follow?[15]

In that moment, Callis conveyed what so many had known for years—George Dixon had died long before his body left the Earth.

Taken as a whole, Dixon was an unmatched talent and innovator, but his willingness to cede control of his life to capitalize on that talent and achieve lofty standing became his greatest weakness and ultimate down-fall. George Dixon never bucked the rising tide of Jim Crow America; instead, his course was navigated for him, and that sacrifice cost him his life and a degree of immortality. Nevertheless, his passage from popular memory should not diminish the victories achieved by this diminutive warrior, a man who set the course for Black sports heroes today—a fight well fought by any measure.

NOTES

Introduction

1. "George Dixon's Belt Rescued during Fire," *Boston Daily Globe*, October 20, 1926.
2. "Doings of the Race," *New Orleans Crusader* editorial as quoted in the *Cleveland Gazette*, July 9, 1892.
3. Robert E. Rinehart, "Beyond Traditional Sports Historiography," in *Deconstructing Sport History: A Postmodern Analysis*, ed. Murray G. Phillips (Albany: State University of New York Press, 2006), 181–202.
4. Rinehart, "Beyond Traditional Sports Historiography."
5. A. J. Liebling, *The Sweet Science* (New York: North Point Press, 1994), 4.
6. Nat Fleischer, *Black Dynamite: Three Colored Aces* (New York: C. J. O'Brien, 1938).
7. Steven Laffoley, *Shadowboxing: The Rise and Fall of George Dixon* (Lawrencetown Beach, Nova Scotia: Pottersfield Press, 2012).
8. Kevin R. Smith, *Black Genesis: The History of the Black Prizefighter, 1760–1870* (Lincoln, NE: iUniverse, 2003), 3.
9. Kevin R. Smith, *Black Genesis: The History of the Black Prizefighter, 1760–1870* (Lincoln, NE: iUniverse, 2003), 3.

Chapter 1

1. "Unjust Treatment Charged," *National Police Gazette*, September 6, 1890.
2. "Dixon Wins the Fight," *National Police Gazette*, November 8, 1890.
3. "Dixon, the Bantam-Weight. The Famous Colored Prize-Fighter Describes His Many Contests," *Baltimore Sun*, November 4, 1890.
4. "The Colored Man in the Ring," *Boston Daily Globe*, April 19, 1891.
5. "The Colored Man in the Ring."
6. Nat Fleischer, *Black Dynamite: Three Colored Aces* (New York: C. J. O'Brien, 1938).
7. John B. McCormick, *The Square Circle: Stories of the Prize Ring* (New York: Continental Publishing Company, 1897).
8. Government of Canada, Library and Archives Canada, Census of Canada 1881, vol. 12, p. 110, microfilm C-13168, image no. e008117604. The 1881 Census marked the second regularly scheduled collection of national statistics in Canada. It officially began April 4, 1881; 205 commissioners were appointed to coordinate the census. Reporting to the commissioners were 3,183 enumerators who were assigned to clearly defined areas. Enumerators visited 192 census districts, divided into 2,139 subdistricts. These units were made

up of cities, towns, groups of townships, First Nations reserves, and other less well-defined areas. Enumerators collected information for 4,278,327 individuals, including 440,558 in Nova Scotia.

9. "The Economy of the Maritimes in the 19th and Early 20th Centuries," Great Unsolved Mysteries of Canadian History, accessed August 2015, http://www.canadianmysteries.ca/sites/jerome/contextes/economie/indexen.html.

10. David Alexander, "Economic Growth in the Atlantic Region, 1880–1940," *Acadiensis Reader, Vol. 2: Atlantic Canada after Confederation* (Fredericton, New Brunswick: Acadiensis Press, 1988).

11. George Dixon, *A Lesson in Boxing* (1893).

12. "Brother of George Dixon, World Champion Boxer, Dies," *Chicago Defender*, April 26, 1930.

13. George Fosty and Darrill Fosty, *Black Ice: The Lost History of the Colored Hockey League of the Maritimes, 1895–1925* (New York: Stryker-Indigo Publishing, 2008).

14. Jane Rhodes, "The Contestation over National Identity: Nineteenth-Century Black Americans in Canada," *Canadian Review of American Studies* 30, no. 2 (2000): 175–86.

15. Robin W. Winks, "The Canadian Negro: A Historical Assessment," *Journal of Negro History* 53, no. 4 (October 1968): 283–300.

16. Lindsay Van Dyk, "Shaping a Community: Black Refugees in Nova Scotia," Canadian Museum of Immigration at Pier 21, accessed August 2015, https://www.pier21.ca/research/immigration-history/shaping-a-community-Black-refugees-in-nova-scotia-0.

17. Rhodes, "The Contestation over National Identity."

18. Van Dyk, "Shaping a Community."

19. Donald Clairmont and Dennis Magill, *Africville: The Life and Death of a Canadian Black Community* (Toronto: Canadian Scholars' Press, 1999), 35–37.

20. Clairmont and Magill, 35–37.

21. Rhodes, "The Contestation over National Identity."

22. Clairmont and Magill, *Africville*, 35–37.

23. Jennifer Nelson, *Razing Africville: A Geography of Racism* (Toronto: University of Toronto Press, 2008).

24. "Under a Northern Star," *Library and Archives Canada*, accessed December 15, 2020, https://www.bac-lac.gc.ca/eng/discover/immigration/history-ethnic-cultural/under-northern-star/Pages/under-northern-star.aspx.

25. Winks, "The Canadian Negro."

26. Harvey Amani Whitfield, *Blacks on the Border: The Black Refugees in British North America, 1815–1860* (Burlington: University of Vermont Press, 2006).

27. Peter McKerrow, *A Brief History of Colored Baptists of Nova Scotia, 1783–1895* (Halifax: Afro Nova Scotian Enterprises, 1976), as quoted by Harvey Amani Whitfield, *Blacks on the Border*.

28. Michael A. Robidoux, "Imagining a Canadian Identity through Sport: A Historical Interpretation of Lacrosse and Hockey," *The Journal of American Folklore* 115, no. 456 (2002): 209–25.

29. "The Halifax Holocaust," *Boston Daily Globe*, November 8, 1882.

30. Elizabeth H. Pleck, "The Two-Parent Household: Black Family Structure in

Late Nineteenth-Century Boston," *Journal of Social History* 6, no. 1 (1972): 3–31.

31. Elizabeth Hafkin Pleck, *Black Migration and Poverty: Boston 1865–1900* (New York: Academic Press, 1979).
32. K. G. Sheard, "Brutal and Degrading: The Medical Profession and Boxing, 1838–1984," *International Journal of the History of Sport* 15, no. 3 (December 1998): 74–102.
33. Kevin R. Smith, *Black Genesis: The History of the Black Prizefighter, 1760–1870* (Lincoln, NE: iUniverse, 2003), 2.
34. "Every American Man and Boy Should Box," *Los Angeles Times*, December 13, 1914.
35. Gerald Early, "The Black Intellectual and the Sport of Prizefighting," *The Kenyon Review* 10, no. 3 (Summer 1988): 102–17.
36. Kevin Smith, *Boston's Boxing Heritage: Prizefighting from 1882 to 1955* (Charleston, SC: Arcadia Publishing, 2002).
37. Stephen Hardy, *How Boston Played: Sport, Recreation and Community* (Knoxville: University of Tennessee Press, 2003).
38. Louis Moore, "Fit for Citizenship: Black Sparring Masters, Gymnasium Owners and the White Body, 1825–1886," *The Journal of African American History* 96, no. 4 (2011): 448–73.
39. "Dixon's Confidence," *Boston Daily Globe*, February 5, 1891.
40. "First Battles of Champion Boxers," *Philadelphia Inquirer*, September 30, 1894.
41. In Charles Dickens's *The Pickwick Papers* (1836), Job Trotter was Mr. Jingle's wily servant, whose true slyness is only ever seen in the first few lines of a scene, before he adopts his usual pretense of meekness.
42. "How Famous Fighters Got Their Start," *National Police Gazette*, June 17, 1905.
43. Guess I should have never questioned "St. Nat." As a member of the International Boxing Research Organization (IBRO), I asked my fellow members if they were familiar with any writing over the last century that explored Nat Fleischer and his accuracy as a historian. I sought a critical examination of his work, especially as it related to the *Black Dynamite* series of books.

   While some members were helpful in pointing to a handful of articles used within the main body of this dissertation, others surprised me at their hardset belief in Fleischer's infallibility. According to IBRO president Dan Couco, "quite a few members" sent emails in support of Fleischer's overall accomplishments for the good of boxing. Some of them stated they would be extremely disappointed if the organization published an article in the *IBRO Journal* criticizing him. One of the letters, whose writer's name is withheld here, read: "What purpose does it serve to take a critical look at the accuracy of the great Nat Fleischer's work? No one else did what he accomplished for boxing. I don't care if he wasn't as accurate in some records. SO WHAT! He was the best thing that ever happened to this sport. He should be deified—not criticized."

   As mentioned previously, Dixon is like many of the boxers of that time in that there is all but nothing in his own voice. That means I depend on secondhand materials. Outside of newspaper clippings, Fleischer's *Black Dynamite* biography on Dixon is the primary source writers have used (either partially or near completely) for the last century. It has been told and retold for generations. Fleischer's writing has shaped how we, today, view Dixon. Therefore, it is important I examine the storyteller just as much as the story he tells—especially for Dixon, for whom race was such an important factor in his portrayal. I cannot take any writer's word as gospel. Even St. Nat.

What has cost sport historians, as a discipline, is our occasional unwavering faith in the accuracy of those who came before us. Sport historians can be stenographers rather than researchers. We should not avoid casting a critical eye and asking hard questions of those who record our history. That should hold true whether an author is writing about Andrew Jackson or Jack Johnson.

44. "Mr. Boxing," *Sports Illustrated*, August 6, 1962.
45. "The Brighter Side," *Idaho Statesman*, September 26, 1944.
46. "Films Explode the Boxing Myth," *New Orleans States-Item*, June 21, 1961.
47. "George Dixon vs. Chester Leon 1906," December 21, 2010, video, 3:28, https://www.youtube.com/watch?v=6foQEfkFHFM.
48. "Films Explode the Boxing Myth."
49. "Dixon World's Greatest Fighter—Bob Armstrong," *Los Angeles Times*, October 4, 1913.

Chapter 2

1. "Corbett's Opinion of Fighters," *National Police Gazette*, July 29, 1906.
2. "Bantam Fight," *Boston Daily Globe*, March 22, 1888.
3. "George Dixon: Greatest, Says Tom O'Rourke," *The Ring Magazine*, October 1936, Don Coleman Collection.
4. "Havlin Open for a Fight," *Boston Daily Globe*, April 11, 1888.
5. "Discoverer of Dixon," *The Ring Magazine*, March 1931, Schutte/Powell Boxing Archives.
6. "Discoverer of Dixon."
7. "Discoverer of Dixon."
8. "Bantam Fight."
9. "Discoverer of Dixon."
10. "George Dixon: Greatest."
11. Neither George Dixon, nor any historian, makes reference to this wife by name or even outside the confines of this story from this clipping. The 1890 census results are difficult to research. Many of the Federal census records were destroyed in a fire at the Commerce Department in Washington, DC, on January 10, 1921. Bits and pieces remain, but out of 62,979,766 people, only the records for 6,160 have survived. Dixon and his "wife" are not among those.
12. "After 800 Battles," *Boston Globe*, January 8, 1900.
13. "A Rash Photographer," *New York Times*, June 11, 1887.
14. "Photographed as Nymphs," *The Atlanta Constitution*, July 18, 1887.
15. "Boston's Extreme Love of Arts," *Chicago Daily Tribune*, June 9, 1899.
16. "Photographed as Nymphs."
17. "Losses by Fire," *New York Times*, January 13, 1903.
18. "Elmer E. Chickering, Photographer, Dead," *Boston Daily Globe*, May 15, 1915.
19. "The Chickering Studios," *Photo-Era Magazine* 42, no. 106 (1919).
20. "Ring Hero Gone," *Boston Daily Globe*," October 18, 1901.
21. "G. Godfrey First Race Fighter," *Chicago Defender*, July 3, 1920.

22. "Godfrey Defeated," *Boston Daily Globe*, August 25, 1888.
23. "G. Godfrey First Race Fighter," *Chicago Defender*, July 3, 1920.
24. Christopher Klein, *Strong Boy: The Life and Times of John L. Sullivan, America's First Sports Hero* (Guilford, CT: Lyons Press, 2013).
25. "Funeral for a Pugilist," *New York Times*, October 21, 1901.
26. "Death of George Godfrey," *Chicago Daily Tribune*, October 18, 1901.
27. "Funeral for a Pugilist."
28. "In the Squared Circle: Real Sports," *Chicago Defender*, May 13, 1922.
29. "Inside the Ropes: George Dixon (Wonder Man of the Ring)," *Chicago Defender*, February 26, 1921.
30. "A Terror of the Prize-Ring," *Chicago Daily Tribune*, November 23, 1890.
31. In official bouts, Dixon fought in two weight classes, bantamweight and featherweight. First established by the *London Prize Ring Rules* in 1860, the bantamweight division was set at a weight limit of 105 pounds. Under Queensberry Rules, it increased to 112 pounds in 1880 and then 115 pounds in 1890. The Amateur Boxing Association set a 118-pound limit in 1890. The National Sporting Club of London set the current 118-pound limit in 1909. The featherweight division, also established by the *London Prize Ring Rules* in 1860, was set at a weight limit of 118 pounds. The Amateur Boxing Association set 126 pounds as its maximum in 1889. Under Queensberry Rules, that changed to 110 pounds in 1889 and then to 115 pounds for the George Dixon–Cal McCarthy bout in 1890. Dixon's manager, Tom O'Rourke, then changed the limit to 120 pounds when Dixon faced Abe Willis in 1891. The National Sporting Club of London set the current 126-pound limit in 1909.
32. "George Dixon Spoiling for a Fight," *Boston Daily Globe*, November 7, 1887.
33. "George Dixon or Little Chocolate," *Chicago Defender*, July 17, 1920.
34. "Fortune Smiled on Dixon until he Began to Drink," *Washington Post*, January 26, 1908.
35. "Rescued men coming home," *Miami Herald*, February 16, 1917.
36. "Clever and Shrewd Diplomats of the Prize Ring of Today," *Duluth News-Tribune*, August 30, 1914.
37. "Aaron P. Ordway a Suicide," *New York Times*, August 17, 1920.
38. "Dave Blanchard Dead: Famous as a Sporting Man in Days Gone by—80 Years Old," *Boston Daily Globe*, June 21, 1907.
39. "Tom O'Rourke," *The Ring Magazine*, September 1936, Schutte/Powell Boxing Archives.
40. "Thos. F. O'Rourke, Dixon's Manager," *San Francisco Bulletin*, August 16, 1897, Schutte/Powell Boxing Archives.
41. "Thos. F. O'Rourke, Dixon's Manager."
42. Loïc J. D. Wacquant, "Pugs at Work: Bodily Capital and Bodily Labor among Professional Boxers," *Body and Society* 1, no. 1 (March 1995): 65–93.
43. "Once a Hero; Dies a Pauper," *Chicago Daily Tribune*, January 12, 1908.
44. "Tom O'Rourke."
45. "Thos. F. O'Rourke, Dixon's Manager."
46. "O'Rourke Accused," *New York Times*, August 8, 1922.
47. "Tom O'Rourke Calls Roosevelt to Aid," *New York Times*, February 14, 1913.
48. "Fortune Smiled on Dixon."
49. Dixon, *A Lesson in Boxing* (1893).

50. "Is George Dixon Still Champion," *National Police Gazette*, March 19, 1904.

51. "Like a Cyclone," *Boston Daily Globe*, December 28, 1889.

52. "Dixon's Confidence," *Boston Daily Globe*, February 5, 1891.

53. "Dixon's Confidence."

54. "Dixon's Confidence."

55. "Like a Cyclone."

56. Nat Fleischer, *Black Dynamite: Three Colored Aces* (New York: C. J. O'Brien, 1938), 21–22.

57. "Cal McCarthy," *BoxRec*, accessed August 2015, http://boxrec.com/boxer/10682.

58. "Lively Bouts," *Brooklyn Daily Eagle*, April 3, 1889.

59. "All for Naught," *Boston Daily Globe*, February 8, 1890.

60. "Lively Bouts."

61. "Fortune Smiled on Dixon."

62. "Lively Bouts."

63. The Undecided McCarthy-Dixon Glove Contest," *National Police Gazette*, March 1, 1890.

Chapter 3

1. "George Dixon Home," *Cleveland Gazette*, August 16, 1890.

2. "Dixon Downs Wallace," *National Police Gazette*, July 12, 1890.

3. "Dixon Downs Wallace."

4. "'Nunc' Weakens," *Boston Daily Globe*, June 28, 1890.

5. "'Nunc' Weakens."

6. "Referee's Remarks," *National Police Gazette*, July 19, 1890.

7. "George Dixon Home."

8. "Dixon Home from Europe," *Wheeling Sunday Register*, August 12, 1890.

9. "George Dixon Home."

10. "Why Not Cover the Entire Country in Your Comment," *Langston City (OK) Herald*, April 9, 1892.

11. "In Their Field," *Cleveland Gazette*, August 23, 1890.

12. "In the College and the Prize Ring," *New York Age*, December 20, 1890.

13. "Correspondence: Letter from Broadbrim," *New Hampshire Sentinel*, August 27, 1890.

14. A deputized posse.

15. "Doings of the Race," *New Orleans Crusader* editorial, as quoted in the *Cleveland Gazette*, July 9, 1892.

16. Ronald L. Jackson II, *Scripting the Black Masculine Body: Identity, Discourse, and Racial Politics in Popular Media* (New York: State University of New York Press, 2006).

17. Established in 1616, the famed London brewery was the largest in the world at that time.

18. "Where's the Nonpareil?" *National Police Gazette*, August 30, 1890.

19. "Dixon Called Down," *Philadelphia Inquirer*, November 21, 1890.

20. "Dixon Called Down."

21. "Dixon Wants More time," *Boston Daily Globe*, October 29, 1890.

22. "Dixon and McCarthy Matched," *Boston Daily Globe*, December 5, 1890.

23. "Crowd Disgusted," *Boston Daily Globe*, February 6, 1891.

24. "Dixon in Good Shape," *Boston Daily Globe*, March 30, 1891.
25. "Dixon in Good Shape."
26. "Dixon Was Handy with His Hands," *National Police Gazette*, April 18, 1891.
27. "Dodged a Paving Stone," *National Police Gazette*, March 31, 1891.
28. "Dixon Was Handy with His Hands."
29. "Fighters I Have Known," *Atlanta Constitution*, June 30, 1907.
30. "Dixon Wins," *Boston Daily Globe*, April 1, 1891.
31. "Dixon Wins."
32. "Dixon Out for Spoils," *Boston Daily Globe*, April 3, 1891.
33. "Dixon Was Handy with His Hands."
34. "Cal McCarthy Buried," *New York Times*, December 2, 1895.
35. "Cal McCarthy Buried."
36. "Fortune Smiled on Dixon until he Began to Drink," *Washington Post*, January 26, 1908.
37. "Prize-Fighting Denounced," *New York Times*, April 9, 1891.
38. "Dixon Was Handy with His Hands." For those interested in Dixon's sartorial selections, the same publication illustrated Dixon from the same fight in different outfits—one image portraying him in the pelvis clothing, others in the traditional black pants.
39. "From the Shoulder," *New York Age*, April 11, 1891.
40. "From the Shoulder."
41. "George Dixon," *Leavenworth (KS) Advocate*, August 15, 1891.
42. David K. Wiggins, "'Black Athletes in White Men's Games': Race, Sport and American National Pastimes," *The International Journal of the History of Sport* 31, no. 1–2 (2014): 181–202.
43. Gerald Early, "The Black Intellectual and the Sport of Prizefighting," *The Kenyon Review* 10, no. 3 (Summer 1988): 102–117.
44. "Reception to Honor Dixon," *Boston Daily Globe*, May 23, 1891.
45. Thomas H. O'Connor, *The Hub: Boston Past and Present* (Boston: Northeastern University Press, 2001).
46. "Reception to Honor Dixon."
47. F. Michael Higginbotham, *Ghosts of Jim Crow: Ending Racism in Post-Racial America* (New York: New York University Press, 2013).
48. Wiggins, "'Black Athletes in White Men's Games.'"
49. Wiggins, "'Black Athletes in White Men's Games.'"
50. William C. Rhoden, *$40 Million Slaves: The Rise, Fall and Redemption of the Black Athlete* (New York: Crown Publishing, 2006), 53.
51. "Black Pugs Have It Hard," *Chicago Daily Tribune*, December 9, 1906.
52. "Color Not Considered," *Washington Post*, February 17, 1908.
53. "The Colored Man in the Ring," *Boston Daily Globe*, April 19, 1891.
54. "The Colored Man in the Ring."
55. "Among the Pugilists," *Wheeling (WV) Register*, November 16, 1890.
56. "Two Fair Prizes," *Boston Daily Globe*, July 27, 1891.
57. "Dixon's Left," *Boston Daily Globe*, July 29, 1891.
58. "Dixon's Left."
59. "A Game Fighter Is He," *The Washington Post*, March 11, 1894.
60. "A Game Fighter Is He."
61. "A Game Fighter Is He."

62. "Wife of Fighter Dixon," *Boston Daily Globe*, July 30, 1891.

63. "Wife of Fighter Dixon."

64. John B. McCormick, *The Square Circle: Stories of the Prize Ring* (New York: Continental Publishing Company, 1897).

65. "Dixon Angry," *Boston Daily Globe*, February 6, 1892.

66. "Dixon Angry."

67. "Dixon Angry."

68. "Dixon and O'Rourke Reconciled," *Philadelphia Inquirer*, February 8, 1892.

69. "General Sporting Notes," *Philadelphia Inquirer*, February 10, 1892.

70. "Many Bouts at the Rink," *Brooklyn Daily Eagle*, October 4, 1892.

71. "Dixon Is Now Champion," *New York Times*, June 28, 1892.

72. "Sporting News," *Topeka Call*, June 19, 1892.

73. "Sporting News."

74. "Sporting News."

75. "Jolts from 'John L.,'" *Boston Daily Globe*, September 22, 1907.

76. "After 800 Battles," *Boston Globe*, January 8, 1900.

77. "Jolts from 'John L.,'" *Boston Daily Globe*, September 22, 1907.

Chapter 4

1. "Bantam's Budget," *Daily Picayune*, August 21, 1892.

2. A career best described as "overshadowed" by his brother, John Wilkes Booth, Abraham Lincoln's assassin.

3. "The Prize Ring," *American Journal of Politics*, October 1892.

4. "The Pugilistic Mania," *Columbus (GA) Enquirer*, September 7, 1892.

5. "The Pugilistic Mania."

6. An archaic term for a person of one-eighth Black ancestry. Also referred to as an octoroon in Dixon's era.

7. As quoted in Joseph R. Roach, *Cities of the Dead: Circum-Atlantic Performance* (New York: Columbia University Press, 1996).

8. Tom Robbins, *Jitterbug Perfume* (New York: Bantam Dell, 1984), 265.

9. Peter Wallenstein, "Did Homer Plessy Die a White Man? Race and Southern History—The State of the Field," *The Georgia Historical Quarterly* 94, no. 1 (Spring 2010): 62–96.

10. Jerah Johnson, "Jim Crow Laws of the 1890s and the Origins of New Orleans Jazz: Correction of an Error," *Popular Music* 19, no. 2 (2000): 243–251.

11. Johnson, "Jim Crow Laws."

12. Michael Dale Somers, *The Rise of Sport in New Orleans, 1850–1900* (Baton Rouge: Louisiana State University Press, 1972).

13. Tim McNeese, *Plessy v. Ferguson: Separate but Equal* (New York: Chelsea House, 2007).

14. Jane Dailey, *The Age of Jim Crow* (New York: W.W. Norton, 2009)

15. Keith Weldon Medley, *We As Freemen* (Gretna, Louisiana: Pelican, 2003).

16. Stuart Omer Landry, *The Battle of Liberty Place: The Overthrow of Carpet-Bag Rule in New Orleans,* (New Orleans: Pelican, 1999).

17. Kenneth T. Walsh, *Family of Freedom: Presidents and African Americans in the White House* (Boulder, CO: Paradigm, 2011), 64–65.

18. Walsh, *Family of Freedom,* 64–65.

19. Johnson, "Jim Crow Laws."

20. Jeffrey T. Sammons, *Beyond the Ring: The Role of Boxing in American Society* (Urbana, IL: University of Illinois Press, 1990).

21. McNeese, *Plessy v. Ferguson*.

22. "John L on Another Spree," *Philadelphia Enquirer*, January 3, 1891.

23. Michael Isenberg, *John L. Sullivan and His America* (Champaign-Urbana: University of Illinois Press, 1994), 285.

24. "Black Pugs Have It Hard," *Chicago Daily Tribune*, December 9, 1906.

25. "Jolts from 'John L.,'" *Boston Daily Globe*, May 14, 1905.

26. "Jolts from 'John L.,'" *Boston Daily Globe*, May 14, 1905.

27. Even John L. Sullivan's namesakes were restless during this time. Take for instance an incident at the Zoological Gardens in Philadelphia, reported by the *Philadelphia Inquirer*, January 5, 1891:

> St. George, "the king of all the garden," set off a frenzy across at the zoo when a stray bone caught in his throat, and sent the aging lion into a panic. Unable to roar, he resorted to a gurgled groan that unnerved his mates. First among his pride, and then among other big cats in the vicinity, the creatures began beating their bodies against the thin iron bars. Hyenas. Panthers. Leopards. All started clanging against their cages as their yelps, snarls, and whines mixed with the roar of lions. The panic then cascaded across the zoo— animals threw themselves against partitions, pawed at the floors, roared and howled. Birds squawked in a frenzy. Monkeys grabbed the hats of young girls and tore then to shreds. That's when John L Sullivan—the "king of a herd of bison" that included the likes of fellow pugilistic namesakes Kilrain and Dempsey—flipped a female of the herd, Mrs. McCaffrey, into the air in an effort to crush the lone fence preventing the beasts from roaming the city freely. Despite his unsuccessful efforts, Bison Sullivan still panicked zoo patrons and sent then rushing from the park.

28. "Sullivan Hit Him," *New Haven Register*, January 9, 1891.

29. Untitled, *Kansas City Star*, January 9, 1891.

30. Untitled, *Tacoma Daily News*, January 4, 1892.

31. "A Louisville Newspaperman Makes a Hero of John L Sullivan," *Duluth Daily News*, March 10, 1892.

32. Untitled, *Tacoma Daily News*, January 19, 1892.

33. "John L. Sullivan Has Taken," *Duluth Daily News*, January 21, 1892.

34. "Sporting Trifles," (St. Paul, Minnesota) *Broad Axe*, February 4, 1892.

35. "John L. Drunk Again," *The State*, February 5, 1892.

36. Untitled, *Wheeling Register*, February 6, 1892.

37. "John L as a Railway Beat," *Kansas Weekly Capital*, February 18, 1892.

38. Untitled, *Philadelphia Inquirer*, March 2, 1892.

39. Jack Anderson, "A Brief Legal History of Prize-Fighting in 19th Century America," *Sport in History* 24, no. 1 (Summer 2004).

40. "Festival Fistic," *Daily Picayune*, September 4, 1892.

41. "How to Handle a Crowd," *Daily Picayune*, March 3, 1892.

42. "The Crown of the Carnival," *Daily Picayune*, March 1, 1892.

43. "Pugilistic Carnival," *Wheeling (WV) Register*, August 21, 1892. Story was later rerun in the *National Police Gazette* on September 10, 1892.
44. Dixon-Skelly, *Mirror of Life and Boxing World*, June 26, 1915.
45. Dixon-Skelly, *Mirror of Life and Boxing World*.
46. Dixon-Skelly, *Mirror of Life and Boxing World*.
47. George Harmon Knoles, *The Presidential Campaign and Election of 1892* (New York: AMS Press, 1942), 138.
48. Stephen A. Jones and Eric Freedman, *Presidents and Black America* (Los Angeles: CQ Press, 2012), 257–58.
49. Knoles, 194.
50. Knoles, 138.
51. Knoles, 138.
52. Knoles, 138.
53. Knoles, 240.
54. Jones and Freedman, 270.
55. Jones and Freedman, 253.
56. "Our Picayunes," *Daily Picayune*, September 5, 1892.
57. "Pugilistic Carnival."
58. "At the Bay," *Daily Picayune*, September 4, 1892.
59. "Pugilistic Carnival."
60. Olympic Club, *The Official Souvenir Program of the Olympic Club, September 5–7, 1892*, Ephemera Collection, Louisiana Research Collection, Tulane University.
61. Olympic Club, *The Official Souvenir Program*.
62. Brook Thomas, *Plessy v. Ferguson: A Brief History with Documents* (Boston and New York: Bedford Books, 1997).
63. Untitled, *Daily Inter Ocean* (Chicago), August 15, 1891.
64. Albion W. Tourgée, *A Fool's Errand by One of the Fools* (Boston: Belknap Press of Harvard University Press, 1961).
65. *Louisiana Laws, 1890*, Citation 111: 153–54 (1890).
66. Rodney A. Smolla, "The Ghost of Homer Plessy," *Georgia State University Law Review* 12, no. 4 (June 1996): 1037–88.
67. Smolla, "The Ghost of Homer Plessy."
68. Thomas, *Plessy v. Ferguson*.
69. Medley, *We As Freemen*.
70. Louise McKinney, *New Orleans: A Cultural History* (New York: Oxford University Press, 2006).
71. "Champion George Dixon: The Greatest of Them All," *National Police Gazette*, March 11, 1899.
72. Lewis A. Erenberg, "More Than a Prizefight: Joe Louis, Max Schmeling and the Transnational Politics of Boxing," in *Beyond Blackface: African Americans and the Creation of American Popular Culture*, edited by W. Fitzhugh Brundage (Chapel Hill: University of North Carolina Press, 2011), 315–56.
73. David K. Wiggins, "'Black Athletes in White Men's Games': Race, Sport and American National Pastimes," *The International Journal of the History of Sport* 31, no. 1–2 (2014): 181–202.
74. "Both Men Are Willing," *Boston Daily Globe*, July 18, 1892.
75. "The Featherweights," *Detroit Plaindealer*, August 5, 1892.

76. "Jack Skelly and George Dixon," *Brooklyn Daily Eagle*, July 29, 1892.
77. "Skelly's Amateur Battles," *Wheeling Sunday Register*, August 28, 1892.
78. "A Sturdy Little Boxer," *Brooklyn Daily Eagle*, September 1, 1892.
79. "The Big Bet on Skelly," *Brooklyn Daily Eagle*, August 2, 1892.
80. "Four of the Champions," *Brooklyn Daily Eagle*, July 30, 1892.
81. "Four of the Champions."
82. "Fighter Jack Skelly," *Wheeling (WV) Register*, August 14, 1892.
83. "The Big Bet on Skelly."
84. "Joins Jack McAuliffe," *Brooklyn Daily Eagle*, August 3, 1892.
85. "Jack Skelly's Confidence in His Ability to Whip Dixon," *Brooklyn Daily Eagle*, August 15, 1892.
86. "A Sturdy Little Boxer."
87. "Fortune Smiled on Dixon until He Began to Drink," *Washington Post*, January 26, 1908.
88. "Fortune Smiled on Dixon."
89. "George Dixon Coming South," *Daily Picayune*, August 7, 1892.
90. "George Dixon Coming South."
91. "George Dixon Coming South."
92. "George Dixon Coming South."
93. "George Dixon Coming South."
94. "George Dixon Coming South."
95. "The Featherweights."
96. "The Featherweights."
97. "A Minor Attraction," *Tacoma (WA) Daily News*, August 17, 1892.
98. "The Featherweights."
99. "Bantam's Budget."
100. "At the Bay," *Daily Picayune*, September 4, 1892.
101. "Jack Dempsey Spars," *Brooklyn Daily Eagle*, April 4, 1888.
102. "Jack Skelly, Former Amateur Champion, 83," *Brooklyn Daily Eagle*, May 26, 1955.
103. "Jack Dempsey's Right Name," *Seattle Daily Times*, May 20, 1909.
104. James Roberts and Alexander Skutt, *The Boxing Register* (Ithaca, NY: McBooks Press, 2011).
105. "Poor Old Jack," *Boston Daily Globe*, January 19, 1895.
106. "Jack Dempsey Insane," *The Washington Post*, February 2, 1895.
107. "Dempsey Physical Wreck," *Boston Daily Globe*, July 13, 1895.
108. "His Last Round," *Boston Daily Globe*, November 2, 1895.
109. "Nonpareil Jack Dempsey," *BoxRec*, last modified July 2, 2020, http://boxrec .com/media/index.php?title=Human:17958.
110. "Memory of Jack Dempsey," *New York Times*, September 4, 1910.
111. "Jack McAuliffe, 71, Ex-ring Champion," *New York Times*, November 5, 1937.
112. "Fighters I Have Known," *Boston Daily Globe*, March 3, 1907.
113. "Jack McAuliffe Beat Mace in First Fight," *Washington Post*, November 8, 1937.
114. "Jack McAuliffe Beat Mace in First Fight."
115. "Sudden Death of a Young Actress," *Washington Post*, October 15, 1890.
116. "Death of McAuliffe's Wife," *Los Angeles Times*, October 15, 1890.
117. "Disease, Not Murder," *Washington Post*, October 16, 1890.
118. "Fought His Last Fight," *Boston Daily Globe*, April 14, 1892.

119. "Bob Cook's Doings," *Boston Daily Globe*, April 15, 1892.

120. "Young Mitchell Done Up," *Washington Post*, February 11, 1894.

121. "Plug-Uglies," *Los Angeles Times*, May 17, 1894.

122. "McAuliffe Married," *Los Angeles Times*, July 31, 1894.

123. "Absolute Divorce," *Los Angeles Times*, May 7, 1898.

124. "Jack McAuliffe, 71, Ex-ring Champion."

125. "Lively Bouts," *Brooklyn Daily Eagle*, April 3, 1889.

126. "Fighter Jack Skelly."

127. "Winters Defeats Thomas," *Brooklyn Daily Eagle*, May 30, 1890.

128. "Hard Fighting with Several Knockouts by Aspiring Boxers," *Brooklyn Daily Eagle*, March 16, 1890.

129. "On a Hot Night," *Brooklyn Daily Eagle*, August 1, 1890.

130. "Fighter Jack Skelly."

131. "Fred Johnson's Boxing Benefit," *Brooklyn Daily Eagle*, July 15, 1892.

132. "Jolts from 'John L.,'" *The State*, May 1, 1905.

133. "Crescent City Sights," *Boston Daily Globe*, September 5, 1892.

134. "Three Great Events," *Boston Daily Globe*, September 5, 1892.

135. "The Three Contests," *Daily Picayune*, September 5, 1892.

136. "George Dixon," *Plaindealer*, August 19, 1892.

137. "Once a Champion," *Boston Daily Globe*, Feb. 27, 1899.

138. "Just before the Fight Began," *Chicago Daily Tribune*, September 6, 1892.

139. "Jack of Fists," *Boston Daily Globe*, September 6, 1892.

140. "Black Wins," *Daily Picayune*, September 7, 1892.

141. "Clever Dixon," *Boston Daily Globe*, September 7, 1892.

142. "Clever Dixon."

143. "Black Wins."

144. "Clever Dixon."

145. "Clever Dixon."

146. "Black Wins."

147. "Clever Dixon."

148. "Fortune Smiled on Dixon."

149. "Clever Dixon."

150. "Clever Dixon."

151. "Clever Dixon."

152. "Our Note Book," *Mirror of Life*, June 26, 1915.

153. "Clever Dixon."

154. "Black Wins."

155. "Clever Dixon."

156. "Dixon's Victory Engenders Bad Feelings at New Orleans between the Races," *Detroit Plaindealer*, September 16, 1892.

157. "Dixon's Victory Engenders."

158. "Fortune Smiled on Dixon."

159. "Dixon's Victory," *Detroit Plaindealer*, September 16, 1892.

160. "Dixon's Victory."

161. "Dixon's Victory."

162. "Champion James Corbett," *Boston Globe,* September 8, 1892.

163. "Champion Corbett," *National Police Gazette*, September 8, 1892.

164. Anderson, "A Brief Legal History."

165. "Sullivan's Night of It," *New Orleans Daily-Picayune*, September 9, 1892.
166. Elliott J. Gorn, *The Manly Art: Bare-Knuckle Prizefighting in America* (Ithaca, NY: Cornell University Press, 1986).
167. "George Dixon," *Cleveland Gazette*, September 10, 1892.
168. "Dixon and Jim Crow," *Cleveland Gazette*, September 10, 1892
169. "George Dixon," *Cleveland Gazette*.
170. "Jolts from 'John L.,'" *Boston Daily Globe*, November 22, 1908.
171. Under the guise of journalism, Sullivan often used his nationally syndicated newspaper column, "Jolts from 'John L.,'" as an arena to settle old scores and promote his own legend and his often hateful ideology. In the earliest days of the modern newspaper, "news" was often indistinguishable from opinion. But by the 1880s, newspaper publishers recognized that rapidly growing populations coalescing around urban areas were creating new shared cultural experiences. They responded to this shift by dividing their publications into sections based on specialized interests. From politics and police, women's issues and society news, to theater reviews and sport, heavier and lighter fare were finding a place side by side on newspaper pages. These various sections soon were seen as essential to attracting a wider audience. As an offshoot, this subdivision created fertile ground for a new era of tastemakers; these were the earliest days of the newspaper columnist.

Enter "Jolts from 'John L.'" These thousand-plus-word rambles appeared in newspapers across the country from 1905 to 1909, surfacing everywhere from Charleston, South Carolina, to San Antonio, Texas, Omaha, Nebraska, to San Francisco, California, Atlanta, Georgia, to Boston, Massachusetts. It had as wide a sphere of influence as any newspaper feature of the day. Sullivan was not the only former pugilist to offer his opinion in a column. Newspapers often recruited fighters, both active and retired, to weigh in on current events within the sport. While many of these articles were penned by managers or journalists who could speak for the fighter, "Jolts" was a syndicated newspaper column unquestionably authored by Sullivan. That kind of bluster and blo-viation could not have been imitated. He was one of the few sports to offer opinions outside the world of sport. That's what made him so attractive to readers and publishers. Sullivan brought exactly what they were looking for in a columnist—a recognizable name to draw eyes, a brash, distinctive voice to draw ears; and a bit of unpredictability and outrageousness to keep them coming back for more.

In one column, recorded here from the *Boston Daily Globe*, October 20, 1907, he recounted a trip aboard a riverboat bound for St. Louis, Missouri, down the Mississippi River, when ten Black men fueled by whiskey attacked him. Sullivan tossed one of the men overboard, only to be attacked by two more, which he also "flooded," and then he was attacked by the remaining seven who "swarmed me like a bunch of monkeys." He wrote of the encounter: "Three more of the colored brothers were thrown overboard, and the rest hammered until they had sense. Those that went overboard, we didn't worry about, as the river negroes can swim like fishes, and they got ashore, I guess. While it lasted, those coons gave me about as much fighting as I'd ever packed into five minutes of time." Of course, as was often the case with Sullivan, his racist views were tinged with an insight into the sport that few offered publicly.

While he was incorrect in discrediting the talent of Black boxers, he was correct in the reason why many of them, especially lesser Black fighters, were pushed forward by their white managers. For Sullivan, the reasoning was more about white opportunists than Black empowerment. He wrote, recorded here from *The State*, December 3, 1905: "One reason the negro has pushed to the front is because he is easy money for the sharp promoters, who can get bigger percentages of profit out of his earnings than white boxers would be fools enough to let them get away with."

172. "Jolts from 'John L.,'" *The State*, July 7, 1907.
173. "Jolts from 'John L.,'" *The State*, April 2, 1905.
174. "Jolts from 'John L.,'" *Boston Daily Globe*, February 9, 1908.
175. "Olympic Club," *Biloxi Herald*, September 10, 1892.
176. "Drawing the Color Line," *Philadelphia Enquirer*, September 30, 1892.
177. "They Say that the Olympic Club," *The Independent: Devoted to the Consideration of Politics, of Social and Economic Tendencies, of History, Literature, and the Arts*, October 6, 1892.
178. "The Prize Ring," *American Journal of Politics*, October 1892.
179. The *Detroit Plaindealer* considered itself an "Afro-American" newspaper, consciously rejecting the term "negro." It ceased operation in 1894.
180. Untitled, *Detroit Plaindealer*, September 23, 1892.
181. "Editorial," *Cleveland Gazette*, September 17, 1892.
182. Untitled, *Detroit Plaindealer*, October 10, 1892.
183. "Dixon Well Received," *Boston Daily Globe*, September 13, 1892.
184. "No Place Like Home," *Brooklyn Daily Eagle*, September 9, 1892.
185. "Many Bouts at the Rink," *Brooklyn Daily Eagle*, October 4, 1892.
186. Thomas, *Plessy v. Ferguson*.
187. Jones and Freedman, *Presidents and Black America*, 268.
188. "Lynch Law," *Chicago Daily Tribune*, September 28, 1893.
189. Frederick Douglass, "Lynch Law in the South," *North American Review* 155 (July 1892), in *The American 1890s: A Cultural Reader*, edited by Susan Smith and Melanie Dawson (Durham, NC: Duke University Press, 2000), 220–26.
190. Jessie P. Guzman, ed., *1952 Negro Yearbook* (New York: Wm. H. Wise & Co., 1952).
191. McNeese, *Plessy v. Ferguson*.
192. "Judge Lynch," *Chicago Daily Tribune*, January 1, 1892.
193. "Daring Display of Lynch Law," *The Manchester Guardian*, March 16, 1891.
194. "The New Orleans Tragedy," *Washington Post*, March 17, 1891.
195. "Why We Have Lynch Law," *Atlanta Constitution*, January 5, 1892.
196. "An Innovation in Louisiana Lynching," *New York Times*, June 25, 1895.
197. Grace Elizabeth Hale, "Without Sanctuary: Lynching Photography in America," *The Journal of American History* 89, no. 3 (2002): 989–94.
198. William James, "A Strong Note of Warning Regarding the Lynching Epidemic (1903)," in *Essays, Comments and Reviews* (Boston; Harvard University Press, 1987).
199. James, "A Strong Note of Warning."
200. Douglass, "Lynch Law in the South."
201. Thomas, *Plessy v. Ferguson*.
202. Thomas, *Plessy v. Ferguson*.

203. Thomas, *Plessy v. Ferguson*.

204. Wallenstein, "Did Homer Plessy Die a White Man?"

205. Thomas, *Plessy v. Ferguson*.

206. Smolla, "The Ghost of Homer Plessy."

207. Smolla, "The Ghost of Homer Plessy."

208. "Equality, but Not Socialism," *Daily Picayune*, May 19, 1896.

209. Thomas, *Plessy v. Ferguson*.

210. Joy J. Jackson, *New Orleans in the Gilded Age* (Baton Rouge: Louisiana State University Press, 1969).

211. Thomas, *Plessy v. Ferguson*.

212. Jeffrey A. Jenkins, Justin Peck, and Vesla M. Weaver, "Between Reconstructions: Congressional Action on Civil Rights, 1891–1940," *Studies in American Political Development* 24 (April 2010): 57–89.

213. David Krasner, "The Real Thing," in *Beyond Blackface: African Americans and the Creation of American Popular Culture*, edited by W. Fitzhugh Brundage (Chapel Hill: University of North Carolina Press, 2011), 99–123.

214. "About," Plessy & Ferguson Foundation, http://www.plessyandferguson.org/. Accessed December 2015.

215. "Olympic Club Netted over $40,000 on the Recent Pugilistic Carnival," *Washington Post*, October 2, 1892.

216. "That Olympic Club Check," *Boston Daily Globe*, October 1, 1892.

217. "Held a Stormy Meeting," *Boston Daily Globe*, October 4, 1892.

218. "A New Club for Pugilists," *New York Times*, November 1, 1892.

219. "Olympics Will Not Quit," *Chicago Daily Tribune*, November 20, 1892.

220. Anderson, "A Brief Legal History."

221. Anderson, "A Brief Legal History."

222. Anderson, "A Brief Legal History."

223. Anderson, "A Brief Legal History."

224. "Andy Bowen May Die," *Chicago Daily Tribune*, December 15, 1894.

225. "Blow Ends His Life," *Chicago Daily Tribune*, December 16, 1894.

226. "What Corbett and Sullivan Think," *Chicago Daily Tribune*, December 16, 1894.

227. "George Lavigne Is Set Free," *Chicago Daily Tribune*, December 28, 1894.

228. "Tells How Andy Bowen Was Killed," *Chicago Daily Tribune*, December 30, 1894.

229. Anderson, "A Brief Legal History."

230. Dale A. Somers, *The Rise of Sports in New Orleans, 1850–1900* (Baton Rogue: Louisiana State University Press, 1972).

231. Anderson, "A Brief Legal History."

232. "Lynched," *The Daily Picayune*, September 9, 1892.

233. "Jack Skelly Ill with Malaria," *New Orleans Daily Picayune*, March 19, 1893.

234. "Two Draws at Coney Island," *New York Times*, March 21, 1893.

235. "It Never Rains," *Brooklyn Daily Eagle*, October 27, 1892.

236. "Fighting Paid Him Better," *Brooklyn Daily Eagle*, October 24, 1893.

237. "Jack Skelly Knocked Out," *Brooklyn Daily Eagle*, October 29, 1894.

238. "When Jack Skelly Prays," *Brooklyn Daily Eagle*, November 8, 1894.

239. "Jack Skelly as an Actor," *Brooklyn Daily Eagle*, May 4, 1896.

240. "The Empire," *Brooklyn Daily Eagle*, May 5, 1896.

241. "The Empire."

242. "The Empire."
243. "The Boxing Bout Fatal," *New York Times*, March 23, 1898.
244. "Boxer Smith Escapes Indictment," *New York Times*, March 25, 1898.
245. "Skelly's Stage Hands Struck," *Brooklyn Daily Eagle*, May 10, 1896.
246. "Jack Skelly, Former Amateur Champion, 83," *Brooklyn Daily Eagle*, May 26, 1955.
247. "Jolts from 'John L.,'" *Boston Daily Globe*, May 31, 1908.
248. "Old-Time Boxer Dies, 83," *New York Times*, May 26, 1953.

Chapter 5

1. George Borden, "Box Me a Tune—George Dixon," *Kola* 11, no. 1 (1999).
2. "Old Chocolate's Jocoserlous Chat," *Chicago Daily Tribune*, November 23, 1889.
3. "At Dixon's Mercy," *Boston Daily Globe*, April 21, 1891.
4. "Dixon Now Is Champion," *New York Times*, June 28, 1892.
5. "The Merry," *Los Angeles Times*, January 27, 1896.
6. "Pugilistic Gossip," *Washington Post*, February 3, 1896.
7. A generation after Dixon, Cuban boxer Eligio Sardiñas Montalvo became known as "Kid Chocolate," or the "Cuban Bon-Bon," during his outstanding career in the 1930s. A handful of generations after that, Peter Quillin's Cuban-born father passed along his love of boxing to his son. It was also Pedro Quillin who gave his son the nickname "Kid Chocolate," in honor of Montalvo, the first Cuban world champion.
8. Loïc J. D. Wacquant, "Pugs at Work: Bodily Capital and Bodily Labor among Professional Boxers," *Body and Society* 1, no. 1 (March 1995): 65–93.
9. Urban, in this case, is defined as an area with a population of more than 8,000 residents.
10. David K. Wiggins, "The Notion of Double-Consciousness and the Involvement of Black Athletes in American Sport," in *Ethnicity and Sport in North American History and Culture*, edited by George Eisen and David K. Wiggins (Westport, CT: Praeger, 1994).
11. "Harry Banks Was Buried," *Boston Globe*, August 25, 1895.
12. "After 800 Battles," *Boston Globe*, January 8, 1900.
13. Louis Moore, "Fine Specimens of Manhood: The Black Boxer's Body and the Avenue to Equality, Racial Advancement and Manhood in the Nineteenth Century," *MELUS* 35, no. 4 (2010): 59–84.
14. John F. Kasson, *Houdini, Tarzan and The Perfect Man: The White Male Body and the Challenge of Modernity in America* (New York: Hill and Wang, 2001).
15. Gale Bederman, *Manliness and Civilization: A Cultural History of Gender and Race in the United States, 1880–1917* (Chicago: University of Chicago Press, 1995).
16. BoxRec, "James J. Jeffries," accessed September 2015, http://boxrec.com /boxer/9022.
17. "Preacher Is Lectured by James J. Jeffries," *Atlanta Constitution*, July 25, 1909.
18. "Preacher Is Lectured By James J. Jeffries."
19. BoxRec, "Queensbury Rules," accessed August 2015, http://boxrec.com/media /index.php/Queensberry_Rules. .

20. Richard Ellmann, *Oscar Wilde* (New York: Random House, 1987).

21. BoxRec, "Queensbury Rules."

22. The Queensbury Rules are as follows:

    1. To be a fair stand-up boxing match in a 24-foot ring or as near that size as practicable;
    2. No wrestling or hugging allowed;
    3. The rounds to be of three minutes duration and one minute time between rounds;
    4. If either man fall through weakness or otherwise, he must get up unassisted, 10 seconds be allowed to do so, the other man meanwhile to return to his corner; and when the fallen man is on his legs the round is to be resumed and continued until the three minutes have expired. If one man fails to come to the scratch in the 10 seconds allowed, it shall be in the power of the referee to give his award in favor of the other man;
    5. A man hanging on the ropes in a helpless state, with his toes off the ground, shall be considered down;
    6. No seconds or any other person to be allowed in the ring during the rounds;
    7. Should the contest be stopped by any unavoidable interference, the referee (is) to name the time and place as soon as possible for finishing the contest, so that the match can be won and lost, unless the backers of the men agree to draw the stakes;
    8. The gloves to be fair-sized boxing gloves of the best quality and new;
    9. Should a glove burst, or come off, it must be replaced to the referee's satisfaction;
    10. A man on one knee is considered down, and if struck is entitled to the stakes;
    11. No shoes or boots with springs allowed; and
    12. The contest in all other respects to be governed by the revised rules of the *London Prize Ring*.

    BoxRec, "Queensbury Rules," accessed August 2015, http://boxrec.com/media/index.php/Queensberry_Rules.

23. Elliott J. Gorn, *The Manly Art: Bare-Knuckle Prizefighting in America* (Ithaca, NY: Cornell University Press, 1986), 66.

24. Moore, "Fine Specimens of Manhood."

25. BoxRec, "Weight Divisions," accessed August 2015, http://boxrec.com/media/index.php/Weight_divisions.

26. Moore, "Fine Specimens of Manhood."

27. "Dixon's Confidence," *Boston Daily Globe*, February 5, 1891.

28. "No, Only Elbow Room in America," *New York Herald*, as reported in the *Detroit Plaindealer*, March 14, 1890.

29. Wacquant, "Pugs at Work."

30. Norman Mailer, *The Fight* (New York: Random House, 1975), 96.

31. Mailer, 96.

32. Mailer, 96.

33. "George Dixon's Method of Training," *Brooklyn Eagle*, September 20, 1893.

34. Dave Day, "'Science,' 'Wind' and 'Bottom': Eighteenth-Century Boxing Manuals," *The International Journal of the History of Sport* 29, no. 10 (July 2012): 1446–65.

35. George Dixon, *A Lesson in Boxing* (1893).

36. Dixon, *A Lesson in Boxing*.

37. Dixon, *A Lesson in Boxing*.

38. Dixon, *A Lesson in Boxing*.

39. Dixon, *A Lesson in Boxing*.

40. M. Bianco et al., "Boxing and 'Commotio Cordis': ECG and Humoral Study," *International Journal of Sport Medicine* 26, no. 2 (2005): 151–57.

41. Dixon, *A Lesson in Boxing*.

42. Cassie Barrett and Danny Smith, "Recognition and Management of Abdominal Injuries at Athletic Events," *International Journal of Sports Physical Therapy* 7, no. 4 (2012): 448–51.

43. "Knockout Blows of 10 Fights," *Philadelphia Inquirer*, January 27, 1895.

44. Dixon, *A Lesson in Boxing*.

45. Dixon, *A Lesson in Boxing*.

46. "What a Fighter Must Do," *Cleveland Gazette*, February 16, 1895.

47. "Points for Pugilists," *Boston Daily Globe*, June 6, 1892.

48. James W. C. Pennington, "The Fugitive Blacksmith" (London: Charles Gilpin, 1849). Accessed via Documenting the American South, http://docsouth.unc.edu.proxy1.lib.uwo.ca/neh/penning49/penning49.html.

49. Stephen C. Kenny, "The Development of Medical Museums in the Antebellum American South: Slave Bodies in Networks of Anatomical Exchange," *Bulletin of the History of Medicine* 87, no. 1 (2013): 32–62.

50. Kenny, "Development of Medical Museums."

51. Guy Reel, "This Wicked World: Masculinities and the Portrayals of Sex, Crime and Sports in the *National Police Gazette*," *American Journalism* 22, no. 1 (2005): 61–94.

52. Reel, "This Wicked World."

53. "It Ended in a Draw," *National Police Gazette*, July 14, 1896.

54. "Champion George Dixon: The Greatest of Them All," *National Police Gazette*, March 11, 1899.

55. "Passing of George Dixon, the Greatest Fighter the World Ever Saw," *National Police Gazette*, February 15, 1902.

56. "Color Line Is Only a Myth," *Los Angeles Times*, April 5, 1914.

57. "Color Line Is Only a Myth."

58. *Encyclopedia of Nineteenth-Century Photography*, vol. 1 (New York: Routledge, 2007), 233.

59. Brian Wallis, "Black Bodies, White Science: Louis Agassiz's Slave Daguerreotypes," *American Art* 9, no. 2 (Summer 1995): 38–61.

60. Harvey Young, "The Black Body as Souvenir in American Lynching," *Theatre Journal* 57, no. 4 (December 2005): 639–57.

Chapter 6

1. Roi Ottley and William J. Weatherby, *The Negro in New York: An Informal Social History* (New York: The New York Public Library, 1967).

2. Lisa Elsroad, "Tenderloin," in *The Encyclopedia of New York City* (New Haven: Yale University Press, 1995), 1161.

3. James Weldon Johnson, *The Autobiography of an Ex-Colored Man* (Boston: Sherman, French and Company, 1912), 103, accessed via Internet Archive, https://archive.org/stream/excoloredman00johnrich/excoloredman00 johnrich_djvu.txt.

4. Ottley and Weatherby, *The Negro in New York.*

5. Ottley and Weatherby, *The Negro in New York.*

6. William C. Rhoden, *$40 Million Slaves: The Rise, Fall and Redemption of the Black Athlete* (New York; Crown Publishing, 2006), 60–68.

7. Rhoden, *$40 Million Slaves*, 60–68.

8. Johnson, *Autobiography.*

9. Ottley and Weatherby, *The Negro in New York.*

10. "George Dixon to Retire and Become a Boniface," *National Police Gazette*, December 30, 1899.

11. "Pugilistic Greatness," *Los Angeles Times*, February 26, 1895.

12. "Three Terrible Blows," *Wheeling Sunday Register*, August 6, 1893.

13. "Three Terrible Blows."

14. "Dixon Still the Champion," *New York Times*, August 8, 1893.

15. "Dixon Still the Champion."

16. "Dixon Still the Champion."

17. "Dixon Still the Champion."

18. "George Dixon's Waterloo," *New York Times*, August 23, 1893.

19. "Plimmer's Victory," *National Police Gazette*, September 9, 1893.

20. "George Dixon's Waterloo."

21. "Plimmer Defeats Dixon," *National Police Gazette*, September 9, 1893.

22. "Dixon Ought to Win," *National Police Gazette*, September 30, 1893.

23. "Dixon Whips 'Solly' Smith," *New York Times*, September 26, 1893.

24. "Billy Murphy Knocked Out," *National Police Gazette*, January 6, 1894.

25. "Champion Jackson Returns to America to Arrange for a Fight with Champion Corbett. His Great," *Cleveland Gazette*, November 5, 1892.

26. "Dixon Knocked Down Again," *Cleveland Gazette*, November 19, 1892.

27. "A Lively Boxing Bout," *Philadelphia Inquirer*, October 30, 1892.

28. "Dixon Says the 'Rosebud' Did Not Down Him," *Cleveland Gazette*, November 19, 1892.

29. "The Rosebud's Great Victory. Champion Dixon Was Knocked out by a Right-Hand Swinging Blow," *Philadelphia Inquirer*, March 24, 1894.

30. "A Running Review of Sporting News," *Philadelphia Inquirer*, March 25, 1894.

31. Display ad, *Boston Daily Globe*, April 1, 1894.

32. "The Sporting World," *Dallas Morning News*, March 27, 1894.

33. "Boxers' Gossip," *Wheeling (WV) Register*, December 25, 1892.

34. "Boxers' Gossip," *Wheeling (WV) Register*, November 27, 1892.

35. "Boxers' Gossip," November 27, 1892.

36. "Boxers' Gossip," December 25, 1892.

37. "Champion George Dixon: The Greatest of Them All," *National Police Gazette*, March 11, 1899.

38. "George Dixon's Company," *Hartford Courant*, January 1, 1895.

39. "Arrested for Assault," *San Francisco Examiner*, November 24, 1893.

40. "Popular George Dixon's Company Amuses Howard Audience," *Boston Daily Globe*, November 1, 1892.
41. "William Delhauer Is Found Dead," *Chicago Daily Tribune*, January 30, 1897.
42. "William Delhauer Is Found Dead."
43. Bridget R. Cooks, "Fixing Race: Visual Representation of African Americans at the World's Columbian Exposition, Chicago, 1893," *Patterns of Prejudice* 41, no. 5 (2007): 435–65.
44. Karen Sotiropoulos, *Staging Race: Black Performers in Turn of the Century America* (Boston: Harvard University Press, 2009).
45. "Fighter Dixon Discharged," *Brooklyn Eagle*, September 4, 1895.
46. "Legal Lore vs. Boxing," *National Police Gazette*, September 7, 1895.
47. "Legal Lore vs. Boxing."
48. "Erne's Clever Defense," *New York Times*, December 6, 1895.
49. "Dixon Ought to Win," *National Police Gazette*, September 30, 1893.
50. "George Dixon under Arrest," *Brooklyn Eagle*, June 9, 1895.
51. "That Little Trouble," *National Police Gazette*, June 9, 1895.
52. "That Little Trouble."
53. "Jolts from 'John L.,'" *Boston Daily Globe*, January 19, 1908.
54. "Can the Phillies Win the Pennant?" *Philadelphia Inquirer*, June 2, 1895.
55. "The World of Fistiana," *Philadelphia Inquirer*, July 19, 1896.
56. "Sporting Notes," *The Freeman*, July 23, 1898.
57. "Jolts from 'John L.,'" *Boston Daily Globe*, January 26, 1908.
58. "George Dixon's Downfall and What It Teaches," *National Police Gazette*, October 14, 1905.
59. "Jolts from 'John L.,'" *Boston Daily Globe*, January 26, 1908.
60. "George Dixon's Downfall."
61. "Opinions of Leading Sporting Writers upon the Dixon-Erne Decision," *National Police Gazette*, December 19, 1896.
62. "Catchweight" describes a fight conducted within a weight limit that does not adhere to the traditional limits for weight classes. In boxing, a catchweight is negotiated prior to weigh-ins.
63. "Greatest Fight of the Century: George Dixon vs. Solly Smith," *Boxing and Wrestling*, April 1956.
64. "A Decision for Dixon," *Brooklyn Eagle*, November 12, 1898.
65. "Pounds Pluto," *Boston Daily Globe*, January 18, 1899.
66. "Dixon Knocks Out Pluto," *New York Times*, January 18, 1899.
67. "Pluto Beaten by His Trainers," *Chicago Daily Tribune*, January 19, 1899.
68. "Santry-Dixon Fight a Draw," *New York Times*, August 12, 1899.
69. "Santry-Dixon Fight a Draw."
70. "Santry-Dixon Fight a Draw."
71. "George Dixon, While Fit and Able . . . ," *National Police Gazette*, September 9, 1899.

Chapter 7

1. "Terry McGovern Objects to Being a Burlesque Star and Is Now Match to Fight George Dixon," *National Police Gazette*, October 14, 1899.

2. "Terry McGovern," last modified March 19, 2017, *BoxRec*, http://boxrec.com/media/index.php?title=Human:9044.

3. Dan Streible, "A History of the Boxing Film, 1894–1915: Social Control and Social Reform in the Progressive Era," *Film History* 3, no. 3 (1989): 235–57.

4. Dan Streible, *Fight Pictures: A History of Boxing and Early Cinema* (Berkeley: University of California Press, 2008), 114, 121–22.

5. Streible, *Fight Pictures*, 103–4.

6. "In Shape," *Boston Globe*, January 9, 1900.

7. "In Shape."

8. "Dixon Passes," *Boston Daily Globe*, January 10, 1900.

9. "George Dixon to Retire and Become a Boniface," *National Police Gazette*, December 30, 1899.

10. "McGovern Conquers Dixon," *New York Times*, January 10, 1900.

11. "Dixon Passes," *Boston Daily Globe*, January 10, 1900.

12. "Echoes of the Fight," *Washington Post*, January 11, 1900.

13. "Dixon Passes."

14. "George Dixon: Greatest, Says Tom O'Rourke," *The Ring Magazine*, October 1936, Don Coleman Collection.

15. "George Dixon: Greatest."

16. "George Dixon in Town," *The Sun*, January 13, 1900.

17. "George Dixon: Greatest."

18. "Dixon Passes."

19. "Dixon Passes."

20. "Echoes of the Fight," *Washington Post*, January 11, 1900.

21. "Dixon Passes."

22. "Dixon Passes."

23. "Dixon Passes."

24. "Sorrow and Praise for George Dixon," *Philadelphia Inquirer*, January 11, 1900.

25. "Sorrow and Praise for George Dixon."

26. "After the Battle," *The Sun*, January 11, 1900.

27. "Dixon Passes."

28. "Fighters Are Hard Losers," *Los Angeles Times*, October 9, 1904.

29. "Sorrow and Praise for George Dixon," *Philadelphia Inquirer*, January 11, 1900.

30. "McGovern Is the Idol," *National Police Gazette*, January 27, 1900.

31. Reading newspapers from the era, it is often difficult to decipher the flowery racist remarks of bygone eras. In the past, some have claimed the "curse of Ham" as biblical justification for imposing slavery or racism on Black people. In his sermon, "Paul's Letter to American Christians," delivered at Dexter Avenue Baptist Church, Montgomery, Alabama, on November 4, 1956, Martin Luther King Jr. called such revisionism "a blasphemy": "I understand that there are Christians among you who try to justify segregation on the basis of the Bible. They argue that the negro is inferior by nature because of Noah's curse upon the children of Ham. Oh my friends, this is blasphemy. This is against everything that the Christian religion stands for. I must say to you as I have said to so many Christians before, that in Christ 'there is neither Jew nor Gentile, there is neither bond nor free, there is neither male nor female, for we are all one in Christ Jesus.'"

32. "Terry Gives a Dinner," *Washington Post*, January 16, 1900.

33. "Model for Pugilists," *Chicago Daily Tribune*, January 11, 1900.

34. "The Passing of George Dixon," *Plaindealer* (Topeka, KS), January 26, 1900.

35. "George Dixon," *Colored American*, January 13, 1900.

36. "Negro must compete in the open market," *Colored American*, February 24, 1900.

37. "Had Their Nerve with Them," *Atlanta Constitution*, January 14, 1900.

38. Clarence Lusane, *The Black History of the White House* (San Francisco: City Lights Publishers, 2010).

39. Lusane, *The Black History of the White House*.

40. "Booker Washington Episode," *Atlanta Journal*, October 22, 1901.

41. "Southern Democrats Berate the President," *New York Times*, October 1, 1901.

42. "Booker Washington Episode."

43. "Both Politically and Socially President Roosevelt Proposes to Coddle Descendant of Ham," *Atlanta Constitution*, October 18, 1901.

44. "McKinley Fails to Meet Prizefighters," *Chicago Daily Tribune*, January 14, 1900.

45. "Had Their Nerve with Them."

46. Brian McKinna, "Marty Bergen," accessed December 25, 2020, *Society for American Baseball Research BioProject*, http://sabr.org/bioproj/person/c19ac6cc.

47. "Black Days for Black Fighters," *Los Angeles Times*, April 26, 1904.

48. William Smith, "Dictionary of Greek and Roman Antiquities" (New York: Little, Brown, 1859) Harvard University Collection.

49. "Callahan Outpointed Dixon," *National Police Gazette*, May 26, 1900.

50. "George Dixon," *Leavenworth Herald*, February 8, 1896.

51. "McGovern Is the Idol," *National Police Gazette*, January 27, 1900.

52. "Dixon Benefit Brought All the Champions Out," *National Police Gazette*, March 17, 1900.

53. "McGovern Is Favourite," *Boston Globe*, February 22, 1900.

54. "After 800 Battles," *Boston Globe*, January 8, 1900.

55. "'Kid' McCoy and George Dixon Hold 'At Homes,'" *National Police Gazette*, March 31, 1900.

56. "'Kid' McCoy and George Dixon Hold 'At Homes.'"

57. "Dixon Decides to Re-enter the Ring," *National Police Gazette*, May 26, 1900.

58. "McGovern Wins over Dixon," *The Washington Post*, June 24, 1900.

59. "Sorrow and Praise for George Dixon," *Philadelphia Inquirer*, January 11, 1900.

60. "Fortune Smiled on Dixon until He Began to Drink," *Washington Post*, January 26, 1908.

61. Streible, *Fight Pictures*.

62. Streible, "A History of the Boxing Film."

63. Streible, *Fight Pictures*.

64. Streible, *Fight Pictures*.

65. Streible, *Fight Pictures*.

66. "Dixon's Friends Urge Him to Quit the Fighting Game," *National Police Gazette*, August 18, 1900.

67. "George Dixon Is Now a Poor Man," *Philadelphia Inquirer*, August 12, 1900.

68. "George Dixon Stranded," *Brooklyn Eagle*, August 20, 1901.

69. "Passing of George Dixon, the Greatest Fighter the World Ever Saw," *National Police Gazette*, February 15, 1902.

70. "Dixon Beat Lenny in 25 Round in a Fast Fight," *National Police Gazette*, December 9, 1899.

71. "Jolts from 'John L.,'" *Boston Daily Globe*, January 26, 1908.

72. Kenneth T. Walsh, *Family of Freedom: Presidents and African Americans in the White House* (Boulder, CO: Paradigm Publishers, 2011), 64–65.

73. Booker T. Washington, "XIV. The Atlanta Exposition Address," in *Up from Slavery: An Autobiography* (New York: Bartleby.com, 2001), http://www
.bartleby.com/1004/14.html. Accessed April 2016.

74. W. E. B. Du Bois, *The Souls of Black Folks* (New York: Oxford University Press, 2007), 27.

75. "Small Purses in England," *National Police Gazette*, June 20, 1903.

76. "To Many Lovers . . . ," *National Police Gazette*, November 28, 1903.

77. "How Dixon Beat Palmer," *National Police Gazette*, December 12, 1903.

78. "Boxing in England," *National Police Gazette*, December 27, 1903.

79. "George Dixon Again Enjoys Prosperity," *National Police Gazette*, January 16, 1904.

80. "George Dixon Again Enjoys Prosperity," *National Police Gazette*, January 16, 1904.

81. "Is George Dixon Still Champion," *National Police Gazette*, March 19, 1904.

82. "George Dixon Again Enjoys Prosperity," *National Police Gazette*, January 16, 1904.

83. Ranking Dixon among the richest Black men in America is not overstatement. For context, in 1909, Booker T. Washington penned *The Story of the Negro: The Rise of the Race from Slavery*. In it, he chronicled James C. Thomas, a New York City undertaker who Washington estimated to be "the richest man of African descent in New York." He wrote, in part:

> James C. Thomas, who, at the time I write, is said to be the richest
> man of African descent in New York, made a large part of his for-
> tune in the under taking business. Mr. Thomas came originally from
> Harrisburg, Texas, where he was born in 1864. In 1881, while he
> was employed by a steamer plying between New Orleans, Mexico,
> and Cuba, yellow fever broke out in New Orleans. The boat he was
> on came to New York to escape the quarantine. It was thus, quite by
> accident, that Mr. Thomas became a New Yorker. There have been
> Negro undertakers in New York, I have been informed, for over
> 150 years. There were several Negro undertakers in New York and
> Brooklyn, at the time Mr. Thomas went into business, but the larger
> part of the trade, which should have come to the colored undertak-
> ers, went to white men.
>
> In 1909, Mr. Thomas had one of the largest businesses of any
> undertaker, white or Black, in the city of New York. He was, in addi-
> tion, the owner of a number of valuable properties in New York
> City and owned stock in the Chelsea National Bank of New York. I
> shall have occasion to make mention, in another connection, of the
> success the Negro has had as a banker, real estate dealer, and as a
> druggist, and in some other forms of business. As illustrating, how-
> ever, the variety of enterprises into which the Negro had entered, I
> might mention the fact that one of the best conducted grocery stores

in the city of Montgomery is run by Victor H. Tulane, who started
in business in 1893 in a little building, twelve by twenty in size, with
no experience and a capital of $90. Mr. Tulane, in 1909, was doing a
business of $40,000 a year. He has been for a number of years one of
the trustees of the Tuskegee Normal and Industrial Institute.

84. "George Dixon Is Home and Broke," *Philadelphia Inquirer*, August 22, 1905.
85. "George Dixon's Downfall and What It Teaches," *National Police Gazette*, October 14, 1905.
86. "George Dixon's Downfall and What It Teaches."
87. "Little Chocolate Wonders If He Could Ever Fight," *National Police Gazette*, March 3, 1906.
88. "Little Chocolate Wonders If He Could Ever Fight."
89. "Passing of a Champion," *Chicago Daily Tribune*, January 14, 1900.
90. "Sporting Salad," *Fort Worth Star-Telegram*, September 16, 1905.
91. "George Dixon's Downfall and What It Teaches."
92. "Pugilistic Doings," *National Police Gazette*, June 9, 1906.
93. "Old George Dixon Again," *National Police Gazette*, January 20, 1906.
94. "He's Not the Dixon of Old," *Boston Daily Globe*, December 11, 1906.
95. "Sullivan, Only Friend of George Dixon, Who Is Now Down and Out," *Wilkes-Barre Times Leader*, December 7, 1907.
96. "About the Boxers," *Boston Daily Globe*, December 13, 1907.
97. "Sullivan, Only Friend of George Dixon."
98. "McGovern, Young Corbett and Dixon Will Meet Tonight," *Boston Daily Globe*, December 12, 1907.
99. "Sporting Notes," *Washington Post*, December 30, 1907.
100. "The Old Sports Musing," *Philadelphia Inquirer*, January 6, 1908.
101. "Long Yale Mascot," *Emporia (KS) Gazette*, January 1, 1908.
102. "Yale's Old Candy Man Dead," *Bridgeport (CT) Herald*, November 17, 1907.
103. "Tom O'Rourke," *The Ring Magazine*, September 1936, Schutte/Powell Boxing Archives.
104. "Dixon Getting the Con Good and Strong," *Boston Daily Globe*, December 8, 1907.
105. "Dixon Getting the Con Good and Strong."
106. "George Dixon Dead," *New York Times*, January 7, 1908.
107. "Hero of Many Battles Will Fight No More," *Boston Daily Globe*, January 7, 1908.
108. "George Dixon Dead," *New York Times*, January 7, 1908.
109. The best-known inflammatory rheumatism is arthritis, also called rheumatoid arthritis.
110. "Four Speedy Fighters Who Have Lost Their Bouts with Drink," *Augusta (GA) Herald*, January 20, 1908.
111. "Jockey 'Pike' Barnes Dead," *The Washington Post*, January 11, 1908.
112. "George Dixon Dead."
113. "Hero of Many Battles Will Fight No More."
114. "Honor Dixon; Booze Defeated Pug," *Atlanta Constitution*, January 8, 1908.
115. "Last Tributes to Little Chocolate," *Hartford Courant*, January 9, 1908.
116. "Dixon's Body Here," *Boston Daily Globe*, January 9, 1908.
117. "Little George Dixon at Rest," *Boston Daily Globe*, January 10, 1908.

118. Callis, in fact, was married to the former Helen Josephine Sprague, a second cousin of Douglas's.
119. "Little George Dixon at Rest."
120. "Little Chocolate's End," *Hartford Courant*, January 11, 1908.
121. "Color Line Is Only a Myth," *Los Angeles Times*, April 5, 1914.
122. "Lessons from Dixon's Career," *Boston Daily Globe*, January 13, 1908.
123. "Once a Hero; Dies a Pauper," *Chicago Daily Tribune*, January 12, 1908.
124. "For Dixon's Monument," *Boston Daily Globe*, January 22, 1908.
125. "Geo. Dixon in Bronze," *Boston Daily Globe*, February 23, 1908.
126. "Monument for George Dixon," *Boston Daily Globe*, May 25, 1909.
127. "George Dixon's Monument Is to Be a Lamppost and Fountain," *Boston Daily Globe*, April 18, 1908.
128. Michele H. Bogart, *The Politics of Urban Beauty: New York and Its Art Commission* (Chicago and London: University of Chicago Press, Press, 2006).
129. Bogart, *The Politics of Urban Beauty*.
130. "In Memory of a Pugilist," *McCook (NE) Tribune*, Sept. 25, 1908.
131. "Horton Law," BoxRec, accessed September 2015, http://boxrec.com/media/index.php/Horton_Law (page discontinued).
132. "'Fake' Fighter Killed Own Game—Now Is a 'Slacker,'" *The Ogden (UT) Standard*, February 10, 1918.
133. "Pugilism Is Popular," *The Washington Post*, April 1, 1900.
134. "Big Fight Investigated," *New York Times*, November 29, 1989.
135. Arne Lang, *Prizefighting: An American History* (New York: Mcfarland & Co. Inc. Publications, 2008).
136. "From a Carr Window," *Los Angeles Times*, February 3, 1913.
137. "From a Carr Window."
138. "From a Carr Window."
139. "Palzer Quits Tom O'Rourke," *Washington Post*, May 26, 1900.
140. "Abe Attell Charges O'Rourke Doped Him," *Gazette Times*, January 23, 1912.
141. "Too Strenuous for Even Tom O'Rourke," *Boston Daily Globe*, August 19, 1922.
142. "Bat Masterson Funeral Services Held in Gotham," *Chicago Daily Tribune*, October 28, 1921.
143. "Tom O'Rourke Dies in Dressing Room," *New York Times*, June 20, 1936.
144. "Tom O'Rourke Piloted Three Great Boxers," July 29, 1936, Schutte/Powell Boxing Archives.
145. "Tom O'Rourke Piloted Three Great Boxers."
146. "Tom O'Rourke Piloted Three Great Boxers."
147. "Tom O'Rourke Piloted Three Great Boxers."
148. "Tom O'Rourke Piloted Three Great Boxers."
149. Patrick Myler, *Ring of Hate: Joe Louis vs. Max Schmeling: The Fight of the Century* (New York: Arcade Publishing, 2005).
150. "Tom O'Rourke Dies in Dressing Room."
151. "Tom O'Rourke," *The Ring Magazine*, September 1936, Schutte/Powell Boxing Archives.
152. "Jolts from 'John L.,'" *The State*, November 17, 1907.
153. George Dixon, *A Lesson in Boxing* (1893).
154. "1908," *Smithsonian,* January 2000.
155. "Jolts from 'John L.,'" *The State*, December 3, 1905.

156. James L. Crouthamel, "The Springfield Race Riot of 1908," *The Journal of Negro History* 45, no. 3 (July 1960).

157. "The Newspapers and the Negro," *Broad Axe* (Chicago), January 25, 1908.

158. Barbara Antoniazzi, "'Unforgiveable Blackness' and the Oval Office," *Race, Gender & Class* 17, no. 3–4 (2010).

159. "Champion Jack Johnson," *The Freeman*, May 1, 1909.

Afterword

1. "George Dixon," *Black Halifax: Stories from Here*, February 28, 2015, https://Blackhalifax.com/portfolio/george-dixon/.

2. Valerie Mason-John, interview by the author, May 20, 2020.

3. "Sports through Edgren's Eyes," *Duluth News-Tribune*, November 14, 1921.

4. "George Dixon's Name CBS Quiz," *Chicago Defender*, December 10, 1955. Psychologist Dr. Joyce Brothers won not once, but twice on the program by putting her boxing trivia knowledge to the test. In December 1955, Brothers won the top prize on *The $64,000 Question*, and then repeated that less than two years later on *The $64,000 Challenge*. In the latter, she competed against a team of seven boxers on boxing lore. Some have credited those appearances for her foray into television, where she found great success for several decades.

5. "Tyson Cave Wins World Boxing Union Super Bantamweight Championship," *CBC News*, November 29, 2015, http://www.cbc.ca/news/canada/nova-scotia/cave-wbu-championship-1.3342282.

6. "Portrait of Africville's George Dixon to Be Unveiled in Halifax," *CBC News*, August 27, 2018, https://www.cbc.ca/news/canada/nova-scotia/george-dixon-boxing-champion-africville-portrait-unveiling-1.4793458.

7. "Sidney Crosby to Headline 'Greatest Sports Dinner' in Nova Scotia," *CBC News*, April 30, 2018, https://www.cbc.ca/news/canada/nova-scotia/sidney-crosby-to-headline-greatest-sports-dinner-in-nova-scotia-1.4641550.

8. Clayton fell short in his effort, fighting only to a majority draw with Kazakhstani boxer Sergey Lipinets.

9. The Canadian Sports Hall of Fame still lists Dixon's date of death incorrectly as 1909.

10. "Does Denzel Always Have to Represent," *Washington Post*, December 23, 2007.

11. Sheryll D. Cashin, "Justice Thurgood Marshall: A Race Man's Race-Transcending Jurisprudence," *Howard Law Journal* 52, no. 3 (Spring 2009).

12. Cashin, "Justice Thurgood Marshall."

13. Cashin, "Justice Thurgood Marshall."

14. The Rev. Henry J. Callis was well known beyond the congregation in front of him. Born in 1858 in Matthew County, Virginia, to Jesse and Nettie (Smith) Callis, Henry Callis fell in with Union soldiers as a young boy and was carried to Yorktown, where Quakers taught him to read and write. He attended Virginia's Hampton Institute, completing his studies in 1879, and took several courses at Cornell University, including political economy, Bible history, and psychology. Callis then pursued theological studies at the University of Rochester. He converted to the African Methodist Episcopal Zion Church and was licensed to preach in 1885.

15. "Lessons from Dixon's Career," *Boston Daily Globe*, January 13, 1908.

BIBLIOGRAPHY

Articles

Anderson, Jack. "A Brief Legal History of Prize-Fighting in 19th Century America." *Sport in History* 24, no. 1 (Summer 2004).

Antoniazzi, Barbara. "'Unforgiveable Blackness' and the Oval Office." *Race, Gender & Class* 17, no. 3–4 (2010).

Bianco, M., et al. "Boxing and Commotio Cordis: ECG and Humoral Study." *International Journal of Sport Medicine* 26, no. 2 (2005): 151–57.

Borden, George. "Box Me a Tune—George Dixon." *Kola* 11, no. 1 (1999).

Bunk, Brian D. "Harry Wills and the Image of the Black Boxer from Jack Johnson to Joe Louis." *Journal of Sport History* 39, no. 1 (Spring 2012): 63–80.

Cashin, Sheryll D. "Justice Thurgood Marshall: A Race Man's Race-Transcending Jurisprudence." *Howard Law Journal* 52, no. 3 (Spring 2009).

Clark, Susan. "Up against the Ropes: Peter Jackson as 'Uncle Tom' in America." *The Drama Review* 44, no. 1 (Spring 2000): 157–82.

Cooks, Bridget R. "Fixing Race: Visual Representation of African Americans at the World's Columbian Exposition, Chicago, 1893." *Patters of Prejudice* 41, no. 5 (2007): 435–65.

Crouthamel, James L. "The Springfield Race Riot of 1908." *The Journal of Negro History* 45, no. 3 (July 1960).

Day, Dave. "'Science,' 'Wind' and 'Bottom': Eighteenth-Century Boxing Manuals." *The International Journal of the History of Sport* 29, no. 10 (July 2012): 1446–65.

Early, Gerald. "The Black Intellectual and the Sport of Prizefighting." *The Kenyon Review* 10, no. 3 (Summer 1988): 102–17.

Fels, Rendigs. "The Long-Wave Depression, 1873–1897." *The Review of Economics and Statistics* 31, no. 1 (February 1949): 69–73.

Hale, Grace Elizabeth. "Without Sanctuary: Lynching Photography in America." *The Journal of American History* 89, no. 3 (2002): 989–94.

Hutchison, Phillip. "Hyping White Hopes: Press Agentry and Its Media Affiliations during the Era of Jack Johnson, 1908–1915." *Journal of Public Relations Research* 23, no. 3 (2011) 325–48.

Jenkins, Jeffrey A., Justin Peck, and Vesla M. Weaver. "Between Reconstructions: Congressional Action on Civil Rights, 1891–1940." *Studies in American Political Development* 24 (April 2010): 57–89.

Johnson, Jerah. "Jim Crow Laws of the 1890s and the Origins of New Orleans Jazz: Correction of an Error." *Popular Music* 19, no. 2 (2000): 243–51.

Kenny, Stephen C. "The Development of Medical Museums in the Antebellum American South: Slave Bodies in Networks of Anatomical Exchange." *Bulletin of the History of Medicine* 87, no. 1 (2013): 32–62.

Kerr, Douglas. "Straight Left: Sport and the Nation in Arthur Conan Doyle." *Victorian Literature and Culture* 38 (2010): 187–206.

Moore, Louis. "Fine Specimens of Manhood: The Black Boxer's Body and the Avenue to Equality, Racial Advancement and Manhood in the Nineteenth Century." *MELUS* 35, no. 4 (2010): 59–84.

Nead, Lynda. "The Cutman: Boxing, The Male Body and the Wound." *Sport, Ethics and Philosophy* 7, no. 4 (2013): 368–77.

Pleck, Elizabeth H. "The Two-Parent Household: Black Family Structure in Late Nineteenth-Century Boston." *Journal of Social History* (Autumn 1972): 3–31.

Poulter, Gillian. "Snowshoeing and Lacrosse: Canada's Nineteenth-Century 'National Games.'" *Ethnicity, Sport, Identity: Struggles for Status* 6, no. 2–3 (2004): 293–320.

Reel, Guy. "This Wicked World: Masculinities and the Portrayals of Sex, Crime and Sports in the *National Police Gazette*." *American Journalism* 22, no. 1 (2005): 61–94.

Reese, Renford. "The Socio-Political Context of the Integration of Sport in America." *Journal of African American Men* 3 (1998): 5–22.

Rhodes, Jane. "The Contestation over National Identity: Nineteenth-Century Black Americans in Canada." *Canadian Review of American Studies* 30, no. 2 (2000): 175–86.

Robidoux, Michael A. "Imagining a Canadian Identity through Sport: A Historical Interpretation of Lacrosse and Hockey." *The Journal of American Folklore* 115 (2002): 209–25.

Sammons, Jeffrey T. "A Proportionate and Measured Response to the Provocation That Is Darwin's Athletes." *Journal of Sport History* 24, no. 3 (Fall 1997): 378–88.

Sheard, K. G. "'Brutal and Degrading': The Medical Profession and Boxing, 1838–1984." *International Journal of the History of Sport* 15, no. 3 (December 1998): 74–102.

Smolla, Rodney A. "The Ghost of Homer Plessy." *Georgia State University Law Review* 12, no. 4 (June 1996): 1037–88.

Streible, Dan. "A History of the Boxing Film, 1894–1915: Social Control and Social Reform in the Progressive Era." *Film History* 3, no. 3 (1989): 235–57.

Taylor, Matthew. "The Global Ring? Boxing, Mobility and Transnational Networks in the Anglophone World, 1890–1914." *Journal of Global History* 8, no. 2 (July 2013): 231–55.

Wallenstein, Peter. "Did Homer Plessy Die a White Man? Race and Southern History—The State of the Field." *The Georgia Historical Quarterly* 94, no. 1 (Spring 2010): 62–96.

Welshman, John. "Boxing and the Historians." *The International Journal of the History of Sport* 14 no. 1 (April 1997): 195–203.

Wiggins, David K. "'Black Athletes in White Men's Games': Race, Sport and American National Pastimes." *International Journal of the History of Sport* 31, no. 1–2 (2014): 181–202.

Winks, Robin W. "The Canadian Negro: A Historical Assessment." *Journal of Negro History* 53, no. 4 (October 1968).

Books

Alexander, David. "Economic Growth in the Atlantic Region, 1880–1940." In
    Acadiensis Reader, Vol. 2: Atlantic Canada after Confederation. Fredericton,
    New Brunswick: Acadiensis Press, 1988.
Bederman, Gale. *Manliness and Civilization: A Cultural History of Gender and Race
    in the United States, 1880–1917*. Chicago: University of Chicago Press, 1995.
Boddy, Kasia. *Boxing: A Cultural History*. London: Reaktion Books, 2008.
Bogart, Michele H. *The Politics of Urban Beauty: New York and Its Art Commission*.
    Chicago and London: The University of Chicago Press, 2006.
Chrysostom, Dio. *The Twenty-Eighth Discourse: Melancomas II*. Loeb Classical
    Library, 1939.
Cornelius, Steven. *Music of the Civil War Era*. Westport, CT: Greenwood Press, 2004.
Dailey, Jane. *The Age of Jim Crow*. New York: W.W. Norton, 2009.
Dixon, George. *A Lesson in Boxing*. 1893.
Du Bois, W. E. B. *The Souls of Black Folks*. New York: Oxford University Press, 2007.
Egan, Pierce. *Boxiana*. London: Virtue, 1824.
Ellmann, Richard. *Oscar Wilde*. New York: Random House, 1987.
Elsroad, Lisa. "Tenderloin." In *The Encyclopedia of New York City*. New Haven: Yale
    University Press, 1995.
Erenberg, Lewis A. "More than a Prizefight: Joe Louis, Max Schmeling and the
    Transnational Politics of Boxing." In *Beyond Blackface: African Americans and
    the Creation of American Popular Culture*, edited by W. Fitzhugh Brundage,
    315–56. Chapel Hill: University of North Carolina Press, 2011.
Fleischer, Nat. *Black Dynamite: Three Colored Aces*. New York: C. J. O'Brien, 1938.
Fosty, George, and Darrill Fosty. *Black Ice: The Lost History of the Colored Hockey
    League of the Maritimes, 1895–1925*. New York: Stryker-Indigo Publishing, 2008.
Gorn, Elliott J. *The Manly Art: Bare-Knuckle Prizefighting in America*. Ithaca, NY:
    Cornell University Press, 1986.
Guzman, Jessie P. *1952 Negro Yearbook*. New York: Wm. H. Wise & Co., 1952.
Hardy, Stephen. *How Boston Played: Sport, Recreation and Community, 1856–1915*.
    Knoxville: University of Tennessee Press, 2003.
Higginbotham, F. Michael. *Ghosts of Jim Crow: Ending Racism in Post-Racial
    America*. New York: New York University Press, 2013.
Hylton, Kevin. *"Race" and Sport*. London: Routledge, 2009.
Isenberg, Michael. *John L. Sullivan and His America*. Champaign-Urbana:
    University of Illinois Press, 1994.
Jackson, Joy J. *New Orleans in the Gilded Age*. Baton Rouge: Louisiana State
    University Press, 1969.
James, William. "A Strong Note of Warning Regarding the Lynching Epidemic
    (1903)." In *Essays, Comments and Reviews*. Boston: Harvard University Press,
    1987.
Kasson, John F. *Houdini, Tarzan and the Perfect Man: The White Male Body and the
    Challenge of Modernity in America*. New York: Hill and Wang, 2001.
Klein, Christopher. *Strong Boy: The Life and Times of John L. Sullivan, America's First
    Sports Hero*. Guilford, CT: Lyons Press, 2013.
Krasner, David. "The Real Thing." In *Beyond Blackface: African Americans and the*

Creation of American Popular Culture, edited by W. Fitzhugh Brundage, 99–123. Chapel Hill: University of North Carolina Press, 2011.

Laffoley, Steven. *Shadowboxing: The Rise and Fall of George Dixon*. Lawrencetown Beach, Nova Scotia: Pottersfield Press, 2012.

Lang, Arne. *Prizefighting: An American History*. New York: Mcfarland & Co. Inc. Publications, 2008.

Landry, Stuart Omer. *The Battle of Liberty Place: The Overthrow of Carpet-Bag Rule in New Orleans*. New Orleans: Pelican, 1999.

Liebling, A. J. *The Sweet Science*. New York: North Point Press, 1994.

Lusane, Clarence. *The Black History of the White House*. San Francisco: City Lights Publishers, 2010.

Mailer, Norman. *The Fight*. New York: Random House, 1975.

Martin, Waldo E. Jr. *Brown vs. Board of Education: A Brief History with Documents*. Boston: Bedford/St. Martin's, 1998.

McCormick, John B. *The Square Circle: Stories of the Prize Ring*. New York: Continental Publishing Company, 1897.

McNeese, Tim. *Plessy v. Ferguson: Separate but Equal*. New York: Chelsea House Publishers, 2007.

McKerrow, Peter. *A Brief History of Colored Baptists of Nova Scotia, 1783–1895*. Halifax: Afro Nova Scotian Enterprises, 1976.

McKinney, Louise. *New Orleans: A Cultural History*. New York: Oxford University Press, 2006.

Medley, Keith Weldon. *We As Freemen*. Gretna, LA: Pelican, 2003.

Metcalfe, Alan. *Canada Learns to Play: The Emergence of Organized Sport, 1807–1914*. Toronto: McClelland & Stewart, 1989.

Moore, Louis. *I Fight for a Living: Boxing and the Battle for Black Manhood, 1880–1915*. Champaign-Urbana: University of Illinois Press, 2017.

Myler, Patrick. *Ring of Hate: Joe Louis vs. Max Schmeling: The Fight of the Century*. New York: Arcade Publishing, 2005.

O'Connor, Thomas H. *The Hub: Boston Past and Present*. Boston: Northeastern University Press, 2001.

Ottley, Roi, and William J. Weatherby. *The Negro in New York: An Informal Social History*. New York: The New York Public Library, 1967.

Pennington, James W. C. *The Fugitive Blacksmith*. London: Charles Gilpin, 1849.

Pleck, Elizabeth Hafkin. *Black Migration and Poverty: Boston 1865–1900*. New York: Academic Press, 1979.

Reel, Guy. *National Police Gazette and the Making of the American Modern Man, 1879–1906*. Basingstoke, UK: Palgrave Macmillan, 2006.

Rinehart, Robert E. "Beyond Traditional Sports Historiography." In *Deconstructing Sport History: A Postmodern Analysis*, edited by Murray G. Phillips, 181–202. Albany: State University of New York Press, 2006.

Robbins, Tom. *Jitterbug Perfume*. New York: Bantam Dell, 1984.

Roberts, James, and Alexander Skutt. *The Boxing Register*. Ithaca, NY: McBooks Press, 2011.

Roberts, Randy. *Joe Louis*. New Haven, CT: Yale University Press, 2010.

Roberts, Randy. *Papa Jack: Jack Johnson and the Era of White Hopes*. New York: Free Press, 1983.

Roberts, Randy, and Andrew R. M. Smith. "Boxing: The Manly Art." In *A Companion to Sports History*, edited by Steven A. Riess, 269–91. Hoboken, NJ: Wiley-Blackwell, 2014.

Runstedtler, Theresa. *Jack Johnson, Rebel Sojourner: Boxing in the Shadow of the Global Color Line*. Los Angeles: University of California Press, 2012.

Sammons, Jeffrey T. *Beyond the Ring: The Role of Boxing in American Society*. Champaign-Urbana: University of Illinois Press, 1998.

Schneider, Mark. *Boston Confronts Jim Crow, 1890–1920*. Boston: Northeastern University Press, 1997.

Smith, Kevin. *Boston's Boxing Heritage: Prizefighting from 1882 to 1955*. Charleston, SC: Arcadia Publishing, 2002.

Smith, Kevin R. *Black Genesis: The History of the Black Prizefighter, 1760–1870*. Bloomington, IN: iUniverse.com, 2003.

Smith, William. *Dictionary of Greek and Roman Antiquities*. New York: Little, Brown, 1859.

Somers, Michael Dale. *The Rise of Sport in New Orleans, 1850–1900*. Baton Rouge: Louisiana State University Press, 1972.

Spencer, Herbert. *The Study of Sociology*. New York: D. Appleton Co., 1873.

Streible, Dan. *Fight Pictures: A History of Boxing and Early Cinema*. Berkeley: University of California Press, 2008.

Sullivan, John L. *Reminiscences of a 19th Century Gladiator: The Autobiography of John L. Sullivan*. Frisco, TX: Promethean Press, 2008.

Thomas, Brook. *Plessy v. Ferguson: A Brief History with Document*. Boston and New York: Bedford Books, 1997.

Thornton, Patricia A. "The Problem of Out-Migration from Atlantic Canada, 1871–1921: A New Look." In *Acadiensis Reader, Vol. 2: Atlantic Canada after Confederation*. Fredericton, New Brunswick: Acadiensis Press, 1988.

Tourgée, Albion W. *A Fool's Errand by One of the Fools*. Boston: Harvard University Press, 1961.

Ward, Geoffrey. *Unforgivable Blackness: The Rise and Fall of Jack Johnson*. New York: Vintage Books, 2004.

Washington, Booker T. *Up from Slavery*. New York: Bartleby.com, 2001.

Whitfield, Harvey Amani. *Blacks on the Border: The Black Refugees in British North America, 1815–1860*. Burlington: University of Vermont Press, 2006.

Wiggins, David K. "The Notion of Double-Consciousness and the Involvement of Black Athletes in American Sport." In *Ethnicity and Sport in North American History and Culture*, edited by George Eisen and David K. Wiggins, 133–56. Westport, CT: Greenwood Press, 1994.

Dissertations

Bennetts, David Paul. "Black and White Workers: New Orleans 1880–1900." University of Illinois, 1972.

Bond, Gregory. "Jim Crow at Play: Race, Manliness and the Color Line in American Sport, 1876–1916." University of Wisconsin–Madison, 2008.

Carey, Kim M. "Straddling the Color Line: Social and Political Power of African American Elites in Charleston, New Orleans and Cleveland, 1880–1920." Kent State University, 2013.

Magazine/Newspaper Articles

Atlanta Constitution
Augusta (GA) Herald
Biloxi (MS) Herald
Boston Daily Globe
Boxing and Wrestling
The Baltimore Sun
Bridgeport (CT) Herald
Broad Axe (Chicago)
Brooklyn Daily Eagle
Chicago Daily Tribune
Chicago Defender
Cleveland Gazette
Colored American (New York Times)
Columbus (GA) Enquirer
Daily Inter Ocean (Chicago)
Dallas Morning News
Detroit Plaindealer
Duluth (MN) News-Tribune
Emporia (KS) Gazette
Fort Worth (TX) Star-Telegram
The Freeman (NY)
Hartford (CT) Courant
Idaho Statesman
Kansas City Star
Kansas Weekly Capital
Langston City (OK) Herald

Leavenworth (KS) Advocate
Los Angeles Times
The Manchester (UK) Guardian
McCook (NE) Tribune
Miami Herald
Mirror of Life and Boxing World
National Police Gazette
New Hampshire Sentinel
New Haven (CT) Register
New Orleans Daily Picayune
New Orleans States-Item
New York Times
The Ogden (UT) Standard
Philadelphia Inquirer
Plaindealer (Topeka, KS)
The Ring Magazine
San Francisco Bulletin
Seattle Daily Times
Smithsonian
Sports Illustrated
The State
Tacoma (WA) Daily News
Topeka Call
Washington Post
Wheeling (WV) Register
Wilkes-Barre (PA) Times Leader

Websites

BoxRec: The Boxing Database. Accessed August 2015. boxrec.com.
Canadian Museum of Immigration at Pier 21. Accessed August 2015. pier21.ca.
Plessy & Ferguson Foundation. Accessed December 2015. plessyandferguson.org.
Society for American Baseball Research BioProject. Accessed December 2015.
    sabr.org/bioproj/person.

Videos

"George Dixon vs. Chester Leon 1906." YouTube, December 21, 2010, 3:28. Accessed
    December 25, 2020. https://www.youtube.com/watch?v=6foQEfkFHFM.

INDEX

Page numbers in *italics* denote illustrations.

image and, 164–65, 173, 217; cor-
ruption and, 243–44; "dark age" of,
7; manuals for, 175–76; promoters
and, 71–72. *See also* bodybuilding;
bout culture; filmmaking; Lewis
Law; London Prizefighting Ring
Rules; prizefighting; Queensberry
Rules; racial divide
Braun, Henry, 157
Brennan, Hank, 44–45
Brooklyn Jacks. *See* Dempsey, Jack
("Nonpareil"); McAuliffe, Jack;
Skelly, Jack
Broughton, Jack, 171
Brown, William Dudley ("Young
Pluto"), 204–5
Brown, Willie, 81, 82–83
Bunce, Capt. George W., 115
Burns, Robert, 63
Burns, Tommy, 234, 250

C

Callahan, Tim, 217, 219, 223
Carney, Jem, 119
Carnival of Champions: aftermath of,
135–38, 154, 158; as national event,
82, 99; Dixon's arrival to, 112–13;
Dixon *vs.* Skelly at, 83, 127–30;
finding opponent for Dixon and,
108–9; McAuliffe *vs.* Myer at,
125–27; program of, 100, *101–2,
103–4,* 105; Sullivan *vs.* Corbett at,
131–33. *See also* Columbus, GA;
New Orleans, LA; Olympic Club
Carroll, Jimmy, 53
Chambers, John Graham, 170
Chapman, Red, 4
Chase, Young, 32
Chickering, Elmer, 34–36
civil rights, 6, 148, 225–27. *See also*
lynching; Niagara Movement;
Plessy, Homer; segregation
Civil War, American, 19–20, 68
Clayton, Custio, 254
Collins, Young, 40
Columbus, GA, 81–83
Colville, James, 33
Connelly, ("One-Eyed"), 123–24

Cooke, Capt. A. W., 41
Corbett, James J. ("Gentleman Jim"):
biography of, 27; bouts of, 153,
243–44; earnings of, 192; mentioned, 28, 194; on Dixon's confidence, 32; picture of, *132,* 183;
support for Dixon and, 232. *See
also* Carnival of Champions
Corbett, Young II, 219, 223, 227, 238
Craig, Frank ("Harlem Coffee Cooler"),
229
Crescent City. *See* New Orleans, LA
Crescent City White League, 144
Crow, Jim, laws of, 146–47, 191, 213,
229, 255. *See also* Ku Klux Klan;
lynching

D

Democratic White League, 88
Dempsey, Jack ("Nonpareil"): bouts of,
94, 126, 158, 246; boxing outfit and,
53; career of, 115–18; picture of,
117. See also McAuliffe, Jack
Denning, Joe, 115
Dixon, Catherine ("Katie"), 73–75, 217
Dixon family: in Canada, 16–17; members of, 14–15; move to Boston of,
21; race and, 12–13
Dixon, George ("Little Chocolate"):
alcohol and, 201–3; appearance
of, 31; as iconic figure, 4–5; biographies of, 8–9; boxing outfit of,
53; career in England of, 227–29;
championship belt of, 3–4; death
of, 234–36; end of career for,
332–33; fame and, 56, 66–67; fighting technique of, 176–78; finances
of, 192, 229; financial support
for, 217–18; first bouts of, 40–41;
funeral of, 237–38; generosity of,
166–67; job at the photo studio
of, 34–35, 36; legacy of, 29–30,
253–57; memorial for, 238–39,
240–41, 242; newspaper coverage
and, 182–83; nickname of, 161–63;
origin story of, 25–26; physicality
of, 173, 179–80, 230–31; picture
of, *2, 10, 48, 80, 159,* 251, *252;* play

about, 154–55; race and, 5–6, 67, 70, 124, 201; ranking of, 27–28; road show of, 197–99; stereotypes and, 250–51; talent of, 32, 178–79; titles of, 60–61, 75–76; video about, 253; visit to the White House of, 214–16; workout regimes of, 174–75. *See also A Lesson in Boxing* (Dixon); Black Bohemia; bout culture; bouts; Carnival of Champions; Dixon, Catherine ("Katie"); Dixon family; O'Rourke, Tom; photo cards; White Elephant saloon

Doherty, Tommy, 40, 41

Douglas, John (9th Marquess of Queensberry), 170–71

Du Bois, W. E. B., 199–200, 225–27, 255

Duffy, Professor, 128

Dunn, Jere, 63

E

Early, Joe, 61

Egerton, Walter ("Kentucky Rosebud"), 195–97

Erne, Frank, 201, 203, 218, 219

F

filmmaking, 207–9, 220–21

Firpo, Luis Angel, 246

Fitzsimmons, Bob: bouts of, 94, 95, 116, 153; mentioned, 28, 99, 170

Fleischer, Nathaniel Stanley: *Black Dynamite* series and, 8–9, 21, 163, 261n43; sport's history and, 26–29

Forbes, James Edward, 44

Foreman, George, 173

Fox, Richard K., 3, 8, 109, 181–82

Fraizer, Bill, 119

Frazier, Joe, 173

Fulijames, George, 115

G

Gans, Joe: mentioned, 69, 248; support for Dixon and, 218, 232, 234; throwing a fight and, 216, 219

Gardner, Oscar, 221

Gilmore, Harry, 119

Goddard, Joe, 135

Godfrey, George ("Old Chocolate"): career of, 36–39; image of, *38*, 183, 187; mentioned, 57, 67, 92; nickname of, 162; relationship with Dixon of, 40

Gorman, Johnny, 123

Goss, Joe, 181

Griffin, Johnny, 111

Griffiths, Albert ("Young Griffo"), 121, 182

H

Hadley, Charles, 37

Hamilton, Elias, 35, 40

Harlan, John Marshall, 145–46

Harris, Sam, 213, 218, 220, 221–22

Hart, Kate, 119–21

Havlin, Jack, 33, 137

Heenan, John ("Benicia Boy"), 41

Hennessey, Patrick, 198

Herman, Pete, 28

Hopper, Jack, 119

Hornbacher, Eugene, 46, 47, 60

Horton Law, 242–43

Hughes, Thomas, 23

Humphreys, Joe, 218, 238

I

Ike Hines Club, 189–90, 191–92

industrialization, 13–14, 165

Inman, Pearl, 121

J

Jackson, Peter: bouts of, 37, 135; image of, 183, *186*; mentioned, 57, 58, 59, 92, 133, 201

Jacobs, Jimmy, 28–29

Jeffries, James J. ("The Heavyweight"), 169–70, 209, 220

Johnson, Fred, 4, 59, 78, *79*, 123

Johnson, Jack: as iconic figure, 6; bouts of, 29, 169, 250–51; compared to Dixon, 255–56; mentioned, 66, 108, 216, 234

Johnson, McHenry, 37

Johnson, Young, 40

92–94; bout attendance and, 4, 194, 205, 210; bouts of, 37, 39; boxing popularity and, 24; Dixon's decline and, 223, 233–34; image of, *90*, 183; mentioned, 123, 152, 235, 238; newspaper column of, 133–34, 271n171; on Dixon's performance, 78–79; on Dixon *vs.* Skelly, 157–58; race and, 91–92. *See also* Carnival of Champions

Sullivan, Tommy, 222

T

Taylor, Bud, 28

Tourgée, Albion Winegar, 105–7, 138, 142–43

Trotter, William Monroe, 226

W

Walcott, Joe: bouts of, 244; Dixon's championship loss and, 212–13; mentioned, 43, 69, 174, 237, 248; picture of, 183; throwing a fight and, 216

Wallace, Nunc, 51, 59, 60, 70, *71. See also under* bouts

Washington, Booker T., 142–43, 215, 225–27, 281n83

Weir, Ike ("Belfast Spider"), 33, 137

Wells, Ida B., 199–200

West, Tommy, 244

White Elephant saloon, 218–19

White, George H., 147, 225

White League, Crescent City, 144

White League, Democratic, 88

White, Tommy, 43, 157

Willamena, Jack, 59

Willard, Jess, 158

Williams, Kid, 28

Willis, Abe, 70, 72–73

Wise, Jimmy, 81, 82–83

Wright, George, 45

Y

Yanger, Benny, 219

Z

Ziegler, Owen, 121

Ziff, Sid, 28–29